Speaking of Liberty

Speaking
of Liberty

Llewellyn H. Rockwell, Jr.

Ludwig
von Mises
Institute
AUBURN, ALABAMA

Patrons

The Mises Institute dedicates this volume to all of its generous donors,
and in particular wishes to thank these Patrons:

Christopher P. Condon, Anthony Deden, Mr. and Mrs. Willard
Fischer / Fisher Printing, Inc., Douglas E. French, Hugh E.
Ledbetter, Frederick L. Maier, Mr. and Mrs. William W. Massey, Jr.,
Roger Milliken, Mr. and Mrs. R. Nelson Nash, Don Printz, M.D.,
Stephenson Family Foundation

James Bailey / James Bailey Foundation, Mr. and Mrs. J.R. Bost,
James W. Frevert, Jule R. Herbert, Jr., Julie Lauer-Leonardi,
Mr. and Mrs. William Lowndes, III,
William S. Morris, III / Morris Communications Corp.,
Donald Mosby Rembert, *top dog*™, James M. Rodney,
Mr. and Mrs. Joseph P. Schirrick in memory of Jeannette Zummo,
Mr. and Mrs. Michael Shaw, Joe Vierra,
Robert H. Walker / Walker Die Casting Company

Andreas Acavalos, Robert B. Allan, Anonymous, Richard Bleiberg,
Dr. V.S. Boddicker, John Hamilton Bolstad, Ronald Bridges,
Paul H. Casey, Mr. and Mrs. John C. Cooke, Kerry E. Cutter,
Carl A. Davis / Davis-Lynch, Inc., Mr. and Mrs. Charles F. de Ganahl,
Eric Englund, Dr. Larry J. Eshelman, Charles Groff, Charley Hardman,
Horace H. Harned, Frank W. Heemstra, Jeremy Horpedahl,
Dr. and Mrs. Robert D. Hurt, Martin Jungbluth, W. Thomas Kelly,
Lucille Lane, Joe R. Lee, John M. Leger, Dr. Floy Lilley,
Arnold Lisio, M.D., Arthur L. Loeb, Björn Lundahl,
Samuel Medrano, M.D., in honor of Lupe C. Medrano,
Joseph Edward Paul Melville, Robert Mish, Brantley I. Newsom,
James O'Neill, Mr. and Mrs. Ronald L. Peterson, Robert M. Richards,
Catherine Dixon Roland, Conrad Schneiker, Mr. and Mrs. Charles R. Sebrell,
Tibor Silber, William V. Stephens, Robert Stewart, George Taylor,
James E. Tempesta, M.D., Lawrence Van Someren, Sr.,
Mr. and Mrs. Quinten E. Ward, Dr. Thomas Wenck,
David Westrate / T and O Foundation,
Arthur Yakubovsky, Dr. Steven Lee Yamshon

To Murray N. Rothbard (1926–1995),
Scholar, Teacher, Gentleman

Cover art courtesy of The Saint Louis Art Museum
(George Caleb Bingham, *Stump Speaking*, 1853–54)

ISBN: 0-945466-38-2

CONTENTS

INTRODUCTION

A common response to a good article is to say to the author: you should write a book! I've heard this for years, but from what I've seen of such efforts, most articles should remain articles. Looking at the corpus of writings in the Austrian tradition, from more than a century ago through the latest books brought out by the Mises Institute, there are more than enough books available, containing systematic expositions of theory and history, that need to be read and studied. There is nothing I could say systematically in a book-length treatment that would add to the articles I write weekly. Articles and books constitute separate literary genres, taking a different pace and designed for different purposes.

The same is true of nonacademic public speeches. They are not designed to give a systematic exposition of ideas but rather to introduce ideas and apply them to the current moment in a way that holds people's attention. The prose takes a different form from the article or the book. It is more immediate and more rhetorical in the classical sense of that term. I have had the pleasure of delivering many of these over the years, to students, supporters of the Mises Institute, financial professionals, and others. Now I've collected them, with little change, into a single volume.

I've made no attempt to disguise the dated material, and thus some do refer to events of the Clinton years without reference to later events. The material on the current state of the economy is subject to withering with time. Some of the material on war predates the change in public sentiment after September 11, 2001—a date which has become something of a hinge of history in American foreign policy.

But there are two senses in which the material itself will always remain relevant. First, the principles are always the same. Second, events tend to repeat themselves. For example, I recently watched a video about the Federal Reserve that the Mises Institute made in the early nineties. It described the recessionary environment of the time. Watching it again in 2003, it seems up to the minute!

I've organized the speeches by topic, though there is plenty of overlap between sections. Economics is tied to politics which leads to issues of war and peace, and back again. I've added neither footnotes nor bibliographies, knowing that Mises.org and Google searches can instantly yield more references for further study than I could possibly add.

Reading through all these, I find common themes: the corruptions of politics, the universality and immutability of the ideas of freedom, the centrality of sound money and free enterprise, the moral imperative of peace and trade, the importance of hope and tenacity in the struggle for liberty, and the need for everyone to join the intellectual fight. These are the themes I hoped to convey in my speeches over the years.

Reading them is no substitute for keeping up with the news through short commentaries, and they are certainly no substitute for extensive reading in the scholarly literature. If someone asked me whether he should read this book or something by Ludwig von Mises or Murray Rothbard, I wouldn't have to consider the question long. It is always better to do deep study.

And yet, I do find value in this genre. I hope you do too. Mostly, I hope you consider supporting the ideas that led me to write them and deliver them. Also, I've included two longer interviews that are a bit more personal.

Many thanks to all those who contributed editorial advice, criticism, and guidance, not all of whom could possibly be named here because so many people have corresponded with me concerning points in this book. But let me mention in particular: Patricia Barnett, Burton S. Blumert, Karen De Coster, Gary North, Chad Parish, David Schatz, James Sheehan, Joseph Stromberg, Judy Thommesen, Jeffrey Tucker, and Kathy White.

A special thank you to all those who have listened over the years, and, in particular, to the patrons of this book and all supporters of the Mises Institute.

Llewellyn H. Rockwell, Jr.
Auburn, Alabama

1. Economics

THE MARVEL THAT IS CAPITALISM

[This speech was given before the Adam Smith Club, Campbell University, Buies Creek, North Carolina, April 4, 2002.]

Free-market economics, of which the Austrian School is the preeminent exponent, asserts that every government intervention in the market generates consequences that are deleterious for prosperity and human liberty. However much such interventions may assist one group in the short run, everyone is made worse off in the long run. Government intervention destabilizes economic life in artificial ways, and ultimately does not work to bring about the results that its proponents claim to desire.

Carl Menger, the founder of the Austrian School of economics, was a firm believer in the law of cause and effect. He believed that economic affairs could be analyzed in these terms as well.

Menger's followers in this tradition of thought, including Ludwig von Mises and Murray N. Rothbard, spelled out the implications of this idea for a huge range of issues that confront us on a daily basis in the world of economics and politics. They focused on universal principles that can be derived from the teachings of economics. The law of supply and demand, for example, cannot be repealed by any legislature or court. Government regulators can impose price ceilings, price floors, or limits to the size of firms like Microsoft, but economic law bites back by yielding shortages, surpluses, and reduced profitability.

It is important that we think of economic life as an intricate global system of exchange, one that works without any central direction, and which generates prosperity and its own form of order within the framework of liberty. This is what is sometimes termed the magic of the marketplace, and we should never underestimate its power. By looking south to Argentina, we can see how a failing economy, one thrown into shock by bad legislation and monetary policy, has destroyed the livelihoods of the entire population.

We are not just talking about the earnings in people's stock portfolio. We are talking about whether mothers can afford to buy milk for their children, and whether the businesses that deliver milk have the freedom to be entrepreneurial and find the least costly methods to make such deliveries possible. When we speak of economics, we are talking about the health of society, and whether medical equipment is working and affordable, and whether the labor market is sufficiently free to permit everyone a place within the division of labor.

People who dismiss the teachings of economics forget that many of the world's wars and ethnic slaughters began with economic intervention. Before ethnic warfare broke out in Yugoslavia in the 1990s, the country was afflicted by one of the most extreme hyperinflations in the history of the world. This literally destroyed the standard of living and helped turn a previously settled society into a killing field.

If we look back at history, we can see that many wars began in trade disputes, when governments attempted to reward some producers at the expense of others. This was the origin of the Civil War, for example. Even in our own times, the perception in the Muslim world that US/UN sanctions against Iraq have slaughtered hundreds of thousands of children has fueled hatred that has culminated in terrorism. The general lesson we can draw is that economics is really just a fancy word for the quality of our lives, and that the quality of our lives has no greater enemy than the governments that attempt to restrict economic liberty.

Looking at people's life spans, we see the hidden history of the rise of economic development. Throughout the first huge period of human history from the beginning until the birth of your father's great-grandfather, the average life span was 20 to 35 years, and a third to half of all children died before reaching the age of five. Economic conditions before very recently in the history of man could not sustain a world population that rose above a few million. Even by the year 1800, the average life span was only 40.

The standard of living for the average person throughout all but the smallest slice of human history can be aptly summed up in the words of Thomas Malthus: "At nature's mighty feast there is no vacant cover for him. She tells him to be gone, and will quickly execute her own orders." That was life as everyone but kings knew it after the Fall and before the Industrial Revolution.

But in the last tiny fragment of the history of the world, life spans have more than doubled and the world population has increased one thousand times. By far the largest improvements in these vital statistics have occurred since 1800, at a time when the division of labor expanded dramatically around the world; when property rights were secure; when capital could be accumulated, invested, and a return paid and reinvested; when technological improvements permitted new forms of productivity. What made this possible was the free market.

We take for granted such luxuries as refrigeration, the air conditioner, the internal combustion engine, and electricity, to say nothing of email, the Web, and fiber-optics. But we rarely reflect on the fact that all of these technologies, so integral to our lives, were absent when our great-great-grandfathers were alive, along with every previous generation in the history of the world. What set this revolution in motion was the world of ideas, when great thinkers began to understand the internal logic of the market economy and its potential for liberating mankind from poverty, dependency, and despotic rule.

Given this history, one might think that everyone would sit and marvel at the products of capitalism. We might think that intellectuals would dedicate their lives to defending this system and explaining its merits. We might imagine that statesmen would dedicate themselves to protecting this system of economic progress from every attempt to curb it or abolish it.

Alas, that is not true. Quite the opposite. The intellectual world often appears to be a conspiracy against market economics, and the media routinely ridicule capitalism. Statesmen spend every waking minute trying to curb, regulate, hamper, or otherwise loot the capitalist system.

Those who attacked the World Trade Center were driven by revenge, but also by a belief that the towering products of the commercial society somehow represent an evil that must be destroyed rather than a virtue that should be emulated. They were merely absorbing a view that is pervasive in our culture today, where the anticapitalistic mentality runs rampant.

In our own times, we have seen the evil produced by this mentality, in the former Soviet Union and in many Third World countries, where politicians do everything possible to keep the entrepreneurial spirit penned up, where property rights are not secure, and where investment for the long term is not permitted. The result is always the same: poverty, despotism, death.

As the founder and president of the Mises Institute, I have a special attachment to the ideas of Mises and to the courageous life he lived in defense of the idea of freedom. He began his career in Vienna, writing about the problem of the business cycle and the role of money and credit in fostering it.

The core point he made in his great 1912 book, the *Theory of Money and Credit*, was that artificial increases in the money supply are not a substitute for real economic production; indeed such increases cause economic damage that can only be rectified through painful economic contractions. His point has continuing relevance.

His next book, from 1919, sought to defend the idea that governments ought to be small and geographically limited, for the sake of social peace. Next, in 1920 and 1922, he proved that socialism could not work as an economic system because it abolished property rights in capital and thus destroyed the system of profit and loss that allows for economic calculation. His methodological and business cycle writings from the 1930s are some of the most profound in the history of the social sciences. Finally in 1940 and 1949, he produced what is quite possibly the finest product of any economist in history: his monumental treatise called *Human Action*.

Incidentally, he wrote most of his treatise while in Geneva, in exile from his native Austria. The invading German armies deemed his work dangerous. They entered Mises's apartment and looted his files and papers. Mises, you see, was against socialism, whether Bolshevik or Nazi. Reflect on that and begin to understand the absurdity of calling communism leftist and Nazism rightist, as if they were polar opposites. They are both varieties of the very opposite of freedom itself.

If I were able to give all college students a reading assignment today, I would recommend *Human Action* above all else. Yes, at nearly 1,000 pages, it can be intimidating, and you will probably need to read it with a dictionary nearby. But it will open up new vistas of thought for you, and help you to rise above conventional wisdom. I continue to believe that this book points the way for us to bring about rising and sustainable prosperity, and also to guard civilization against its enemies.

The headlines of the business pages have been trumpeting the arrival of recovery from March 2001 until the present—so far, the entire length of the downturn. How do the experts decide when recession has turned to recovery? By looking at the data, which come in packages labeled in various ways: the GDP, the leading indicators, the unemployment rate, industrial production, housing starts, commercial borrowings, office vacancy rates, and a host of other considerations. If these tend in the negative direction, we are said to be entering a downturn. If they move in a positive direction, it is said that we are recovering.

Let's grant, first, that the larger the data set, the more subject to manipulation it is. We can count housing starts, but measuring something like national productivity is very tricky business. The great scandal of the way that Gross Domestic Product is collected is that it does not measure wealth destruction, as caused by something like the attacks on September 11 or the 40 percent of private wealth consumed by government at all levels every year. Neither does it make a distinction between private production and outright government spending. Because of this, looking at the data alone, without a proper theory of economics, can produce a highly misleading picture.

For many months, the government has been engaged in a serious effort to bring us out of recession through a variety of fiscal and monetary policies. If recovery is really here, can we say that these policies have worked? Not necessarily, because we must establish a firm relationship between cause and effect to draw such a conclusion. The economy might have recovered without such stimulus efforts. In fact, such stimulus efforts might make the recovery weaker than it otherwise might be.

A more serious possibility is that the stimulus efforts have actually created an illusion. While everyone is celebrating the unexpected economic recovery, which is also unexpectedly robust, it serves us to look beneath the surface. There are aspects of this recovery that are highly unstable because they were brought about through artificial means. There are also certain policy trends which suggest that it might not last or that it will not be as robust as it might otherwise be.

The Congressional Budget Office points out that new government spending has surpassed the amounts envisioned in the stimulus measures proposed in 2001 and 2002, exceeding what even the most spendthrift lawmakers dared demand. The spending surge along with consumer debt helps to explain why the recession seemed mild and why everyone is talking about recovery.

A major increase in government spending, which has very quickly redirected $100 billion into the economy, began in October 2001. Outlays went up over 2001's increases by 13.1 percent. In terms of GDP, it accounts for fully 1 percent. As for consumer spending, it is financed almost entirely by new borrowing fueled by artificially lower interest rates.

Looking even deeper, we can see that Federal Reserve policy has been astonishingly loose since the beginning of 2001, reaching as high as 20 percent per annum by some measures. Let's say I set out to stimulate economic production in a college classroom. We could all gather together to write some software that is valued by the market, or we could teach each other new skills that increase our labor productivity.

But what if I stood there with a photocopying machine and made a thousand copies of a $20 bill, passed them around, and then announced that we are all $20,000 richer than before? Everyone would be rightly skeptical of this claim. When the Federal Reserve does this same thing with its money-creation machine, we should be skeptical also.

While recognizing that some of the rebound may consist of sustainable investment begun after the great shakeout of 2000, these factors just cited strongly suggest that the current economic recovery consists of more myth than reality. We need to ask ourselves whether and by what means it can be sustained. . . . The only means for doing so is for it to be supported through strong economic development and sound investment—investment that is borne out in consumer purchases and long-term profits.

It turns out, however, that the federal government has done everything possible to undermine the likelihood of a sustainable recovery. In 2002, the US imposed a 30-percent tariff on steel. The idea here was to help one inefficient, bloated, and pampered industry at the expense of all US consumers of steel, including US businesses, and all producers in Europe, Asia, Brazil, and Australia. This is brazen protectionism, deeply harmful all around, not to mention morally repugnant.

Did it help the steel industry? In the short run, yes. But we have to ask ourselves whether this kind of help is a good thing in the long run. The tariffs permit an inefficient industry to continue to produce inefficiently, and forestall improvements in technology and cutbacks in wages that are necessary if the industry is to adjust to 21st-century realities. There is no virtue to keeping dying and inefficient technology humming along so that workers who would be better employed elsewhere can continue to enjoy fat checks doing outmoded work.

How long must such tariffs remain in place? The steel industry says they are only necessary in order to get it back on its feet. But that belies that question of what, precisely, is going to inspire this sector to clean up its act? Protecting an industry from competition is a method that permits everything wrong with the industry to persist and not change. Either this tariff will have to be in place permanently, or the industry will have to be shaken up.

If you think about it, Soviet socialism survived for 74 years on precisely such policies. The Soviet State protected all its industries from market competition under the alleged need to build socialism. Factories were never closed, and workers were never let go except for political reasons, when their services were employed in the Gulag. The system worked only if the standard was not efficiency but merely the guarding of the status quo. Eventually this system collapsed, as statist systems must, and the Soviets woke up to a world that was backward and decayed.

The steel tariff imposed by the Bush administration is different from Soviet socialism only in degree, not in kind. It is an attempt to circumvent the market process through a centrally administered system of rewards and subsidies for industry to abide by political priorities rather than market dictates. In the meantime, all purchasers of steel, whether consumers or other businesses, are harmed by being forced to pay a higher price for an inferior product.

Also in 2002, the US imposed massive punitive duties on softwood imports from Canada. Why? Because Canada refused to obey a US demand that it place a new tax on its softwood. The new duties raise the price of softwood, used for building nearly every home in America, by 27 percent. This is going to distort the housing market, among many other sectors that use wood. Higher prices for steel and wood put additional pressure on other businesses that use these products in production.

In economic terms, tariffs are indistinguishable from sales taxes. They take people's property by force by requiring businesses and consumers to pay higher prices for goods than they would otherwise pay in a free market. To that extent, they harm the prospects for economic growth. If anyone says otherwise, he is ignoring hundreds of years of scholarship and the entire sorry history of government interference with international trade.

The repercussions of these two actions are already being felt via damaged relations in Latin America and Europe. The World Trade Organization will likely give the green light for retaliation. Protectionist lobbies all over the world are rushing to take advantage of the opportunity. The EU has imposed tariffs on US steel, and Canada is considering retaliatory measures. This way lies trade war, which is the worst thing that can happen to an economy, other than hot war.

Another policy that endangers recovery is the war on terrorism. I'm not taking issue with the need for justice after September 11, but it seems clear that the government used this tragedy as an excuse to vastly increase spending and regulation over the American and world economy. President Bush, who campaigned on a platform of cutting government, has asked for another $28 billion to pour into the military, even as he is pushing for more regulations on banks and financial privacy in the name of rooting out terrorism. The total increases for 2002 and 2003 could be as high as $300 billion, depending on whom the US plans to conquer next.

Here again, this spending can create the illusion of prosperity, but we must also remember that first lesson of economic science: the world is a finite place where the use of any and all resources are constrained by scarcity. This is just another way of saying that you can't always get what you want, and when you do, it must come from somewhere. When the government spends resources, it must drain them from the private economy through taxation, borrowing, or inflating the money supply to pay for the new spending.

Economics doesn't deny that redirecting resources from one sector where they are valued by consumers, to another sector where they are valued by government, can create pockets of expansion. What economics suggests is that this is not an efficient or sustainable use of such resources. Only the unhampered competitive market economy, with its system of market prices, profits, and losses, can reveal to us with any certainty the most desirable destination of economic goods.

But in the examples I have just given, you can see how government intervention is redirecting resources from consumers' most desired uses to purposes deemed desirable by political planners. The politicians believe that the military needs resources more than you and I, so they take them. They believe that the profits of the steel industry are more important than the international division of labor, so they protect that industry. They believe that the softwood industry deserves to obtain the highest possible prices for its products, so they intervene to hamper imports.

As for the explosion of consumer spending that has taken place over the course of the downturn, this does indeed encourage businesses to expand. If low interest rates are encouraging consumers to dig deep to borrow for and buy new homes, this will encourage more investment in housing on the production side as well, and this too will be encouraged by the interest rates being depressed by the Federal Reserve. Artificially low interest rates also tend to discourage savings, and encourage people to put money back into the stock market where, they hope, it can earn a higher rate of return.

If credit expansion, protectionism, and government spending were a path to prosperity, mankind would have long ago created heaven on earth. But the politicians engaged in these activities have to contend with reality, and the reality is that economic forces in society must be mutually sustaining. To have production and borrowing, there must be savings, which only occur when people forgo consumption today to prepare for tomorrow, and when investment pans out in the form of consumption. Absent such conditions, economic growth lacks a foundation in reality and turns to dust when economic conditions change.

We have seen many examples of this in recent years. The Internet bubble was one such case. There was nothing unreal about technology or its potential to provide massive gains in efficiency, as well as a vibrant new commercial marketplace and information delivery service. Nor was there anything ignoble about investors who pumped money into dot-coms on the promises of future profits. What distorted the picture was too much credit, courtesy of the Federal Reserve, chasing too few capitalized companies.

When the Fed began to reduce the pace of monetary pumping, lenders pulled back, investors pulled out, and dot-coms and their support infrastructure found themselves overextended, well beyond what the market would have borne if it had not been subsidized by a reckless Fed policy.

The collapse of the Nasdaq was nothing more than reality reasserting itself. Some malinvestments were cleaned out and the ground was prepared for new investment.

Dot-coms weren't the only ones affected by the bubble. Enron is another famed case in point. This company profited and dramatically expanded at a time when investors were encouraged to recklessly purchase stocks without regard to balance sheets. The auditors are catching the blame, but the truth is that Enron profited in a time when portfolio managers weren't paying very close attention either. The only way such a "cluster of errors" comes to predominate in a market economy is when the central bank unleashes new money and credit beyond anything that the market can sustain for long.

Prior to our own bubble, we saw a similar situation in Asia, and, before that, in Mexico. In each of these cases, what we find is not market failure but a failure of the system of money and credit to provide reliable signals for investors and lenders. It is helpful to think of the interest rate as a price signal, so that Fed attempts to drive down rates simply misprice credit. In the same way that a government price ceiling would cause overconsumption of any good—whether eggs, gas, or electricity—distortions of the interest rate encourage overconsumption of credit.

It is not surprising, then, that we are seeing a spending boom take place today among consumers even as producers are pulling back in many areas. Certain sectors have prospered since the reflation began after mid-2001. Housing, in particular, has boomed all out of proportion to what it would otherwise do in a free market. If any sector is being set up for a fall today, it is this one.

Regardless of the fallout from day-to-day economic affairs, Mises believed that no power on earth is as strong as ideas. You live in the world of ideas, so take your responsibilities very seriously. The achievements of freedom *should* speak for themselves, but sadly they do not. Freedom needs courageous individuals who are willing to stand apart from the mob and state an unconventional truth.

A SECRET HISTORY OF THE BOOM AND BUST

[This text is drawn from the keynote address at the Sage Capital Management Conference in Houston, Texas, March 12, 2003.]

The Austrian economists tell us that a price is more than a price. It is an objective expression of subjective judgments concerning human wants, now and in the future. It conveys information to us about how we ought to conduct ourselves: where capital should be directed, how much of what should be consumed now or later, which jobs to take and which to pass over. In short, prices provide the roadmap to the successful navigation of the material world.

How striking it is to see stock prices respond so actively to the war on Iraq, the dominant event of the day. Since the war began, prices rose in response to the prospect that war would end soon and sank on the prospect that the war will go on and on. What does this price information convey? Most likely, it reflects an inchoate sense that this war would do nothing to bring us out of economic contraction and into recovery.

That is precisely true. Wars often result in severe setbacks, not only prolonging the contraction, but deepening it as well. To hear official voices talk, however, we have not been going through the longest recession in the postwar period. Instead, we have been through a 24-month "slow recovery." It is also called a "sagging economy with sound fundamentals."

Greenspan has made references to a "soft patch" in a foundation supposedly as hard as stone.

Indeed, in the effort to avoid using the term recession, the Federal Reserve has become a business-cycle phrase mill. Thus, according to the Fed, this is a "soft economy," a "subpar economy," a "skittish economy," an economy "weighed down by weak expenditures," an economy of "persistent weakness," or, my favorite, an economy facing "formidable barriers to vigorous expansion." Call it what you want, but don't call it a recession. As for the D-word, depression, don't even think it!

With the latest data on the producer price index, the commodity price index, and the increase in oil prices, we are starting to see other tortuous linguistic devices at work. It is not inflation; it is "sector-specific price pressure." In the old days, rising unemployment, sinking production, and price inflation combined to create what was called "stagflation." What will it be called this time? Something rather ingenious, no doubt.

The National Bureau of Economic Research officially dates the contraction from March 2001, fully six months before 9-11. Not a day has gone by in the last two years when some commentator hasn't either denied we are in downturn, claimed we are already out of the contraction, or cited evidence that the recovery is underway and demanded that everyone admit it already. In fact, I believe our time will be recorded as a period of general economic meltdown. How much worse will it get and how much longer will it last? We cannot know for sure, but we do know that right now the government is doing everything in its power to make it worse.

Those of us who warned in the 1990s that the stock-price mania could not last were accused of spreading "gloom and doom." Our warnings were considered self-evidently ridiculous, because, of course, it was said that we were in a New Economy, and such things as profitability and earnings and savings were old hat and had no bearing on the cyberworld being created before our eyes. Only the Austrian School economists seemed to wonder who or what was behind the frenzy.

In contrast to the 1980s, when everyone was watching the money supply, the markets were suspiciously uninterested in what the Fed was up to in the 1990s. It funded a bailout of Mexico, then a bailout of East Asia, and then a bailout of a crazy Connecticut hedge fund that believed it could predict the future by paying Nobel laureates vast sums to concoct a mathematical model that perfectly predicted the past.

But still, hardly anyone cared. The phrase "money supply" elicited yawns. The *Wall Street Journal*, meanwhile, ran a few articles explaining why there is no longer any such thing as risk. It was only the Austrians who seemed to take notice when money creation rates began to take off in 1995, and climbed to 15 percent in late 1998 and 1999, taking the bull market on its wildest-ever ride. Monetary expansion rates settled down a bit in 2000, a trend which at first seemed merely inauspicious—like a tiny tap on a domino lined up against a thousand others.

Once the bear market began, there was no turning back, no matter how much the Fed inflated. Instead of stabilizing downward as they had in Clinton's first term, money-creation rates shot up again, reaching an astounding 22 percent in December 2001 from a year earlier, and then fell back down again, creating a double-dip bear market in the course of a mere 24 months. In these numbers we find the secret history of the great boom and bust of our time. Let me give a brief outline of why, and try to explain why it is that so few seemed to pick up on it.

At the dawn of the century of central banking, an economist named Ludwig von Mises set out to rewrite the theory of what money is and how government can seriously distort its workings. Among the puzzles he sought to solve was one that most economists, including Karl Marx, had noticed: swings in business activity from boom to bust.

Marx said that cycles are endemic to capitalism, and a sign of the final crisis that will sweep in the age of socialism. In contrast, Mises found that the business cycle is a symptom not of the free market but of attempts to manipulate the market through unsound monetary practices. Moreover, he found that these cycles are self-correcting, provided that the government doesn't attempt to forestall the necessary correction that follows an artificial boom.

Mises concluded by looking carefully at the relationships among the financial sector, money and banking, and the structure of production itself. On the free market, he said, the interest rate reflects the extent to which people are willing to forgo current consumption for later consumption. The more businesses and holders of money are willing to put off consumption, the lower the rate will be. A low borrowing rate for business, which spurs investment, reflects a high rate of consumer savings, which reflects a willingness of consumers to purchase the products made in lengthy production processes.

In testimony the other day, Greenspan claimed the following: "Economists understand very little about how technological progress occurs." Perhaps he should have said that he, Greenspan, knows little about how technological progress occurs. At least as regards the Austrian economists, his statement is false. Within the framework of the freedom of exchange, entrepreneurs make judgments about what consumers might want in the future, including new technologies.

Capitalists and investors assume the risk, employing private property. Investments that are profitable attract more resources and those that yield losses are shelved.

This is the free-market capital structure at work in a complex economy. It is truly a miracle of coordination—extending through all sectors and across a huge range of time horizons—with no central management, and needing none. It balances human needs with the availability of all the world's resources, unleashes the amazing power of human creativity, and works to meet the material needs of every member of society at the least possible cost.

It does this through exchange, cooperation, competition, entrepreneurship, and all the institutions that make possible capitalism—the most productive economic system this side of heaven. This system of capital coordination not only works without central management; government's attempt to manage it creates dislocations across sectors and across time.

Let us never underestimate the social benefits that flow from this seemingly technical mechanism. The market economy has created unfathomable prosperity and, decade by decade, century by century, miraculous feats of innovation, production, distribution, and social coordination.

To the free market, we owe all material prosperity, all leisure time, our health and longevity, our huge and growing population, nearly everything we call life itself. Capitalism and capitalism alone has rescued the human race from degrading poverty, rampant sickness, and early death.

In the absence of the capitalist economy and all its underlying institutions, the world's population would, over time, shrink to a small fraction of its current size, with whatever was left of the human race systematically reduced to subsistence, eating only what could be hunted or gathered. The institution that is the source of the word civilization—the city—depends on trade and commerce, and cannot exist without them.

And this is only to mention the economic benefits of capitalism. It is also an expression of freedom. It is not so much a social system but the natural result of a society wherein individual freedom is respected, and where businesses, families, and every form of association are permitted to flourish in the absence of coercion, looting, and war.

Capitalism protects the weak from the strong, granting choice and opportunity to the masses, who once had no choice but to live in a state of dependency on the politically connected and their enforcers.

But capitalism has many enemies, among them those who would attempt to gin up economic production through loose credit. What Mises focused on in his book on money was the effects of this particular attack on the free market: expansion of money and credit by the central bank, and, in particular, the attempt to drive down the price of credit to spur business investment.

Doing this through the interest rate requires injections of new money into the economy. One effect of this has been known for centuries: it causes prices to rise. But the other effect Mises discovered: it subsidizes long-term capital investment in a manner that cannot be supported by the patterns of consumption and saving. As one Austrian economist puts it, when the central bank drives down interest rates, it causes the economy to bite off more than it can chew.

The effect of artificially inflating the economy can be rising prices. But as we saw in the late 1920s and other times since, that is not always the case. It often causes a kind of investment euphoria that leads people to believe that nothing can go wrong.

The monetarists, for example, believe that so long as prices remain in check, there is no problem associated with money expansion. The supply-siders, though sound on many issues, have an unfortunate faith in the power of loose credit to make bread from stones.

Mises developed his theory throughout the 1920s and warned of the coming of the 1929 stock market crash. His work was carried forward by F.A. Hayek throughout the 1930s. Hayek later received the Nobel Prize for this. Indeed, the theory was widely embraced until Keynes dreamed up an alternative view that resurrected all the old fallacies about the miracles of money creation and centralized economic management.

Then the Misesian theory languished for decades until the current downturn. Today it is getting new attention as the leading explanation of the insanity of the late 1990s and the current bust. Only the Austrians said all along that reality would strike back.

The Fed and the administration have worked ever since, using the only tools they have—regulation, spending, and credit expansion—to reverse the course of the recession.

When I think of the Fed's spreading money far and wide, I think of the government in Huxley's *Brave New World* handing out soma pills or spreading soma vapors to distract people from reality, drugging them so they will be content despite the surrounding disaster. If they start to resist, out comes the soma until the crowds collapse in kisses and hugs.

It is always an illusion to believe that more money is the answer. The federal funds rate is at a 40-year low, and that hasn't done the trick. During the 1990s, the Bank of Japan tried again and again to manufacture a recovery through absurdly low rates, but that didn't work either. There is no evidence from either theory or history that pounding interest rates into the ground can create anything resembling a sustainable prosperity. And yet, people believe it, or want to believe it, because it seems better than the alternative.

This entire affair illustrates the underlying reality of American political and economic life: the State's ability to create money and credit. All other powers of government—regulatory, fiscal, even military—pale in comparison to this. Despite that, the Fed is the least controversial institution in American political life. Apart from Ron Paul of Texas, no national politician understands how it works. When Greenspan comes before Congress, he is treated like a minor god.

If this worship is ever tempered with skepticism, it is on grounds that he is not inflating enough, that he is somehow being stingy and not spreading the wealth. Tragically, there is no organized constituency in American politics for tighter money, less credit, or sounder finance.

Mises distinguishes three varieties of inflationism, that is, the demand that the State work with the banking industry to flood the economy with credit. The first is naïve inflationism that sees no real downside to monetary expansion; the second is inflationism intended to reward debtors at the expense of creditors; and the third sees disadvantages to an expansionary policy, but believes that the advantages outweigh them.

The US is right now in the grip of the worst form: naive inflationism, which, as Mises says "demands an increase in the quantity of money without suspecting that this will diminish the purchasing power of the money. It wants more money because in its eyes the mere abundance of money is wealth. Fiat money! Let the State 'create' money, and make the poor rich, and free them from the bonds of the capitalists!"

And here we are today enduring the longest recession in postwar history, a Nasdaq off 75 percent from its highs and a Dow off 40 percent, and the government is still issuing buy signals.

Imagine if you had used George W. as your portfolio manager. You would have bought stocks when he became president, held onto them through 9-11 and then bought more and more afterwards.

Incidentally, you'll notice that the official rationale for buying stocks has changed. Whereas once it was said that you should buy because the economy is on a permanent growth path, after September 11, it was said that you should buy to display your patriotism. If that isn't a sell signal, I don't know what is.

Of course no one in his right mind would let the president of the United States manage his stock portfolio. Why, then, do we trust his government to spend wisely the $2.5 trillion it will extract from the private economy this year? Of course, we don't really trust the government to do that, but we do not have much choice in the matter. This money is taken from us through force and is thereby, by definition, directed toward uses that are not those which owners would choose. This is power, not market, at work.

What is striking to note, however, is all the ways in which power is not only destructive but also ineffective against the market economy. The government did not know that firms such as Enron and WorldCom were unviable. All the regulators put together could not anticipate the consequences of what private traders alone were to discover: that these businesses had wildly overextended themselves.

Leaving aside questions of ethical lapses at these companies, the most significant lesson we should learn from their collapse is that the market economy has built within it a fabulous internal check against illusion. Companies that could not sustain themselves on their own merits were simply abandoned by investors. It counts toward the enduring shame of the Bush administration that it attempted to blame the market for the bust of so many companies, rather than having given credit to the market for having discovered the problem in the first place and having done something about it.

But as FDR demonstrated after the Depression, there are political points to be made by skewering the private sector in order to distract from the failures of the public sector. The alleged crime the Bush administration seized on was "accounting fraud"—even though it is not at all clear that what WorldCom, Enron, Computer Associates, Global Crossing, or Qwest did, often with the blessing of respected auditors, amounts to that at all.

In each case, the accusation was similar: their books counted spending as profitable investment before the revenue was in the bag, and when the economic tables turned, their optimistic projections proved unsound and even, in retrospect, absurd.

WorldCom was the worst case of the batch, which is why the government has made such a big deal out of the arrest of two former executives. Their spectacular shifting of a total of $3.8 billion from expenses to capital began small, in mid-2000 as the bust was hitting and their financial statements were starting to appear unimpressive.

No one disputes the facts. WorldCom's expenses for last-mile leases on other companies' communications networks were rising very quickly. Managers wanted to move these expenses off of the profit and loss statement and onto the balance sheet, thus reflecting a more profitable appearance.

Now, understand that there was no lying going on, and no graft or theft or anything else of that nature. What we have here is an imprudent reclassification designed to impress investors who, at the height of the bubble, demanded nothing less. Unless you are an accounting whiz, there is no way to say that this is *a priori* evil. In any case, it didn't fool everyone. Many skeptics drew attention to the crazy finance of World-Com's books. But in the boom times made possible by the Fed, most people didn't care.

Most of the other cases of corporate fraud that came under the microscope were far less serious than WorldCom, and none are obvious cases of theft or fraud. Mostly it was just bad forecasting reflected in optimistic accounting methods. The supposed damage caused by their behavior was that their dressed-up books kept their stock price rising even as the financial condition of the company deteriorated. That's probably true, but it is also a short description of what it means to be in a bubble economy. If this is fraud, the entire economic boom was fraud.

Hitting closer to the truth, the *New York Times* called DC's antibusiness frenzy "the vital center of the administration's strategy for reducing the political vulnerability for the White House." In other words, the Republicans were up to their old trick of behaving even worse than the Democrats in order to keep the Democrats from coming to power. If you disagree with this approach, you must be some sort of libertarian utopian who doesn't understand the need for compromise.

The underlying assumption was the view that it is always a terrible thing for a business to go under, which in fact it is not. It is merely a reflection of human preference as expressed in buying and selling decisions. The only alternative to going under, in some cases, is to operate uneconomically. But that is precisely what the government had in mind for the steel sector last year.

Recession, inefficiency, and bankruptcy are not the only man-made disasters with which government threatens us. Hardly a day goes by when the government doesn't issue some maniacal warning about an impending terror attack. And the sense of uncertainty and confusion that follows can only forestall recovery.

How much is real and how much is propaganda or merely bureaucratic risk aversion? We cannot know. They recently urged us to buy duct tape to seal the windows in our house in order to protect ourselves from chemical warfare. They also told us that they may use nuclear bombs against enemies real and imagined.

When the warning was given in February, gullible Americans cleaned out the stores of duct tape. Buried in the news a week later was the fact that the person who gave the tip that led to the orange alert was lying. Of course, the revelation didn't do the government much harm, and the crisis environment that the tip engendered did much good for our masters, who want to keep us in a relentless state of insecurity, and therefore dependent on them.

That helps them keep doing what they want to do anyway: for example, spend money and inflate away the debt thereby incurred. Politicians say they must run deficits of hundreds of billions of dollars to avert an impending calamity that will make 9-11 look like a warmup. They say this, but have yet to issue a sell signal.

The government continues to downplay the economic calamity before our eyes while talking up the prospects for a calamity that can only be solved, they say, by use of the biggest big-government program of them all: war.

At the end of the Cold War, many of us hoped that normalcy would return, that the US would once again become a peaceful commercial republic. But Bush the elder had a different idea. He decided to bomb Iraq and to impose sanctions that would last 12 years, kill untold hundreds of thousands, inspire terror plots all over the Muslim world, and provide a new rationale for why the US must continue to squander hundreds of billions a year on military public-works programs.

We are often told we must go to war because some swarthy, foreign head of state is not a big fan of the US president. In 2003, the person fitting that description is Saddam Hussein. Before that it was the Mullah Omar. A few years earlier, it was Milosevic. Before that, it was some ward-heeler in Somalia. Moving backward in time, we had to take out the strongmen in Panama and Haiti. The story goes on and on. It seems that the US government is addicted to conflict. It just can't seem to give it up.

Now, I know there will be plenty of disagreement when I say we ought to be trading with Iraq, not bombing it. But let's at least be clear on what we are talking about when we refer to the US military machine. The US will spend $400 billion on its military this year—and that doesn't include VA hospitals, most spying, the atom-bomb building at the Energy Department, the military part of Nasa, or the Pentagon's huge "black" or secret budget.

The second highest military budget in the world is Russia's. Going down the list, next comes China, then Japan, then the UK. You have to tick through 27 countries and add their total spending together to equal what the US spends per year. Not since the Roman Empire has a single country been so militarily dominant.

Let's look at the relative strength of the US versus Iraq in particular. Quantitatively, before the war, Iraq spent one quarter of one percent of what the US government spends on its military. Qualitatively, the Iraqi military machine was already crippled, with no spare parts for its ancient equipment. The soldiers are teenage conscripts in rags with old rifles. The idea that this is a fair fight is a joke.

Those who worry about Iraq over-arming itself ought to look a bit closer to home. As for the shooting war, some military commentators have compared its ease to drowning puppies. Thanks to a combination of misrule and punishing sanctions, this once prosperous country has been reduced to rubble. The US has reduced it further, though in doing so the US faces a difficult foe: the desire of a people not to be invaded by a foreign army, and the unpredictability of political forces.

The longtime emphasis of the old liberal tradition with regard to war is this: even the victor loses. We lose resources. We lose tax dollars. We lose trading relationships and good will around the world. Most of all, we lose freedom. And herein lies the biggest cost of war to us, for there is no way that the US can maintain a free market that is the foundation of prosperity while at the same time attempting to create a global military central plan.

Big government abroad is incompatible with small government at home. To the extent we cheer war, we are cheering domestic socialism and our own eventual destruction as a civilization. But perhaps you do not need persuading on any of these matters. I know many people who look at the economy and the military belligerence of the US government and they react with despair. I reject this posture. For one thing, I am firmly convinced that the government has reached too far.

When you consider the full range of social, economic, and international planning on which it has embarked, you can know in advance that this cannot work. Government is not God, nor are the men who run it impeccable or infallible, nor do they have a direct pipeline to the Almighty. The method they have chosen to bring about security and order is destined toward failure.

The war against terrorism is a good example. Everyone in Washington is terrified of the next attack. To shore up the war, there has been no shortage of rhetoric. No expense is spared on arms escalation. There is no lack of will. The effort has the aid of plenty of smart people. It is backed by threats of massive bloodshed.

What is missing is the essential means to cause the war to yield beneficial results. With all the millions of potential terrorists out there, and the infinite possibilities of how, when, and where they will strike, there is no way the State can possibly stop them.

Behind terrorism is political grievance. This is not speculation. This is the word of the terrorists themselves, from Timothy McVeigh to Osama bin Laden to the suicide bombers.

The pool of actual terrorists (like the pool of the poor in the War on Poverty) is limited and can be known, and they are the ones the State focuses on. But the pool of potential terrorists (and potential poor people) is unlimited, and unleashed by the very means the State employs.

Hence, not only does the State not accomplish its stated goals, it recruits more people into the armies of the enemy, and ends up completely swamped by a problem that grows ever worse, as the target population is able to make a mockery of the State through sheer defiance.

In the War on Poverty, as more and more were added to the ranks of the poor, and the intended beneficiaries of the programs themselves began to mock the State's benevolence, people began to speak of the failure and collapse of the Great Society. Of course the welfare state still exists, but the moral passion and ideological fervor are gone. In the same way, we will soon begin speaking of the collapse of the War on Terror.

Bin Laden is still on the loose, and everyone knows that there are hundreds or thousands of replacement bin Ladens out there. Terrorism has increased since the war began. Israel suffers daily, and in constantly changing ways, ways in which even the most famous and empowered intelligence and military units cannot anticipate or prevent.

But can't the State just kill more, employ ever more violence, perhaps even terrify the enemy into passivity? This cannot work. Even prisons experience rioting. A bracing comment from Israeli military historian Martin van Creveld: "The Americans in Vietnam tried it. They killed between two-and-a-half and three million Vietnamese. I don't see that it helped them much." Without admitting defeat, the Americans finally pulled out of Vietnam, which today has a thriving stock market.

Can the US just back out of its War on Terror? Wouldn't that mean surrender? It would mean that the State surrenders its role, but not that everyone else does. Had the airlines been in charge of their own security, 9-11 would not have happened. In the same way that the free market provides for all our material needs, it can provide our security needs as well.

The War on Terror is impossible, not in the sense that it cannot cause immense amounts of bloodshed and destruction and loss of liberty, but in the sense that it cannot finally achieve what it is supposed to achieve, and will only end up creating more of the same conditions that led to its declaration in the first place.

In other words, it is a typical government program, costly and unworkable, like socialism, like the War on Poverty, like the War on Drugs, like every other attempt by the government to shape reality according to its own designs. The next time Bush gets up to make his promises of the amazing things he will achieve through force of arms, how the world will be bent and shaped by his administration, think of Stalin speaking at the 15th Party Congress, promising "further to promote the development of our country's national economy in all branches of production." Everyone applauded, and waded in blood, pursuant to that goal, but in the end, even if he did not know it, it was impossible to achieve.

Mises, who was so brilliant when it came to issues of money and credit, also saw the need for a thriving economy to operate amidst an environment of peace. "War," he said, is harmful, not only to the conquered but to the conqueror. Society has arisen out of the works of peace; the essence of society is peacemaking. Peace and not war is the father of all things. Only economic action has created the wealth around us; labor, not the profession of arms, brings happiness. Peace builds, war destroys.

Our age is dominated by the state and its errors. The state has given us recession and war, while liberty has given us prosperity and peace. Which of the two paths prevails in the end depends on the ideas we hold about freedom, capitalism, and ourselves.

May we never forget the great truth that our founding fathers worked so hard to impart: tyranny destroys, while liberty is the mother of all that is beautiful and true in our world. I make no apologies for being a champion of prosperity and its source, the free-market economy. It is what gives birth to civilization itself. It is fashionable to reject concerns about the economy as narrow and uninteresting, a merely bourgeois interest. If this attitude comes to prevail, we have great reason to be concerned about our present age.

If, on the other hand, we can educate ourselves about the workings of economic forces, and the way in which they are the foundation of freedom and peace, we will not only emerge from this recession prepared to enter onto a new growth path; we will have gone a long way to protecting ourselves from future assaults on our right to be free.

WHY AUSTRIAN ECONOMICS MATTERS

[Based on a lecture given as part of the Heritage Foundation Resource Bank Series in Washington, DC, December 10, 1995.]

Economics, wrote Joseph Schumpeter, is "a big omnibus which contains many passengers of incommensurable interests and abilities." That is, economists are an incoherent and ineffectual lot, and their reputation reflects it. Yet it need not be so, for the economist attempts to answer the most profound question regarding the material world.

Pretend you know nothing about the market, and ask yourself this question: how can society's entire deposit of scarce physical and intellectual resources be assembled so as to minimize cost; make use of the talents of every individual; provide for the needs and tastes of every consumer; encourage technical innovation, creativity, and social development; and do all this in a way that can be sustained?

This question is worthy of scholarly effort, and those who struggle with the answer are surely deserving of respect. The trouble is this: the methods used by much of mainstream economics have little to do with acting people, and so these methods do not yield conclusions that have the ring of truth. This does not have to be the case.

The central questions of economics have concerned the greatest thinkers since ancient Greece. And today, economic thinking is broken into many schools of thought: the Keynesians, the Post Keynesians, the New Keynesians, the Classicals, the New Classicals (or Rational Expectations School), the Monetarists, the Chicago Public Choicers, the Virginia Public Choicers, the Experimentalists, the Game Theorists, the varying branches of Supply Sideism, and on and on it goes.

Also part of this mix, but in many ways apart from and above it, is the Austrian School. It is not a field within economics, but an alternative way of looking at the entire science. Whereas other schools rely primarily on idealized mathematical models of the economy, and suggest ways the government can make the world conform, Austrian theory is more realistic and thus more socially scientific.

Austrians view economics as a tool for understanding how people both cooperate and compete in the process of meeting needs, allocating resources, and discovering ways of building a prosperous social order. Austrians view entrepreneurship as a critical force in economic development, private property as essential to an efficient use of resources, and government intervention in the market process as always and everywhere destructive.

The Austrian School is in a major upswing today. In academia, this is due to a backlash against mathematization, the resurgence of verbal logic as a methodological tool, and the search for a theoretically stable tradition in the madhouse of macroeconomic theorizing. In terms of policy, the Austrian School looks more and more attractive, given continuing business-cycle mysteries, the collapse of socialism, the cost and failure of the welfare-warfare regulatory State, and public frustration with big government.

In its 12 decades, the Austrian School has experienced different levels of prominence. It was central to the price theory debates before the turn of the century, to monetary economics in the first decade of the century, and to the controversy over socialism's feasibility and the source of the business cycle in the 1920s and 1930s. The school fell into the background from the 1940s to the mid-1970s, and was usually mentioned only in history of economic thought textbooks.

The proto-Austrian tradition dates from the 15th-century Spanish Scholastics, who first presented an individualist and subjectivist understanding of prices and wages. But the formal founding of the school dates from the 1871 publication of Carl Menger's *Principles of Economics*, which changed economists' understanding of the valuing, economizing, and pricing of resources, overturning both the Classical and the Marxian view in the "marginal revolution."

Menger also generated a new theory of money as a market institution, and grounded economics in deductive laws discoverable by the methods of the social sciences. Menger's book, said Ludwig von Mises, made an economist of him, and it is still of great value.

Eugen von Böhm-Bawerk was the next important figure in the Austrian School. He showed that interest rates, when not manipulated by a central bank, are determined by the time horizons of the public, and that the rate of return on investment tends to equal the rate of time preference. He also dealt a deadly blow to Marx's theory of capital and exploitation, and was a key defender of theoretical economics at a time when historicists of every stripe were trying to destroy it.

Böhm-Bawerk's greatest student was Ludwig von Mises, whose first major project was the development of a new theory of money. The *Theory of Money and Credit*, published in 1912, elaborated on Menger, showing not only that money had its origin in the market, but that there was no other way it could have come about. Mises also argued that money and banking ought to be left to the market, and that government intervention can only cause harm.

In that book, which remains a standard work today, Mises also sowed the seeds of his business-cycle theory. He argued that when the central bank artificially lowers interest rates, it causes distortions in the capital-goods sector of the structure of production. When malinvestments occur, an economic downturn is necessary to wash out bad investments.

Along with his student F.A. Hayek, Mises established the Austrian Institute for Business Cycle Research in Vienna, and he and Hayek showed that the central bank is the source of the business cycle. Their work eventually proved to be most effective in combating Keynesian experiments in fine-tuning the economy through fiscal policies and the central bank.

The Mises-Hayek theory was dominant in Europe until Keynes won the day by arguing that the market itself is responsible for the business cycle. It didn't hurt that Keynes's theory advocating more spending, inflation, and deficits was already being practiced by governments around the world.

At the time of the business cycle debate, Mises and Hayek were also involved in a controversy over socialism. In 1920, Mises had written one of the most important articles of the century: "Economic Calculation in the Socialist Commonwealth," followed by his book, *Socialism*. Until then, there

had been many critiques of socialism, but none had challenged socialists to explain how their economy would actually
work absent free prices and private property.

Mises argued that rational economic calculation requires
a profit-and-loss test. If a firm makes a profit, it is using
resources efficiently; if it makes a loss, it is not. Without such
signals, the economic actor has no way to test the appropri-
ateness of his decisions. He cannot assess the opportunity
costs of this or that production decision. Prices and the profit-
and-loss corollary are essential. Mises also showed that private property in the means of production is necessary for these
prices to be generated.

Socialism holds that the means of production should be
in collective hands. This means no buying or selling of capital goods and thus no prices for them. Without prices, there is
no profit-and-loss test. Without accounting for profit and loss,
there can be no real economy. Should a new factory be built?
Under socialism, there is no way to tell. Everything becomes
guesswork.

Mises's essay ignited a debate all over Europe and America. One top socialist, Oskar Lange, conceded that prices are
necessary for economic calculation, but he said that central
planners could generate prices out of their own heads, watch
the length of lines at stores to determine consumer demand,
and provide the signals of production themselves. Mises countered that "playing market" wouldn't work either; socialism,
by its own internal contradictions, had to fail.

Hayek used the occasion of the calculation debate to
elaborate upon and broaden the Misesian argument into his
own theory of the uses of knowledge in society. He argued
that the knowledge generated by the market process is inaccessible to any single human mind, especially that of the central planner. The millions of decisions required for a prosperous economy are too complex for any one person to
comprehend. This theory became the basis of a fuller theory

of the social order that occupied Hayek for the rest of his academic life.

Mises came to the US after fleeing the Nazis and was taken in by a handful of free-market businessmen, preeminently Lawrence Fertig. Here he helped build a movement around his ideas, and most free-market economists acknowledge their debt to him. No one, as Milton Friedman has said, did as much as Mises to promote free markets in this country. But those were dark times. He had trouble finding the paid university post he deserved, and it was difficult to get a wider audience for his views.

During these early years in America, Mises worked to rewrite his just completed German-language treatise into *Human Action*, an all-encompassing work for English-language audiences. In it, he carefully reworked the philosophical grounding of the social sciences in general and economics in particular. This proved to be a significant contribution: long after the naïve dogmas of empiricism have failed, Mises's "praxeology," or logic of human action, continues to inspire students and scholars. This *magnum opus* swept aside Keynesian fallacies and historicist pretensions and ultimately made possible the revival of the Austrian School.

Until the 1970s, however, it was hard to find a prominent economist who did not share the Keynesian tenets: that the price system is perverse, that the free market is irrational, that the stock market was driven by animal spirits, that the private sector should not be trusted, that government is capable of planning the economy to keep it from falling into recession, and that inflation and unemployment are inversely related.

One exception was Murray N. Rothbard, another great student of Mises, who wrote a massive economic treatise in the early 1960s called *Man, Economy, and State*. In his book, Rothbard added his own contributions to Austrian thought. Similarly, the work of two other important students of Mises, Hans F. Sennholz and Israel Kirzner, carried on the tradition. And Henry Hazlitt, then writing a weekly column for

Newsweek, did more than anybody to promote the Austrian School, and made contributions to the school himself.

The stagflation of the 1970s undermined the Keynesian School by showing that it was possible to have both high inflation and high unemployment at the same time. The Nobel Prize that Hayek received in 1974 for his business-cycle research with Mises caused an explosion of academic interest in the Austrian School and free-market economics in general. A generation of graduate students began studying the work of Mises and Hayek, and that research program continues to grow. Today, the Austrian School is most fully embodied in the work of the Mises Institute.

The concepts of scarcity and choice in a world of uncertainty lie at the heart of Austrian economics. Man is constantly faced with a wide array of choices. Every action implies forgone alternatives or costs. And every action, by definition, is designed to improve the actor's lot from his point of view. Moreover, every actor in the economy has a different set of values and preferences, different needs and desires, and different time schedules for the goals he intends to reach.

The needs, tastes, desires, and time schedules of different people cannot be added to or subtracted from other people's. It is not possible to collapse tastes or time schedules onto one curve and call it consumer preference. Why? Because economic value is subjective to the individual.

Similarly, it is not possible to collapse the complexity of market arrangements into enormous aggregates. We cannot, for example, say the economy's capital stock is one big blob summarized by the letter K and put that into an equation and expect it to yield useful information. The capital stock is heterogeneous. Some capital may be intended to create goods for sale tomorrow and others for sale in 10 years. The time schedules for capital use are as varied as the capital stock itself. Austrian theory sees competition as a process of discovering new and better ways to organize resources, one that is fraught with errors but that is constantly being improved.

This way of looking at the market is markedly different from every other school of thought. Ever since Keynes, economists have developed the habit of constructing parallel universes having nothing to do with the real world. In these universes, capital is homogeneous, and competition is a static end state. There are the right number of sellers, prices reflect the costs of production, and there are no excess profits. Economic welfare is determined by adding up the utilities of all individuals in society. The passing of time is rarely accounted for, except in changing from one static state to another. Varying time schedules of producers and consumers are simply non-existent. Instead, we have aggregates that give us precious little information at all.

A conventional economist is quick to agree that these models are unrealistic—ideal types to be used as mere tools of analysis. But this is disingenuous, since these same economists use these models for policy recommendations.

One obvious example of basing policy on contrived models of the economy takes place at the Justice Department's antitrust division. There the bureaucrats pretend to know the proper structure of industry, what kinds of mergers and acquisitions harm the economy, who has too much market share or too little, and what the relevant market is. This represents what Hayek called the pretense of knowledge.

The correct relationship between competitors can only be worked out through buying and selling, not bureaucratic fiat. Austrian economists, in particular Rothbard, argue that the only real monopolies are created by government. Markets are too competitive to allow any monopolies to be sustained.

Another example is the idea that economic growth can be manufactured by manipulating aggregate demand curves through more and faster government spending—considered to be a demand booster instead of a supply reducer or government bullying of the consuming public.

If the hallmark of conventional economics is unrealistic models, the hallmark of Austrian economics is a profound appreciation of the price system. Prices provide economic actors with critical information about the relative scarcity of goods and services. It is not necessary for consumers to know, for example, that a disease has swept the chicken population to know that they should economize on eggs. The price system, by making eggs more expensive, informs the public of the appropriate behavior.

The price system tells producers when to enter and leave markets by relaying information about consumer preferences. And it tells producers the most efficient, that is, the least costly way to assemble other resources to create goods. Apart from the price system, there is no way to know these things.

But rational prices must be generated by the free market. They cannot be made up the way the Government Printing Office makes up the prices for its publications. They cannot be based on the costs of production in the manner of the Post Office. Those practices create distortions and inefficiencies. Rather, prices must grow out of the free actions of individuals in a juridical setting that respects private property.

Neoclassical price theory, as found in most graduate texts, covers much of this territory. But typically, it takes for granted the accuracy of prices apart from their foundation in private property. As a result, virtually every plan for reforming the post-socialist economies talked about the need for better management, loans from the West, new and different forms of regulation, and the removal of price controls, but not private property. The result was the economic equivalent of a train wreck.

Free-floating prices simply cannot do their work apart from private property and concomitant freedom to contract. Austrian theory sees private property as the first principle of a sound economy. Economists in general neglect the subject, and when they mention it, it is to find a philosophical basis for its violation.

The logic and legitimacy of "market failure" analysis, and its public-goods corollary, is widely accepted by non-Austrian schools of thought. The notion of public goods is that they cannot be supplied by the market, and instead must be supplied by government and funded through its taxing power. The classic case is the lighthouse, except that, as Ronald Coase has shown, private lighthouses have existed for centuries. Some definitions of public goods can be so broad that, if you throw out common sense, everyday consumer goods qualify.

Austrians point out that it is impossible to know whether or not the market is failing without an independent test, of which there is none outside the actions of individuals. The market itself is the only available criterion for determining how resources ought to be used.

Let's say I deem it necessary, for various social reasons, that there be one barber for every 100 people and, as I look around, I notice that this is not the case. Thus I might advocate that a National Endowment for Barbers be established to increase the barber supply. But the only means for knowing how many barbers there ought to be is the market itself. If there are fewer than one per hundred, we must assume that a larger number is not supposed to exist by any reasonable standard of efficient markets. It is not economically proper to develop a wish list of jobs and institutions that stands apart from the market itself.

Conventional economics teaches that if the benefits or costs of one person's economic decisions spill over onto others, an externality exists, and it ought to be corrected by the government through redistribution. But, broadly defined, externalities are inherent in every economic transaction because costs and benefits are ultimately subjective. I may be delighted to see factories belching smoke because I love industry. But that does not mean I should be taxed for the privilege of viewing them. Similarly, I may be offended that most men don't have beards, but that doesn't mean that the clean-shaven ought to be taxed to compensate me for my displeasure.

The Austrian School redefines externalities as occurring only with physical invasions of property, as when my neighbor dumps his trash in my yard. Then the issue becomes crime. There can be no value-free adding-up of utilities to determine subjective costs or benefits of economic activity. Instead, the relevant criterion should be whether economic actions occur in a peaceful manner.

Another area where Austrians differ is how the government is supposed to go about the practical problem of correcting for market failures. Granted that somehow the government can spot a market failure, the burden of proof is still on the government to demonstrate that it can perform the task more efficiently than the market. Austrians would refocus the energy that goes into finding market failures to understanding more about government failures.

But the failure of government to do what mainstream theory says it can is not a popular subject. Outside of the Public Choice schools, it is usually assumed that the government is capable of doing anything it wants to do, and of doing it well. Forgotten is the nature of the State as an institution with its own pernicious designs on society. One of the contributions of Rothbard was to focus Austrians on this point, and on the likely patterns interventions will take. He developed a typology of interventionism, and provided detailed critiques of many kinds of interventions and their consequences.

The question is often asked, in James Buchanan's famous phrase, What Should Economists Do? Mainstreamers answer, in part: forecast the future. This goal is legitimate in the natural sciences, because rocks and sound waves do not make choices. But economics is a social science dealing with people who make choices, respond to incentives, change their minds, and even act irrationally.

Austrian economists realize that the future is always uncertain, not radically so, but largely. Human action in an uncertain world with pervasive scarcity poses the economic problem in the first place. We need entrepreneurs and prices to help overcome uncertainty, although this can never be done completely.

Forecasting the future is the job of entrepreneurs, not economists. This is not to say that Austrian economists cannot expect certain consequences of particular government policies. For example, they know that below-market price ceilings always and everywhere create shortages, and that expansions of the money supply lead to general price increases and the business cycle, even if they cannot know the time and exact nature of these expected events.

One final area of theoretical concern that distinguishes Austrians from the mainstream is economic statistics. Austrians are critical of the substance of most existing statistical measures of the economy. They are also critical of the uses to which they are put. Take, for example, the question of price elasticities, which supposedly measure consumer responsiveness to changes in price. The problem lies in the metaphor and its applications. It suggests that elasticities exist independent of human action, and that they can be known in advance of experience. But measures of historical consumer behavior do not constitute economic theory.

Another example of a questionable statistical technique is the index number, the prime means by which the government calculates inflation. The problem with index numbers is that they obscure relative price changes among goods and industries, and relative price changes are of prime importance. This is not to say the Consumer Price Index is irrelevant, only that it is not a solid indicator, is subject to wide abuse, and masks highly complex price movements between sectors.

And the Gross Domestic Product statistic is riddled with composition fallacies inherent in the Keynesian model. Government spending is considered part of aggregate demand, and no effort is made to account for the destructive costs of taxation, regulation, and redistribution. If Austrians had their way, the government would never collect another economic statistic. Such data are used primarily to plan the economy.

For Austrians, economic regulation is always destructive of prosperity because it misallocates resources and is extremely destructive of small business and entrepreneurship.

Environmental regulation has been among the worst offenders in recent years. Nobody can calculate the extraordinary losses associated with the Clean Air Act or the absurdities associated with wetlands or endangered species policies. However, environmental policy can do what it is explicitly intended to do: lower standards of living.

But antitrust policy, in contrast to its stated policy, does not generate competitiveness. Such bogeymen as predatory pricing still scare the bureaucrats at Justice, whereas simple economic analysis can refute the idea that a competitor can sell below his cost of production to take over the market and then sell at monopoly prices later. Any firm that attempts to sell below the costs of production will indefinitely suffer losses. The moment it attempts to raise prices, it invites competitors back into the market.

Civil-rights legislation represents one of the most intrusive regulatory interventions in labor markets. When employers are not able to hire, fire, and promote based on their own criteria of merit, dislocations occur within the firm and in labor markets at large. Moreover, civil rights legislation, by creating legal preferences for some groups, undermines the public's sense of fairness that is the market's hallmark.

There is another cost of economic regulation: it impedes the entrepreneurial discovery process. This process is based on having a wide array of alternatives open to the use of capital. Yet government regulation limits the options of entrepreneurs, and erects barriers to the exercise of entrepreneurial talent. Safety, health, and labor regulations, for example, not only inhibit existing production, they impede the development of better production methods.

Austrians have also developed impressive critiques of redistributionism. Conventional welfare theory argues that if the law of diminishing marginal utility is true, then total utility can be easily increased. If you take a dollar from a rich man, his welfare is slightly diminished, but that dollar is worth less to him than to a poor man. Thus, redistributing a dollar from a rich man to a poor man increases the total utility between the two. The implication is that welfare can be maximized through perfect income equality. The problem with this, say Austrians, is that utilities cannot be added and subtracted, since they are subjective.

Redistributionism takes from property owners and producers and gives, by definition, to nonowners and nonproducers. This diminishes the value of the property that has been redistributed. Far from increasing total welfare, redistributionism diminishes it. By making property and its value less secure, income transfers lessen the benefits of ownership and production, and thus lower the incentives to both.

Austrians reject the use of redistribution to stimulate the economy or otherwise manipulate the structure of economic activity. Increasing taxes, for example, can do nothing but harm. A shorthand for taxes is wealth destruction. They forcibly confiscate property that could otherwise be saved or invested, thus lowering the number of consumer options available. Moreover, there is no such thing as a strict consumer tax. All taxes decrease production.

Austrians do not go along with the view that deficits don't matter. In fact, the requirement that deficits be financed by the public or foreign bond holders drives up interest rates and thus crowds out potential private investment. Deficits also create the danger that they will be financed through central-bank inflation. Yet the answer to deficits is not to increase taxation, which is more destructive than deficits, but rather to balance the budget through necessary spending cuts. Where to cut? Anywhere and everywhere.

The ideal situation is not simply a balanced budget. Government spending itself, regardless of deficit or surplus, should be as small as possible. Why? Because such spending diverts resources from better uses in private markets.

We hear talk of this or that "government investment." Austrians reject this term as an oxymoron. Real investment is taken on by capitalists risking their own money in hopes of satisfying future consumer demands. Government limits the satisfaction of consumer demands by hampering production in the private sector. Besides, government investments are notorious wastes of money, and are in fact consumption spending by politicians and bureaucrats.

Mainstream economists hold that the government must control monetary policy and the structure of banking through cartels, deposit insurance, and a flexible fiat currency. Austrians reject this entire paradigm, and argue that all are better controlled through private markets. In fact, to the extent that today we have serious and radical proposals for having the market play a greater role in banking and monetary policy, it is due to the Austrian School.

Deposit insurance has been on the public mind since the collapse of the S&L industry. The government guarantees deposits and loans with taxpayer money, so this makes financial institutions less careful. Government effectively does to financial institutions what a permissive parent does to a child: encourages poor behavior by eliminating the threat of punishment.

Austrians would eliminate compulsory deposit insurance, and not only allow bank runs to occur, but appreciate their potential as a necessary check. There would be no lender of last resort, that is, the taxpayer, in an Austrian monetary regime, to bail out bankrupt and illiquid institutions.

Much of the Austrian critique of central banking centers around the Mises-Hayek business cycle theory. Both argued that the central bank, and not the market itself, is responsible for the cyclical behavior of business activity. To illustrate the theory, Austrians have undertaken extensive studies of many historical periods of recession and recovery to show that each was preceded by central-bank machinations.

The theory argues that central-bank efforts to lower interest rates below the free-market's level causes borrowers in the capital goods industry to overinvest in their projects. A lower interest rate is normally a signal that consumers' savings are available to back up new production. That is, if a producer borrows to build a new building, there is enough savings for consumers to buy the goods and services that will be made in the building. Projects undertaken can be sustained. But artificially lowered interest rates lead businesses into undertaking unnecessary projects. This creates an artificial boom followed by a bust, once it is clear that savings weren't high enough to justify the degree of expansion.

Austrians point out that the Monetarists' growth rule ignores the "injection effects" of even the smallest increase in money and credit. Such an increase will always create this business-cycle phenomenon, even if it works to maintain a relatively stable index number, as in the 1920s and 1980s.

What then should policy makers do when the economy enters recession? Mostly, nothing. It takes time to wipe out the malinvestment created by the credit boom. Projects that were undertaken have to go bankrupt, employees mistakenly hired must lose their jobs, and wages must fall. After the economy is cleansed of the bad investments induced by the central bank, growth can begin anew, based on a realistic assessment of the future behavior of consumers.

If the government wants to make the recovery process work faster if, say, there is an election coming up, there are some things it can do. It can cut taxes, putting more wealth into private hands to fuel the recovery process. It can eliminate regulations, which inhibit private-sector growth. It can cut spending and reduce the demand on credit markets. It can repeal antidumping laws, and cut tariffs and quotas, to allow consumers to buy imported goods at cheaper prices.

Central banking also creates incentives toward inflation-ary monetary policies. It is not a coincidence that ever since the creation of the Federal Reserve System, the value of the dollar has declined 98 percent. The market did not make this happen. The culprit is the central bank, whose institutional logic drives it toward an inflationary policy, just as a counter-feiter is driven to keep his printing press running.

Austrians would reform this in fundamental ways. Roth-bardians advocate a return to a 100-percent gold coin stan-dard, an end to fractional-reserve commercial banking, and the abolition of the central bank, while Hayekians advocate a system where consumers select currencies from a variety of alternatives.

Today, Austrian economics is on the upswing. Mises's works are read and discussed all over Western and Eastern Europe and the former Soviet Union, as well as Latin Amer-ica and North Asia. But the new interest in America, where the insights of the Austrian School are even more sorely needed, is especially encouraging.

The success of the Ludwig von Mises Institute is testi-mony to this new interest. The primary purpose of the Insti-tute is to ensure that the Austrian School is a major force in the economic debate. To this end, we have cultivated and organized hundreds of professional economists, provided scholarly and popular outlets for their work, educated thou-sands of graduate students in Austrian theory, distributed mil-lions of publications, and formed intellectual communities where these ideas thrive.

Every year we hold a summer instructional seminar on the Austrian School, called the Mises University, with a fac-ulty of more than 25, and top-flight students from around the country. We also hold academic conferences on theoretical and historical subjects, and the Institute's scholars are fre-quent participants at major professional meetings. The Mises Institute assists students and faculty at hundreds of colleges and universities. We have a program for visiting fellows to complete dissertations, and for visiting scholars to pursue new research, as well as being a major center for graduate students.

New books on the Austrian School appear every few months, and Austrians are writing for all the major scholarly journals. Misesian insights are presented in hundreds of economics classrooms all over the country (whereas just 20 years ago, no more than a dozen classrooms presented them). Austrians are the rising stars in the profession, the economists with the new ideas that attract students, the ones on the cutting edge with a promarket and antistatist orientation.

Most of these scholars have been cultivated through the Mises Institute's academic conferences, publications, and teaching programs. With the Institute backing the Austrian School, tradition and constructive radicalism combine to create an attractive and intellectually vibrant alternative to conventional thought.

The future of Austrian economics is bright, which bodes well for the future of liberty itself. For if we are to reverse the trends of statism in this century, and reestablish a free market, the intellectual foundation must be the Austrian School. That is why Austrian economics matters.

THE VIABILITY OF THE GOLD STANDARD

[This speech was delivered at the Burton S. Blumert Gold Conference in San Mateo, California, September 14, 2002.]

In the 19th century, notes Murray N. Rothbard, debates on monetary issues were highly public and intensely controversial. Do you favor the national bank? The gold standard? Bimetallism? What is your opinion of the free silver movement? What is most important: a highly liquid money stock that can prop up commodity prices, or a sound dollar that promotes thrift and discourages debt accumulation? Should the monetary system reward debtors or creditors?

These were issues debated in the nation's newspapers, discussed in political meetings, and raged on in the streets. Every educated man had an opinion. Part of the reason is that, frankly, people were much better educated in those days. It is astonishing to imagine today, but average people had the mental equipment to enable them to understand these complicated issues, if not always to arrive at the right conclusions.

The federal government had long been involved in money precisely because this is one of the first areas a government likes to get its grubby hands on when it takes power. The US government was no exception, despite constitutional provisions that would appear to restrict its monetary power.

Matters are radically different today. It is very rare to ever see an article addressing the money question in the nation's newspapers. Debates and discussions are left to the academic journals or the self-published tracts of money cranks—with the major exception of the Austrian economists, who continue to believe that the money issue is both academically important and politically crucial.

This is why the Mises Institute has been sponsoring research and writing on the gold standard, and promoting an idea that most public intellectuals find absurdly anachronistic: that a gold standard is better than our current monetary system. What's more, we not only believe that the gold standard had a better record historically, we believe that we ought to institute a gold standard right now.

Even many libertarians find themselves mystified by our focus. Who cares about these arcane issues of monetary policy? What does it have to do with the fate of human liberty? Could we pick a policy agenda that is more unlikely to come about? Are we just gluttons for political failure? Why not trim our ambitions to political reality?

It is true that not a soul in Washington apart from our heroic Congressman from Texas, Ron Paul, says a word about the gold standard. Even Alan Greenspan, who once wrote that freedom is inseparable from the gold standard, dreads being asked about the subject. To him, it is entirely theoretical with no practical import. In any case, he doesn't want people looking too closely at the kinds of things he does at the Fed, any more than the Wizard of Oz wanted anyone to pull back the curtain.

Most economists have no interest in the issue. What's more, the most influential economist of the last century, John Maynard Keynes, hated the gold standard with astonishing intensity, and he considered it his great accomplishment in life to have assisted in its destruction. Even to this day, his influence is immense, with most economists accepting the broad framework he laid out in his work, and sharing his conviction that the worst thing that could befall any society is for the government to lose its power to manage economic life.

There are many objections to the conventional view of the gold standard, but let me just respond to the point about realism. There are a lot of policies which seem unrealistic to promote. We can admit that there is little prospect that the post office will be privatized anytime soon, but that fact does not diminish our responsibility to push the idea. Nothing could be more obvious than admitting that private enterprise would do a better job of delivering letters than the government. But if no one says it—if people are not willing to state what is true, again and again—all hope for change is lost. And sometimes, just stating what is true is enough to bring about change when conditions are ripe for it.

In the debate on the post office, we have the added advantage of being able to point to a superior and very well developed sector of private package and letter delivery. The reason it is thriving is due to loopholes in the law, which these companies exploit. If the letter statutes were repealed, I have no doubt that first-class letters would be deliverable by private enterprise within days. That is precisely why the post office is so anxious to hold onto its legal privileges.

In any case, as with the gold standard, it might be said that advocating privatization is politically unrealistic and therefore a waste of time. What's more, we might say that by continuing to harp on the issue, we only marginalize ourselves, proving that we are on the fringe. Again, I submit that there is no better way to assure that an issue will always be off the table than to stop talking about it.

This applies to the gold standard too. The case for radical monetary reform is as obvious as the need to sell the post office. Every year or 18 months, the world goes through some sort of monetary convulsion. In the last 10 years, we've seen it in Mexico, all through Asia, and now Latin America. To one degree or another, there are few problems of international economics that are not traceable to the grave limitations of a world fiat money system.

This includes the problem of the business cycle itself. In the 2001 and following economic downturn, unlike any I can remember, the Austrian theory of the trade cycle has received a fantastic amount of public commentary and attention. The core idea of this theory is that Fed-created credit is responsible for the boom and bust, and it has been embraced by top economists at some of the largest and most prestigious investment houses.

The Mises Institute has done a fine job in getting the word out about the true cause of the business cycle, but the real reason it is getting such attention is that it provides such a compelling explanation of the 1990s bubble and the later crisis. Neither do most of these economists doubt that financial bubbles would not be a problem under the gold standard, even if they believe the gold standard introduces problems of its own.

Far from being an arcane and anachronistic issue, then, we can see that the gold standard and the issues it raises get right to the heart of the current debate concerning the future of the world economy and its reform. What the critics who denounce gold are really saying is that the government and its friends don't like the idea of the gold standard, so therefore they are not going to favor one.

Why do the government and its partisans dislike the gold standard? It removes the discretionary power of the Fed by placing severe limits on the ability of the central bank to inflate the money supply. Without that discretionary power, the government has far fewer tools of central planning at its disposal. Government can regulate, which is a function of the police power. It can tax, which involves taking people's property. And it can spend, which means redistributing other people's property. But its activities in the financial area are radically curbed.

Think of your local and state governments. They tax and spend. They manipulate and intervene. As with all governments from the beginning of time, they generally retard social progress and muck things up as much as possible. What they do not do, however, is run huge deficits, accumulate trillions in debt, reduce the value of money, bail out foreign governments, provide endless credits to failing enterprises, administer hugely expensive and destructive social insurance schemes, or bring about immense swings in business activity.

State and local governments are awful, and they must be relentlessly checked, but they are not anything like the threat of the federal government. Neither are they as arrogant and convinced of their own infallibility and indispensability. They lack the aura of invincibility that the central government enjoys.

Why is this? You might say it is because the federal government already does these things, but no government has ever been troubled by the prospect of providing redundant services. You might say that state-level constitutions restrict their activities, but our experience with the federal government demonstrates that constitutions can't restrain a government by themselves. The main reason, I believe, is that the state and local governments do not issue their own currencies controlled by central banks.

It is the central bank, and only the central bank, that works as the government's money machine, and this makes all the difference. Now, it is not impossible that a central bank can exist alongside a gold standard, a lender of last resort that avoids the temptation to destroy that which restrains it. In the same way, it is possible for someone with an insatiable appetite to sit at a banquet table of delicious food and not eat.

Let's just say that the existence of a central bank introduces an occasion of sin for the government. That is why, under the best gold standard, there would be no central bank, gold coins would circulate as freely as their substitutes, and rules against fraud and theft would prohibit banks from pyramiding credit on top of demand deposits. As long as we are constructing the perfect system, all coinage would be private. Banks would be treated as businesses, no special privileges, no promises of bailout, no subsidized insurance, and no connection to government at any level.

This is the free-market system of monetary management, which means turning over the institution of money entirely to the market economy. As with any institution in a free society, it is not imposed from above, dictated by a group of experts, but is the *de facto* result that comes about in a society that consistently respects private-property rights and encourages enterprise.

Money is not something chosen by social managers but the consequence of economic development as society moves from barter to indirect exchange. One commodity that is widely in demand comes to operate as a medium of exchange, a commodity for which any good or service can be traded with the expectation that this commodity will be demanded by others in future exchanges. Precious metals, gold in particular, have traditionally served as the money of choice.

As Rothbard explained, the institutions we call banks serve a dual function in a free-market system. First, they provide safekeeping for one's money, and offer money substitutes that they certify really do represent money in the vault. And second, they provide credit services, both to savers who would like to see money risked in the loan market and to borrowers who need cash for purposes of consumption or investment. The banks work as brokers between these parties to effect mutually beneficial exchanges.

If any market-chosen commodity can perform the function of money, why are we Austro-libertarians focused on gold? It is often said that we have an obsession with gold and a fixation on the subject of money. To some degree, however, this alleged obsession has been shared by popular culture and by financial markets, as a continuing testimony to the power of the idea of gold as a guarantor of value.

Whenever a writer wants to convey the idea that something sets the highest standard, he refers to it as the gold standard. I was amused the other day to read in the London *Daily Telegraph* an article on grade inflation in British schools, in which the writer counterpoised the grading gold standard of the past. The metaphor seems quite apt.

As for financial markets, events this year have again underscored the underlying obsession, if you want to call it that, that the world's financial markets have with gold. It is not a coincidence that gold-mining stocks were the best performing during the bust period of this business cycle. And earlier this summer, we saw spot prices of gold begin to move very rapidly in response to the growing perception that the financial sector was far from bottoming out. Try as it might, the establishment just can't seem to crush the perception that gold is more reliable than government's paper money.

Indeed, gold continues to be seen as a standard of soundness, as the commodity to flee to in times of emergency, as the last store of value that can be counted on. Neither are these emergencies unknown in the modern world. In Latin America this summer, we witnessed governments prohibiting withdrawals from banks during financial crises, just as we saw in the early days of the Great Depression in the United States. Gold continues to be perceived as a safe haven from the wiles of political opportunism and violence.

J. Bradford DeLong, former assistant US Treasury Secretary, wrote the following just the other day:

> Eighty years ago, John Maynard Keynes argued that governments needed to take responsibility for maintaining full employment and price stability, that the pre-World War I gold standard had not been the golden age people thought it was, and that its successes were the result of a lucky combination of circumstances unlikely to be repeated. Keynes was an optimist in believing that governments could learn to manage the business cycle.

DeLong continues to point out that the record of post-gold currencies has been a disaster as compared with their promise.

In this respect, fiat currency has much in common with socialism. They both failed to live up to their promises, and, indeed, failed miserably by every standard. But they both long outlived their failures, simply because political elites had too much invested in them to change the system, and the intellectual class worked overtime to shore up support for the failed system. Eventually, of course, full-blown socialism collapsed, just as I believe that fiat currency systems will.

Murray Rothbard has written:

> It might be thought that the mix of government and money is too far gone, too pervasive in the economic system, too inextricably bound up in the economy, to be eliminated without economic destruction. . . . In truth, taking back our money would be relatively simple and straightforward, much less difficult than the daunting task of denationalizing and decommunizing the Communist countries of Eastern Europe and the former Soviet Union.

And for all the reasons that gold eventually emerged as the money of choice thousands of years ago, it continues to have the properties that make it the best money of choice today. It is portable, divisible, fungible, durable, and has a high ratio of value per unit of weight. It is as compatible with today's economy, driven by information technology and lightning quick financial transactions, as it was compatible with the 19th-century economy of heavy industry and agriculture. It is not technical limitations that prevent the dollar from being redefined as a unit weight of gold, but political ones.

The monetary benefits of a gold standard are clear enough, and they include life without inflation, an end to the business cycle, rational economic calculation in accounting and international trade, an encouragement to savings, and a dethroning of the government-connected financial elite.

But it is also political considerations that draw people to support the gold standard. Gold limits the power of the State and puts power back in the hands of the people.

Once you begin to understand the role of the monetary regime in the building of the modern statist enterprise—in providing the means of funding for the entire welfare-warfare state, in generating financial instability, in destroying savings, and undermining living standards—you realize that there is far too little interest in the subject in the mainstream press. You begin to realize that the 19th-century focus on the money issue was entirely appropriate.

Once having read Mises or Rothbard or any number of great monetary theorists, you begin to realize that understanding the monetary regime is the key that unlocks the mysteries of political control in our time. The Fed was created not to scientifically manage the economy—as the journals claimed at the time—but because it met the institutional needs of both the government and the banking industry. The government sought a means of finance that didn't depend on taxation, and the banking industry sought what Rothbard called a cartelization device. That is to say, the banking industry was seeking some way to prevent competitive pressures between banks from limiting their ability to expand credit.

Well, the central bank fit the bill. A central bank managing a currency that is not tied to anything real fits the bill even better. If a little power to inflate is good for the government and its connected banking and financial interests, a lot of power to inflate is even better. For this reason, it was very likely that the gold standard could not have survived the creation of a central bank, and, for the same reason, the creation of a new gold standard will have to do away with the central bank that would always threaten to bring it down.

The power to create fiat money is the most ominous power ever bestowed on any human being. This power is rightly criminalized when it is exercised by private individuals, and even today, everyone knows why counterfeiting is wrong and knavish. Far fewer are aware of the role of the federal government, the Fed, and the fiat dollar in making possible the largest counterfeiting operation in human history, which is called the world dollar standard. Fewer still understand the connection between this officially sanctioned criminality and the business cycle, the rise and collapse of the stock market, and the continued erosion of the value of the dollar.

In fact, a sizeable percentage of even educated adults would be astounded to discover that the Federal Reserve does more than manage the nation's money accounts. In fact, its main activity consists in actually creating money that distorts production and creates inflation and the business cycle. In fact, I would go further to suggest that many educated adults believe that gold continues to serve as the ultimate backing of our monetary system, and would be astonished to discover that our money is backed by nothing but more of itself.

We have our work cut out for us, to be sure, mainly at the educational level. We must continue to state the obvious at every opportunity, that the fiat system is exactly what it is, a system of paper money backed by nothing of real value. We must continue to point out that because of this, our economic system is not depression-proof, but rather highly vulnerable to complete meltdown. We must continue to draw attention to the only long-term solution: a complete separation of money and State based on the commodity that the market has always chosen as money, namely, gold.

Apart from making the intellectual case, the biggest obstacle we currently face is that most all theoretically viable plans for radical monetary reform depend heavily on those who are currently in charge of mismanaging our money being the ones to manage a transition. In many ways, this is akin to expecting the politburo to have instituted a free-market economy in Russia before the great counterrevolution. Can we really expect that Alan Greenspan is going to wake up one day and decide to do the right thing? It is possible, but I seriously doubt it.

I recognize that this problem is a real one, but it is no different from the rest of the practical problems of instituting freedom. When we call for spending cuts, we are implicitly calling on Congress to do something that is against its self-interest. When we call for deregulating financial markets, we are expecting the SEC to do the very thing it is least likely to do from a bureaucratic pressure-group perspective. And when we call for sound money, we are similarly expecting those who currently benefit from the present system to have a change of heart and mind, and to act against their own interests.

This takes us back to our original question: is the gold standard history? Is it so preposterously unrealistic to advocate it that we might as well move on to other things? It won't surprise you that my answer is no. If there is one thing that a long-term view of politics teaches, it is that only the long-term really matters.

Back in 1997–98 you were considered a crabby kook, and behind the times, to warn that the bull market in tech stocks could not last. But economic law intervened, and fashions changed. Back in those days, too, had you suggested that the business cycle had not been repealed, you would have been dismissed out of hand. But economic law intervened.

In the same way, there will come a time when the current money and banking system, living off credit created by a fiat money system, will be stretched beyond the limit. When it happens, attitudes will turn on a dime. No advocate of the gold standard looks forward to the crisis nor to the human suffering that will come with it. We do, however, look forward to the reassertion of economic law in the field of money and banking. When it becomes incredibly obvious that something drastic must replace the current system, new attention will be paid to the voices that have long cast aspersions on the current system and called for a restoration of sound money.

Must a crisis lead to monetary reforms that we will like? Not necessarily, and, for that matter, a crisis is not a necessary precursor to radical reform. As Mises himself used to emphasize, political history has no predetermined course. Everything depends on the ideas that people hold about fundamental issues of human freedom and the place of government. Under the right conditions, I have no doubt that a gold standard can be completely restored, no matter how unfavorable the current environment appears toward its restoration.

What is essential for us today is to continue the research, the writing, the advocacy for sound money, for a dollar that is as good as gold, for a monetary system that is separate from the State. It is a beautiful vision indeed, one in which the people and not the government and its connected interest groups maintain control of their money and its safekeeping.

What has been true for hundreds of years remains true today. The clearest path to the restoration of economic health is the free market undergirded by a sound monetary system. The clearest path toward economic destruction is for us to stop working toward what is right and true.

WHAT CAUSES THE BUSINESS CYCLE?

*[This speech was given at the Mises Institute's "Austrian Econom-
ics and Investing" Conference, Vienna, Austria, May 25, 1988.
(Some information has been updated.)]*

The greatest mystery in the history of economic theory, and still the most unresolved controversy in the economics profession, is the nature and source of the business cycle. Why do recessions occur and why do booms occur? Why do they tend to follow each other with some degree of regularity?

Solving the mystery of the business cycle is a different task than confronted Adam Smith and the classical economists. They sought to answer the question of how economies grow. They concluded that free exchange and capital accumulation are the sources. But the mystery of the business cycle deals with a far more complex problem of why growth seems to occur intermittently. This is a question that only began to absorb economists in the middle of the 19th century.

Part of the reason is that business cycles simply didn't exist in the prior centuries. We get a clue to the ultimate resolution of this problem by noting that central banks didn't exist before business cycles began to be noticed. But it took economists a very long time before they put two and two together to understand that it is the activities of the central bank itself that bring about the trade cycle.

Business cycles raise a particular question. It is not why businesses fail. We know that in a vibrant market economy, businesses do fail. Entrepreneurial forecasting ability is not perfect, innovation disrupts plans, and consumer demand is always changing. The only economies where businesses do not fail are stagnant, socialist ones. Thus, to the question of why businesses start and fail, we already have the answer: the market rewards only those who serve the consuming public, and not all businesses do so all the time.

The question that the business cycle asks is different. Why do business errors often occur in clusters? Why do entrepreneurs make mistakes on an aggregate level? Why, if you look at macroeconomic data, do we see these large swings in economic activity that have come to be called booms and busts?

In Karl Marx's view, the business cycle was an inherent part of the capitalist economic system and a signal of its fundamental instability. He foresaw cycles worsening, with each recession worse than the last, and ultimately leading to the breakdown of capitalism itself. For decades socialists echoed his forecast, and attempted to reinterpret every cycle as a millennial sign that the capitalist system was being trampled by forces of history.

The cycle theories of Marx were far from the only reason his ideas came to be accepted by intellectuals. The real source of attraction to Marxism was its promise of an egalitarian society, one that operated without traditional restraints on economic and sexual behavior. Envy-ridden intellectuals, forever believing themselves to be underpaid and overworked, were attracted to the idea of expropriating the capitalist class and enjoying the proceeds. Since then, these intellectuals have learned they can do this without bringing about the breakdown of capitalism. They can work through Congress and state legislatures to bring about the same result.

The Great Depression seemed to confirm Marx's view of the business cycle and gave a boost to the socialist cause. Beginning in the early 1930s, a huge debate ensued between market advocates like Henry Hazlitt, author of *Economics in One Lesson*, and socialist intellectuals writing in the pages of leftist weeklies like the *Nation*. The socialists pointed to the declining share of the return on capital enjoyed by the workers and the rising profits of the exploiter class. They said that the Great Depression ensued when workers no longer had the means to purchase products of their own making. The only answer, then, is to redistribute property from the capitalists to the workers, and insure that society, as embodied by the State, and not private owners of capital, would control the means of production.

Here again, over time, the socialists learned that it was not necessary to bring about a revolution to achieve this end. Congress, the executive branch, and state legislatures were all that was necessary to prevent owners of capital from controlling the uses of their own property.

For a time, it appeared that the socialist interpretation of the Great Depression was winning out. And even to this day, the interpretation is underscored in John Kenneth Galbraith's interesting but wrongheaded book on the Great Depression, and in countless PBS documentaries. The fallacy with all of these accounts is that they deal with the downturn, as if it is the only issue worth examining, but not with the larger perspective of the cycle in general. Only by broadening our horizons to understand the boom phase of the cycle as well can we arrive at reasonable conclusions and solid recommendations for minimizing the role of cycles.

In 1936, John Maynard Keynes came out with his *General Theory*, which came to dominate macroeconomic thinking for decades following. Though his original work is rarely read by professional economists, and virtually never discussed in the classroom setting, the assumptions behind his theory still dominate much of economic thinking.

In Keynes's theory, like Marx's, business cycles are an inherent part of the market economy. But he argued it was not necessary to overthrow property and markets in order to control them. The government, working hand in glove with Keynesian economists of course, could pursue policies that would keep business cycles at bay. The problem, said Keynes, was fundamentally twofold.

First, the price system doesn't work very well or reflect real economic needs. Prices and wages often do not adjust in ways that coordinate the economy. But by manipulating prices, mainly through inflation, the system could be fixed up.

Second, the investment sector is fundamentally irrational. Animal spirits periodically sweep through markets, causing businesses to underinvest in things that are needed and over-invest in things that are not.

Keynes offered two ways out of this problem. We can live with the resulting business cycles, but this creates its own problems since the price system is so deeply flawed. Or we can manipulate the demand side of the economy to force it into coordination with the supply side. As a result of this Keynesian-style analysis, the government now had an intellectual justification for the huge New Deal machinery that had been established to manage the economy. After the war, this Keynesian machinery became a permanent part of government policy.

Economists deluded themselves into thinking they could smooth out business cycles by managing countercyclical fiscal and monetary policies. The idea was this: in an economic downturn, the government could goose the money supply and run a deficit to lift the economy back into normalcy. Once recovered, the government would drive up interest rates again and run a budget surplus. It would be as simple as managing the gears on a stick-shift car while driving through mountain terrain.

The result, of course, was far different. In the postwar period, business cycles became progressively worse, with every attempt to manage them seeming to create its own problems, among them inflation, hyperinflation, enormous government debts, and rising deficits. I think we should also include, as a cost of Keynesian policy, the loss of freedom that Americans experience. No longer did we have a government that largely stayed out of economic policy. Rather, we had a government that regarded itself as all-knowing and regarded the market economy as essentially stupid.

It is often said that John Maynard Keynes and the New Deal saved capitalism from itself. In fact, his ideas radically distorted what we *call* capitalism. The US government is the biggest, most powerful government in human history. To this day, it is involved in every area of American economic life. It has veto power over the hiring and firing decisions of virtually every business in the country. It tells people how old they must be to work, how much they must be paid, what benefits they must be provided, and taxes a third or more of their income. The government regulates, in minute detail, the architecture of every commercial building in the country. With its antitrust laws and taxing power, it can make or break huge corporations. Recently we've seen the Justice Department attempt to guide the direction of software development, even threatening to bar the introduction of newer generations of software.

Yet despite all this, the US is widely seen today as the paragon of capitalism. A century-and-a-half ago, all this would have been seen as the embodiment of wild-eyed socialist experimentation. But a century that has been dominated by the State as much as this one has changed everyone's standards of what constitutes freedom.

Is the business cycle truly a natural part of the free market? Ludwig von Mises explored this question in his 1912 book called the *Theory of Money and Credit*. He first explored the possibility that discoordinations in gold flows between countries, caused by bad monetary policies, might be the source of booms and busts. And while he concluded that this is the root of international business cycles, he said this doesn't explain how a business cycle could be created in a single country. In exploring this issue, he went much further in his analysis than any previous thinker.

His resultant theory is called the Austrian theory of the business cycle. The Austrian theory notes that it is crucial to understand the boom times in order to understand the bust. To generate an economic boom, the central bank artificially lowers interest rates, creating the illusion of increased savings. Faced with new credit availability, the business sector borrows to expand production and begin long-term investment projects. The boom continues for as long as interest rates remain artificially held down. Businesses continue to invest in projects for which there is no real, underlying economic demand or rationale. This type of investment is what Mises called malinvestment.

Note that during this period, the increase in money and credit doesn't necessarily result in higher prices. The monetary inflation is bringing about a fundamental structural change in the economy, but it is not creating any visible ill effects. Production is expanding, unemployment is down, interest rates are low, the stock market is booming, and everyone appears to be getting richer. We can recognize this in the US and Britain in the 1920s, Asia in the 1980s and early 1990s, and quite possibly the US today.

But this boom is not self-sustaining. When businesses bring products to the market at the end of the production process, they are met with consumers who have neither the savings nor the income to purchase them. Once prices eventually do begin to creep up, the discoordinations between the investment and spending sector begin to be revealed. The central bank raises rates to prevent conspicuous declines in the purchasing power of money, and the boom begins to reverse itself. This process can occur over six months or 15 years (Japan). There is no set formula. The timing is largely unpredictable as well, especially in a global economy.

But these business cycles do terrible damage to the economy. They bankrupt businesses that were only trying to follow the market's signaling devices. Businessmen could not have known with certainty that the Fed was manipulating the signals. Business cycles throw people out of work, not because managers or the owners of businesses were engaged in inefficient production, but because everyone was dealt a bad hand by the money managers at the top of the central bank.

This is essentially what brought about the Great Depression. Throughout the 1920s, the Fed engaged in an expansionist monetary policy, giving stocks, real estate, and heavily capitalized businesses an artificial shot in the arm. When the stock market finally crashed, and the bubble burst, the exaggerated investment was exposed as a fraud. Thus, we can see that it is not the market that is the source of business cycles. Rather, the business cycle is the working out of a market attempting to correct for the failures of central bankers and the government officials who cheer them on.

The central bank has long felt the pressures of politics to keep interest rates unnaturally low. These pressures come from both the president and the Congress. The president, of course, is concerned about keeping rates low before elections. Quite often, presidents are willing to tolerate a recession after election to their first term. But they will not tolerate one leading up to the election itself. The Fed chairman, who frequently proclaims his independence from politics, is in fact utterly dependent on favors from the White House. In order to maintain the Fed's much ballyhooed independence, it must do what the president wants.

The central bank also faces pressures from its member banks, who profit from the boom created by lower rates.

Congress also has an impact. If we ever see the Fed chairman threatened with investigations into the Fed's secrecy, or badgered in front of committees, it is nearly always done in times when interest rates are high. Special interest groups—from large manufacturers to farmers—lobby their Congressmen to intervene. There are very few politicians who call the Fed to complain when it is keeping the lid on interest rates.

Of course, the media play a role in the interest-rate conspiracy as well. They are always ready to tell the public about the sad plight of borrowers who are being squeezed by high interest rates. Telling the story of a structure of production that has fallen into misalignment because of artificially low rates just doesn't make good copy. The media fan the flames during recessions, especially when every business failure is considered to be a national tragedy instead of part of the natural cleansing process of the market economy.

The media also add to the general sense that the boom phase of the cycle is the good phase and the bust is the bad phase. In fact, looked at from an economic perspective, the boom phase is the one that should worry us. It is during these times that borrowers are being misled and economic misalignments are taking place. The bust represents a period of honesty and decency, when at last reality is catching up to the lies that low interest rates have been telling.

The common misperception that economic booms should go on forever is what gives impetus for governments to intervene. But any intervention designed to soften the blow of a recession can only end up prolonging the agony, just as it did during the Great Depression, and as such efforts are doing today in Asia. What should government do during a recession? The short answer is nothing. It should take care to ensure there are no obstacles to the downward adjustment of wages and that the market is free to generate entrepreneurial opportunities, but otherwise it should stay out of the way.

Compare the actions of Warren G. Harding with those of Herbert Hoover. In 1921, the US experienced a major economic downturn, which was a direct result of the inflationized economy of wartime. Unemployment reached 11.7 percent, even as high as 15 percent, and output crashed. This was after unemployment had fallen to 1.4 percent in 1919. Economists generally rank the severity of this depression more extensive than even the one that would follow a decade later.

There was no shortage of advice given to the Harding administration. Henry Ford and Thomas Edison wanted to create fiat money on a huge scale. The secretary of commerce, Herbert Hoover, wanted a massive public-works program. Labor leaders demanded make-work programs.

In the end, however, before these plans could be implemented, the economy began to rebound. By 1922, unemployment was back down to reasonable levels, output was expanding, and the economy was rebounding across the board. This was *laissez-faire* at work. The politicians could not act fast enough, and thank goodness. The depression was over in a year.

Compare that to the actions of the Hoover administration. Despite his reputation as a do-nothing president, he did far too much. He attempted to keep wages propped up and to stop business failures. He embarked on a massive public works spending program and erected high tariff barriers. He may have been living out a fantasy first developed when he was secretary of commerce, but the economy was the victim. We did not enter recovery as we should have and could have, and instead we got a national socialist as president for four straight terms.

Let me proceed, then, to an analysis of where we are today [1998]. There is no shortage of New Era thinking. The line you read again and again in the pages of the *Wall Street Journal* is that the business cycle has been abolished, and that we have entered into a new paradigm of permanent prosperity. This kind of talk worries me. It is precisely what we had heard about Asia for the last several years. And it is what was said in 1920s America.

The bottom line is that there ain't no such thing as a New Era. As long as we live on this earth, there are certain fixed cause-and-effect relationships at work that cannot be repealed. Among them is this: an economy pumped up by artificial credit will eventually enter recession. When it happens and what the effects will be are open questions. But that it will happen should not be in dispute.

Can we know where we are in a cycle? We can get an inkling by looking at the data, particularly Federal Reserve money supply figures, savings rates, and basic stock indicators. We first have to ask ourselves: where are the excesses? Inflation is low and business investment doesn't appear to be particularly overblown. But look at the stock market. We've experienced astounding increases, with stock prices having quadrupled since 1990. The price/earnings ratios are now at a historic high of 28, from a postwar average of 14. At the same time, personal saving has fallen rather dramatically. In 1992, personal saving was 6.2 percent of disposable income. By 1997, it had fallen to 3.8 percent of disposable income. This is the lowest rate since 1946.

Greenspan has not abolished business cycles. But he has been lucky enough to preside over a new era in monetary affairs, one in which the dollar has been catapulted from a regional currency to the world's reserve currency. The dollar's hegemonic reign has allowed him to conduct a reckless policy of socializing investment risk while not paying the price. From the end of 1990 to the end of 1996, the Fed used its open market operations to increase the monetary base (MB), which is currency plus bank reserves, by 55 percent. Currency itself increased 60 percent.

As Jeffrey Herbener of Grove City College has pointed out, the dollar-reserve system of the "global economy" of the 1990s is the resurrection of Keynes's Bretton Woods system without gold. Under the "gold-reserve" system of Bretton Woods, each country's currency had a fixed exchange rate against the dollar, and foreign governments could redeem the dollar at the US Treasury for gold at the fixed rate of $35 an ounce.

The linchpin of the Bretton Woods agreement was the fixed rate of redemption between the dollar and gold. The Fed undermined this link by accelerating monetary inflation in the 1960s to help finance expenditures for the Great Society and the Vietnam War. From the beginning of 1960 to the end of 1964, the Fed increased the money base 3 percent per year, but from the beginning of 1965 to the end of 1970, the Fed more than doubled the rate of increase to 6.3 percent. The average annual rate of price inflation went from 1.3 percent in the earlier period to 4.2 percent in the latter one.

After increasing the monetary base 8.7 percent per year from 1971 to 1974, the Fed accelerated the rate to 10.4 percent from 1975 to 1981. But after the debacle of the first half of the 1970s, it was difficult to convince foreigners to hold more dollars as reserve. Accelerating monetary and credit inflation by the Fed led to severe domestic price inflation (average annual rates of 11.2 percent), soaring interest rates (peaking in 1981 at a 14 percent 3-month rate), collapsing capital values (from 1976 to 1982, the Dow lost 22 percent and stood at 774 in 1982), and higher unemployment (peaking at 9.7 percent in 1982, a rate not seen since 1941).

This entire scenario is precisely the reverse of the American economy in the 1990s. From 1982 through 1990, the dollar began to regain its status as the world's reserve currency. The Fed expanded the monetary base 11 percent per year in the 1980s, but the demand to hold dollars overseas helped soak up the monetary inflation, and the American economy experienced economic growth with low levels of price inflation. The annual rate of price inflation was only 5.9 percent. But the improved performance of the economy in the 1980s was only a foretaste of the renaissance of dollar dominance in the world.

American supremacy in the wake of the collapse of communism allowed the Fed to fully exploit the international dollar-reserve system. The new system opened up a vast new vista for overseas dollar holdings. From Russia and Eastern Europe to China and East Asia, the governments of former communist countries began to soak up dollars to hold as official reserves as they became part of the American, "global" system. From the beginning of 1991 to the end of 1996, the Fed increased the monetary base 9.1 percent per year, while price inflation ran only 3.6 percent annually.

Like Bretton Woods, the new regime depends on foreigners' willingness to hold dollars and use them as the basis for their own domestic monetary inflation and credit expansion. Only with harmonized monetary policies can the system survive.

But therein lies the great danger of the system to the American economy. A rogue nation will be tempted to defend its currency and stave off devaluation by spending its dollar reserves. Any significant disgorging of dollars would threaten to ignite price inflation in America if the dollars were repatriated. Significant domestic price inflation would, at best, bring a repeat of the 1970s, and, at worst, a hyperinflation.

This danger explains the US interest in promoting IMF austerity policies and bailouts. The bailouts are intended to soften the blow of devaluation and price inflation. In exchange for taxpayers subsidizing banks and large corporations, and other key beneficiaries of the system, the IMF can use the bailout money as leverage to impose conditions favorable for the future of the dollar-reserve system.

In the last three years, the system has faced a $50 billion bailout of Mexico, a $57 billion bailout of South Korea, $43 billion for Indonesia, $18 billion for Thailand, for a total of $118 billion in Asia (some estimate that it will eventually rise to $160 billion) to fend off its own destruction. But by delaying the day of reckoning with bailouts, the international mountain of dollars and debt grows, making the inevitable collapse all the more devastating.

The system will not be able to prevent the disgorging of dollar reserves to fend off Asian-style financial debacles in China, South America, Russia, and a repeat performance in Mexico. If the euro becomes the common currency of the EU, its members replace their dollar reserves with euros. And if Japan recovers, the yen will become the reserve currency across Asia. Global dollar hegemony will be at an end.

The Fed has overseen the best of times for the American economy in the 1990s, a period of rapid monetary inflation and credit expansion with current benefits of low interest rates, high earnings, soaring capital values, low unemployment, and steady economic growth. It has come courtesy of foreigners who have absorbed enormous quantities of dollars and, in so doing, kept the business cycle at bay.

Don't count on that to last forever.

We could abolish business cycles if we had the will. It would require extreme monetary discipline, an end of risky socialism, the abolition of institutions like deposit insurance and fractional-reserve banking that sustain essentially bankrupt banks and investment houses, and finally, the institution of a true world money based on gold. Until then, we can expect that our troubles are far from over. We can only hope that when the inevitable recession does set in that Greenspan won't do something stupid like bail out the stock market, attempt to defend the dollar internationally, or keep banks from failing. Sadly, given his close working relationship with the White House, and the fecklessness of the GOP, the next downturn of the business cycle is likely to look less like 1921 and 1922 and more like 1931 and 1932.

[Note: In the recession of 2001–2003, Greenspan has done all of the above.]

Is Inflation Dead?

[Based on a speech delivered at the Mises Institute Supporters Summit, Palm Springs, California, February, 27, 1998.]

Wall Street remains constantly worried about two forces in American economic life, inflation and deflation. These days, fear of one does not necessarily exclude fear of the other. It seems Wall Street worries about inflation on Monday, Wednesday, and Friday. On Tuesday and Thursday, it worries about deflation. Or perhaps it worries about both at the same time.

Just what is the concern? Of course, inflation is one of the most destructive forces in all of human history. In order for an economy to function, money must be sound and its value must be honestly come by. For most of human history, soundness and honesty were guaranteed because money was just another name for the most valuable commodity, namely gold. Gold was ideal money because it was portable, durable, divisible, fungible, and scarce. Above all, scarce.

Gold has been money throughout most of our nation's history. The government had little to no control over its supply and therefore its value. But around 1913–1918, in the midst of wartime, the foundation of money in gold began to be frittered away. Over the decades, the link became progressively less secure until, in 1973, the last remnants of the gold standard were done away with. If you put a dollar in a mattress in 1970, and pulled it out today, it would be worth less than a quarter.

Why? The monetary authorities have conducted a 35-year war against the sound dollar, which is precisely what we would expect given that the dollar no longer has any link to gold. The result has been theft on a grand scale. In fact, the government has extracted more from us in inflation than it has in tax increases over this same period. The government and its friends, and not the American people, benefit from inflation, for reasons I'll explain shortly.

The demise of the gold standard is what made this extortion possible. Under a gold standard, there are strict limits on how much money can be created. Under the paper money standard, there are no limits. It always surprises me when I talk to college students, businessmen, and even to bankers, that not everyone understands this. They do not understand that there is no gold backing up the nation's currency at all. There is no limit on how much of it must be created by the government and the banking cartel. Thus there is no limit to the extent to which money can continue to be watered down by monetary authorities. The only real restraint on monetary growth today is fear of a backlash by the financial community.

But Wall Street rarely takes the long view. So when inflation worries begin to dominate the market, it is not the fear of what further monetary depreciation might mean to American families that is the primary concern. Rather, traders are often concerned about the Federal Reserve's response to renewed inflation. They are concerned the Fed might raise interest rates in an effort to counter inflation tendencies. And higher interest rates mean less borrowing, less credit expansion by the banking system, and thus represent a potential end to the decade-long party on Wall Street.

And what about the threat of deflation? This term, which hasn't been heard in public for many years, first started being drummed lately when the price indexes first recorded a drop in selected consumer and producer prices. In common parlance, dating back to the Great Depression, deflation is supposed to be as much a threat to economic stability as inflation. The reasons the financial markets fear it have as much to do with the new uncertainties widespread deflation introduces, as much as they have to do with the real effects of deflation.

What are the real effects of deflation? A common myth is that it leads to lower profitability, and possibly even recession or depression. Is this true? A good way to tell is to set aside macroeconomic data like the consumer and producer price index, and look at a particular industry. Consider the price of computer hardware. For 20 years, the prices of computers have been falling while quality has been rising, and memory and speed have increased at a breakneck pace. Yet the industry is also among the most profitable.

Falling prices typically signal rising prosperity, just as they did in the latter half of the 19th century. In fact, if we had a truly free market coupled with a gold standard of sound money, falling prices would become the norm. You might be able to keep that dollar in your mattress and pull it out 25 years later only to discover it has more purchasing power than it had when you first squirreled it away. Sadly, this is not a luxury any of us has yet experienced. Even in the midst of all this talk about deflation, we have yet to see any kind of secular slide in prices that has lasted longer than a few weeks.

Part of the reason for this is that Washington apparently hates and fears lower prices. A few years ago, the price of beef took another tumble, causing ranchers around the country to worry about their own profitability. They lobbied Washington, as people are apt to do these days, and persuaded the secretary of agriculture to intervene. He bought up millions of dollars of what the ranchers called excess beef and gave it away to the poor for free.

As a beef lover, I would have loved to have benefited from low priced beef, and would have been even happier to get it for free. Sadly, I have not benefited from the secretary of agriculture's actions. He was effectively stealing the benefit of lower prices from consumers and handing it over to a special interest group, all at the behest of well-heeled lobbyists in Washington.

I mentioned the Great Depression earlier. This is typically attributed to the falling price level of the 1930s, as if this were a cause of general economic downturn. In fact, falling prices were the one aspect of the Depression that helped mitigate the effects of a deep productivity crash that was brought about and sustained by government intervention in the price system. Falling prices meant that the dollars that people did own were becoming more and more valuable over time. But Washington, in its infinite wisdom, worked for the better part of a decade to pump the price level back up again, thereby ensuring that the real cause of the depression would not be addressed.

Before we leave the general topic of what is inflation, let me say a few words about the great CPI controversy. Early in the second term of the Clinton administration, Treasury Department and Fed officials began to wonder whether the inflation indexes being used to calculate inflation were really telling the truth. They announced that they were pretty sure that the CPI overestimates inflation by nearly a percentage point, or perhaps by as much as two points.

Now, consider what this would mean. The Bureau of Labor Statistics employs thousands of people to do nothing but examine prices paid for goods and services at all levels of industry. They calculate data from every conceivable source, and present it in myriad ways to the public. They break down the data in every conceivable way. But somehow, said the Clinton administration, in the voice of Stanford University's Michael Boskin, along the way, mistakes are being made. The Bureau of Labor's statisticians are overestimating inflation.

The question to ask Boskin is: how can you know for sure? To say that you know the BLS is making a mistake is also to say that you know with certainty what the correct inflation rate is. You have to have a benchmark to say that something doesn't measure up. And if Boskin knew the truth, why not just abolish the BLS once and for all? If we need to know any economic data, we could just email Boskin, and he could consult his astrologer or swami or whomever he relies on for his revelations. Paying him half-a-million per year would save taxpayers billions.

In justifying his view, Boskin spent less time explaining his methodology than attacking the BLS's own. He pointed out that it doesn't make very much sense to aggregate prices that are stable and fixed—say for instance those of commodities—with those that change because of technological shifts or changes in relative scarcities. For example, what if I decided to calculate the 10-year inflation rate using three goods: private-school tuition, handheld calculators, and gasoline. I might end up with an index number of 0. Yet that conceals an enormous amount of information. And let's say I want to throw in the price of real estate in Greenwich Village. We might get a soaring rate of inflation.

Boskin is right that the inflation rate is highly dependent on precisely what is in and what is out. It is difficult to adjust for price changes that come about from technology. The basket of goods that is included in the CPI is constantly changing, but not because science necessitates this. It changes because the BLS watches politics very carefully, and politics necessitates that the government always generate a lower and lower inflation rate.

The purpose of all this data collection is to discover the mysterious and highly elusive thing called the price level. The trouble is that there ain't no such thing as a price level. Prices do not move up and down like the sea level. They always move relative to each other and in odd and unpredictable ways. Monetary inflation causes many if not most of them to rise, but calculating to what extent is a very tricky business. The only thing we can know for sure about monetary inflation is that it waters down the purchasing power of our money, and does so in an insidious and deadly way. Try to make a science out of finding out precisely how much, and you are headed for trouble.

Economists who favor monetary manipulation have a good reason to always talk about prices instead of purchasing power. It helps distract attention away from the real culprit, the real source of inflation. It's not a mysterious rise and fall of the price level that can be more precisely measured by better data collection. In fact, the cause of inflation is not mysterious at all. It consists of the nation's central bank adding to the stock of dollars in the economy by artificial means. The Fed can do this in three ways: lowering the discount rate, buying assets on the open market, and lowering the reserve ratio on bank deposits.

It is impossible to think about the nature of inflation and monetary manipulation in general without understanding what the Fed is all about. If you like conspiracy theories, you'll love the history of the Fed. When talking about the Fed as a conspiracy against the public interest, however, we are not really talking about theory. We are talking real-world history. When the Fed was set up before World War I, it was designed by the banking and corporate elites, mostly consisting of a collaborative effort between the Morgan and the Rockefeller financial empires, with one purpose in mind: to make possible a more elastic currency. What does elastic currency mean? Well, let's just say it's something we would all like to have on a household level. Can't pay the bills? If your household income is elastic, you just add a zero or two to your bank ledger. Elastic effectively means the ability to print more money when it turns out that you haven't managed your accounts well.

That is precisely what the Fed was founded to make possible. It cartelized the banking system and allowed for coordinated inflation and credit expansion. It cut the necessary minimum reserve requirements, provided added bailout guarantees, and allowed banks to pyramid loans on top of Fed reserves. This was a tremendous benefit to the banking industry, and to the government which needed financing to enter the world war, but it forecast disaster for the soundness of currency. After the Great Depression, the same elites conspired again to institute new protections for the banking industry, giving us Glass-Steagall, deposit insurance, and watering down the gold standard ever more.

For most of the second half of the 20th century, a debate has raged about who precisely is to blame for inflation. This debate usually began with the assumption that if one party is not to blame it is the Federal Reserve. It is not only Greenspan who has a reputation as a great inflation fighter, but every previous Fed chairman. They are all described in the usual monetary histories as hard-nosed opponents of inflation. But how can this be? There is only one force that can cause the purchasing power of existing dollars to systematically decline, and that force is an expansion of the existing dollar stock through artificial means. There is only one power on earth that brings that about and that is the Federal Reserve.

Has some sneaky guy at the Fed been coming in after hours, after all the members of the board of governors have gone home, to print up money, buy and sell assets, raise and lower discount rates, and generally subsidize certain banks at the expense of others? Not at all. This has been a systematic policy. Large banks enjoy having the power to inflate for the same reason the counterfeiter values his printing machine. And in this, the Fed and its banks work hand in hand with the government.

The loss of the value in the dollar benefits debtors, and there's no bigger debtor than the federal government. An elastic currency permits the expansion of debt to a huge extent, and makes it possible for the government to be the one and only entity that can make an ironclad promise to make good on its debts. Thus, its bonds carry no risk premium. They will always be paid, but always at someone else's expense.

Not that the Fed has always intended to bring about large-scale monetary depreciation. It can set out to expand credit without warrant, and to grow the money supply to bring about an economic boom, but the consequences of those actions are not felt immediately and they are not always predictable. Moreover, the Fed is always anxious to separate itself from the effects of its policies.

Even today, Greenspan the Great frequently goes before Congressional committees and solemnly declares to what extent he thinks current rates of economic growth risk setting off inflation. But economic growth itself cannot set off inflation. Economic growth is neither a necessary nor sufficient cause for inflation. In fact, given the economists' famous equation of exchange, economic growth tends to make goods and services cheaper, since the same amount of money is doing more work.

Why does Greenspan mislead people? The Fed always wants to avoid the tail of price inflation pinned on its own behind. In this, it shares an interest with government generally. Government blames unions. It blames businessmen. In the next round of price inflation, it will undoubtedly blame the soaring stock market, and the regular Americans who threw caution to the wind to invest in booming stocks.

There are generally four schools of thought on whether price inflation is good or bad for the economy. The first is the Keynesian School, which has generally celebrated inflation as a means of bringing markets back into equilibrium when they have been thrown out by the business cycle. In the Keynesian theory, you can reduce unemployment by increasing inflation.

You can reduce inflation, but only if you are willing to tolerate higher unemployment. In the choice between people and money, people won every time . . . by losing sound money.

Of course this tradeoff ended up being shown to be completely mythical. There is no relationship between inflation and unemployment. Developments of the mid-1970s, in which inflation and unemployment moved up together, dealt a substantial blow to the theory. And today, we've witnessed dramatic declines in both; the theoretical apparatus behind Keynesian macroeconomics lies in tatters.

But the soundness of economic theories alone does not determine whether it is useful for the power elite. Keynesian economic theory was well supplemented by a leftist theory that favored redistribution of all wealth, especially taking from producers and giving to nonproducers. Inflation does this, as well as taxation and the welfare state. It punishes savers and makes economic calculation difficult. Inflation shortens time horizons of people in society and thus weans them of bourgeois values. It punishes enterprise with capital and rewards those with debt. This is why egalitarians have always celebrated inflation, and why you are more likely to hear the case for inflation being made by a socialist than a believer in free enterprise.

Yet not all backers of inflation favor redistribution and leftism. The Supply-Siders are great on the need for tax cuts. But if you look at the works of Jude Wanniski, the politics of Jack Kemp, or the recommendations of the editorial page of the *Wall Street Journal*, you see a single fallacy repeated again and again: economic growth must be backed by monetary growth. Or put in an even more dangerous phrase: restrictive monetary growth holds back economic growth. This is merely another version of the old fallacy that prosperity can come from the printing press.

In a slightly different way, the Chicago School or Monetarist approach advocates a fixed rate of growth for the money supply, neither undershooting nor overshooting the rate of economic growth and thereby achieving a stable price level. Now, as we already discussed, the notion of a stable price level is unachievable. The very nature of prices is that they adjust up and down, relative to each other, to reflect changes in resources, tastes, and technology.

So this supposed ideal of stable money is not only impossible to achieve, but it robs people of the opportunity to experience a rising purchasing power of money. The Monetarist plan also imposes a kind of collateral damage on the economy that the theory doesn't take account of. All new money injections distort the pricing signal of the interest rate. It causes some industries to undertake borrowing and business expansion they would not otherwise undertake. The new money works as a subsidy for some kinds of projects but not to others. As a result, even the Monetarist proposal sets in motion an artificial boom in some sectors of the economy.

Monetarism can be particularly dangerous in periods of deep recession, when economists of this school typically recommend gunning the money supply, as Milton Friedman recently did with respect to Japan. But gunning the money supply does nothing to correct the underlying structural problems that lead to business downturns in the first place. What an economy in recession needs more than new money is time and freedom. Time and freedom to clean out bad investments, time and freedom for wages to adjust, and time and freedom for the investment sector to align itself with the spending and savings sectors.

But what I'm speaking about here relates more to business cycles than inflation as such. And in order to understand them both, we need a richer and more complete view of the monetary side of the economy. That is where we turn to the writings of Murray Rothbard, Ludwig von Mises, F.A. Hayek, and the Austrian School of economics generally. For most of the 20th century, the Austrian School fought against monetary depreciation and for the gold standard. Only the Austrian School accurately predicted the consequences of fiat money and warned against the perils of inflation, not only its effect but also its cause.

The Age of Greenspan is considered to be one of sound money and low inflation. But consider a more fundamental change that has taken place in the monetary regime in the last decade. The Federal Reserve has long considered the banking system to be too big to fail. But with Greenspan, many more institutions have been added to the list. He intervened in 1987 to pull the stock market up from failure. He has intervened several times since then to bolster buying in the bond market and in the commodity futures market. During the Mexican peso crisis, he committed resources from the Fed to propping up the investments of US banks in Mexico, and then later combed the halls of Congress agitating for a bailout. He intervened after the dot-com bust and September 11. Finally, he has been the major force behind arguing for an expansion of the IMF, along with an implicit promise to bail out the IMF should its resources run dry.

In effect, Greenspan has instituted a too-big-to-fail doctrine for Wall Street and even whole governments. The consequence of this is to dramatically subsidize the willingness of traders and governments to take risks. They can safely assume a bailout will be forthcoming. It is difficult to imagine a more dangerous move on the part of any central banker. If you wonder about the future of inflation, I consider this to be a very strong indicator that we are not done with it yet.

What should the US do now? We should enjoy whatever deflation we can get right now. The government should not try to sustain high prices on any goods or services, but rather let them fall. That will allow us to prepare for a time when the dollar faces a challenge as the world reserve currency, and the monetary expansion of the last 10 years comes home to roost.

If we want to eliminate inflation forever, there is an easy step we can take. We can resecure the dollar to its historical foundation in gold and suppress the issuance of any more artificial money and credit. We could separate the monetary regime from the State entirely, and build a firewall between the dollar and politics. Only that step will provide permanent protection.

Until then, I would not suggest we become sanguine about the prospects of inflation, but prepare ourselves, not only for another bout, but also for the shock that comes with the realization that the laws of economics have not been repealed after all.

THE ECONOMICS OF DISCRIMINATION

[Based on a speech delivered at the Georgia State University School of Law in Atlanta, April 1992.]

The Fabian Society of Great Britain held to three central doctrines of political economy. First, every country must create its own form of socialism. Second, socialism imposed slowly is more permanent than the revolutionary sort. Third, socialism is not likely to succeed in Western countries if it appears undemocratic or authoritarian.

Using this formula, the Fabians achieved their dream in Britain. They used labor unions to socialize the workforce, the state to nationalize basic industries, and social insurance schemes to collectivize the property that was left. In addition, they relied on soft-planning, a government-run medical industry, and middle-class income redistribution to build the state sector. It was still socialism, however, and it nearly destroyed the country.

According to the Fabian formula, the American form of socialism would also need to be different from the Bolshevik model. If you understand this, you can understand the essence of American politics from at least the 1960s.

In the early days of the Clinton administration, White House aides visited Daniel Patrick Moynihan's Senate office to explain their proposal for so-called empowerment zones. These are sections within major cities targeted for a mass dumping of welfare dollars and business subsidies. When Moynihan heard the plan, he exclaimed: "That sounds Fabian!" The *New York Times* reported that Clinton's aides assumed he meant this as a compliment.

No one, certainly not the Clintons, could win the presidency of this country on a program of revolutionary socialism. If the opponents of property and markets are to succeed, they must create a peculiar form. It must be well suited to political and demographic conditions that are distinctively American.

We have little reason to fear nationalized industries or comprehensive planning. Labor union power is on the decline. Americans bristle at any hint of direct controls over production decisions. Environmental socialism has probably peaked. And fully socialized medicine failed last year because of massive public resistance to such a step-up in government power.

We don't have British socialism. We don't have the British style. But we do have a problem with socialism. It takes many forms, but the form I'd like to concentrate on today relates largely to labor markets and the rights of business.

First let's get our terms straight. One sort of property is private. That means it is owned by private individuals and should be controlled by them. This type of property is the basis of all market exchange.

Another kind of property is public property. The term is a misnomer, of course. Public property is sometimes the least accessible to the public. Yet we know what this term means: property owned by the state. It is not subject to market conditions. No individual can choose to use it or to sell it as he sees fit.

But US political culture has created a third and far more insidious type of property. It is called commercial property. It includes all private and public property used for exchange in the free market. Included in this category is most everything but private homes and clubs, and secretive government bureaucracies. This means that the following institutions are so-called commercial property: hotels, restaurants, bookstores, manufacturing plants, computer retailers, universities, and so on.

Being classed in this way subjects this form of property to a variety of civil-rights laws. When examined from a philosophical standpoint, such laws are nothing more than the legal right to trespass. A qualified individual may demand service against the will of the owner. He may demand to be hired, or not to be fired, against the will of the owner. He may demand a higher salary or a promotion, against the will of the owner.

If the free market embodies the idea of contract, civil rights embodies what Barry Smith has called the spromise. A spromise commits a third party to act against his will. As the owner of the business, you may wish to stop paying an employee and terminate his employment. Civil rights say you may not, without the permission of the government.

Civil rights, and the right of trespass it implies, is a major part of American socialism, a carefully tailored product indeed. It is designed to fit with America's excessive devotion to the ideals of democracy and equality. It is designed to exploit the demographic heterogeneity of America's population. And its implementation relies on America's traditionally sanguine view of centralized executive power.

We could argue about when American socialism first took root. Many say it began with the Great Society. Others trace it to the New Deal. There's a good case to be made for tracing it to the Lincoln presidency, which also used the language of democracy and egalitarianism, exploited America's hetero-geneity, and dramatically centralized power in an imperial executive. That period also provided a test run for inflation-ary monetary policy and income taxation, two institutions that the Progressive Era entrenched, and which provide the fuel for American socialism today.

The symptoms of American socialism are easy to identify. They appear in legislation like the Americans with Disabili-ties Act, the limitless amendments to the Civil Rights Act, the Community Reinvestment Act, and all manner of interfer-ence with the freedom of association.

In addition, regulatory agencies issue tens of thousands of regulations each year to manage the private lives of citizens and the conduct of private business. Of all the menacing fed-eral agencies, the socialism I am speaking about has been expertly practiced by the Department of Housing and Urban Development, the banking regulators at the Federal Reserve, and the bureaucrats at the Equal Employment Opportunity Commission.

The result has been a degree of tyranny. Civil rights law-suits are shutting down businesses daily. Many potential cap-italists decide not to open businesses for fear of the govern-ment's equality police.

Small companies routinely do anything within the law to avoid advertising for new positions. Why? Government at all levels now sends out testers to entrap businesses in the crime of hiring the most qualified person for a job. Pity the poor real estate agent and the owner of rental units, who walk the civil rights minefield every day. If any of these people demonstrate more loyalty to the customer than to the government, they risk bringing their businesses to financial ruin.

The restaurants Denny's and Shoney's, two great examples of capitalism in action, know all about this. In the last two years, they were both hit with class-action suits alleging discrimina-tion. It didn't matter that the plaintiffs were all trumped up, and the specific cases cited were patently fraudulent. For example, one plaintiff found a foreign object in her hash-browns, and claimed it was put there on grounds of race. Both companies decided to settle out of court, establish extensive quota programs, pay off all plaintiffs, and set up new minority-owned franchises. They did so not because they were guilty, but because the so-called justice system is stacked against them.

Just recently, 99 white male troopers in Maryland collected $3,500 each in back pay on grounds that they had been discriminated against in promotions. I don't doubt that they were, but I'm suggesting a more peaceful solution. Let's return to the market all decisions about hiring, firing, promotion, and access. That means getting the government and the courts out of the business of enforcing equality once and for all.

But that solution is nowhere in sight. The courts enforce an egalitarianism that tolerates no acknowledgment of differences among people. This denies the obvious. People do differ radically in their talents and weaknesses, their determinations to succeed, their mental facilities, their attitudes and character, their physical abilities, their environments, and their physical makeup. Moreover, these differences appear not only in individuals but also appear systematically among groups.

Men as a group, for example, are different from women as a group. Northerners are different from Southerners. Californians are different from Texans. Catholics are different from Baptists. Blacks are different from whites. Immigrants are different from natives. The rich are different from the poor. These differences should not be denied, but celebrated, for they are the very source of the division of labor.

Yet our central government attempts to stamp out all these differences by forcing individuals and businesses to act as if they do not exist. The primary means has been the criminalization of our most serious secular sin: discrimination. There can be no actions in American life—save the decision of whom to marry—that discriminates on the grounds of any number of criteria as defined by the government. If anyone commits this sin, he can forget the confessional or forgiveness. The heavy penance is cash handed over to the government and the special interests, with half going to the lawyers who arranged the transfer.

To see just how serious the government takes this sin, and how absurd are the results, consider disabilities law. Most people think of the Americans with Disabilities Act as a law forcing public and private facilities like courthouses and shopping malls to accommodate wheelchairs and the like. In fact, the Act is much broader. Since the ADA went into effect, less than one-quarter of the ADA-related complaints filed with the federal government concern such public and private facilities. The vast majority relate to employment.

Tens of thousands of such complaints, which are threatened lawsuits, have been filed with the EEOC. For example, a Florida district appeals judge was caught shoplifting a remote control, so the Florida Supreme Court dismissed him from the bench. He says this violates the ADA, which indeed it does, for he stole the device because he was depressed that his son was getting bad grades.

Mental illness is protected under the Americans with Disabilities Act. You cannot fire or refuse to hire a person who is "otherwise qualified" by the government's standards. What is official mental illness? The EEOC suggest we consult the Diagnostic and Statistical Manual of Mental Disorders. According to the DSM, protected symptoms include "confused thinking," "consistent tardiness or absences," "lack of cooperation or inability to work with co-workers," "reduced interest in one's work," and "problems concentrating."

Before the ADA, these were reasons for booting a person off the payroll. Today, they bestow rights against employers, rights that sane people do not have. Nor does it count when, as a result, ADA-afflicted businessmen experience symptoms of DSM mental illness themselves: "anxiety, fear, anger, suspicion."

The authors and enforcers of the ADA are not concerned with quadriplegics. Their goal is sinister to the core: removing the last vestiges of employers' legal rights, and replacing them with civil rights, which trump all considerations of private property. Just as landlords no longer have an effective legal right to evict nonpaying tenants, so employers cannot shop for the best workers. In this subtle form of socialism, nearly everyone has a veto over the free choices of the capital owner. The workplace is ruled by a victimocracy.

Unlike the Clean Air Act and similar bills, the ADA is not industry specific. It affects every business in the country with 15 or more employees, forcing owners and managers to pretend that the physically, mentally, and emotionally disabled (and "disabled") are identical to the nondisabled, and to spend to make it so.

Say you're a small businessman, barely alive thanks to regulations and high taxes, and a man who can't see applies for the job of office manager. You cannot turn him down on that ground, even though the job requires some reading, for that would violate his civil rights. You have to hire another employee to read to him. If you hesitate, you pay back wages and, thanks to the Civil Rights Act of 1991, massive damages.

If a supermarket manager refuses to hire a bum to ring the cash register, he can be taken to court. A sales manager may prefer salesmen who can remember customers' names and preferences, not to mention his own products, but discrimination against those with low IQs or the memory impaired is not allowed.

If a thousand-mile stare makes you uneasy, you're out of luck, for this is no longer a chilling quirk, but a certified disability. Would you rather not hire a nightwatchman with a history of drug use? If he's not on crack today, he's on your payroll. For this reason, drunkards are daily suing for their right to go off on a toot and not be kicked off the payroll.

Say the applicant is a dyslexic with a history of drug addiction who not only has trouble reading, but can't learn or reason well thanks to minor brain damage. If he applies, you have to hire him, and make what the government calls "necessary accommodations."

The public accommodations provisions of the ADA are nothing to shake a stick at. A man in a wheelchair, for example, sued for the right to coach third base on a Little League baseball team. A girl with a steel walker sued for the right to skate during prime hours at a public skating rink. A blind man sued for the right to be a firefighter. People of low intelligence are suing for more time to take tests. On and on it goes.

In each of these cases, businesses and other organizations usually settle out of court. They find that's cheaper than taking the case to trial. But the settlements themselves have caused a wealth loss, which is vast and growing. And with the ADA, there is no way to comply, because there is no way to prepare for every possible contingency, every possible lawsuit, every possible government trick. Doggerel.

Businesses can try to escape some of this by requiring certain abilities in a written job description. But they must be able to show, in a court of law, that the requirements are essential to the job. Businesses do not always know ahead of time what a person will be required to do. So they look for qualities like character and attitude. But these are unquantifiable. To the government, they are irrelevant, as you can tell by visiting any government office.

One way the ADA is enforced is through the use of government and private "testers." These actors, who will want to find all the "discrimination" they can, terrify small businesses. The smaller the business, the more ADA hurts. That's partly why big business supported it. How nice to have the government clobber your up-and-coming competition.

How could this nutty and dangerous legislation have passed? In Washington, DC, economics has always taken a backseat to special-interest lobbying. But when something is labeled civil rights, especially when it harms small businessmen and tramples on the freedom to exclude, it flies through Congress. Only four people in the Senate voted against the bill. Editorially, not even the *Wall Street Journal* spoke out against it when it mattered.

The ADA illustrates an important point about antidiscrimination law. Contrary to myth, rules against discrimination never create a level playing field. Forbidding one form of discrimination must necessarily compel another form of discrimination.

If an owner is forbidden to discriminate in hiring on grounds of sex or race, the government can only discover a violation of the law by looking at who is hired. This compels active discrimination against people on grounds of their sex or race. It is a zero sum game, where one person's winnings come from another's losses.

Still fewer are willing to speak openly about what has happened to the banking industry in the last few years. Once upon a time, the credit rating was the primary means by which bankers and other lenders assessed creditworthiness. But this is under assault today. Along with other institutions essential to the functioning of a free market, sound credit standards are being sacrificed on the political altar.

The operative test of a bank's political correctness is its Community Reinvestment Act (CRA) rating. The ratings, mandated by Congress and the Bush administration in a bill affixed to the S&L bailout legislation in 1989, categorizes lending by race, sex, and income level. Using nebulous CRA requirements, regulatory control, and the threat of merger rejection, government officials exercise remarkable control over the lending policy of banks.

Last year, for example, Shawmut National Corp. of Connecticut wanted to acquire New Dartmouth Bank of New Hampshire. The Federal Reserve Board, which must approve all bank acquisitions, foiled Shawmut's plans in a split vote.

The banks were not undercapitalized. The proposed merger did not violate antitrust law. There were no allegations of fraud. Instead, Shawmut was under investigation by the Department of Justice for violating fair-lending laws. In the first decision of its kind, the Federal Reserve thwarted the acquisition on those grounds at the behest of the Department of Justice. I guess that's part of the price for retaining its "independence."

Shawmut never admitted guilt. But the bank had to spend a minimum of $960,000 on rejected minority applicants. With claims averaging $10,000 to $15,000 per plaintiff, the final price was much higher. In addition, Shawmut was forced to set aside $85 million in loanable funds solely for privileged applicants.

Shawmut is not even allowed to attach a risk premium to interest rates on loans given to questionable applicants so long as they are privileged by government. Instead, it must make these loans at below market rates, therefore subsidizing them with other depositors' money.

When Fleet Financial Group, New England's largest bank holding company, fired 3,000 people and reduced its operating expenditures by $300 million, the business pages featured the story. But the media did not ferret out who had downsized the institution. One month before the layoffs, Fleet had suffered a similar shakedown.

A Boston "community activist" and self-described "urban-terrorist" named Bruce Marks heads a group called the Union Neighborhood Assistance Corp. He began making noise when Fleet was planning to buy the failed Bank of New England. Marks noted that Fleet wasn't directly backing loans in Boston's Roxbury, Dorchester, and South End. Instead, to comply with the CRA, it subsidized other mortgage companies that lent at higher rates. Marks convinced some people who held these mortgages that they were being ripped off.

Marks then got local reporters, always anxious for a new victim, to make a fuss about the matter. After *60 Minutes* ran an attack, Fleet agreed to stop purchasing loans from third-party lenders in the inner city. That, of course, wasn't enough. Marks and his Union wanted Fleet to make the loans itself—and give the Union cold hard cash.

Over two years, Marks's band of brigands disrupted luncheons, breakfast meetings, press conferences, and speeches. Once Marks and his Union members burst into a hearing of the Senate Banking Committee where they filled the room and sang gospel songs. It was the kind of display that makes corporate big shots cower, politicians swoon, and regulators cheer. In the end, Fleet had to give Marks a cool $140 million.

Fleet also agreed to set aside $7.2 billion in loans for "low-income" borrowers, plus another $800 million in programs and payoffs for other "inner-city borrowers." Fleet was attacked for loansharking, but the real sharks were those who looted the bank vault with the permission of government regulators.

Studies that purport to show discrimination rarely look at individual loan applications. Instead, they consider only carefully selected neighborhoods. Typically they fail to count minorities living in predominantly majority areas. And they look only at the lending record of banks and S&Ls, and not other mortgage lenders. However flawed, the studies always make a splash in the dangerous waters of politics.

Another voice added to this cacophony of credit confusion is Ralph Nader's. Nader likes to cite a now-famous 1992 Boston Federal Reserve study by Alicia Munnell, then director of research and now Clinton's assistant Treasury secretary for economic policy. It was supposed to adjust for more factors than any other study and still recorded a 6-point lending gap, a 17-percent versus 11-percent turndown rate by race.

Peter Brimelow of *Forbes* was the only one to call her bluff. He confronted her with the fact that her data also revealed identical default rates, which, he pointed out, implied a racially impartial application of standards of credit-worthiness.

When confronted with the implications of this data, she collapsed. "I do not have evidence," she admitted. "No one has evidence," she continued in her own defense. Her admission hasn't stopped her from continuing to make the charge, and from ordering changes in the way banks make loans.

What's at stake here is not fairness in lending. Everyone acknowledges as an empirical fact that whites on average are more eligible for credit than blacks on average, just as Asians are more eligible than whites. What's at issue is the transfer of the welfare function from fiscal policy to banking policy. The pool of loanable funds has become a convenient substitute for direct welfare benefits.

Tens of billions have been doled out to satisfy civil rights groups who cry discrimination. This has an industry-wide chilling effect. It scares banks negotiating reorganizations and freezes up available capital that deserving families need in purchasing new homes.

Civil-rights socialism in banking wastes scarce resources and punishes achievement and responsibility. It harms the very groups it claims to help, by driving away market-specific solutions. Rechanneling funds makes the economy operate less efficiently and rightly angers property owners and depositors.

In a similar way, civil rights lawsuits alleging some kind of racial and sexual discrimination are shutting down businesses every day.

Let's return to the Denny's and Shoney's cases of judicial aggression. Flagship, Denny's' parent company, was forced to settle a pile of litigation, including two class-action lawsuits—pushed by a combine of the Justice Department, the NAACP, and a bunch of liberal lawyers—for a total payout of $54 million. The Oakland, California, law firm that handled the largest suit got $8.7 million.

More than 4,300 people signed up as anti-Denny's plaintiffs. The *New York Times* even published a toll-free number to dial up and try your chances at some of the loot. Of the thousands of cases of alleged discrimination, news accounts and plaintiffs' lawyers focused on two of the supposed worst incidents, which supposedly prove the perfidy of Denny's. In Annapolis, Maryland, in May of 1993, six Secret Service agents were assigned to President Clinton's security detail for a speech in that city. They entered the local Denny's restaurant at noon.

Several media outlets said the agents were "refused a table." The charge was a lie, made possible only because of the lack of accountability in civil-rights suits. The president was speaking nearby, meaning the restaurant was crowded. The agents were seated. The agents were served, but late.

Everyone has experienced late service, even watching someone who came in after us getting their food before we've ordered. Yet at the first sign of delay, agent Robin Thompson marched up to the waitress and demanded the food. The waitress said it was on the way. Thompson demanded to see the manager. He was on the phone. The highly paid gun-toting Secret Service agent was yelling, and the waitress was alleged to have rolled her eyes after he left. This was one of the charges that grew into a nationwide class-action suit.

On that very day, Denny's had settled another suit in California alleging discrimination for $34.8 million, including $6.8 million for that California firm. A federal judge claimed he had to wait for a table, and that diners chanted racial epithets at him.

Regardless of the facts, how is this Denny's' fault? It's one of the peculiar aspects of civil rights laws under commercial property.

As part of the settlement, Denny's had to hire a full-time civil rights monitor, introduce a system of private spies to ferret out any internal "discrimination," run re-education programs for all nonminority employees, turn over a set number of franchises to minorities for free, and put a hostile person on its board of directors. As part of the same suit, the NAACP pressured Denny's to spend at least $1 billion to find and hire minority managers and turn over restaurants to them.

Why couldn't Denny's have told the agitators to hit the road? In a word: fear. Business can no longer risk taking these cases to trial. Even huge settlements like these are likely to be less expensive.

The cost to the overall economy is incalculable. How many companies will refuse to go public for fear that it makes them easy pickings for liberal lawyers? How many people, shocked by the gross unfairness of this ruling, will choose not to expand their businesses? How many potential entrepreneurs will be turned off from business altogether? When whole businesses are looted, the country is not safe for free enterprise.

We cannot have free labor markets so long as we don't have the freedom to hire and fire. It is as essential that women's health clubs be allowed to exclude men as it is for Korean restaurants to be able to hire and promote only Koreans. These are the rights and privileges that come with private property. If we limit them, we destroy markets and replace them with civil rights socialism.

In *Forbidden Grounds*, University of Chicago law professor Richard Epstein refutes some of the myths of civil rights. Epstein points out an obvious fact that somehow goes unnoticed: antidiscrimination laws intervene in the freedom of contract, the legal right to use one's own property as one sees fit. Additionally, there is no reason to think that such legal restrictions generate any social benefit.

Epstein uses the methodology of the Chicago School, whose theory of welfare attempts to derive social utility mathematically. But the question can also be approached, and far more effectively, from the deductive standpoint of the Austrian School.

Free exchange produces the highest social utility, since both parties benefit to the maximum extent possible, or the exchange would not have taken place. If the most-preferred choice on a person's rank of preferences is outlawed as discriminatory, maximum benefit is denied to him.

Consider this example. John is an employer who wants to hire Jim, and Jim wants to be hired. This is probably because John values Jim's labor, but it may also be because they are old college buddies. Jane wants the job too, but she is passed over, and she thinks the exchange between John and Jim injures her right to partake in the exchange.

In the free market, it is not enough to assert your right to be hired; Jane would have to offer some conditions of exchange to make herself relatively more attractive to John than is Jim. For example, Jane could lower the price of her labor to make it more competitive. If Jane's labor is of no value or even negative value to John, then she would have to consider an apprentice relationship or possibly even offer a negative wage, that is, pay John to let her work. Or she could just give up and take a job somewhere else at what she regards as her true market worth.

No matter how the transaction ends up in this free market—whether John hires Jim or Jane—two parties are definitely better off, and the nonparticipating third party no worse off than he or she would be otherwise. We cannot know by how much John and the hired employee are better off, since utility is purely subjective and cannot be added and subtracted. We can only know that with voluntary market arrangements, and a free-floating wage system in this case, social utility is maximized no matter who is hired.

But say that Jane is passed over, and demands that the government step in on the grounds that John should not be allowed to discriminate in favor of Jim. Compelled to do so, John hires Jane, even though her services are less in demand

and Jim, whose services are more in demand, is left out in the cold.

Under this compulsion model, John is coerced into hiring someone he prefers less, Jim is forcibly shut out of the exchange, and only Jane gets her way. We cannot know mathematically how much Jane benefits from the exchange. We can only know that in this example she would not have been hired in the absence of government intervention, and that when she is hired by force, John and Jim are made worse off. The lower valued labor has been employed over the higher valued labor. We can definitely say that overall social utility in this three-person economy is diminished.

Civil rights laws force a similar outcome. They compel exchanges that would not have taken place under a voluntary system. We can thus immediately cut through the claims of civil-rights supporters that antidiscrimination laws guarantee rights, but do not themselves discriminate. By their own logic, civil rights laws compel discrimination.

The language of Title VII of the 1964 Civil Rights Act seems innocuous, but it is enough to bring serious harm to the social order and the free market. The law reads:

> It shall be an unlawful employment practice for an employer to fail or refuse to hire or to discharge any individual, or otherwise to discriminate against any individual with respect to his compensation, terms, conditions, or privileges of employment, because of such individual's race, color, religion, sex, or national origin.

The Civil Rights Act ostensibly did not allow government to change the private pattern of employment. The assurances of Senator Hubert H. Humphrey (D.-Minn.) were especially powerful:

> Employers may hire and fire, promote and refuse to promote for any reason, good or bad, provided only that individuals

may not be discriminated against because of race, religion, sex or national origin.

On another occasion, Humphrey made a famous promise:

> If the Senator [George Smathers] can find in Title VII . . .
> any language which provides that an employer will have to
> hire on the basis of percentage or quota related to color, race,
> religion, or national origin, I will start eating the pages one
> after another.

But the authors of the law did not state their aims openly; they opted for a more subtle form of egalitarian behavior control. The civil rights legislation did not explicitly outlaw certain market outcomes, but only made actionable certain subjective states of mind: people cannot discriminate "on the basis of" or "on the grounds of" some physical attribute. It is not the action itself which is made illegal, but the motive.

Let's say that Congress is disgusted by the number of divorces in the nation. It concludes that many result from shotgun marriages. So it decides to pass the following law: "All marriages contracted by parties under the age of 26 must be based on love, not mere infatuation." The law is actionable in court, and enforced by a $5,000 penalty.

What happens? Does the divorce rate go down? Perhaps, but not because young marriages are more loving. It is because people decide to play it safe. They wait until the age of 26 to get married.

What's being outlawed here is not an action as such, but a motivation. But to keep the motivation from being detected, people change their behavior. For this same reason, antidiscrimination law has led to quotas. For fear of the government, people change their behavior.

To illustrate further how civil rights laws are logically inseparable from reverse discrimination, quotas, and government control of labor markets, consider this additional thought experiment. Say a Catholic requests a job, but is told: no Papists need apply.

In announcing his policy, the employer reveals his motivation for not hiring the man. The government then passes a law making such a motivation illegal, so the employer knows he must hide his true feelings. He assures the authorities that he has had a change of heart about Catholics, whom he now regards as deserving of equal rights. Then he rejects a long series of applicants on the grounds that he doesn't like the look in their eyes. But it turns out that all the rejected applicants were Catholics. Even so, he assures the authorities, that is not why they were rejected.

The trouble for the authorities is that the employer seems to be fulfilling the language of the law—he is no longer discriminating "on grounds" of a person's belonging to the Catholic Church—yet Catholics are still not being hired in this person's firm. Allowing the situation to continue would defeat the purpose of the law, since there would have been no point in its having been passed if it were only going to produce the same result.

Predictably, the authorities conclude that he is still engaging in illegal discrimination. They further conclude that in the future he will be evaluated in terms of how many Catholic employees he has hired and promoted, and fined heavily and perhaps jailed if he does not comply. To comply, the employer realizes, he must reject non-Catholics in favor of Catholics. In effect, he has been forced to establish *de facto* hiring quotas. Catholics now have privileges and non-Catholics are discriminated against. We can't expect any other outcome.

But what if it turns out that the reason the employer disliked Catholics, though he had never thought about it before, was that most Catholics do indeed have a funny look in their eyes? In other words, he was using their Catholicism as a proxy for other behaviors he found unattractive.

In fact, the Catholics he discriminates against may have many traits that link them besides their religion: unassimilated ethnicity, hard-to-understand accents, chips on their shoulders, or whatever. These traits do not have to apply to every Catholic; they need only apply to the ones he has known. In fact, they need not apply even to a majority of those he has known. Because all economic decisions take place on the margin—that is, he makes choices among several seemingly desirable ends—he has only to find one characteristic that falls along group lines to make his discriminatory decision rational.

So the authorities must either outlaw discrimination on every possible ground that links Catholics together as a group, or they can specify that only certain criteria are legal in decisions to hire, fire, pay, and promote. Furthermore, these criteria must be distributed relatively evenly among Catholics and non-Catholics. Given the tendency of groups to have much in common that will be marginally job relevant, or else they would not be considered a group in need of protection, this could be difficult.

Say the authorities choose the criterion of education as a worthy hiring standard. If, over time, it turns out that education is not distributed evenly among Catholics and non-Catholics, the authorities must select a new criterion. Or they could claim that educational institutions are guilty of discrimination, and enact draconian controls over them. If the differences persist, the authorities will have to undertake increasingly extreme measures to bring about the desired result.

Whatever path is taken, to the extent that the original form of discrimination was rational and pervasive, the authorities will be forced to seek a near-total takeover of the labor markets to ensure "fairness" for Catholics. A law mandating "religion-blind" hiring must be enforced as "religion-conscious" hiring if it is to have any effect. This follows from the simple act of forbidding discrimination on grounds of religion.

There is no rational ground on which to exclude civil rights laws from the same sort of analysis. Their goal was not a level playing field; that was already in place in the labor markets. The goal was to redistribute wealth through government from one group to another group, and to enhance government control over the labor markets.

Civil rights laws, moreover, may actually increase discrimination. Employers forced to pay or promote people out of fear of the government will tend to avoid hiring them in the first place. And those who do get hired under such circumstances will be the cream of the labor pool, further marginalizing the least skilled and least experienced.

There is good reason to question the alleged policy ideal of sameness throughout the economy. Consider living arrangements. Good sense tells us that retired people sometimes want to live in adult-only complexes. Running, yelling children can pose a physical danger or just get on older people's nerves. So Congress passed a law in 1988 that makes it illegal to discriminate in housing against families with children, even though such discrimination can be perfectly rational.

Civil rights laws are one of the paths to socialism because they overthrow the freedom of association and the employers' freedom to choose. How crucial are these to preserving prosperity, freedom, and civilization itself? We'll find out if the central government succeeds in stamping them out entirely.

If we are ever to reverse our current course, we must pay closer attention to the wisdom of Edmund Burke, Alexis de Tocqueville, John C. Calhoun, John Randolph of Roanoke, Lord Acton, Helmut Schoek, Bertrand de Jouvenel, Ludwig von Mises, Murray N. Rothbard and all the others who have taught that liberty and equal outcomes are incompatible goals. One always comes at the expense of the other. For a variety of reasons, this lesson has been forgotten in our times.

The free-market economy has a record like no other of offering economic advancement for everyone no matter what his station in life. However, it does not offer equality of result or even equality of opportunity. The free market offers not a classless society, but something of much greater value: liberty itself.

No reform of these laws will get to the root of the problem unless it is the repeal of all civil rights laws.

We are all familiar with Joseph Schumpeter's paradoxical prediction that socialism would win out over capitalism. We also thought that the events of 1989 disproved him. In light of our present situation, let's revisit Schumpeter.

The capitalist or commercial society, he says, is defined by two elements: first, private property in the means of production; second, regulation of the productive process by private contract, management, and initiative. By Schumpeter's definition, we only have capitalism in the first sense. We have private property, but no longer can we govern the productive process by private contract, management, and initiative. The government exercises veto power over all matters of economic management.

By socialist society, he further writes, he means an institutional pattern in which the control over the means of production is vested with a central authority, or as a matter of principle, the economic affairs of society belong to the public and not to the private sphere.

Which does our society most closely resemble: Schumpeter's commercial society or Schumpeter's socialist society? Whatever our answer, we know where the trend line is pointing.

We need to reevaluate Schumpeter's famous prediction about the US:

> It is only socialism in the sense defined in this book that is so predictable. Nothing else is. In particular there is little reason to believe that this socialism will mean the advent of the civilization of which orthodox socialists dream. It is much more likely to present fascist features. That would be a strange answer to Marx's prayer. But history sometimes indulges in jokes of questionable taste.

MEDICINE AND THE STATE

[This speech was delivered before the Association of American Physicians and Surgeons in St. Louis, Missouri, on October 26, 2000.]

Throughout the 19th century, socialist ideology gained ground among intellectuals who were attempting to revive ancient dreams of a total State that managed every aspect of people's lives. The critics, too, weighed in to explain that socialism has ethical and practical limitations. If you abolish private property, which socialism proposes to do, you abolish economic exchange, which is a source of social peace. In addition, you eliminate the profit motive, which is a major factor in spurring people on to work and produce.

The major limitation to this dominant mode of criticism is that it was narrowly focused against the idea of completely eliminating private property. In addition, the 19th-century economic criticisms of socialism did not get to the heart of the matter, which is that *any* attempt to curb the workings of economic exchange forces resources into uneconomic uses. An economy is defined as a system in which human energies and resources are employed toward their most productive purposes, according to consumers' spending. Not only socialism, but all interventions in the free market redirect resources in ways that are counterproductive—away from the voluntary sector of society and into the State sector.

The history of socialist theory is bound up with policies toward the medical marketplace. To control people's access to medical care is to control their very lives, so it is no wonder that this is the goal of every State. In the course of a century we have taken a long march from a largely free system of medical provision to one dominated by unfree programs and mandates.

And yet, I'm sorry to report, the US, despite huge interventions on a scale unimaginable in an era of free markets, remains freer than most places in the world. Privatization of medical provision isn't on the radar screen of the world's politicians, even after manifest failures. Even after the collapse of all-out collectivism in the Soviet Union and Eastern Europe, there has been precious little movement toward reform in the medical sector.

We are a long way from clear thinking on the subject of medical care (the realization that the provision of medical services of every kind is best left to the forces of the market economy and the charitable sector than placed in the hands of the regulating, taxing, intruding State).

Ludwig von Mises was socialism's greatest critic, having written the decisive attack in 1922. His book, *Socialism*, is usually credited for proving why Soviet-style socialism could never work. But less known is the fact that he attacked the entire panoply of what he called "destructionist" policies, which included the medical policies of the social welfare states in the German-speaking world at the time. Mises had a way of getting to the heart of the matter, so his comments on socialized health insurance apply to our own situation. Reviewers at the time noted his opposition and decried them as the ravings of an extreme classical liberal. If so, I am happy to rave myself.

Allow me to quote his remarks in full:

> To the intellectual champions of social insurance, and to the politicians and statesmen who enacted it, illness and health appeared as two conditions of the human body sharply separated from each other and always recognizable without difficulty or doubt. Any doctor could diagnose the characteristics of "health." "Illness" was a bodily phenomenon which showed itself independently of human will, and was not susceptible to influence by will. There were people who for some reason or other simulated illness, but a doctor could expose the pretense. Only the healthy person was fully efficient. The efficiency of the sick person was lowered according to the gravity and nature of his illness, and the doctor

was able, by means of objectively ascertainable physiological tests, to indicate the degree of the reduction of efficiency.

Now every statement in this theory is false. There is no clearly defined frontier between health and illness. Being ill is not a phenomenon independent of conscious will and of psychic forces working in the subconscious. A man's efficiency is not merely the result of his physical condition; it depends largely on his mind and will. Thus the whole idea of being able to separate, by medical examination, the unfit from the fit and from the malingerers, and those able to work from those unable to work, proves to be untenable. Those who believed that accident and health insurance could be based on completely effective means of ascertaining illnesses and injuries and their consequences were very much mistaken. The destructionist aspect of accident and health insurance lies above all in the fact that such institutions promote accidents and illness, hinder recovery, and very often create, or at any rate intensify and lengthen, the functional disorders which follow illness or accident. . . .

Feeling healthy is quite different from being healthy in the medical sense, and a man's ability to work is largely independent of the physiologically ascertainable and measurable performances of his individual organs. The man who does not want to be healthy is not merely a malingerer. He is a sick person. If the will to be well and efficient is weakened, illness and inability to work is caused. By weakening or completely destroying the will to be well and able to work, social insurance creates illness and inability to work; it produces the habit of complaining—which is in itself a neurosis—and neuroses of other kinds. In short, it is an institution which tends to encourage disease, not to say accidents, and to intensify considerably the physical and psychic results of accidents and illnesses. As a social institution it makes a people sick bodily and mentally or at least helps to multiply, lengthen, and intensify disease.

Thus spake Mises. He was observing that there is a moral hazard associated with socialized and subsidized medicine.

Because there is no clear line between sickness and health, and where you stand on the continuum is bound up with individual choice, the more medical services are provided by the State as a part of welfare, the more the programs reinforce the conditions that bring about the need to make use of them. This one insight helps explain how socialized medicine takes away the incentive to be healthy, and maximizes the problem of overutilization of resources. Hence, socialized medicine must fail for the same reasons all socialism must fail: it offers no system for rationally allocating resources, and instead promotes the overutilization of all resources, ending in bankruptcy.

And now consider the presidential campaign of the year 2000. The most medically dependent group in the country is seniors, who also happen to be, at once, the most government-addicted and financially well-off members of society. Their medical care is largely paid through public dollars. And yet this group is nearly united in the claim that it is not enough. They demand that their drugs be free or at least be as cheap as fruits and vegetables at the grocery store. And the candidates respond not by pointing out the unreality and illegitimacy of their demands, but by competing to see who can provide free drugs more quickly through one or another central plan.

Can anyone doubt that Mises was right, that socialized medicine has led to a sickly frame of mind that has swept and now dominates the culture? The habit of complaining is endemic to this sector of society. Never have so many rich people who have been given so much by government demanded so much more. And the politicians are not pilloried for pandering to them but rewarded to the degree that they can dream up central plans that accommodate the complaining class through ever more freebies.

And when does it stop? When the coffers run dry. Until then, the subsidies work to distort the market and distort people's sense of life's limits. And no one has pointed out during this presidential campaign what this program would mean for drug manufacturers. It would essentially nationalize them by mandating that they work first for the government that is subsidizing drug purchases and only second for the consumer. But this is the path that all steps toward socialized medicine take: instead of physicians and patients engaging in cooperative exchange, we get government standing between them and dictating medical care.

Now, it is sometimes said that medical care is too important to be left to the market, and that it is immoral to profit from the illnesses of others. I say medical care is too important to be left to the failed central plans of the political class. And as for profiting from providing medical care, we can never be reminded enough that in a free society, a profit is a signal that valuable services are being rendered to people on a voluntary basis. Profits are merely a by-product of a system of private property and freedom of exchange, two conditions which are the foundation of an innovative and responsive medical sector.

In the recent century, however, these institutions have been attacked and subverted at every level. In the medical-care market, the process began in the late 19th century with the policies of Germany's Otto von Bismarck, who sought a third way between the old liberalism and communism. As the originator of national socialism designed to foil international socialism, he claimed credit for being the first to establish a national health care system—thus adopting the very socialism he claimed to be combating.

Politicians ever since have followed this lead, continuing with Emperor Francis Joseph of Austria-Hungary, Wilhelm II of Germany, Nicholas II of Russia, Lenin, Stalin, Salazar of Portugal, Mussolini of Italy, Franco of Spain, Yoshihito and Hirohito of Japan, Joseph Vargas of Brazil, Juan Peron of Argentina, Hitler, and FDR. What a list! As individuals, most have been discredited and decried as dictators. But their medical-care policies are still seen as the very soul of compassionate public policy, to be expanded and mandated, world without end.

In each case, the national leader advertised the importance of centralized medical welfare for the health of the nation. But what was always more important was the fact that such policies reward the politicians and parties in power with additional control over the people, while dragging the medical profession—an important and independent sector that is potentially a great bulwark against State power—into a government system of command and control.

Before coming to power, Hitler's party, for example, made statements condemning socialized medicine and compulsory social insurance as a conspiracy to soften German manhood. But once in power, they saw the advantages of the very programs they condemned. As Melchior Palyi argued, Hitler saw that the system was actually a great means of political demagoguery, a bastion of bureaucratic power, an instrument of regimentation, and a reservoir from which to draw jobs for political favorites. By 1939, Hitler had extended the system of compulsory insurance to small business and tightened the system in Austria. One of his last acts in 1945 was to include workers from irregular types of employment in the system, socializing medical care even in his last days.

After the war, the Social Democratic Party charged with de-Nazification immediately expanded his system to further centralize the medical sector. On the medical care front, Hitler may yet achieve his 1,000-year Reich.

The Soviet Union adopted a more radical course. This was the first country to adopt all-round socialized medical care—the dream of the Democratic Party in this country. In 1919, Lenin signed a decree that said every Soviet citizen had a right to free medical care. By 1977, this right had dramatically expanded to become the right to health itself—language now regularly employed by US politicians.

During the in-between years, the Soviet Union became host to one of the most backward, murderous, and coercive systems of medical provision ever concocted. The country trained more doctors than any in the world, but the vital statistics showed a more complete picture. Lifespans averaged 10 to 20 years less than in western countries. Infant mortality was twice as high. By the time of the collapse of socialism, 80 million people were said to have chronic illnesses, and up to 68 percent of the public was health-deficient by international standards. Mental retardation afflicted nearly a quarter of the children—a consequence of serious deprivation.

It was impossible for ordinary people to gain access to decent drugs. Stores carried only the most primitive medicines. However, the country was flooded with penicillin, as ordered in the central plan, a plan which was not altered even after the citizens became resistant to it. The hospitals housed 12 to 16 patients per room. More than a third of rural hospitals had no running water. Syringes were reused an average of 1,000 times. To keep up with the planned death rate, hospitals routinely threw people out before they died so that the hospital wouldn't go beyond its quota of corpses.

Of course most real care went underground, where bribing for anaesthesia was common. Former Soviet economist Yuri N. Maltsev points out that this method was even used in the case of abortion, which was the most common surgical procedure in the Soviet Union. After Maltsev emigrated to the US, he was astonished to see that the US was adopting many of the principles that drove the old Soviet system. But in the US, it is not called socialism or communism. It is called insurance.

All Western systems have been based on a deeply flawed notion of insurance. After Hillary's outrageous medical plan came out in 1993, I appeared on panels at *National Review* and the Claremont Institute on the subject, and explained what insurance is and what it is not. Hillary's plan was not insurance. It was regimentation through welfare. Other panelists were aghast that I was criticizing not just Hillary's plan but the very principle of government insurance, dating back to Bismarck. So that we are not confused, let me explain.

The world is full of risks, among which are those that are inherent in the nature of things, and those which can be increased or decreased according to human will. The risks against which you can insure yourself are those over which you can have no control. You can't stop a hurricane from destroying your house. The chances of this happening to a pool of homeowners are calculable. Hence you can be protected against losses through insurance with reasonable rates, set according to the risk factor. If you take actions that bring about the destruction of yourself and try to collect, however, you are committing insurance fraud. That is because outcomes that can be directly controlled by the insured are not insurable.

The risk of getting sick combines random and nonrandom variables. Catastrophic illnesses occur predictably in groups and thus can be insured against. But routine maintenance follows many predictable lines that must be reflected in premiums. The most cost-effective way to pay for medical care is the same way car maintenance is paid for: a fee for service. In a free market, this would be the dominant way medical care is funded. Prices would be aboveboard and competitive, and there would be a range of quality available for everyone. There would be no moral hazard. This was largely the system before the Blues (Blue Cross and Blue Shield), of course.

What is called health insurance in the US consists of two types: one provided by employers in which the insurer is not permitted to discriminate too severely in light of individual risks. The other is not insurance at all but a straight-out welfare payment mandated by the State: this is Medicare, Medicaid, and the huge range of programs delivering aid to individuals. None has much to do with a free-market provision of medical services.

As a result, the consumer has fewer rights than ever. Physicians are caught up in an awful web of regulations and mandates. Business is saddled with huge burdens that have nothing to do with satisfying consumer demands. And innovation is limited by an array of penalties, subsidies, and regulations. The failures of the present system create constant pressure for ever more legislation that further socializes the system, which produces more failure and so on and so on.

For the most part in the US, the long march toward medical socialism has taken the path of least political resistance. Public outrage at the Hillary Clinton health plan of 1993 was a beautiful thing to behold, and with the help of the Association of American Physicians and Surgeons (AAPS), this outrage forced the administration to back down. But in the meantime, the regulatory State has taken steps toward imposing some of the mandates Hillary favored.

In some ways, the Republicans are as bad as the Democrats. For instance, throughout the 1990s the GOP has backed legislation that can best be described as Hillary-lite, complete with restrictions on the ability of insurers to discriminate, premium caps on some groups, penalties for noncompliance, mandatory portability, and on and on. As bad as the legislation passed in the 1990s has been, we can be thankful that gridlock prevented a comprehensive plan from passing.

Government intervention in the US medical market began in the late 19th century, first in the form of government regulations on medical schools. No one dreamed where this would eventually lead. Moreover, no one would have thought to call such intervention a species of socialism.

Socialism, it was believed, was Plato. It was Marx. It was not the American Medical Association. The AMA was about insuring quality, not equalizing wealth or expropriating the expropriators.

In fact, the empowerment of this physician cartel was the original sin of American medicine. Through its ability to limit supply and outlaw competition, organized medicine has punished its customers, although the word is never used so as to disguise what is, after all, an economic relationship.

Competition among providers leads to rational pricing and maximum consumer choice. But this is exactly what the AMA has always sought to prevent. The AMA, founded in Philadelphia in 1847, advanced two seemingly innocent propositions in its early days: that all doctors should have a "suitable education" and that a "uniform elevated standard of requirements for the degree of MD should be adopted by all medical schools in the US." These were part of the AMA's real program, which was openly discussed at its conventions and in the medical journals: to secure a government-enforced medical monopoly and high incomes for mainstream doctors.

Membership in the new organization was open only to "regular" physicians, whose therapies were based on the "best system of physiology and pathology, as taught in the best schools in Europe and America." Emphatically not included among the "best" were the homeopaths. How the "regulars" came to crush the homeopaths and other competitors, and penalize patients in the process, is a story of deception and manipulation, of industry self-interest and State power. The organization knew it needed more than persuasion to secure a monopoly, so it also called for a national bureau of medicine to oversee state licensing and other regulations.

In those limited-government days, however, the idea went nowhere. But in the statist Progressive Era after the turn of the century, anticompetitive measures became respectable, and the AMA renewed its drive for a cartel, spurred on by the popularity of self-medication and the increasing number of medical schools and doctors. Then the AMA's secretary N.P. Colwell helped plan (and some say write) the famous 1910 report by Abraham Flexner. Flexner, the owner of a bankrupt prep school, had the good fortune to have a brother, Simon, who was director of the Rockefeller Institute for Medical Research.

At his brother's suggestion, Abraham Flexner was hired by the Rockefeller-allied Carnegie Foundation, so that the report would not be seen as a Rockefeller initiative. AMA-dominated state medical boards ruled that in order to practice medicine, a doctor had to graduate from an approved school. Post-Flexner, a school could not be approved if it taught alternative therapies, didn't restrict the number of students, or made profits based on student fees.

The Flexner Report was more than an attack on free competition funded by special interests. It was also a fraud. For example, Flexner claimed to have thoroughly investigated 69 schools in 90 days, and he sent prepublication copies of his report to the favored schools for their revisions. So we can see that using lies to advance political goals long predated the Gore campaign.

With its monopoly, the AMA sought to fix prices. Early on, the AMA had come to the conclusion that it was "unethical" for the consumer to have any say over what he paid. Common prices were transmuted into professional "fees," and the AMA sought to make them uniform across the profession. Lowering fees and advertising them were the worst violations of medical ethics and were made illegal. When fees were raised across the board, as they frequently could be with decreased competition, it was done in secret.

Then there was the problem of pharmacists selling drugs without a doctor's prescription. This was denounced as "therapeutic nihilism," and the American Pharmaceutical Association, controlled by the AMA, tried to stamp out this low-cost, in-demand practice. In nearly every state, the AMA secured laws that made it illegal for patients to seek treatment from a pharmacist. But still common were pharmacists who refilled prescriptions at customer request. The AMA lobbied to make this illegal, too, but most state legislatures wouldn't go along with this because of constituent pressure. The AMA got its way through the federal government, of course.

By the end of the Progressive Era, the AMA had triumphed over all of its competitors. Through the use of government power, it had come to control education, licensure,
treatment, and price. Later it outcompeted fraternal medical
insurance with the state-privileged and subsidized Blue Cross
and Blue Shield. The AMA-dominated Blues, in addition to
other benefits, gave us the egalitarian notion of "community
rating," under which everyone pays the same price no matter
what his condition.

When you see the bait, expect a trap. A cartelized profes-
sion is one that is easier to control and nationalize. Thus, the
New Deal brought us massive national subsidies. The Great
Society brought us the disastrous welfare systems of Medicare
and Medicaid. There were also the HMO subsidies from the
Nixon administration's monstrous Health Care Financing
Administration. The employer-mandates that make life so
difficult for small business and led to the creation of more
HMOs resulted from the lobbying of large corporations wanting to impose higher costs on their competitors, and labor
unions attempting to cartelize the labor force and keep out
low-price labor services.

And today, both major parties say all this apparatus is
wonderful and should be protected and expanded until the
end of time. It is true that there are some wonderful efforts
afoot to resist further socialization of medical care. But there
are no active political movements alive that are making any
progress toward a fully free market in medicine, toward a full
de-Nazification, a complete de-Sovietization, and a total de-
AMAization.

Several years ago, in the midst of the early 1990s' medical
care battles, UNLV economist Hans-Hermann Hoppe developed a plan that is extreme in its simplicity and radical in its
implication. Let me present that plan to you today.

1. Eliminate all licensing requirements for medical
schools, hospitals, pharmacies, and medical doctors and other
medical-care personnel. This would cause the supply to

increase. Prices would fall, and a greater variety of medical care services would appear on the market, many provided the way they are now but others provided through innovative new techniques. Many underground treatments would appear above ground.

And, yes, quackery would thrive. But as with other professions, competing voluntary accreditation agencies would take the place of compulsory government licensing, because consumers care about reputation, and are willing to pay for it. Consumers can make discriminating medical-care choices, just as they make discriminating choices in every other market.

2. Eliminate all government restrictions on the production and sale of pharmaceutical products and medical devices. This means no more Food and Drug Administration, which presently hinders innovation and increases costs. Costs and prices would fall, and a wider variety of better products would reach the market sooner, particularly through online delivery sources. The market would force consumers to act in accordance with the market's risk assessment. And competing drug and device manufacturers and sellers, to safeguard against product liability suits as much as to attract customers, would provide increasingly better product descriptions and guarantees.

3. Deregulate the medical insurance industry. A person's health or lack of health lies increasingly within his own control, thanks to the proliferation of health information. Instead of subsidizing uninsurable risks, "insurance" would involve the pooling of individual risks. "Winners" and "losers" are distributed according to the law of large numbers. There would be unrestricted freedom of contract: a health insurer would be free to offer any contract whatsoever, to include or exclude any risk, and to discriminate among any group of individuals. On average, prices would drastically fall, and the reform would restore individual responsibility in medical care.

Also, patients would be free to sign contracts with their doctors agreeing not to sue except in the case of real negligence, and never for a less-than-happy outcome.

4. Eliminate all government subsidies to the sick or unhealthy. As Mises said, subsidies create more of whatever is being subsidized. Subsidies for the ill and diseased breed illness and disease, and promote carelessness, indigence, and dependency. If we eliminate them, we would strengthen the will to live healthy lives, and to work for a living. In the first instance, that means abolishing Medicare and Medicaid. Because medicine is an economic service, rules of demand and supply apply to it as they do to everything else.

As long as those choices are made in an unhampered market, and as long as people needing medical care can freely choose among alternatives, the system will work as smoothly as any other market. The so-called crisis in medicine stems not from any peculiarities in the service itself but rather from the way that politicians have decided that medical care will be both produced and distributed.

We need to reject the principles that drive socialized medicine. These include the ideas of equality and universal service as mandated by the State, as well as the view that it is the responsibility of business and not that of the individual to pay the costs of medical care. Above all, we need to understand that medical care is a right only in this sense: the right of provider and patient to negotiate. Every service should be protected as this kind of right. Medical care is no different.

What about those who cannot afford much needed services? During the campaign, George W. had finished his speech and a hand shot up from a young lady who proceeded to complain that she could not afford a special device that would permit her to overcome her visual disability. Still relatively new to the campaign trail, Bush asked her how much the device would cost. She responded that it would cost about $400. W. then asked for someone in the audience to help this girl with the expenses, and in a few minutes, there was enough money pledged to make it possible for the girl to purchase the device.

The national press hooted and howled at the incident. They claimed that he missed the point, which was not to provide for the girl's particular need but rather to develop a national plan using the girl as a political prop. Actually, I liked Bush's idea better. He was suggesting that the girl had no natural right to the device. He believed it ought to be provided in the way all such luxuries are provided in a free market—through purchase or charity.

Judging from his more recent behavior, I don't believe we are justified in being optimistic about his plans for medical care. Neither do I believe that there is much hope in reforms that pretend to use market principles to better distribute medical care in the present system. Realistically, the best we can hope for is legislative gridlock, based on the principle that, first, do no more harm. To live by this principle means that you must ignore the partisan slogans that dominate the rhetoric of any proposed reform. Instead, you must live by this rule: carefully read any legislation before you offer your support.

Quite often some reforms sound great in principle—and I'm thinking here of gimmicks like educational vouchers and social security privatization—but once you look at the details, you find that the legislation would make the present system even worse. This was the case with the Republican health bill of the mid-1990s, which the AAPS fought so valiantly. I have no doubt the same is true of various proposals for Medical Savings Accounts. The power elite love nothing better than to turn a good reform idea into a cover for an increase in State power. Keep a watchful eye, and never believe the rhetoric until you see the bill itself.

Oh, yes, I am pessimistic about the legislative process. However, in the long term, I am cautiously optimistic about our overall situation. The exploding power of the market economy, and its ability to outrun and outperform the planners, is as evident in medical care as in every other industry. We've already begun to see the way in which the Web has presented serious challenges to conventional forms of medical-care delivery.

The future will offer other opportunities. And we should seize each one, on the principle that all forms of welfare and state regulation deserve to be tossed in the dustbin of history along with the ideological system that gave birth to them. Until that day, if you want to stay out of the trap, ignore the bait.

2. War

WAR AND FREEDOM

[A version of this talk was delivered at the Freedom Summit in Phoenix, Arizona, on October 12, 2002.]

Concerning the Bush administration's foreign policy, I'm not sure that most libertarians—to say nothing of most Americans—have considered the full extent of what we are dealing with here. On television, Bush promised war against Iraq and war-crimes trials for any Iraqi military leader who follows orders, if Iraq failed to meet a series of demands. One of them was as follows: Iraq "must stop all illicit trade outside the oil-for-food program."

Consider what this meant. The US threatened total war against a country if it permits its citizens to exercise their natural right to trade and improve their lot in life. This is not just contrary to free-trade principles. It is contrary to all standards of human decency. Quite frankly, a more despotic demand is hard to imagine.

Bush says there "can be no peace if our security depends on the will and whims of a ruthless and aggressive dictator." If others take that statement differently from the way he intended it, they may be forgiven.

Before Bush gave his speech, the Bush administration had issued a *National Security Strategy for the United States*—a blueprint for domestic and global conquest by the US government—of free markets and free trade. It asserts the right of the US to deliver a preemptive strike against any country anywhere that gets on Washington's nerves, and lays out a blueprint for permanent military occupation of the entire world by the US.

In the 1990s, when the US was busy looking for war rationales and throwing itself into every conflict it was fortunate enough to discover or create, Murray N. Rothbard wrote a satirical piece called: "Invade the World." He wrote:

> We must face the fact that there is not a single country in the world that measures up to the lofty moral and social standards that are the hallmark of the USA. . . . There is not a single country in the world which, like the US, reeks of democracy and "human rights," and is free of crime and murder and hate thoughts and undemocratic deeds. Very few other countries are as Politically Correct as the US, or have the wit to impose a massively statist program in the name of "freedom," "free trade," "multiculturalism," and "expanding democracy." And so, since no other countries shape up to US standards—in a world of Sole Superpower—they must be severely chastised by the US. I make a Modest Proposal for the only possible consistent and coherent foreign policy: the US must, very soon, Invade the Entire World!

It would seem that the Bush administration received a copy of this article and used it as a working model for its own foreign policy. Just as Rothbard suggested, the invade-the-world strategy is taking place in the name of freedom. It is therefore incumbent on those of us who love free markets and free trade to speak out, not only against the despotic ambitions of this document itself, but also on behalf of the real meaning of economic freedom. We must fight our way through the thicket of rhetoric, political grandstanding, and moral hypocrisy to preserve some sense of the meaning of freedom itself.

This is not usually a problem when a president of the Democratic Party is in control. Given their constituents and rhetorical apparatus, the Democrats will not usually promote global empire while singing the praises of free markets, entrepreneurship, private property, and low taxes. What we get instead, as we did under Carter and Clinton, is talk of welfare rights, the urgency of redistribution, public education, labor rights, and the like.

And there is a certain honesty to this approach, for big government abroad and big government at home are a suitable match. There is no strict line of political demarcation between a government that minds its business at home or abroad. Internationally expansionistic states are not usually humble at home, and, as a matter of history, international and national socialist states have tended to be expansionist beyond their borders insofar as they have had the resources to do so. All this stands to reason.

What is more troubling, and far more difficult to unravel, is the situation we currently face, in which a regime knows and embraces a partisan language of economic liberty while promoting the opposite. Though the Republicans have been generally derided as the Stupid Party, in fact this approach of doublespeak is far shrewder than the approach of the other party. When Republicans promote big government as liberty, it is intimidating to the opposition, which finds itself robbed of its only opposition tactic, even as it is rhetorically compelling to those generally disposed to support the ideals of freedom.

Here is one example of what I mean. The Bush document says:

> The concept of "free trade" arose as a moral principle even before it became a pillar of economics. If you can make something that others value, you should be able to sell it to them. If others make something that you value, you should

be able to buy it. This is real freedom, the freedom for a person—or a nation—to make a living.

Now, it is hard to disagree with that. In fact, it might be seen as a summary of the libertarian economic credo. And yet, the United States imposes trade sanctions on half the countries of the world, and the sanctions against Iraq in particular have resulted in mass human suffering. The very administration that preaches the libertarian line on trade has imposed high tariffs on steel and timber, and pushed massive agricultural subsidies that blatantly violate all international trade treaties to which the US has become party. What we have here are actions that are the very opposite of the rhetoric, and yet the rhetoric plays the role of distracting people from what is really going on.

There are many other examples. The document preaches fiscal prudence, from an administration that has expanded government spending more dramatically and on more fronts than even LBJ. It preaches free markets but endorses the internationalization of US labor and environmental controls. It rails against centralized economic planning, but embraces global efforts to cut "greenhouse gases," even going so far as to brag of spending the largest sum ever spent to stop alleged climate change. The document calls for free enterprise, but also a 50-percent increase in foreign aid slated for development assistance. It decries World Bank subsidies of the past, but calls for the World Bank to spend more on public schools and promises a 20-percent increase in the money contributed by the US toward that end.

In sum, we have here something worse than a wolf in sheep's clothing. We have a wolf that has also learned to b-a-a-a-h. Even aside from partisan considerations, the permanent governing regime always needs an ideological rationale for maintaining control over the population, and a continuing supply of resources to feed all the pressure groups that live off the taxpayer. Even apart from elections, which change the flavor of government control but not its underlying reality, this permanent regime, which we can call the State, always seeks to expand.

For all the partisan bickering in Washington, all groups are pleased to cooperate in the overall mission of insuring the health of the State, and the best way is what they call bipartisanship: each votes the other's priorities in exchange for having its own met. Thus does the welfare-warfare State thrive.

It is no surprise that today the great rationale of the proposed expansion of the State is the fight against terrorism, which doesn't only mean stopping those who seek to harm US citizens on American soil, but encompasses some sort of blueprint for complete global domination. The war on terrorism is not just about stopping real threats, if it involves that at all. It is about securing the authority of the US government against anything and everything that might threaten its interests. That threat could be swarthy teams of violent criminals hailing from far-flung parts of the world. But, from the point of view of the State, the threat also comes from any political activist or even intellectual apparatus that does not unquestioningly yield to the power of the State.

This is most clear in an offhanded comment the document has on Colombia. It reads: "In Colombia, we recognize the link between terrorist and extremist groups that challenge the *security of the State* and drug trafficking activities that help finance the operations of such groups." Thus we see here that the mere production of goods that people want to buy, combined with a political stance the US opposes, can get you branded a terrorist. If this is true in Colombia, where the document promises that the US government will provide "basic security to the Colombian people," it is far more true right here at home.

The Bush document lays out a variety of criteria for distinguishing the good states from the bad states that the US now swears it can destroy on a whim. The document decries any State that tramples on what it calls the "nonnegotiable demands of human dignity," among which are the rule of law, limits on the absolute power of the State, free speech, freedom of worship, equal justice, respect for women, religious and ethnic tolerance, and respect for private property.

It is not an objectionable list, though only the hopelessly naïve could possibly believe that the US has any intention of sticking by this list. US allies in the Near East and North Africa stand in constant violation of these principles. For that matter, the United States itself has a less than stellar record in defense of private property—after all, this is a country that takes up to 40 percent of your income. And you may notice that while the US decries those who have no limit on the absolute power of the State, there is no call for what the American colonists favored: a strictly limited State power.

In fact, a new doctrine has developed in Washington that says, in the words of this document, "weak states . . . can pose as great a danger to our national interests as strong states." And with all the foreign aid, military assistance, multilateral lending support, and military mandates that the US is imposing around the world, you can be sure that America is doing everything possible to prevent the formation of weak states around the world. It is quite a transition from the 18th century, when we went about creating a State that was deliberately weak, while warning against foreign entanglements, to the current situation in which a strong State at home goes on an imperial rampage to create subservient copies of itself around the world.

September 11 represented a horrible loss of life and property, but it also represented what many in the United States government considered to be a new lease on life. Osama bin Laden, having long left the public eye, even though he was blamed for the attacks, remains at large. The government is using the event as an excuse to trample on rights and liberties and vastly expand itself.

In every event, even the most calamitous, there are certain people and institutions that end up benefiting, so let us think about what institution has benefited the most from the events. What institution has accumulated more power and money and public respect? The answer is obvious: it is the State itself. One might think that this would be a problem for the Bush doctrine.

After all, if some other major institution, such as a church or company, uses a disaster it is responsible for, to claim that it should be given more money and power, we suspect its motives and certainly do not grant automatic deference. Why are so many willing to do this with the State? In part it comes down to the magic plural pronoun: "we." In page after page, the Bush administration document uses this word to imply that the interests of the State are identical to the interests of the American people. It follows that whatever the government decides to do, whatever it deems to be in the public interest, must be the right thing. If you disagree, then you are opposing the public interest and you might just be a threat to public order itself. At the very least, the burden of proof is on you to explain why you might oppose the idea of a permanent wartime economy.

There is a revealing passage about halfway through the Bush administration's manifesto. It reads as follows: "It has taken almost a decade for us to comprehend the true nature of this new threat." What happened 10 years ago? The Cold War had vanished because of the sudden and unexpected dissolution of the Soviet Union, and so too the main ideological rationale for the buildup of the biggest, richest, most powerful State apparatus the world had ever seen. The history of the last 10 years can be read as a struggle between citizens to regain control of their lives and property against an immense governmental structure that seemed to lack a believable reason for its existence.

Then came September 11, 2001. The Bush document describes this event as has become customary: a hinge of history that forced the United States to rethink its place in the world and the meaning of freedom itself. It is not described as what it was: a wholly preventable hijacking by Saudi nationals trained in the US and motivated by revenge at US foreign policy. Had the pilots of the planes been armed, as they would have been, had federal regulations not prevented it, the hijackers would have been dealt with long before they could have wrecked the buildings.

Before this happened, the post-Cold War welfare-warfare State had many rationales to justify its continuation. Clinton attempted to merge a British-style paternalism with a US-style focus on international human rights. The great threat at home and abroad that had to be defeated was abstract and ideological: concerns like unfairness and injustice. This did not gain many converts, especially since it meant converting the US armed forces into a glorified corps of international social workers. There were a series of invasions and operations to stop alleged ethnic cleansing, to impose democracy, to end warlordism, and the like. There were the inevitable worries about China becoming too big for its britches.

None of these served as a replacement for the communist menace as a viable excuse for the permanent war economy. The military-industrial elites that live off the war threat were very worried about their long-term status, especially because internal polling continued to reveal a systematic and growing loss in confidence in government as an institution. Panic over the pace of private-sector technological development further worked to alarm the government, which still populated its offices with IBM Selectrics as Windows 98 was being shipped to customers. As Social Security became a laughingstock, and Clinton's Monica problem did the same for the chief executive, US foreign policy came to be subject to withering critiques by a diverse group of intellectuals from the left and right.

To the government, September 11 meant an end to all of this. It held out the hope that something could be seen as a scarier threat to the public than government itself. It worked to transform public opinion about the government itself, from a menace to a savior. To be sure, this step was wholly unwarranted. It was the government that banned guns on planes, the government that ran airport security, the government that antagonized the hijackers, the government that created and sustained what became al-Qaeda, the government that received the advance warnings and did nothing, and the government that had promised and failed in every way to deliver security. September 11 was a spectacular government failure.

In order to distract us from this conclusion, the government has created the illusion that the greatest threat we face is somewhere out there, and we must trust the government to tell us from day to day what that threat is. Among them is what has come to be known as the rogue state.

The Bush document includes a fascinating definition of what constitutes a rogue state.

- A rogue state, it says, brutalizes its own people and squanders its national resources for the personal gain of its rulers. Check.

- It displays no regard for international law, threatens its neighbors, and callously violates international treaties to which it is party. Check.

- It is determined to acquire weapons of mass destruction, along with other advanced military technology. Check.

- It sponsors terrorism around the globe. Given that Osama and his men were once on the CIA payroll, and given what most of the Arab world believes about the US role in the Middle East, we have to say, check.

• Finally, the document says, almost in anticipation of this manner of critique, a rogue state hates the United States and everything for which it stands.

And in this last sentence we find the real definition: a rogue state is a state that our State hates and visa versa. We are back to the age-old problem of which true libertarians are all too aware: the State itself is the greatest source of conflict ever known to man.

The right response to September 11 would have been for government's entire security apparatus to be dismantled, and to allow the airlines and other firms to provide their own security. But, of course, it had all the earmarks of a crisis, and history shows that crises are great opportunities for the State. The voices of clarity on this issue have been overwhelmed by those who have belligerently asserted that the government must do something, anything, in retaliation for 9-11.

Most tragically, the need for war was asserted by people who called themselves libertarians, people who otherwise claimed to understand the nature of government.

Without naming the guilty here, let me just say that only four institutions—to my knowledge—were willing to take a principled stand after 9-11: the Independent Institute, the Foundation for the Future of Freedom, the Center for Libertarian Studies, and the Mises Institute—four of the least well-connected among the hundreds of free-market organizations in this country. Once having signed up for the war on terrorism, mainstream libertarian organizations find themselves in an intellectual bind, fearing to criticize the foundations of the policy and enjoying the newfound access to power that the initial endorsement of the war gave them.

And yet, we should not be surprised at the failure of the mainstream libertarian movement to provide a voice of sanity in these times. For too long, they have seen the problem of government power not as a moral or principled concern but as something to be worked out among policy elites, among which they have wanted to include themselves. They have promoted the view that the means of achieving our ends is through joining the governing elites in their salons of DC, and impressing power holders with your intellectual agility. What could possibly beat cocktails with DeLay, Greenspan, and von Rumsfeld?

The moral courage that motivated the American colonists, Cobden and Bright, the war resisters, the tax protesters, the anti-New Deal writers, the anticommunist and anti-Nazi intellectuals—none of this experience has informed the dominant libertarian strategy of our age, so, of course, the libertarians have been largely and tragically co-opted.

There is a further intellectual problem at work among the mainstream of libertarians, and it is captured in the chart that purports to summarize all political ideology according to one's opinion concerning the balance of civil and economic liberty. Nowhere on the chart is there anything about foreign policy or war—the murder end of the State. Quite frankly, libertarians just haven't cared that much about the issue, even though war is the health of the State.

After a lifetime of activism in libertarian circles, Murray Rothbard came to observe that most people in the libertarian movement have no real interest in the issue, even though it can be said that war is by far the gravest threat to liberty mankind has ever known. There are many reasons for this oversight, among which is that we all tend to take the path of least resistance, and it is far easier to analyze a telecommunications bill than to denounce the CIA and the war power.

But, as Mises argued, if we hate socialism, we must also hate war. "Military Socialism is the Socialism of a state in which all institutions are designed for the prosecution of war," he wrote.

> The military state, that is the state of the fighting man in which everything is subordinated to war purposes, cannot admit private ownership in the means of production.

Standing preparedness for war is impossible if aims other than war influence the life of individuals. . . . The military state is a state of bandits. It prefers to live on booty and tribute.

Mises is right: if we libertarians tolerate war, we tolerate tyranny.

But if the libertarians have shown a lack of courage stemming from intellectual failure, the American conservatives have been far worse. From the pages of the *Wall Street Journal* to *National Review*, there is one thing we can count on: bone-chilling calls for international bloodshed at the hands of the US State. It was bad enough during the Cold War, when American conservatives cheered on the warfare state—the emergence of a totalitarian bureaucracy within our shores—as a supposedly temporary measure to fight a particular enemy.

But nowadays, American conservatives have come to define themselves as the people least wary of using nuclear weapons and the most ready to cheer the death of innocents. The moral hypocrisy of these people—who think nothing of running an article calling for an end to abortion next to a piece defending the deaths of hundreds of thousands of foreigners, unborn and born—takes one's breath away.

We have dealt here with three groups—the Bush administration, the libertarian mainstream, and American conservatives—that use the language of liberty to promote or defend its opposite. What about those of us who remain, those whose commitment to the free society is implacable, even in these times? I know this. There are more of us than the media take account of. The Bush document includes a passage that strikes me as true: "no people on earth yearn to be oppressed, aspire to servitude, or eagerly await the midnight knock of the secret police." I would only add that this includes the American people.

Beneath all the hoopla of this past September 11, beneath the sickening displays of celebration for the government and the complete absence of commentary on most victims of 9-11, who, after all, were engaged in the peaceful, civilizing business of commerce, I did detect growing public frustration with the direction the warfare state is going. Apart from all the bombs, billions, and baloney, the only thing the federal government seems to have done to protect us from terrorism is make our airports even more inconvenient, and institute a perfectly ridiculous color-coded chart to tell us just how close the next terrorist threat allegedly is.

We are far from the time when a majority of public opinion will come to understand the real nature of the threat we face, and the real ideological foundations of the struggle in which our epoch has plunged us. But just as the partisans of the welfare-warfare State say that their reign must last the duration of our lifetimes, let us all commit to making sure that the resistance lasts just as long. Even if we do not achieve victory in our lifetimes, we might slow down the advance of tyranny and therefore have done good. If we do not even manage that, we can know that we have done the right thing, the moral thing, the courageous thing.

But is final victory really so unthinkable? In the 18th century, had the opponents of British imperial rule given up in 1750, there would have been no 1776. Had the anticommunists in Russia thrown in the towel in 1950, when Soviet rule seemed implacably secure, there would have been no 1989. Neither will we be intimidated and neither will we despair, because we are fighting the biggest of all big lies, the idea that the State is a means of security and salvation. In addition, we have on our side the greatest forces for good in human history: the ideas of liberty and the demand for freedom. From these principles, we will not be moved.

In the meantime, Bush threatens war. For my part, I favor the proposal of the Iraqi vice president that Bush and Saddam have a private duel. Choose your weapons, fellas, and leave the rest of us out of it.

FREE TRADE VERSUS WAR

[This speech was presented at the Mises Institute's "Costs of War" Conference in Atlanta, Georgia, on May 22, 1994.]

P olitics, like war, robs words of their meaning. This is especially true of the language of economics. For example, economists know what *investment* means and that it's good for the economy; but the government uses *investment* to mean its profligate spending projects which are, of course, harmful to the economy. In 18th-century America, our forefathers knew what was meant by the word *rights*. When Thomas Jefferson and others used it, it meant limitations on government power. In today's America, however, the word *rights* has become synonymous with government power. A *violation of rights* has come to mean the exercise of liberty.

So it is with the phrase *free trade*. Politics, and in particular that most concentrated form of politics—war, have ruined its meaning. In the 18th and 19th centuries, the term described the economic regime under which people could buy and sell across the borders without penalty from the government. The case for free trade was the case for free markets. When the government interferes in the freedom to contract, it benefits some—that is, powerful special interests, at the expense of others—that is, the people. Under free trade, on the other hand, the general good is served.

Originally, free trade was not like mercantilism, where the government monopolizes and otherwise hinders the right to trade across borders. Free trade was not like an export policy where domestic producers are subsidized so they can push their goods on consumers abroad at the expense of taxpayers at home. Free trade was not like a producer policy where large producers conspire with the government to decide what goods will be allowed to cross borders. Free trade was not like an industrial policy where large corporations are given investment guarantees in the disguised form of aid to foreign regimes. Free trade was not like imperialism, where a more powerful government imposes its will on a less powerful one through intimidation and force. Free trade was an ideal that grew out of the vision of liberty.

The same freedom that governs the market at home, its proponents believed, ought to govern trade across borders. Just as private parties negotiate their contracts for their goods and services at home, they would do so abroad. In the 18th and 19th centuries, to be a free trader meant to apply pressure to try to bring about this ideal through intellectual persuasion and political lobbying. Free traders brought that pressure to bear against their own government. That was where their moral obligation began and ended.

What about the term *protectionism?* It meant government manipulation of trade on behalf of particular interest groups. Governments can do this alone by erecting tariffs, quotas, and sanctions. Governments can engage in protectionism in cahoots with other governments as in Nafta or Gatt; but, however it is achieved, protectionism constitutes intervention in the natural order of liberty. To be consistent with history and theory, people who claim to favor free trade should be agitating against the US's protectionist policies and US support of the protectionist policies of others.

Instead, many of the free traders commit much of their energies to lobbying for Nafta and Gatt, which represent the opposite of free trade. These agreements are mercantilist because they exalt the right of government to hinder trade. They support an export-driven policy under which producers are subsidized. They embody industrial policy where large corporations are paid off. They are imperialistic with regulations on labor and the environment to be harmonized across borders.

How did this all begin? When did *free trade* come to mean its opposite? As with so much else, it was World War II that changed everything. The trust and deference that the

American people gave the government during the war spilled over to the postwar plans for carving up the spoils. At the Bretton Woods conference in 1944, trade came to mean investment guarantees and global bureaucracies in statist treaties between governments. This was central planning exalted to new heights.

As F.A. Hayek wrote in the neglected conclusion to his 1944 book, the *Road to Serfdom*, "If international economic relations, instead of being between individuals, become relations between whole nations organized as trading bodies, they will inevitably become the source of friction and envy." Ludwig von Mises concluded in his 1944 book *Omnipotent Government: The Rise of the Total State of Total War* with a similar warning. "The establishment," he said, "of an international body for foreign trade planning will end in hyperprotectionism." These two great free marketeers understood how government uses the period immediately following a war as it does the war itself for State power and special-interest rewards.

The Wilson administration attempted this after World War I. An early draft of the League of Nations treaty included a world trade tribunal. After World War II, Mises and Hayek did not want such a thing to be imposed on us. Instead they wanted to recreate the 19th-century ideal. And thanks to the work of Mises and other partisans of the free market, when the Truman administration emerged from negotiations in Havana with something called the International Trade Organization, free-market advocates were ready. We had had the World Bank and the International Monetary Fund foisted on us, but free traders did stop the ITO.

The lobbying efforts of Philip Cortney, under the influence of Henry Hazlitt, proved definitive. In his book, the *Economic Munich: The I.T.O. Charter, Inflation or Liberty, the 1929 Lesson*, Cortney explained the dangers of turning over trade policy to an international body. "In the long run," he said, "a centralized trade authority will globalize protectionism."

Cortney cited the charter of the International Trade Organization to make his point. It endorsed demand-side management and full-employment policies, which Cortney rightly regarded as code words for government planning. Thanks to such intellectual leaders and the Old Right in Congress, the ITO went down to defeat.

Of course, during the debates, the elites never missed a chance to smear the ITO opponents, and the language of trade was permanently subverted. Advocates of global bureaucracies began calling themselves free traders. The ITO, they said, would save free trade from itself just as the New Deal had saved capitalism from itself. The opponents of world bureaucracies, no matter how much they favored free trade, were called *isolationists* and *protectionists*—words drawn from recent war propaganda. As true believers in trade, the Old Right would not accept the term *isolationist*. And as opponents of mercantilism, of course, they rejected the word *protectionist*.

Centralizing bodies managing trade are, of course, not compatible with self-determination, even if erected in the name of free trade. In holding this view, the Old Right was in a great American tradition: Southern free traders from Jefferson to Calhoun. This tradition was not rooted in an internationalist ideology, obviously; neither did its proponents push for global treaties that violate sovereignty. The tradition was based on a hard-nosed understanding of the nature of power and a devotion to federalism and local control. When power is centralized, they argued, it expands and will be used against the people.

The best way to limit power is to limit centralization. For example, it is in the economic interest of smaller political units to maintain open trading relationships. The larger the political unit, as Hans-Hermann Hoppe has shown, the more enlightening a policy of autarchy can appear. The Southern free traders linked their economic doctrine with states' rights as embodied in the Constitution, and with a noninterventionist foreign policy and severe limitations on what they call *consol-idation*, that is *centralization*.

These ideas melded on a theoretical level because they speak to the right of individuals and communities to be free of arbitrary powers of distant rulers. Among the reasons the Declaration of Independence gave for overthrowing King George III was that he was "cutting off our trade with all parts of the world." Jefferson presents a more elaborate argument in his 1774 essay *Summary View of the Rights of British America*. The outrages of the Sugar Act and the Townsend Duties demonstrated that Britain was willing to use coercion to deny Americans the liberty to trade—meaning to buy, to sell to any-one that they pleased. Jefferson regarded this as the essence of tyranny intolerable enough to warrant a violent overthrow of the government. "Single acts of tyranny may be ascribed to the accidental opinion of the day," he wrote in 1774, "but a series of repressions begun in a distinguished period and pur-sued unalterably through every change of ministers plainly prove the deliberate systematical plan of reducing us to slav-ery." To ensure the right of trade among other rights, the founders established, not a central government, but a federal one. It was a union among states, and these individual states would protect the people against the centralization of power by jealously guarding states' rights and privileges.

Trade became an issue again in the debates of the Con-stitution, however. The so-called Federalists, actually the cen-tralizers, accused the states of erecting barriers to trade under the Articles of Confederation. This was among the most seri-ous accusations that could be made. It implied that the states were doing to each other what King George had done to America. The Federalists argued that the Constitution was necessary to bring about free trade among the states. In partic-ular, they argued, the commerce clause would be the essential guarantee of a free flow of goods. The anti-federalists, really the anticentralists—official monikers being a prime example of the misuse of language—countered that the commerce clause conflicted with another valued precept of American liberty, that is, states' rights.

The anti-federalists warned that the freedom of trade, like all freedoms, was best protected by the decentralized Articles of Confederation, or something similar, rather than by a new central government with central powers, especially the power to conduct trade policy. The anti-federalists argued that this clause could, and therefore, would be abused to the advantage of one sector as opposed to another. But the Constitution passed upon James Madison's promise that this would never be so. "The commerce clause," he said, "would forever be used to protect the liberty of every American to trade in an unhindered way just as every other American."

Of course, history did not turn out that way. After the overthrow of the king, the partisans of Northern industrial and banking interests began agitating to abandon the principles of the Declaration. The Hamiltonians wanted the powers of King George to be exercised by the president in violation of the principles agreed upon in the Constitution. Their goal was the enrichment of special interests—manufacturing and banking—at the expense of the Southern states. The great statesmen of the first half of the 19th century, free traders to a man, were devoted to stopping the Hamiltonian power policy of executive power, entangling alliances and war, taxes, and protectionism to benefit northern elites.

The old Republicans wanted the political victory of 1800 used to roll back the centralizing that had taken place since 1787. Their goal was to secure a permanent victory over the Hamiltonians, who were both pro-State and pro-war, as well as pro-tariff.

Among the greatest of the Southern republicans was John Randolph of Roanoke—the aristocratic libertarian. He said,

> Let us adhere to the policy laid down by the second, as well as by the first, founder of our republic. By the Camillus as well as the Romulus of the infant state to the policy of peace,

commerce, and on friendship of all nations entangling alliances with none.

He was among the earliest and most hard core of the antiprotectionists of the Old South. His reasons were part philosophical, part economic, and part political. As a partisan of states' rights, he saw no justification for granting an external power the right to interfere with commerce and the use of private property; yet Randolph was also a centralist of a particularly American sort. "When I speak of my country," he wrote John Brockenborough, "I mean the commonwealth of Virginia. I was born in an allegiance to George III. My ancestors threw off the oppressive yoke of the mother country, but they never made me subject to New England in the matters spiritual or temporal, neither do I mean to become so voluntarily."

Another great old Republican was John Taylor of Caroline. He was not only a brilliant political philosopher; he led the opposition to the Northern protective tariff. "Give us a free and open competition in our own market," he said, "and we fear not to encounter like competition in the general market of the world." Taylor saw the tariff as part of the apparatus of statist domination. The interest groups behind it were northern industrialists who wanted to feed their private greed at public expense. Rather than selling their wares on a level playing field of free competition, they sought government privilege. In 1821 the Congressional Committee of Manufacturers issued a report calling for protective tariffs to expand industry. In today's language, men call this growing the economy, expanding trade, enacting fair trade, or any of another number of other chivalrous methods used to centralize trade authority. But Taylor saw the real motive of tariffs. They were a power grab.

But the manufacturers sought to gain from what came at the South's expense in two respects. First, economically, the tariff harmed agriculture and transferred wealth. Second, politically it was contrary to the free-trade sentiments of the Old South, and it subverted Southern rights of political self-determination and was, therefore, a violation of the original federal compact.

Taylor was a lover of peace, so the industrialists were his natural enemies. As is so often the case, the pro-tariff party was also the pro-war party. The industrialists favored Hamilton's attempt to foment a war with France to enhance the Executive. Taylor noted that the industrialists' 1821 report complained that, "We flourished in war and are depressed in peace because manufacturers then flourished and now are depressed." They hoped that the tariffs would similarly enhance their profits. If only today's war and tariff party were half that honest! Taylor responded as follows: "They say," he said, "we flourished in war. Who are we? Not the people of the states generally. They were loaded with taxes, deprived of commerce, and involved in debt. The families, which flourished in war, were the contracting and [industrialist] families, the latter by loans and premiums and the selling the wares of their factories at the profit of fifty or an hundred per centum. Had the great family of the people flourished," said Taylor, "they would not have hailed peace" and trade.

The industrialists wanted to revive what Taylor had called the "property transferring policy which operated so delightfully in war." Taylor said, "It is a consequence of war to transfer property. And this has hitherto been considered one of its evils." But the Northern industrialists wanted to redefine redistribution as a virtue of war—with themselves on the receiving end of the loot, of course.

A third great Old South free-trade theorist was John C. Calhoun. He, too, denounced the tariff imposed by the Northern usurpers. "By a perversion of the powers of the Constitution, which was intended to protect the states of the Union in enjoyment of their natural advantages, they have stripped us of the blessings bestowed by nature and converted them to their own advantage. Restore our advantages by giving us free trade with the world, and we would become what they are now by our own means—the most flourishing people on the globe."

In contrasting himself with his opponents, Calhoun said, "We want free trade, they restrictions. We want moderate taxes, frugality in the government, economic accountability, and a rigid application of the public money to the payment of debt." Calhoun granted that the Constitution allowed the central government to impose a duty on imports for revenue purposes, but his analysis of power politics led him to believe that more was involved. Neither the tax imposed nor the revenue collected were being used for the general interest. They were being used by one group to destroy another. The tariff, therefore, violated the Constitution by benefiting one group at the expense of another without the exploited group's consent.

Calhoun was, in addition to all of his other achievements, an impressive economist theorist. He defended free trade as necessary to the division of labor. As he explained, the South has

> from soil and climate, a facility in rearing certain great agricultural staples. While other and older countries with dense population and capital greatly accumulated have equal facility in manufacturing various articles suited to our use. And thus a foundation is laid for an exchange of the products of labor mutually advantageous.

The tariff, he argued, acted as a tax on his trade. And a tax hurts the producer, he said, whether it is laid on the vender or the purchaser. It doesn't matter whether the tax is a consumption tax or a production tax. In the end it hurts production because, he said, the tax must always eat into profits and therefore future capital. "The effect on us," he wrote, "is to compel us to purchase at a higher price both what we obtain from them and from others without receiving a corresponding increase in the price of what we sell."

Calhoun developed a unique way of thinking about the tariff that turned it into a populist issue. If the tariff is one-third, it is the same as the government taking one-third of what the producers raise in cotton, rice, and tobacco. Whether the goods are coming into the country or leaving it, a tariff of one-third is the theft of one-third. To Calhoun this meant that one-third of the toil and labor of the people of the South was being transferred to the North to build Northern industry and to feed a hostile government. "We are the serfs of the system," he announced, "out of whose labor is raised, not only the money paid into the Treasury, but the funds out of which are drawn the rich rewards of the manufacturer associates and interests. Their encouragement is our discouragement."

The survival of the South is at stake in this issue, he said. "The last remains of our great and once flourishing agriculture must be annihilated in the conflict. In the first instance, we will be thrown on the home market which can not consume a fourth of our products; and instead of supplying the world as we would with free trade, we would be compelled to abandon the cultivation of three fourths of what we now raise and receive for the residue whatever the manufacturers, who would then have their policy consummated by the entire possession of our market, might choose to give."

Free trade, Calhoun believed, represented the ultimate safeguard of political rights. Without such trade, the South would become a captive nation, enserfed for a cabal of Northern industrialists tied to and dependent upon government power. His solution, of course, was to insert the right of interposition whereby South Carolina would stand as a buffer between the individual and the central government. To protect the Constitution, that is, Calhoun advocated disobedience to central government. That's a sound principle.

Let's compare Calhoun's arguments against the tariff of abominations with Jefferson's summary view. Both argued against violations of free trade. Both argued against a centralized government. Both argued that tariffs were taxation without representation. Both argued that this is tyranny, and both argued that radical means were justified in overthrowing the oppressor. This is one of the reasons that the founding fathers of the Confederacy felt themselves to be the heirs of the original founders. Tariff taxes precipitated both independence movements, and both were based on the view that liberty and free trade were of a piece. If Randolph, Taylor, Calhoun, and all their followers had been able to repeal the tariffs and prevent their reimposition, the war between the states might never have occurred. So many young men might never have died, and our nation might still be free.

Instead, after a reprieve in 1833, the central government engaged in more and more trade protectionism and centralized tyranny, which helped lead to war. In his seldom quoted first inaugural address, Abraham Lincoln pledged, "no bloodshed or violence," but he also promised to "collect the duties in the impost no matter what." He effectively announced that he planned to tax the South to death, and as soon as he was able to do so, Lincoln imposed the highest tariff in US history, doubling the rates to 48 percent. It's no wonder that when Edmund Ruffin fired the first shot in the beginning of the war between the states, he aimed at a customs house—Fort Sumter.

The war is also appropriately called the War of Federal Aggression. And one aggression occurred in 1861 with the passage of the Morrill Tariff. The South made the choice for liberty through secession, and the Confederate Constitution specifically forbade high tariffs. At the beginning of the war, a revealing Boston newspaper editorial accused the South of the gravest crime of all, which the editorialist called the cause of the war. The South, said the editorial, wanted a system "verging on free trade. If the Southern Confederation is allowed to carry out a policy by which only a nominal duty is laid upon import, no doubt, the business of the chief Northern cities will be seriously injured." Alas, the South was not allowed to carry out its policy of free trade, and the nation paid a terrible price.

It is a price that we are still paying, and we are repeating the same errors with regard to current trade policy. Despite the rhetoric we hear from Washington, there is no threat that free trade is going to break out anytime soon. A true regime of free trade, as Murray Rothbard has pointed out, would be greeted by Washington, DC, with about the same enthusiasm as the repeal of the income tax.

Let's consider the linguistic categories that govern the great trade debates of our time— Nafta and Gatt. The media and the government have successfully created a political split of Manichean proportions. On one side we have the representatives of pure light—multinational corporations, every executive branch agency, the leaders of both parties of both houses of Congress, the media, all the ex-presidents, respected public intellectuals, Beltway think tanks, professors at every top university. They are called the free traders. On the other side, we have almost everyone else. Public opinion has been solidly against both Nafta and Gatt at least before it has been shaped by those on the other side. We can add to the public a handful of columnists and academics who have actually bothered to look at the documents in question. The people of light say that this latter group represents the forces of darkness— isolationists and reactionary opponents of free trade and progress.

Let's look at how reality changes this conventional grouping. Nafta established a trade block primarily to benefit government-connected corporations and banking interests. It invested new powers in the Executive to interfere with trade from non-North American nations. It's a natural consequence of Nafta that the US government would threaten trade war with Japan. It's a natural consequence of Nafta that the US would set up a multibillion dollar fund to support the Mexican peso. It's a natural consequence of Nafta that unprecedented levels of foreign aid would flow to Mexico City.

Like Hamilton's domestic policy, Nafta is statist to the core. The Congressional Research Service tells us that under Nafta we cannot reduce regulation on labor or the environment even to retain investment. The labor side tells us that we are to have equal wages between men and women, which not even Hamilton would have favored imposing by Executive fiat. The Nafta-ites tell us that we retain our sovereignty under Nafta. It is partially true. We retain our sovereignty to increase our restrictions on business, to increase labor and environmental regulations, but we do not retain our rights to reduce them without monetary and trade penalties from trinational secretariats.

Nafta is imperialist. It preaches to other countries about what kinds of laws and regulations they should have—the social democratic mixed economy that is impoverishing us. Nafta is, of course, not the free trade of Jefferson, Randolph, Taylor, and Calhoun. It is trade for the few and not the many, for the particular interests and not the general interests.

What about Gatt and the World Trade Organization it proposes to establish? Same is true. It is sold as free trade, yet it represents something else entirely. It enshrines the principle of manipulating economies by demand-side management. It embraces so-called *sustainable development*, which is a code word for the entire environmentalist agenda. The World Trade Organization comes complete with a new ministerial conference, a director general, a secretariat plethora of committees, councils, and review bodies, and a bunch of new, fancy office buildings in Geneva. WTO's mission will not be the lowering of trade barriers, but rather its stated goal of "achieving greater coherence in global economic policy making." As

US trade representative Mickey Kantor was toasting the end of the Gatt negotiations in December, the *New York Times* hailed the WTO as the trade equivalent of the World Bank and the International Monetary Fund.

Jefferson, Taylor, Randolph, and Calhoun were right. Centralized government is the tyrant. These free-trade revolutionaries found the remedy in a love of liberty and a willingness to fight for independence. Like Mises writing in his 1919 work *Nation, State, and Economy*, they believed that "no people or part of a people should be held against its will in a political association that it does not want."

For Jefferson, Randolph, Taylor, and Calhoun, the cause of independence was the force powerful enough to rally the public against distant rulers. But their desire for independence was not, of course, directed against any other country, and free trade was a key to this. As Calhoun said when he wrote to the Manchester Anti-Corn Law League in 1845, "I regard free trade as involving considerations far higher than mere commercial advantages as great as they are. It is, in my opinion, emphatically the cause of civilization and peace."

But, civilization and peace are threatened. In Jefferson's day the tyranny was centered in the British Crown. In our day the tyranny is centered in Washington, DC, and in New York, and in Geneva. We are surrounded by DC bureaucrats, Nafta bureaucrats, UN bureaucrats, bureaucrats with the World Bank and the IMF, and assorted scalawags on the pay of the governing elites. If we are to restore liberty, limited and local government, free enterprise, and, yes, free trade, we must begin by understanding the power that a legitimate regionalism and an old-fashioned devotion to independence will have in uniting us against the forces of central control. In doing so, we will stand with the author of the Declaration of Independence, with the republicans of the Old South, and with the signers of the Confederate Constitution.

TIME TO END PERPETUAL WAR

[This speech was delivered at the Center for Libertarian Studies and Rothbard-Rockwell Report *Conference on the Warfare State, San Mateo, California, February 21, 1998.]*

Is the US world empire decaying? At first glance, this may seem an odd time to be asking the question. The US is prepared to embark on an openly political war with no basis in just war theory. It can only end in further massive suffering for the Iraqi people, and a further diminution of American liberty. And yet it may be going forward, with American tax dollars being chewed up by a horrible war machine on an imperialist adventure.

Right now, no single country in the world is sufficiently powerful to challenge US hegemony and military might. Public opinion seems to be little help. Three in four Americans say they would back bombing raids and ground troops if the Clinton administration orders them. At a time when public respect for government in domestic affairs is at historic lows, the foreign-policy apparatus of the empire seems to have escaped serious public scrutiny.

All of this is true at one level. Yet below the surface, we see a different reality. The foundations of empire have begun to crack. US military actions since the end of the Cold War have not replenished the stock of public good will toward the warfare State. On the contrary, they have drawn down the capital built up over the prior 40 years when Americans were convinced that the warfare State was all that stood between them and nuclear annihilation by foreign powers. Public enthusiasm for the empire, while still far too high, has waned as compared with 20 years ago, and even since the first war against Iraq.

Virtually every country in the world has announced its resentment against the US attempt to run the world. In particular, the US's position on Iraq is in the extreme minority.

The US does not enjoy a consensus at the UN; world opinion on US global hegemony ranges from hired tolerance to extreme opposition. Pro-peace and anti-US groups are now active in every country where US bases exist.

Important members of the pundit class have already defected, especially from this most recent campaign against Iraq. The military itself is in disarray, crippled by a combination of affirmative action, feminization, and welfare dependency. And the US presidency, which has traditionally given direction and meaning to the empire, now lacks the moral legitimacy to lead the troops, much less to sustain a viable New World Order. Important elements of the establishment itself have split away from the globocop consensus. As a result of all these developments, the US empire is shakier than it has been since World War II.

Surely all of these developments count as bullish for American liberty, because in the final analysis, there can be no reconciling empire and freedom. Either one or the other must go. Either the US government can invade Iraq on a whim or our homes and businesses will be free from invasion by agents of the State. Either the US government will have bases in a hundred countries or our communities will not be permanently occupied by agents and judges working for Leviathan.

The framers intended to keep the US out of foreign wars. They understood that a government that goes in search of monsters to destroy will end up destroying its own people. The foreign-policy apparatus of today inflicts a horrible cost on the world. But the greatest cost of all—or at least the one that should matter to us the most—is the cost to the liberty that is our birthright. Though the American empire will not go without a fight, and the end could be years in the future, its collapse provides us with a great opportunity to do the hard work of restoring our liberty right here at home.

Of course to hear the spokesman for the empire tell it, everything about the global project is in full working order, a line which the media gladly parrot. But it is the nature of the

State to lie. It lies about why it is taxing us. It lies about who is getting the money. It lies about its motives for regulating us. It lies about the legitimacy of its power. But no State lies nearly so much as an empire in the conduct of its foreign policy.

So, let's examine the structural setting in which the US foreign policy of war and militarism is currently being conducted, beginning first with the domestic political setting. President Clinton, the man who denies having had sexual relations with Monica Lewinsky, has tried to persuade the American public that Saddam represents a direct threat to our country. But by now, as much as people prefer Clinton to his likely successors of Gore and then Gingrich, he has a serious credibility problem.

One wonders if any president could make a morally credible case for invading Iraq now. Think back to 1990, when George Bush had to make a case for war. He had several huge advantages that Clinton does not have. Iraq had invaded Kuwait. It was a fact. It's true that Iraq may have had a credible case for doing so. The two countries are only separate because of arbitrary lines drawn by the British, and, besides, Kuwait was drilling for oil in Iraqi territory. Plus, the US ambassador to Kuwait, April Glaspie—and this is not in dispute—had already given the go-ahead to our then-ally Saddam.

Nonetheless, Iraq had invaded Kuwait, and once Bush decided he wanted to boost his standing in the polls, that invasion gave the US a clear objective, which was actually rather limited. According to the UN mandate, it was to get Iraq out of Kuwait and restore the ruling family to power. Even so, it wasn't enough to garner support from Congress or the American public. Saddam had to be portrayed as an evil dictator—the new Hitler—wrecking the lives of his own people.

Then the Bush administration had to resort to a series of wild claims that Saddam had nuclear weapons, that he was tossing babies out of their incubators in Kuwait, and that Iraq would also invade Saudi Arabia, monopolize oil, and drive up the price of gasoline. This in turn could bring on a deep recession. As James Baker famously said, this splendid little war was about "jobs, jobs, jobs."

Of course, the result was that the US forcibly kept Iraqi oil off the world market, a result far more restrictive of supply than any scare scenario cooked up by the Bush administration. The US government has gone from warning the world that Iraq may not sell oil to denouncing Iraq for wanting to sell oil, and forcibly preventing it from doing so. The warfare State is capable of stunning levels of perfidy. It is US sanctions, not Saddam's attempt to cartelize Arab oil markets, that have kept Iraqi oil off the market.

Gulf War One, said George Bush at the time, was a test case for the New World Order. With the Cold War over and the economic basketcase enemy of international communism vanquished, the US would not dismantle its military empire but would find new uses for it. US foreign policy elites announced that they were the world's only indispensable nation, the only force standing between order and international chaos. American taxpayers would be looted until the end of time for the sake of this order.

The US continued the Iraq war by another means. That way we could have an enemy—a man who can be relied upon to denounce the US in passionate tones—anytime the president in power happened to need one. To achieve this end, the US decided it would be best to commit genocide, to starve the people of Iraq and encourage them to die from disease as well (that's why US bombers targeted sewage treatment plants, to poison the water supply). This has resulted in 1.4 million deaths, most of them children and old people denied access to food and medicine. But the power elite got what they wanted: a permanent enemy in a world where threats to US interests appear increasingly remote.

When compared to Gulf War One, Gulf War Two has no clearly defined objective. It is not going to provide greater access to sites for UN investigators. It is not going to make Saddam less belligerent. It's not going to make him less popular with his own people and thereby undermine his rule. Quite the opposite; Saddam is given credit by his own people for having the courage to stand up to the evil empire.

In the official rationale for this war, Iraq is very mad at the US because Iraq doesn't want Americans on the UN inspection team looking for chemical and biological weapons. Iraq says they might be spies, an accusation that is supposed to prove what a paranoid maniac Saddam is. From listening to his crazed rantings, you might think the US had it in for him.

Yet as Jeffrey Smith pointed out in the *Washington Post*, if US military planners do attack Iraq, they will be drawing on data about Iraqi capabilities and targets collected by UN inspection teams. Are UN inspectors spies? No one doubts it.

So far, the only credible excuse the US can come up with for attacking Iraq is that of supposed chemical and biological warfare. Yet even if Saddam did use these against the Kurds and threatens their use against Israel, are they a direct threat to Americans? Of course not. If a Texan or a Marylander told you he had bought a gas mask to protect himself from Saddam's weapons of mass destruction, you would likely think him nuts.

But let's just say Saddam did have the military technology to launch chemical weapons against the US. What better way to provoke such an attack than a 7-year economic embargo that has reduced Iraq's once-thriving middle class to the status of hunters and gatherers? There is one better way: have the Secretary of State say on national television that she regards the death of 1.4 million civilians in Iraq as an "acceptable price to pay." That is precisely what Madeleine Albright said in a televised interview in December 1996.

It takes a pretty nasty foreign government to be a greater threat to people than their own government. Yet we have to ask ourselves: which is the greater threat to the livelihood of the Iraqi people? Saddam? Or US bombs and embargoes? By any measure, it is the latter, and this is a national disgrace.

Another difference between then and now is the proximity to the Cold War, which had acculturated the public to the idea of empire. Bush's war came a mere 20 months after the unraveling of socialism in Eastern Europe, and before so-called isolationist sentiment began to rise to the surface of public opinion.

But the Cold War ended a decade ago. People now in junior high school have no memory of it, and thus no memory of a time when the US military empire successfully portrayed itself as a messianic force for good in the world.

And think of this. In every past war, the US has gone out of its way to show its enemies as the aggressors, even if it has to phony up the charge. Ft. Sumter, the *Maine*, the *Lusitania*, Pearl Harbor, the Gulf of Tonkin, the Berlin nightclub, the invasion of Kuwait—in all of these, the US has gone out of its way to portray itself as the avenger of foreign aggression, which ultimately desires only peace and justice.

But not this time. As the *New York Times* put it, this is an openly political as versus defensive war. The Clinton administration is seeking to use the US warfare machine to punish a government headed by a man the White House does not like. It has gone so far as to intervene to scuttle diplomatic efforts at peace. Never before have the aggressive intentions of US foreign policy been so open.

Lacking a precipitating outrage against justice, it has been considerably more difficult for the Clinton administration to whip up public enthusiasm for this war. Of course public opinion polls show public approval of a war to oust Saddam from power. But as the *New York Times* has also warned, polls on politics increasingly reveal the answers people think they are supposed to give. What is unclear is how well they measure people's actual opinions. This is especially true in times when politics is no longer a public preoccupation.

Reading the polls with this mind—that they are likely to measure more of what people think people think than what they really think—you get some interesting results. For example, support for a military solution against Iraq has dropped nine points since November, when the policy elites first began to call for Saddam's head on a platter. A two-month public relations campaign to oust Saddam not only failed to whip up war fever; it actually had the reverse effect, at least for a time.

This reflects something more profound than that people think bombing is not a good idea. It reveals that a fundamental shift in the climate of opinion is taking shape, a shift that is likely to have far-reaching effects on the ability of US empire to function with confidence in the future.

Running an empire based on war requires more, much more, than tacit approval from the taxpayer public. It requires the public be charged up and cheering both the objective and the methods of war. When the public is so charged, the State is provided some public-opinion capital to spend when casualties and bills begin arriving. This is the real point of military parades, war drums, and the symbolic displays of patriotism required by the modern totalitarian project.

In the movie *Wag the Dog*, the main responsibility of the team manufacturing a war with Albania is goading public opinion in the right direction. For their purposes—which was to create a massive public distraction from the president's peccadilloes—passive interest was not enough. So the hired team commissioned two popular songs—one rock and one folk—invented phony heroes for the public to love, and primed the pump on certain popular sacrificial rituals. The point of all this is to divert the public from thinking too carefully about the lies and false morality of the war itself.

The same pitch is necessary whether we're dealing with a war made in Hollywood, as it was in the movie, or a real war involving actual people halfway around the world. In either case, public enthusiasm and calls for foreign blood are necessary to the warfare project. But in post-Cold War times, the drumbeat doesn't always succeed in getting people to dance. In Gulf War Two, the long drumbeat to war has failed to even interest the public in any intense way.

As Meg Greenfield writes in her *Newsweek* column,

> I can't remember a run-up to a war—or whatever it is we are about to have with Iraq—as strong as this. It seems to have all the urgency for people of a once-a-week seminar on international relations. . . . There have been no constituencies, no sides, no hotly held positions. There are, instead, just desultory statements, odd articles and speculations and musings. The controversy, to the extent there is one, goes in no direction, takes no shape, commands no silent, grim attention of the kind people give when they believe themselves to be in the presence of a large, consequential and risky national undertaking.

The political parties have been surprisingly silent on the Iraq matter. The Democrats make perfunctory statements in defense of the White House's position. And the Republicans are all over the map, on one hand calling for caution and on the other demanding the immediate murder of Saddam Hussein. But notice that resolutions, for or against any aspect of this Iraq war, were not voted on before Congress could recess for the Valentine's Day week. They decided it was politically safer to make love than war.

This has provided a wonderful opportunity for the forces opposed to war to step into the vacuum and have our voices heard. A prominent Associated Press story last week led with the heroic efforts of Congressman Ron Paul of Texas to prevent Clinton from using force in the Gulf absent a Congressional declaration of war. He introduced emergency legislation to this effect.

Paul, you see, is old-fashioned enough to believe in the Constitution. This is the action of a real statesman, a man of courage willing to stand up to presidential power grabs, and

say: absolutely not. That is not the way war is conducted in a
civilized society. Ron has received more attention and support
on this issue than any other he has addressed since he reen-
tered political life two years ago.

Contrast this to Gingrich, the man whose constitutional
responsibility it is to check the power of the White House. But
in the case of Iraq, he has given Clinton, his supposed political *bête noire*, complete backing for anything this administration wants to do. Speaking for the entire Republican Party,
Gingrich has threatened political retaliation only if Clinton
does not go far enough. He has even said that he will not look
too carefully into this Lewinsky matter because that would be,
at this time, unpatriotic.

Outside the United States, it turns out, there are quite a
few Ron Pauls, statesmen willing to stand up to the US global
hegemon. In fact, the single most remarkable aspect of this
run-up to war has been the utter isolation of the US. After
years of propaganda about the glories of the international
community, about the United Nations and our allies hither
and yon, the US can now only consistently count on Britain
and Israel as accomplices.

And it's not clear how this action can be good for either
Britain—which has a strong interest in keeping the peace in
its neck of the woods—or Israel. This week in Bethlehem,
some 900 schoolchildren and university students defied a government ban and marched in support of Iraq. "O Saddam our
dear, hit Tel Aviv. O Saddam our dear, hit with chemicals,"
they chanted, according to press reports. The students also
burned the US and Israeli flags, shouting "Death to America,
death to Israel." As you can see, the peace process is coming
along nicely.

It was several weeks after the US and British governments announced their planned war against Iraq before the
international coalition backing the idea began to solidify.
First, a trusted and valiant ally came forward: Canada. Then
Australia, a country with a huge stake in the outcome. Finally,

and most impressively, the great nation of Oman joined our coalition. It was probably the first time in its history that the word "Oman" was said on national radio.

In Gulf War One, using the usual combination of threats and bribes, the US was able to put together a multilateral fig leaf for its little war. Crucially, this coalition included Arab states. But for the present war, there have been few foreign policy adventures of the US that have so thoroughly united the Arab world against us. Not even the billions upon billions the US has slathered supposed allies with has paid off this time. It's a measure of how utterly implausible US foreign policy has become—not only implausible but also deeply unwelcome around the world, and conspicuously immoral to anyone who still cares about justice.

Japan has officially backed US military intervention, but with a surprising degree of reticence. Support among the people of Japan is thin to nonexistent, a fact of which the ruling party must take note. Organizations within Japan devoted to kicking out the US military are growing all the time, particularly where US bases are located.

These groups are taking out advertisements in American newspapers to make the case against US imperialism. They mention the rise of crime and auto accidents where bases are located, the noise and danger associated with US overflights, the subsidization of prostitution and cultural degradation that come with the military presence. Americans who live near military bases on our own soil can relate.

This very day, demonstrations are taking place in Tokyo to protest US attacks on Iraq. There have been protests in front of a Yokosuka Army base every day since February 3. On February 6, 56 Japanese peace organizations filed a protest with the American Embassy. In Hiroshima, petitions circulate in shopping malls every day in protest, and they are then faxed every day to the White House. These petitions not only call for the US to leave Iraq, but also for the US to leave Japan.

The following letter was sent by the Japanese Network for Disarmament, the leading antimilitarist Japanese organization, to the White House:

To Bill Clinton:

The difference between now and the Gulf War seven years ago is that the current crisis is being staged unilaterally by yourself and the US military which you command, not by an invasion or violation of international law on the part of Saddam Hussein.

On this day, prior to imminent strikes against Iraq announced by you, you must make it clear that no support or agreement whatsoever can be found among the Japanese public for such militaristic adventures and mass slaughter. . . .

Military attacks not only result in the loss of lives; they are nothing less than the worst form of international terrorism which prevents Iraqis from exercising their right to reform Iraqi society by themselves. . . .

We are aware that the US itself believes in weapons of mass murder and mass destruction. Has the US not turned its back on the ruling by the International Court of Justice that the use of nuclear weapons is against international law, by, still today, filling its arsenals with more than 15,000 nuclear warheads?

Which "dictatorship" has violated the spirit of the International Test Ban Treaty, again and again, with so-called subcritical nuclear tests? Which country continues to arm destroyers and aircraft and tanks with radiological arms, even after having killed numerous Iraqi children and harmed its own soldiers with depleted uranium weapons? Which country is opposed to a ban . . . of such weapons? Was it not you, President Clinton, who ordered the decision not to sign the treaty banning antipersonnel landmines? . . .

[W]e cannot suppress our astonishment and anger in regard to the fact that the US is intending to use the people of Iraq as guinea pigs for testing newly developed weapons. . . . We strongly oppose the use of US bases in Japan for such inhuman militaristic adventures. . . .

We know that the new base which you are about to build in Nago, Okinawa . . . is intended to serve the projection of national power and a policy of military intervention. Along with the people of Okinawa, we will say again and again that the elimination of these bases, not their relocation, is the solution.

The letter ends with the exhortation: "DO NOT KILL!"

So there's no reason to take Japan's backing of the US war plot too seriously. It demonstrates the extent to which the ruling party is wholly owned by the US and certainly not enthusiastic for the war. Protests against US military bases are taking place in Germany, Italy (where hotdogging Marine pilots just killed 20 people on the Northern Italian ski slopes), France, Spain, Scandinavia, and the US as well. Not even at the height of the Cold War had the US faced such intense international opposition.

The leaders of Russia have been especially resistant to US demands for total global power. For a day or two, US militarists tried to portray Boris Yeltsin as crazy and Yevgeny Primakov as a new Hitler. But there was a problem: their arguments against the Iraq war make an unusual amount of sense, so the only solution was to ignore the screams of protest coming from our on-again-off-again ally in a century of wars. As for Primakov being the new Hitler, an additional problem emerged: it turns out that he is Jewish. But this fact didn't stop the *Wall Street Journal* from describing him as an Arabist, a mysterious term left over from the Cold War years meaning a critic of US Mideast policy.

Why does it matter that the US is increasingly isolated in running a global imperial campaign? As de la Boétie, Hume, Mises, Rothbard, and many others have emphasized, all government must ultimately rest on the consent of the governed for one clear reason: government represents a tiny minority of the population and the governed represent the great majority. When that consent is withdrawn, the government must necessarily collapse. It issues orders and no one obeys.

In our lifetimes, we have witnessed many examples of this, and, if you are like I am, you feel a surge of joy anytime a government anywhere collapses. It's a reminder that no matter how impenetrable and ominous a government can seem, it is ultimately a fragile institution that must constantly tend to its public image to shore up confidence and legitimacy.

It turns out that this Hume-Mises insight also applies on the international scale. The US has long dreamed of establishing a world government. With the collapse of the Soviet Union, the prospect seemed to be at hand. The dream of the social democratic, redistributionist, regulatory, welfare-warfare State run by what Clinton calls the indispensable nation seemed close to becoming a reality.

What is the role of the UN in this enterprise? To operate as a democratic fig leaf for US control. Just like domestic government, world government also needs consensus to survive and thrive. Without that consensus, the US may find itself issuing orders, like Ceausescu in his palace, but with no one obeying. With the growing global resistance to the Iraqi adventure, we are witnessing something like a withdrawal of consent that threatens the very existence of the world State.

A global government run by the US in the manner proposed by Clinton is a fragile project, even more so than the British empire of the 19th century. Britain frequently used native troops, usually from racial and ethnic minorities, to run its colonies. They were highly trained and managed by British officers. But the troops at least had some connection to the cultures they were ruling. Conflicts were handled by local troops and they chose their battles with an eye to not undermining political support for the British regime.

The US empire of our time consists entirely of US troops, periodically touched up by a smattering of players from governments the US keeps on its payroll. Such an empire is as unviable in the long run as socialism itself. It is hardly surprising there is growing resistance, and it is resistance that the US has neither anticipated nor has any way to meet on a civil level.

Most impressively, this resistance is not only political; it is also moral. And here we must give due credit to Pope John Paul II, and indirectly to the US bishops, for protesting this war at every step. The Pope was a leading critic of the last Gulf War, and despite neoconservative attempts to silence him in this country, he helped prepare Christians around the world to say no to the US-run New World Order.

Immediately after leaving Cuba, where his visit has stirred up opposition to communist control and another US embargo, he went to work trying to bring a peaceful resolution to the Iraqi conflict. The Pope has demanded that the US "swear off" military options, and succeeded in persuading Kofi Annan to visit Iraq, thereby forestalling strikes for a bit longer.

Some US commentators say the Pope's interests in this are merely parochial. He knows that Christians are well-treated in Iraq, at least as compared with every other Arab nation. He is concerned for their fate with continued sanctions and military strikes. By describing these concerns as parochial, the intention is to dismiss them, as if to say US political concerns are far more important than the lives of any foreign Christians.

In fact, the Pope's concerns reflect a long-standing Catholic concern that the conduct of war accord with the Augustinian-Thomist doctrine of the Just War. War must be defensive. It must never target civilians. Its means must be proportional to the threat. It must be a last resort. Peace must be established and kept as soon as the fighting is over. Revenge against a defeated enemy is ruled out of order. The US campaign against Iraq must be regarded as profoundly unjust according to every one of these tenets.

The US bishops have exercised uncharacteristic courage in opposing this war, and all seven active Cardinals have signed a letter saying that military force would be "difficult if not impossible to justify" morally. They specifically call for "widening the participation of other governments, especially Arab states, in the concerted effort to bring about Iraqi compliance on these issues."

The ranks of the dissidents on this war contain some interesting new recruits. Tony Snow, the neoconservative columnist, has expressed profound skepticism about the war. Robert Novak has been as sound as Joe Sobran and Ron Paul. I'm pleased to see Pat Buchanan, who seemed to have gone soft on the empire insofar as it is cracking down on supposedly unfair traders, has solidly opposed the Clinton war on Iraq.

Jude Wanniski led the way in condemning the embargo, and has written memo after memo attacking US policy on Iraq. I'm also pleased to announce that William F. Buckley has criticized the idea of bombing Iraq and even suggested loosening the embargo. He has retained some conscience, even after everything.

Just to prove that no one is beyond redemption, Jack Kemp has said of this war:

> I don't want to bomb. And I believe the debate right now is between the bombers and those who want to bomb even more. My hope would be that we would exhaust all diplomatic efforts. So I advance that concept in the hopes that we could get out of this cul-de-sac without putting American troops, men and women, on the ground into Iraq.

Good for Kemp. He may be a big-government conservative. He may think that government can work domestic wonders through big-spending HUD programs. But he at least has some skepticism about the ability of Madeleine Albright or anyone else to run the world via bombing campaigns. If forced to choose between a cheesy welfare program like enterprise zones and a murderous global military empire run at my expense, I'll take the enterprise zones any day. Meanwhile, Steve Forbes has called for the assassination of Saddam and a massive air war. I think all of us need to hold off when it comes to whom to support in the next election.

Tom Clancy, the warmongering novelist, has also had a change of heart, asking in the *New York Times*:

> Who has told us that it is O.K. to kill women and children? ... Who has prepared us and the world for the unpalatable consequences of even a successful attack? What exactly would we be trying to accomplish? What constitutes success? How likely is failure, and what would be the consequences? Have any of these questions been answered at all, much less sufficiently to take human life? If so, it has escaped my notice.

We must also credit the John Birch Society and its magazine, *New American*, which has been vehement in editorializing against the bloody operation. They point out that Saddam is just the kind of foreign enemy an empire on the march likes to have to justify its power. What a nice contrast with the blood-thirsty thirty-somethings at the *Weekly Standard*, who equate the slaughter of innocents with national greatness.

In fact, outside the Kristolians, I must say there has been a dearth of commentators on the right whooping it up for war. This is a great step. But even so, there has been far too much silence. *National Review* says nothing. The Cato Institute has said nothing. The Heritage Foundation called for Saddam's head in November, and has said nothing since. Neither has R. Emmett Tyrrell.

It's sad to say that the Monica Lewinsky matter, just as it has persuaded Clinton to embark on the war as many in his administration have wanted, has also provided a nice distraction for many people on the right to not talk about what is ultimately a far more important matter. Impeach Clinton, yes, but for what? For having a dalliance and lying about it, just like almost every other powerful man in Washington, or for conducting an unconstitutional military campaign against a starving country and risking, as Boris Yeltsin says, a new world war?

There are plenty of officers and enlisted men in the military who would like to see Clinton impeached for any reason at all. Sexual harassment is the biggest issue in the military today. Any officer who tried to do with his staff what Clinton has done with his would be strung up. Officers know this; it is a continuing threat. The trials that have led high-ranking people to court martial have traumatized an entire generation that thought the military and sexual license were a natural combination.

And now Clinton dares to contemplate sending troops into a ground war to Iraq? He dares tell them what to do? As anyone in the military can testify, the worst thing for morale is the perception that the decision-makers are exempt from the strictures that govern those who take orders. We must never forget, too, that Clinton is widely resented for having skipped out of the draft himself.

An additional difficulty is the interesting split in the US establishment itself. Bill Clinton, it has been noted quite often, is not a favorite of the Georgetown social set and is an infrequent visitor to the Council on Foreign Relations. His interest group is not the CFR but a younger and more reckless group of social planners, baby boomers who see government as their playground and global social democrats who care nothing about concepts like the long term. These are not the cautious diplomats and wise men of old, constructing the world order according to plan. They are ideologues who have little understanding that power has its limits.

In today's issue of *Foreign Affairs*, the journal of the CFR, you are far more likely to see articles warning of the pitfalls of a global democratic outlook and US imperial power than in the past. Richard Betts, in his article "The New Threat of Mass Destruction," warns that

US military and cultural hegemony—the basic threats to radicals seeking to challenge the status quo—are directly linked to the imputation of American responsibility for maintaining world order. Playing Globocop feeds the urge of aggrieved groups to strike back." Betts warns that the US hegemon actually risks fueling an increase in domestic terrorism, and suggests the US needs to "tread more cautiously, especially in the middle east.

Thomas Friedman, writing in the *New York Times,* warns of another potential cost of unrestricted Middle East interventionism. He points out that if it's nuclear proliferation that concerns us, we still have a problem with Russia. Why would we want to continue to irritate a country that has thousands of nuclear weapons floating around, unmanaged and unattended? Is nuclear war an acceptable risk to take simply to expand that part of the empire called Nato? Arabist or not, Russia is deeply resentful that the US wants to dictate the terms on which that country can trade with countries like Iran and Iraq.

The problem for the future of American liberty is that the type of domestic terrorism warned about here also provides a convenient excuse for further crackdowns on political dissidents and individual freedom at home. Finally, let me say a few words about the prospect that this entire Iraqi war is intended to distract from the Monica Lewinsky matter. The answer is exactly as the foreign press describes it: of course it is intended to distract. But that is not the same thing as saying that Lewinsky is the only reason the US is prepared to bomb.

At the Pentagon and the State Department, there are people who have long believed that without a major war of Manichaean proportions, the US empire will whither and die. It was the Lewinsky matter that persuaded Clinton to pay closer attention to them. If his poll ratings weren't as high as they are, he might have begun bombing a month ago.

No one knows whether in the short run, the peacekeepers or the warmongers will prevail. But as bumpy as this road to war has been, it is more likely to harm the empire than beef it up. For the sake of American liberty, we must do everything in our power to stop this war, to oppose it now and even when the bombs start falling and the troops hit the Iraqi sands. Not for us is this line that there shall be no criticism of the president once the shooting starts. There's no more important time to denounce war than in its midst.

Empire is contrary to the American ethos. The American people have made exceptions in this century: the Hitler threat and the Communist threat. But there is no threat on the world scene to our families and property greater than that posed by the US government itself.

In order to beat back the real threat, it will be necessary to expose the phony ones and put obstacles in the way of the empire's global ambitions. Every voice raised in opposition contributes to a more peaceful world in the future, contributes to bringing down the US empire, and, therefore, contributes to the restoring of the liberty from government oppression that is our inheritance.

DOWN WITH THE PRESIDENCY

[This speech was delivered at a meeting of the John Randolph Club in Arlington, Virginia, October 5–6, 1996.]

The modern institution of the presidency is the primary evil Americans face, and the cause of nearly all our woes. It squanders the national wealth and starts unjust wars against foreign peoples that have never done us any harm. It wrecks our families, tramples on our rights, invades our communities, and spies on our bank accounts. It skews the culture toward decadence and trash. It tells lie after lie. Teachers used to tell schoolkids that anyone can be president. This is like saying anyone can go to Hell. It's not an inspiration; it's a threat.

The presidency—by which I mean the executive State—is the sum total of American tyranny. The other branches of government, including the presidentially appointed Supreme Court, are mere adjuncts. The presidency insists on complete devotion and humble submission to its dictates, even while it steals the products of our labor and drives us into economic ruin. It centralizes all power unto itself, and crowds out all competing centers of power in society, including the church, the family, business, charity, and the community.

I'll go further. The US presidency is the world's leading evil. It is the chief mischief-maker in every part of the globe, the leading wrecker of nations, the usurer behind Third-World debt, the bailer-out of corrupt governments, the hand in many dictatorial gloves, the sponsor and sustainer of the New World Order, of wars, interstate and civil, of famine and disease. To see the evils caused by the presidency, look no further than Iraq or Serbia, where the lives of innocents were snuffed out in pointless wars, where bombing was designed to destroy civilian infrastructure and cause disease, and where women, children, and the aged have been denied essential food and medicine because of a cruel embargo. Look at the human toll taken by the presidency, from Dresden and Hiroshima to Waco and Ruby Ridge, and you see a prime practitioner of murder by government.

Today, the president is called the leader of the world's only superpower, the "world's indispensable nation," which is reason enough to have him deposed. A world with any super-power at all is a world where no freedoms are safe. But by invoking this title, the presidency attempts to keep our attention focused on foreign affairs. It is a diversionary tactic

designed to keep us from noticing the oppressive rule it
imposes right here in the United States.

As the presidency assumes ever more power unto itself, it
becomes less and less accountable and more and more tyrannical. These days, when we say the federal government, what
we really mean is the presidency. When we say, national priorities, we really mean what the presidency wants. When we
say national culture, we mean what the presidency funds and
imposes.

The presidency is presumed to be the embodiment of
Rousseau's general will, with far more power than any
monarch or head of state in pre-modern societies. The US
presidency is the apex of the world's biggest and most powerful government and of the most expansive empire in world
history. As such, the presidency represents the opposite of
freedom. It is what stands between us and our goal of restoring our ancient rights.

And let me be clear: I'm not talking about any particular
inhabitant of the White House. I'm talking about the institution itself, and the millions of unelected, unaccountable
bureaucrats who are its acolytes. Look through the US government manual, which breaks down the federal establishment into its three branches. What you actually see is the
presidential trunk, its Supreme Court stick, and its Congressional twig. Practically everything we think of as federal—
save the Library of Congress—operates under the aegis of the
executive.

This is why the governing elites—and especially the foreign policy elites—are so intent on maintaining public respect
for the office, and why they seek to give it the aura of holiness.
For example, after Watergate, they briefly panicked and worried that they had gone too far. They might have discredited
the democratic autocracy. And to some extent they did.

But the elites were not stupid; they were careful to insist
that the Watergate controversy was not about the presidency
as such, but only about Nixon the man. That's why it became

necessary to separate the two. How? By keeping the focus on Nixon, making a devil out of him, and reveling in the details of his personal life, his difficulties with his mother, his supposed pathologies, etc.

Of course, this didn't entirely work. Americans took from Watergate the lesson that presidents will lie to you. This should be the first lesson of any civics course, of course, and the first rule of thumb in understanding the affairs of government. But notice that after Nixon died, he too was elevated to godlike status. None other than Bill Clinton served as high priest of the cult of president-worship on that occasion. He did everything but sacrifice a white bull at the temple of the White House.

The presidency recovered most of its sacramental character during the Reagan years. How wonderful, for the sake of our liberties, that Clinton has revived the great American tradition of scorning tyrants. In some ways, he is the best president a freedom lover can hope for, more well known for his private parts than his public policies. Of course, someday, Clinton too will ascend to the clouds, and enter the pantheon of the great leaders of the free world.

The libraries are filled with shelf after shelf of treatises on the American presidency. Save yourself some time, and don't bother with them. Virtually all tell the same hagiographic story. Whether written by liberals or conservatives, they serve up the identical Whiggish pap: the history of the presidency is the story of a great and glorious institution. It was opposed early on, and viciously so, by the anti-federalists, and later, even more viciously, by Southern Confederates. But it has been heroically championed by every respectable person since the beginning of the republic.

The office of the presidency, the conventional wisdom continues, has changed not at all in substance, but has grown in stature, responsibility, and importance, to fulfill its unique mission on earth. As the duties of the office have grown, so has the greatness of the men who inhabit it. Each stands on the shoulders of his forerunners, and, inspired by their vision and decisiveness, goes on to make his own contribution to the ever-expanding magisterium of presidential laws, executive orders, and national security findings.

When there is a low ebb in the accumulation of power, it is seen as the fault of the individual and not the office. Thus the so-called postage-stamp presidents between Lincoln and Wilson are to be faulted for not following the glorious example set by Abe. They had a vast reservoir of power, but were mysteriously reluctant to use it. Fortunately that situation was resolved, by Wilson especially, and we moved onward and upward into the light of the present day. And every one of these books ends with the same conclusion: the US presidency has served us well.

The hagiographers do admit one failing of the American presidency. It is almost too big an office for one man, and too much a burden to bear. The American people have come to expect too much from the president. We are unrealistic to think that one man can do it all. But that's all the more reason to respect and worship the man who agrees to take it on, and why all enlightened people must cut him some slack.

The analogy that comes to mind is the official history of the popes. In its infancy, the papacy was less formal, but its power and position were never in question. As the years went on and doctrine developed, so too did the burdens of office. Each pope inherited the wisdom of his forbears, and led the Church into fulfilling its mission more effectively.

But let's be clear about this. The church has never claimed that the papacy was the product of human effort; its spiritual character is a consequence of a divine, not human, act. And even the official history admits the struggles with anti-popes and Borgia popes (and someday Vatican II popes).

Catholics believe the institution was founded by Christ, and is guided by the Holy Spirit, but the pope can only invoke that guidance in the most narrow and rare circumstances. Otherwise, he is all too fallible. And that is why, although allegedly an absolute monarch, he is actually bound by the rule of law.

The presidency is seemingly bound by law, but in practice it can do just about anything it pleases. It can order up troops anywhere in the world, just as Clinton bragged in his acceptance speech at the Democratic convention. It can plow up a religious community in Texas and bury its members because they got on somebody's nerves at the Justice Department. It can tap our phones, read our mail, watch our bank accounts, and tell us what we can and cannot eat, drink, and smoke.

The presidency can break up businesses, shut down airlines, void drilling leases, bribe foreign heads of state or arrest them and try them in kangaroo courts, nationalize land, engage in germ warfare, firebomb crops in Colombia, overthrow any government anywhere, erect tariffs, round up and discredit any public or private assembly it chooses, grab our guns, tax our incomes and our inheritances, steal our land, centrally plan the national and world economy, and impose embargoes on anything anytime. No prince or pope ever had this ability.

But leave all that aside and consider this nightmare. The presidency has the power to bring about a nuclear holocaust with the push of a button. On his own initiative, the president can destroy the human race. One man can wipe out life on earth. Talk about playing God. This is a grotesque evil. And the White House claims it is not a tyranny? If the power to destroy the entire world isn't tyrannical, I don't know what is. Why do we put up with this? Why do we allow it? Why isn't this power immediately stripped from him?

What prevents fundamental challenge to this monstrous power is precisely the quasi-religious trappings of the presidency, which we again had to suffer through last January. One man who saw the religious significance of the presidency, and denounced it in 1973, was—surprisingly enough—Michael Novak. His study, *Choosing Our King: Powerful Symbols in Presidential Politics*, is one of the few dissenting books on the subject. It was reissued last year as—not surprisingly—*Choosing Our Presidents: Symbols of Political Leadership*, with a new introduction repudiating the best parts of the book.

Of course, none of the conventional bilge accords with reality. The US president is the worst outgrowth of a badly flawed Constitution, imposed in a sort of coup against the Articles of Confederation. Even from the beginning, the presidency was accorded too much power. Indeed, an honest history would have to admit that the presidency has always been an instrument of oppression, from the Whisky Rebellion to the War on Tobacco.

The presidency has systematically stolen the liberty won through the secession from Britain. From Jackson and Lincoln to McKinley and Roosevelt Junior, from Wilson and FDR to Truman and Kennedy, from Nixon and Reagan to Bush and Clinton, it has been the means by which our rights to liberty, property, and self-government have been suppressed. I can count on one hand the actions of presidents that actually favored the true American cause, meaning liberty. The overwhelming history of the presidency is a tale of overthrown rights and liberties, and the erection of despotism in their stead.

Each president has tended to be worse than the last, especially in this century. Lately, in terms of the powers they assumed and the dictates they imposed, Kennedy was worse than Eisenhower, Johnson was worse than Kennedy, Nixon was worse than Johnson, Carter was worse than Nixon, and Reagan—who doubled the national budget and permanently entrenched the warfare State—was worse than Carter. The same is true of Bush and Clinton. Every budget is bigger and the powers exercised more egregious. Each new brutal action breaks another taboo and establishes a new precedent that gives the next occupant of the White House more leeway.

Looking back through American history, we can see the few exceptions to this rule. Washington wrote an eloquent farewell address, laying out the proper American trade and foreign policy. Jefferson's revolution of 1800 was a great thing. But was it really a freer country after his term than before? That's a tough case to make. Andrew Jackson abolished the central bank, but his real legacy was democratic centralism and weakened states' rights.

Andrew Johnson loosened the military dictatorship fastened on the South after it was conquered. But it is not hard to make the country freer when it had become totalitarian under the previous president's rule. Of course, Lincoln's bloody autocracy survives as the model of presidential leadership. James Buchanan made a great statement on behalf of the right of revolution. Grant restored the gold standard. Harding denounced US imperialism in Haiti. But overall, my favorite president is William Henry Harrison. He keeled over shortly after his inauguration.

There have been four huge surveys taken of historians' views on the presidents: in 1948, in 1962, in 1970, and in 1983. Historians were asked to rank presidents as Great, Near Great, Average, Below Average, and Failure. In every case, number one is Lincoln, the mass murderer and military dictator who is the real father of the present nation. His term was a model of every despot's dream: spending money without Congressional approval, declaring martial law, arbitrarily arresting thousands and holding them without trial, suppressing free speech and the free press, handing out lucrative war contracts to his cronies, raising taxes, inflating the currency, and killing hundreds of thousands for the crime of desiring self-government. These are just the sort of actions historians love.

The number two winner in these competitions is FDR. Moreover, Wilson and Jackson are always in the top five. The bottom two in every case are Grant and Harding. None bothered to rate William Henry Harrison.

What does greatness in the presidency mean? It means waging war, crushing liberties, imposing socialism, issuing dictates, browbeating and ignoring Congress, appointing despotic judges, expanding the domestic and global empire, and generally trying his best to be an all-round enemy of freedom. It means saying with Lincoln, "I have a right to take any measure which may best subdue the enemy."

The key to winning the respect of historians is to do these things. All aspirants to this vile office know this. It's what they seek. They long for crisis and power, to be bullies in the pulpit, to be the dictators they are in their hearts. They want, at all costs, to avoid the fate of being another "postage-stamp president." Madison said no man with power deserves to be trusted. Neither should we trust any man who seeks the power that the presidency offers.

Accordingly, it is all well and good that conservatives have worked to discredit the current occupant of the White House. Call him a philanderer, a cheat, and a double-dealer if you want. Call him a tyrant too. But we must go further. The answer to restoring republican freedom has nothing to do with replacing Clinton with Lott or Kemp or Forbes or Buchanan. The structure of the presidency, and the religious aura that surrounds it, must be destroyed. The man is merely a passing occupant of the Holy Chair of St. Abraham. It is the chair itself that must be reduced to kindling.

It was never the intention of the majority of framers to create the mess we have, of course. After the war for independence, the Articles of Confederation had no chief executive. Its decisions were made by a five-member Confederation. The Confederation had no power to tax. All its decisions required the agreement of 9 of the 13 states. That is the way it should be.

Most of the delegates to the unfortunate Philadelphia convention hated executive power. They had severely restricted the governors of their states after their bitter experience with the colonial governors. The new governors had no veto, and no power over the legislatures. Forrest McDonald reports that one-quarter of the delegates to the convention wanted a plural executive, based loosely on the Articles model. But those who planned the convention—including Morris, Washington, and Hamilton—wanted a single, strong executive, and they out-maneuvered the various strains of anti-federalists.

But listen to how they did it. The people of the several states and their representatives were suspicious that Hamilton wanted to create a monarchy. Now, there's much mythology surrounding this point. It's not that the anti-federalists and the popular will opposed some guy strutting around in a crown. It was not monarchy as such they opposed, but the power the king exercised.

When they said they didn't want a monarch, they meant they didn't want a King George, they didn't want a tyrant, a despot, an autocrat, an executive. It was the despotic end they feared, and not the royal means.

Indeed, formally, the Constitution gives few powers to the president, and few duties, most of them subject to approval by the legislature. The most important provision regarding the presidency is that the holder of the office can be impeached. It was to be a threat constantly hanging over his head. It was, most framers thought, to be threatened often and used against any president who dared gather more power unto himself than the Constitution prescribed.

In one famous outburst, Hamilton was forced to defend himself against the charge that the new office of the presidency was a monarchy in disguise. He explained the difference between a monarch and a president. But as you listen to this, think about the present executive. Ask yourself whether he resembles the thing Hamilton claimed to have created in the office of the presidency, or whether we have the tyrant he claimed to be repudiating.

Among other points, Hamilton said in "Federalist 69":

> The President of the United States would be liable to be impeached, tried, and, upon conviction . . . removed from office; and would afterwards be liable to prosecution and punishment in the ordinary course of law. The person of the

king of Great Britain is sacred and inviolable; there is no
constitutional tribunal to which he is amenable; no punishment to which he can be subjected. . . .

The President will have only the occasional command of
such part of the militia of the nation as by legislative provision may be called into the actual service of the Union. . . .
[The power] of the British king extends to the *declaring* of
war and to the *raising* and *regulating* of fleets and armies—
all which, by the Constitution under consideration, would
appertain to the legislature. . . .

The President is to have power, with the advice and consent
of the Senate, to make treaties, provided two thirds of the
senators present concur. The king of Great Britain is the sole
and absolute representative of the nation in all foreign transactions. He can of his own accord make treaties of peace,
commerce, alliance, and of every other description. . . . The
President is to nominate and, *with the advice and consent of
the Senate*, to appoint ambassadors and other public ministers. . . . The king of Great Britain is emphatically and
truly styled the fountain of honor. He not only appoints
to all offices, but can create offices. He can confer titles of
nobility at pleasure . . . and . . . [even] make denizens of
aliens. . . .

[The President] can prescribe no rules concerning the
commerce or currency of the nation; [the king] is in several respects the arbiter of commerce, and in this capacity
can establish markets and fairs, can regulate weights and
measures, can lay embargoes for a limited time, can coin
money. . . . What answer shall we give to those who
would persuade us that things so unlike resemble each
other?

Well, we can debate all day whether Hamilton was naïve
about the imperial office he was in fact creating, or whether
he was a despicable liar. But the fact remains that in his writings, despite his reputation as a backer of the exalted presidency, he is by today's standards a Congressional supremacist.

For that matter, and in comparison with today's presidency, so was the British king.

Most historians agree that there would have been no presidency apart from George Washington, who was trusted by the people as a true gentleman, and was presumed to understand what the American revolution was all about. But he got off track by attempting to suppress the Whisky Rebellion, although he at least acknowledged that his actions went beyond the strict letter of the Constitution. But though the presidency quickly spun out of control, at its antebellum worst it had nothing in common with today's executive State.

In those days, you could live your life and never even notice that the presidency existed. You had no contact with it. Most people couldn't vote anyway, thank goodness, and you didn't have to, but certain rights and freedoms were guaranteed regardless of whoever took hold of this—by today's standards—largely ceremonial position. The presidency couldn't tax you, draft you, or regulate your trade. It couldn't inflate your money, steal your kids, or impose itself on your community. From the standpoint of the average American, the presidency was almost invisible.

Listen to what de Tocqueville observed in 1831:

> The President is . . . the executor of the laws; but he does not really cooperate in making them, since the refusal of his assent does not prevent their passage. He is not, therefore, a part of the sovereign power, but only its agent. . . . The president is placed beside the legislature like an inferior and dependent power. . . .

> The office of president of the United States is

> temporary, limited, and subordinate. . . . [W]hen he is at the head of government, he has but little power, little wealth, and little glory to share among his friends; and his influence in the state is too small for the success or the ruin of a faction to depend upon his elevation to power. . . . The influence

which the President exercises on public business is no doubt feeble and indirect.

Thirty years later, all this would be destroyed by Lincoln, who fundamentally changed the nature of the government, as even his apologists admit. He became a Caesar, in complete contradiction to most of the framers' intentions. As Acton said, he abolished the primary contribution that America had made to the world, the principle of federalism. But that is an old story.

Less well known is how Wilson revived Lincoln's dictatorial predilections, and added to them an even more millennial cast. Moreover, this was his intention before he was elected. In 1908, while still president of Princeton, he wrote a small book entitled the *President of the United States*. It was a paean to the imperial presidency, and might as well have been the bible of every president who followed him. He went beyond Lincoln, who praised the exercise of power. Wilson longed for a Presidential Messiah to deliver the human race.

> There can be no successful government, without leadership or without the intimate, almost instinctive, coordination of the organs of life and action. . . . We have grown more and more from generation to generation to look to the President as the unifying force in our complex system. . . . To do so is not inconsistent with the actual provisions of the Constitution; it is only inconsistent with a very mechanical theory of its meaning and intention.

The president must be a

> man who understands his own day and the needs of the country, and who has the personality and the initiative to enforce his views both upon the people and upon Congress. . . . He is not so much part of its organization as its vital link of connection with the thinking nation . . . he is also the political leader of the nation. . . . The nation as a whole has chosen him. . . . Let him once win the admiration and confidence of the country, and no other single force can withstand

him, no combination of forces will easily overpower him.
His position takes the imagination of the country. He is the
representative of no constituency, but of the whole people . . .
the country never feels the zest of action so much as when its
President is of such insight and caliber. Its instinct is for unified action, and it craves a single leader. . . .

The President is at liberty, both in law and conscience, to be
as big a man as he can. His capacity will set the limit . . . he
is the only spokesman of the whole people. [Finally, Presidents should regard] themselves as less and less executive
officers and more and more directors of affairs and leaders
of the nation—men of counsel and of the sort of action that
makes for enlightenment.

This is not a theory of the presidency. It is the hope for a
new messiah. That indeed is what the presidency has come to.
But any man who accepts this view is not a free man. He is
not a man who understands what constitutes civilized life.
The man who accepts what Wilson calls for is an apostle of
the total State and a defender of collectivism and despotism.

Conservatives used to understand this. In the last century,
all the great political philosophers—men like John Randolph
and John Taylor and John C. Calhoun—did. In this century,
the right was born in reaction to the imperial presidency. Men
like Albert Jay Nock, Garet Garrett, John T. Flynn, and Felix
Morley called the FDR presidency what it was: a US version
of the dictatorships that arose in Russia and Germany, and a
profound evil draining away the very life of the nation.

They understood that FDR had brought both the Congress and the Supreme Court under his control, for purposes
of power, national socialism, and war. He shredded what was
left of the Constitution, and set the stage for all the consoli-
dation that followed. Later presidents were free to nationalize the public schools, administer the economy according to
the dictates of crackpot Keynesian economists, tell us who
we must and who we must not associate with, nationalize
the police function, and run an egalitarian regime that extols

nondiscrimination as the sole moral tenet, when it is clearly not a moral tenet at all. Later conservatives like James Burnham, Wilmoore Kendall, and Robert Nisbet, understood this point too.

Yet who do modern conservatives extol? Lincoln, Wilson, and FDR. Reagan spoke of them as gods and models, and so did Bush and Gingrich. In the 1980s, we were told that Congress was the imperial branch of government because Tip O'Neill had a few questions about Reagan's tax-and-spend military buildup, and his strategy for fostering global warfare while managing world affairs through the CIA. All this was bolstered by books by Harvey Mansfield, Terry Eastland, and dozens of other neoconservatives who pretended to provide some justification for presidential supremacy and its exercise of global rule. More recently even Pat Buchanan repeated the "Ask not . . . " admonition of John F. Kennedy, that we should live to serve the central government and its organizing principle, the presidency.

What the neocon logic comes down to is this: The US has a moral responsibility to run the world. But the citizens are too stupid to understand this. That's why we can't use democratic institutions like Congress in this ambition. We must use the executive power of the presidency. It must have total control over foreign affairs, and never bow to Congressional carping.

Once this point is conceded, the game is over. The demands of a centralized and all-powerful presidency and its interventionist foreign policy are ideologically reinforcing. One needs the other. If the presidency is supreme in global affairs, it will be supreme in domestic affairs. If it is supreme at home, there will be no states' rights, no absolute property rights, no true liberty from government oppression. The continued centralization of government in the presidency represents the end of America and its civilization.

A key part of the theory of presidential supremacy in foreign affairs is the idea that politics stops at the water's edge. If you believe that, you have given up everything. It means that foreign affairs will continue to be the last refuge of an omnipotent scoundrel. If a president can count on the fact that he won't be criticized so long as he is running a war, he will run more of them. So long as he is running wars, government at home cannot be cut. As Felix Morley said, "Politics can stop at the water's edge only when policies stop at the water's edge."

Sadly, the Congress for the most part cares nothing about foreign policy. In that, it reflects the attitude of the American voter. The exception is the handful of Congressmen who do speak about foreign issues, usually at the behest of the State Department, the CIA, the Pentagon, and the increasingly global FBI. Such men are mere adjuncts of presidential power.

In fact, it is the obligation of every patriot not only to denounce a president's actions at home, but to question, harass, and seek to rein in the presidency when it has sent troops abroad. That is when the watchful eye of the citizenry is most important. If we hold our tongues under some mistaken notion of patriotism, we surrender what remains of our freedoms. Yet during the Gulf War, even those who had courageously opposed this intervention in advance mouthed the old clichés about politics and the water's edge and "supporting the troops" when the presidency started massacring Iraqis. Will the same happen when the troops are sent to China, a country without a single aircraft carrier, in retaliation for some trumped-up incident in the tradition of the *Maine*, the *Lusitania*, Pearl Harbor, and the Gulf of Tonkin?

If there is ever a time to get behind a president, it is when he withdraws from the world, stops wars, and brings the troops home. If there is ever a time to trip him up, question his leadership, and denounce his usurpations, it is when he does the opposite. A bipartisan foreign policy is a Napoleonic foreign policy, and the opposite of that prescribed by Washington in his farewell address.

In the midst of America's war against Britain in 1812, John Randolph wrote an open letter to his Virginia constituents, pleading with them not to support the war, and promising them he would not, for he knew where war led: to presidential dictatorship: "If you and your posterity are to become hewers of wood and drawers of water to the modern Pharaoh, it shall not be for the want of my best exertions to rescue you from cruel and abject bondage."

Sixty years ago all conservatives would have agreed with him. But the neoconservative onslaught has purged conservatives of their instinctive suspicions of presidential power.

By the time 1994 had come around, conservatives had been thoroughly indoctrinated in the theory that Congress was out of control, and that the executive branch needed more power. The leadership of the 104th Congress—dominated to a man by neocons and presidential supremacists—bamboozled the freshmen into pushing for three executive-enhancing measures.

In one of the Congress's first actions, it made itself subject to the oppressive civil rights and labor laws that the Executive enforced against the rest of the nation. This was incredibly stupid. The Congress was exempted from these for a reason. It prevented the Executive from using its own regulatory agencies to lord it over Congress. By making itself subject to these laws, Congress willingly submitted itself to implicit and explicit domination by the Department of Labor, the Department of Justice, and the EEOC. It imposed quotas and political correctness on itself, while any dissenters from the presidential line suddenly faced the threat of investigation and prosecution by those they were attempting to rein in.

The imposition of these laws against Congress is a clear violation of the separation of powers. But it would not be the last time that this Congress made this mistake. It also passed the line-item veto, another violation of the separation of powers. The theory was that the president would strike out pork, pork being defined as property taken by taxation and redistributed to special interests. But since pork is the entirety of the federal government's $1.7 trillion budget, this has given the president wide latitude over Congress. It takes away from Congress the right to control the purse strings.

Also part of the Contract with America was term limits for Congress. This would represent a severe diminution of Congressional power with respect to the presidency. After all, it would not mean term limits for the permanent bureaucracy or for federal judges, but only for the one branch the people can actually control. Thank goodness the self-interest of the politicians themselves prevented it from coming into being.

After that initial burst of energy, this Congress surrendered everything to the Clinton White House: control of the budget, control of foreign affairs, and control of the Federal Reserve, and the FBI. The Justice Department operates practically without oversight, as does the Treasury, HUD, Transportation, Commerce, EPA, the SEC, the FTC, and the FDA.

Congress has given in on point after point, eventually even granting the presidency most of what it demanded in health-care reform, including mandated equal coverage of the mentally ill. Chalk it up to long-term planning. They came into office pledging to curb government, but are as infatuated with the presidency as Clinton himself. After all, they hope their party will regain the office.

Then the Republicans had the audacity to ask in bewilderment: why did the president beat Dole? What did we do wrong? The real question is what have they done right? James Burnham said that the legislature is useless unless it is curbing the presidency. By that measure, this Congress has been worthless. It deserves to lose its majority. And its party deserves to lose the presidency, whose powers they are so anxious to grab for themselves.

The best moments in the 104th Congress were when a few freshmen talked quietly of impeachment. Indeed it is their responsibility to talk loudly, openly, and constantly of impeachment. Today's presidency is by definition in violation of the Constitution. Talk of impeachment ought to become routine. So should ridicule and humiliation. For if we care about liberty, the plebiscitory dictatorship must be reined in or tossed out.

John Randolph had only been a Senator for a few days when he gave an extraordinary speech denouncing John Quincy Adams. "It is my duty," said Randolph,

> to leave nothing undone that I may lawfully do, to pull down this administration. . . . They who, from indifference, or with their eyes open, persist in hugging the traitor to their bosom, deserve to be insulted . . . deserve to be slaves, with no other music to soothe them but the clank of the chains which they have put on themselves and given to their off-spring.

John Randolph said this in 1826. This was a time, writes de Tocqueville, when the presidency was almost invisible. If we cannot say this and more today, when the presidency is dictator to the world, we are not authentic conservatives and libertarians. Indeed, we are not free men.

WAR AND THE CAPITALIST PRESS

[This speech was given at the Center for Libertarian Studies and Rothbard-Rockwell Report Conference Against U.S. Aggression, San Mateo, California, June 12, 1999.]

To make a case against the Nato killers who have laid waste to Yugoslavia, it might be enough to simply quote Bill Clinton. "Our children are being fed a dependable daily dose of violence," the president said. "And it sells." Further, it "desensitizes our children to violence and to the consequences of it."

But in these comments, presumably, he wasn't revealing the essence of his war, and its convenient effect of eclipsing Monica as his legacy to the world and its dreadful consequence to imparting an example of violence and bloodshed to anyone who still looks to the government for moral example. Rather, it turns out, he was leveling an attack on the private sector, which entertains us with movies and video games. He says it is the movie and video-game industries, not real-life wars, that are corrupting morals.

And yet the violence being inflicted and the blood being spilled by the troops Clinton commands are real. It is foolish to believe that this does not have an effect on the children of this country. It is sadly true that the behavior of the president still has an undue influence on those who yet believe the civics-text lie that the office is the most morally exalted in the land. The most corrupt media mogul does far more good, and far less harm, than the president.

But for those who still believe in the modern civic religion, it is the president who sets the moral tone, and the boundaries of right and wrong. It is no wonder, then, that one of the killers at Columbine had widely proclaimed his desire to drop some bombs on Serbia. Neither should we forget that the man convicted of bombing the Oklahoma City federal building received his training in how to kill during the war on Iraq, ordered up by the last madman to hold the office.

But it is not only the killers themselves who must be held accountable. It is also those who would attempt to put the best possible spin on the killing machine, trying to make its actions morally justifiable, and putting in print calls for wartime escalation rather than peace. They serve as handmaids to the warfare state and as megaphones for the Leviathan State, and I don't care if their politics are from the Left or the Right: they must be held to account.

Two unfortunate facts undergird the thesis and argument of this talk. First, the *Wall Street Journal* is seen the world over as the preeminent capitalist organ of opinion, one that is seen to speak for the American tradition of free enterprise. Second, of all leading publications, it has proven to be the most aggressive in its promotion of the blood-soaked war on Yugoslavia. Since the war began, the *Journal* has been unswervingly enthusiastic, tolerated no dissent of its pro-war position in its news, its editorial pages, or its op-ed pages. Its content wouldn't have been different if the most hawkish division of the State Department had been exercising full editorial control.

How can these two disparate positions of free enterprise and imperialism be reconciled? The Left has a ready answer. In the Leninist tradition, Marx's failure to predict the overthrow of capitalism can be explained by reference to the international policy of the capitalist nations. Once the capitalists had fully exploited the workers at home, they would seek out foreign markets to exploit and impose their will using war and imperialism.

Thus ran Lenin's analysis in August 1915:

> Imperialism is the highest stage in the development of capitalism, reached only in the twentieth century. Capitalism now finds that the old national states, without whose formation it could not have overthrown feudalism, are too cramped for it. Capitalism has developed concentration to such a degree that entire branches of industry are controlled by syndicates, trusts and associations of capitalist multimillionaires and almost the entire globe has been divided up among the "lords of capital" either in the form of colonies, or by entangling other countries in thousands of threads of financial exploitation.

> Free trade and competition have been superseded by a striving towards monopolies, the seizure of territory for the investment of capital and as sources of raw materials, and so on. From the liberator of nations, which it was in the struggle against feudalism, capitalism in its imperialist stage has turned into the greatest oppressor of nations. Formerly progressive, capitalism has become reactionary; it has developed the forces of production to such a degree that mankind

is faced with the alternative of adopting socialism or of experiencing years and even decades of armed struggle between the "Great" Powers for the artificial preservation of capitalism by means of colonies, monopolies, privileges and national oppression of every kind.

Now, before we all convert to Leninism, let's admit that he was not wrong on the facts, but remember that he made a grave categorical error, as explained by Ludwig von Mises in his 1922 book *Socialism*. Free trade and free enterprise are not aggressive; they are the global font of cooperation and peace. When conflicts do arise in the free market, they are settled based on the terms of contract. So long as the State does not intervene, private property and free enterprise ensure peaceful cooperation among men and nations. What Lenin identified as attributes of capitalism were in fact attributes of the State, particularly the State which claims to be master of economic affairs. As Mises explained:

> Military Socialism is the Socialism of a state in which all institutions are designed for the prosecution of war. It is a State Socialism in which the scale of values for determining social status and the income of citizens is based exclusively or preferably on the position held in the fighting forces. The higher the military rank the greater the social value and the claim on the national dividend.

> The military state, that is the state of the fighting man in which everything is subordinated to war purposes, cannot admit private ownership in the means of production. Standing preparedness for war is impossible if aims other than war influence the life of individuals. . . . The military state is a state of bandits. It prefers to live on booty and tribute.

Pairing the Leninist with the Misesian position on the ideological basis of imperialism helps illuminate the crucial framework for understanding this war. As Hans-Hermann Hoppe has explained, the great intellectual error of classical liberalism was its Hobbesian concession in favor of what it believed could be a limited State. In reality, the State is far more dangerous in a productive, capitalist society than it is in an impoverished, socialized society, simply because it has far more private resources to pillage and loot for the State's own benefit. Availing itself of the vast fruits of private production, the State engages in self-aggrandizement, expansion, and, inevitably, imperialism.

By way of illustration, in the US today, we have two economies, one free and one unfree. The free one has given us the great abundance of consumer goods, the widest distribution of wealth, and the fastest pace of technological innovation known in the history of man. The unfree one—characterized by the two trillion dollar federal budget and the more than one-quarter of that spent on apparatus that builds and administers weapons of mass destruction—has produced what we have been reading about in the headlines for the last two months. Military Socialism, which exists by pillaging the free economy, is responsible for a brutal and immoral war on a civilian population halfway around the world—the destruction of hospitals, churches, nursing homes, residential neighborhoods, and town squares.

In an ideal world, the daily newspaper focusing on American economic life would celebrate the free economy, which the *Wall Street Journal* does on occasion, but also condemn the unfree one, which the *Wall Street Journal* does not. There is a reason why this is not the case. The horrible reality is that the unfree economy may be murderous and wasteful but it also makes many people very rich. The stocks of the companies that build the bombs and enjoy the booty after the war is over, are publicly traded, in the same manner as the stocks of real capitalist companies. When the *Journal* celebrates this war, it is speaking on behalf of the companies that stand to benefit from the war.

But that doesn't inoculate the newspaper from moral responsibility for backing the bloodshed. And it doesn't shield it from open displays of confusion, as when the paper's support for free enterprise conflicts with its support for Military Socialism. For example, the paper recently editorialized about the Clinton administration's drafting of pilots and technicians in the form of an order prohibiting their leaving. Think of it as the nationalization of talent, or simply a stopgap measure to stop the drain from the public to the private sector.

Incidentally, not only should the pilots in the armed forces be allowed to resign for the private sector anytime they want to, actually, these pilots have a moral obligation to resign. They must not use their considerable flying talents to commit the war crimes they are being ordered to commit. They have a moral obligation not to murder and destroy property, a moral obligation not to aggress. By prohibiting them from changing jobs, Clinton is coercing these pilots into committing gravely evil acts.

But somehow, even though pilot resignations would benefit the private sector, the editors at the *Wall Street Journal* couldn't bring themselves to condemn Clinton's tyrannical action. Instead, it suggested various incentive programs that would cause pilots to be less likely to abandon their nation-building, or nation-destroying actions. The paper suggested higher pay and a greater clarity of mission. In this case where the interests of the free and unfree economies collide, the *Wall Street Journal* sides with War Socialism.

And just so we are clear on how bad things have gotten at the *Journal*, let's sample some of the analysis that it has printed over the last several months. No journalist today has provided analysis of the high-tech world as trenchant as that of the *Journal*'s regular columnist George Melloan. When he writes about the free economy, he is usually level-headed and morally sound. But on the matter of war, he has epitomized the capitalist-imperialist mode denounced by Lenin.

Melloan writes that the purpose of this war is "something far more ambitious than pacification. It is trying to civilize Serbia." If this be civilizing, God save us from barbarism, and from warfare statists masquerading as advocates of free enterprise.

What about the US bombing of the Chinese embassy, which would have been perceived as a world-historic crime and act of war if a US embassy had been the target? "The [embassy] bombing," Melloan writes, "was clearly the kind of accident that happens in war." Besides, he further opined, "the Chinese government clearly gives aid and comfort to the Serbian barbarian, Slobodan Milosevic. It has joined with Russia to try to sway United Nations Security Council votes in his favor."

Well, clearly then, murder and destruction are just what the State orders for anyone who would give aid and comfort to the Serbian barbarian. In fact, can't we say that anyone who isn't on board with this war is giving aid and comfort to the enemy? Shouldn't their voices be quelled? Can we really say they don't deserve to be bombed? It's all part of the civilizing process.

The day after the bombing, there was no time for regrets at the *Wall Street Journal*. No, the editorial page used the occasion to spread the war fever. After all, the *Journal* said of the bombed embassy, "War is dangerous, and while Nato has sought to avoid civilian casualties, clearly people have died on the ground. [Catch the responsibility-shedding passive voice?] An obvious question may dawn on Chinese people eventually," the *Journal* continued, "Why, in the middle of such a war, did their government choose to keep all those people in its embassy and potentially in harm's way?"

Imagine that. The US has never declared war on Belgrade. The State Department never demanded that all diplomats leave the city. It promised at the outset only to hit military targets of the Yugoslav army. And yet when the US bombs the Chinese embassy, according to the *Journal*, it is the fault of the Chinese diplomats in Belgrade.

Along these lines, imagine further the future of death coverage in the *Journal*. Those kids in the Littleton High

School: what were they doing there anyway? Don't they know that school can be dangerous? Those people murdered by an immigrant on the Long Island Railroad: didn't they know the New York metropolitan area is a place not unfamiliar with killing?

This is the moral reasoning of a blunted conscience, one no longer struck by the pain of human suffering and the evil of violence except when affecting the appearance of shock serves a political purpose. This illustrates a broader point: in American public life today, there are two kinds of death. Death caused by the US government is justifiable, as Madeleine Albright tells us about the death of children in Iraq. Only death caused by enemies of the US government is considered an atrocious and intolerable act that cries out for vengeance. The operating principle here is not the sanctity of life but the sanctity of the nation-State that determines which kind of life is valuable and which is not.

And yet this cannot be the entire answer to the mystery of why bloodshed would be overlooked by the *Journal*. We've all been struck by the mystery of how otherwise sensible people could come to support a holocaust to achieve their own view of political utopia. I can't say I have the answer. How were US communists able to reconcile themselves with the mass bloodshed wrought by the Bolshevik revolution and its aftermath? How were German intellectuals and religious leaders able to justify in their own minds the bloodshed wrought by the Nazi dictatorship? How were US citizens able to observe the bombings of Dresden, Hiroshima, and Nagasaki, and the mass ethnic cleansing of German civilians after World War II, and call it patriotism in action?

It will always be something of a mystery, but if you want to see the same moral blindness at work right now, look no further than the early column by Max Boot, whose usual beat is the litigation explosion. Writing on the *Journal*'s op-ed page, which he edits, he praised this war on grounds that "humanitarianism truly is in the driver's seat." He speaks for many in the pundit class, who regard this war as uniquely motivated by a moral end. Similarly, Robert Samuelson wrote in the *Washington Post* the other day that "Kosovo may represent the first war in US history that has been undertaken mostly for moral reasons."

There are several problems with this theory, aside from the fact that the families of the 2,000 civilians killed do not likely consider their deaths the consequence of humanitarianism. First, the Clinton regime has made an appeal, not only to the well-being of the Kosovars, but to American interests as well. Clinton himself says we all have an interest in a stable world where Europe is not embroiled in war. On Memorial Day, he even vaguely suggested that if we don't stop Milosevic now, he and his armies will someday come attacking US shores.

Second, no one can convince me that charity and love are the driving forces behind a war in which tens of billions may eventually be transferred from taxpayers to the merchants of death. Perhaps greed also plays a role?

Third, every war I can think of, as far back as you look in US history or world history, has been justified under some moral theme. The enemy must always be demonized and the home government sanctified, if only to provide a necessary ethical coating to the nasty business of mass murder. The pundits who say the moral themes of this war are unique are only displaying their historical ignorance.

Finally, Boot's phrase about humanitarianism reminds me of Isabel Paterson's brilliant chapter in her book, the *God of the Machine* entitled "The Humanitarian With the Guillotine." She argued that the great evils of holocausts and mass slaughter could not thrive anywhere in the world unless they were given a benevolent public face.

> Certainly the slaughter committed from time to time by barbarians invading settled regions, or the capricious cruelties of avowed tyrants, would not add up to one-tenth the horrors perpetrated by rulers with good intentions.

She pointed to the example of Stalin:

> we have the peculiar spectacle of the man who condemned millions of his own people to starvation, admired by philanthropists whose declared aim is to see to it that everyone in the world has a quart of milk.

In a similar way, we are rattled on a daily basis by the atrocities committed by our own government, justified in the name of *ending* atrocities. Asked about the mounting civilian casualties—first denied, then called mistakes, later dubbed military targets—Nato spokesman Jamie Shea finally, if implicitly, admitted the existence of the bloodshed that has shocked the world. "There is always a cost to defeat an evil," he responded. "It never comes free, unfortunately."

Doing evil so that good may come of it, using evil means to accomplish good ends—these are condemned by the Western religious tradition, particularly in light of the rethinking of public morality after the rise and fall of totalitarianism. Hence, many around the world are already comparing the US with Hitler's army, including Alexander Solzhenitsyn. I wonder why. Perhaps because General William Odom, director of the National Security Agency under Reagan, urged copying German military tactics in a ground invasion of Belgrade. Also, writing—where else?—in the *Wall Street Journal*, the general praised the Nazis who "swept down this corridor in World War II, taking the whole of Yugoslavia in a couple of weeks."

The *Journal* editors were similarly jingoistic as the prospect of peace raised its ugly head. They raise the horrible prospect, only recently considered an essential feature part of the democratic system, that Milosevic "will remain in power unless his own people throw him out." The *Journal* just presumes that it is somehow up to the US to decide who gets to be president in faraway sovereign countries.

One wonders how it is possible that in wartime, all the normal rules of civilized life, all the lessons learned from history, all the checks on power that have been established over the centuries, are thrown onto the trash heap. It's a question to ask Carlos Westendorp, who calls himself the "High Representative of the International Community for the Civil Implementation of the Dayton Peace Accords." Also writing in the *Wall Street Journal*, he says that after the Serbs have been defeated "a full international protectorate is required. It may last for a few years. Yes, this disregards the principles of sovereignty, but so what? This is not the moment for post-colonial sensitivities."

There we have it. It is not just democracy, the very principle of sovereignty itself that is reduced to a mere "sensitivity" not suitable in emergency times such as these. Thus the *Wall Street* warriors were among the first to call for arming anyone but Serbs, and, in this war, demanding that the US put together an invasive army to conquer the country and overthrow the government—a plan now summed up as "ordering up ground troops." By calling for ground troops, and criticizing anyone who might be skeptical of the idea, the *Journal* is able to maintain its anti-Clinton posture and appeal to what it believes is the latent hawkishness of its readership.

On the very day that the *New York Times* reported progress in the desperate attempt by non-British European governments and Russia to broker something of a peace agreement, the *Journal* at last conceded that too many innocents were dying in this war. "Of its nature, war is about suffering," the comfy editors typed into their word processors.

Modern war, the editors continued, is particularly irritating because "we now live in an age in which television brings the inevitable ruins of war into everyone's living room every night." This has forced a national conversation about whether blowing up civilian infrastructure is morally wise. Further, the publicity given to civilian killings—no thanks to the *Journal* here—is "creating divisions inside Nato itself." Interesting how the *Journal* can muster more moral pathos over divisions within an aggressive military pact than over the death of 2,000 innocents, and the destruction of the property of millions.

So how does this bit of soul searching on the part of the editors end? With—you guessed it—another call for ground troops, which they now claim would have prevented civilian casualties. "What the American people do not want are casualties for no purpose," says the *Journal*. Besides, "going to Belgrade and throwing out a war criminal is not going to lose elections. And while it would involve casualties, it would bring the destruction and killing to an end."

The use of language here is strange: note the supposed distinction between mere casualties and killing. That one sentence is a case study in the language of imperialist propaganda. Opposite the editorial page on the same day, a pollster named Humphrey Taylor mulls over the question of popular support for the war, noting that this one has been seriously lagging in that area. The reason, he concludes, is that there have actually been too few casualties on our side. He ends with this stirring call to arms: "It's quite possible that casualties could strengthen, not weaken, American resolve to defeat Slobodan Milosevic."

Yes, it's true. This sentence appeared in a respectable newspaper, the voice of capitalism in our times. Thank goodness for the pollsters and their advice!

You know, I've been thinking. Clinton says he needs to draft pilots to conduct his war, but this is bad for morale. Shouldn't those who are most enthusiastic for ground troops be the first ones forced into combat? If we are to reinstate the draft, I say let's start by drafting the people who write this drivel and give them the opportunity to become the war heroes they so badly want to be. Let's institute another Lincoln Brigade, staffed by the *Journal*'s own editors, that will make all the necessary sacrifices to save the world for social democracy.

I've only scratched the surface of the *Journal*'s two-month-long campaign for US war. True, I have left out the pretentious prattle of a certain Margaret Thatcher, who wrote on its pages in favor of "the destruction of Serbia's political will, the destruction of its war machine and all the infrastructure on which these depend." She could have just summed it up by calling for a wholesale ethnic cleansing of Serbs from Serbia.

Also, I have left out the ridiculous parodies written by some British fellow calling himself Winston Churchill, Jr., who appears to be trying, without success, to turn some history-making phrase. In sum, let me say that in these last 70 days, the only truthful statement on the war from the *Journal*'s editorial page came on May 13: "Propaganda, especially in wartime, knows no bounds."

All this war propaganda might be expected from the likes of the *New Republic*. But for the *Journal* to beat the drums louder than anyone does great damage to the cause of free enterprise. It links capitalism and imperialism in the public mind, and fans the flames of Leninist theory in the academy and abroad. This damage is deepened by the broader problem that it is not just the *Journal* that is perceived to be a defender of economic freedom; the US itself, particularly at the end of the Cold War, was, until recently, perceived to be the standard bearer of liberalism.

Here is where this war has been so costly. Liberal reform movements in China, Romania, Greece, Serbia, and many other places in the world, have suffered serious blows to their credibility, because their cause is treated under the general rubric of Americanization. The bombs that fall on innocents have the indirect effect of fanning the flames of anti-Americanism, which translates into antiliberalism. To the extent that America still represents the hope of freedom in the world, this war is very harmful to the cause of liberty, free trade, and human rights.

How can such a result benefit Wall Street? Well, there's another side effect of the defeat of liberal reform movements in such places as Serbia and other European and Asian states. The end result of this war is likely to be the rearming of the world, after a period in which it appeared that we were in for a long period of disarmament. You can only imagine yourself as the head of any State that has had difficult relations with the US in the past—and that is most. You might draw from this experience the crucial lesson that States without nuclear weapons, such as Yugoslavia, are vulnerable to the most brutal forms of imperial assault.

The only way to forestall this result would be for Congress to take a drastic step and eviscerate the military budget, refusing to pay for this or any future war. But this will not happen, due to a deep intellectual incoherence at the heart of the Republican party. It was only days after the GOP voted not to endorse the war that it voted to double the fiscal outlay to pay for the war. But this is no different from scolding the local gang for their pillaging while giving it the key to a weapons stockpile. If the warfare State has funding and armaments, it is naturally going to go looking for enemies on which to use them. Every bureaucrat knows that he must justify this year's budget in order to position himself for next year's budget battles.

Isn't it time the Republicans fundamentally rethink their pro-military bias? Hardly a day goes by when I don't hear some conservative spokesman, GOP presidential hopeful, or right-wing commentator complain about how Clinton has supposedly gutted our defenses. But look at the facts. The US will spend more than $300 billion on the military this year. The second highest military spending in the world comes from Russia, which spends the equivalent of $60 billion. Scary imperialist China spends $37 billion. Just from looking at these numbers, the US could slash the military budget by two-thirds, and still spend well more than any other country.

The conservative attachment to militarism has doomed the program to cut government in the entire postwar period. The *Journal's* own editorial position—favoring huge tax cuts and equally huge spending increases—illustrates the problem. This view is rightly denounced as hypocritical by the Left who point out that the American Right is only for limiting government spending when it goes to the wrong people, but all for the tax-and-spend agenda when it buys military hardware.

The usual response to this in the past is that defense is a legitimate constitutional function, whereas welfare redistribution is dubious at best. But there is nothing constitutional about the biggest and most destructive cache of weapons of mass destruction ever held by a single government, much less controlled by a single man we call the president.

The original constitutional vision was of states that protected themselves from invasion through local militias. The function of the federal government was to intervene only when this proved insufficient in the case of an invasion. There is no more constitutional justification for the warfare state than the welfare state.

In the past, we have been able to count on a large peace movement to oppose US foreign policy adventures. But for reasons that are still not entirely clear to me, the soft Left has gone AWOL in its responsibilities, leaving only the truly principled Left and the truly principled Right to stand up against the massive nuclear arsenal of the world's biggest power. But it can be done, provided we don't shrink from our responsibilities.

Some people have complained that in condemning the US intervention in the Balkans, the antiwar movement has ignored the atrocities of Milosevic. In the first place, it is very difficult to verify claims in wartime, though since Milosevic is both a nationalist and an avowed socialist of the old school, not to mention an elected politician, I can readily believe he is capable of doing all that he is accused of doing.

Similarly, I am also quite willing to believe the worst that is said about the US head of state. People in power are not like the rest of us. In their careers, the ordinary vices and evils are rewarded as political successes, an incentive structure that tends to insure that the higher you go in politics, the less you believe you are bound by the moral tenets of the mortal class.

At the same time, I do not believe that we, as Americans, have an obligation to denounce all tyrants with equal moral passion. No foreign tyrant ever killed anyone while invoking my name and my heritage. But a long string of American presidents have done so, and one is doing so now.

As citizens of this country, as a part of our civic duty, if not as the sum total of our civic duty, we must do our best to denounce and restrain our own tyrants. We cannot stop bloodshed in Rwanda or ethnic conflict in Turkey, but our voices can make a real difference in what our own government is allowed to get away with. When a regime that rules in our name engages in any form of mass killing, the primary question that will be asked of us is: did you speak out against it? Did you do all that you could do to stop it? Or did you remain silent?

Near the turn of the last century, two months into the US war on Spain, Charles Eliot Norton of Harvard gave an address that ended this way:

> My friends, America has been compelled against the will of all her wisest and best to enter into a path of darkness and peril. Against their will she has been forced to turn back from the way of civilization to the way of barbarism, to renounce for the time her own ideals. With grief, with anxiety must the lover of his country regard the present aspect and the future prospect of the nation's life. With serious purpose, with utter self-devotion he should prepare himself for the untried and difficult service to which it is plain he is to be called in the quick-coming years.

> Two months ago America stood at the parting of the ways. Her first step is irretrievable. It depends on the virtue, on the enlightened patriotism of her children whether her future steps shall be upward to the light or downward to the darkness.

3. Ludwig von Mises

MISES AND LIBERTY

[The keynote address at the Mises Institute's new building dedication in Auburn, Alabama, June 6, 1998.]

We come together at a crucial time in the history of the Mises Institute and the history of liberty. This weekend, we dedicate a new home, which we see as a new headquarters of the Austrian School of economics and the scholarship of liberty. We are deeply grateful to all who have made it possible. You show your commitment to the ideas that underlie the free and prosperous commonwealth of Mises's vision.

The autobiography of Milton and Rose Friedman tells a story about Ludwig von Mises that was retold in the Sunday *New York Times* book review. In 1947, some free-market economists, including Friedman and Mises, came together to form the Mont Pelerin Society. But Mises was clearly agitated at the ideological tenor of the discussion. Finally, he stood up and shouted, "you are all a bunch of socialists," and stamped out. In the story, the Mont Pelerin Society went on to glory as the fountainhead of the classical-liberal revolution.

The point of the anecdote is to make Mises appear to be a fanatical ideologue, and Friedman a man of reason. It assumes that for Mises, sticking to principle was some sort of

fetish that prevented him from thinking strategically or coop-
erating with like-minded scholars. It conveys the message that
adherence to strict standards of truth is the enemy of practi-
cality.

Mises's adherence to such standards assured that his audience would be limited to a small set of followers, and that his
way of thinking would be ignored by intellectual leaders and
statesmen who could actually make a difference in the world.
Now, I've heard this kind of talk for years, and some of the
same accusations are leveled at the Mises Institute. So, I would
like to take up the task of defending firm adherence to principle, and of speaking honestly and forthrightly, and respond to
the charge that Mises and the Misesians marginalize themselves by being inflexible. I would like to show, instead, that
truth is our greatest weapon, and that ideological pragmatism
works against the cause of liberty in the long run.

First, let's clear up some matters of fact. It turns out there
is much more to Friedman's story, and the details illustrate
why Mises, in his life and in his work, continues to be an
inspiration.

The event happened, not at the opening meeting of the
Mont Pelerin Society in 1947, but in the mid-1950s, as the
Chicago School was gaining dominance over the free-market
movement, and the Mont Pelerin Society was falling under
their sway.

Mises knew then what has become obvious today, namely
that it's a long, long way from Chicago to Vienna. The
Chicago School has long embraced a positivist methodology,
which claims that all questions of theory and policy must be
submitted to empirical testing. We cannot know in advance
whether a tight price ceiling will lead to shortages; we can
only try it, and observe the results. This application of positivism to economic theory and policy has been a bad development for liberty.

As James Glassman pointed out at the Austrian Scholars
Conference, this accounts for why so much policy debate boils

down to a pointless numbers game. When someone suggests raising the minimum wage, interest groups inundate Congress with supposedly scientific empirical tests designed to show that such a raise would have no effect, or even lead to more employment.

Opponents of the wage increase then attempt to debunk the assumptions of these studies and trot out their own, showing the opposite effect for this specific raise. The battle rages back and forth, but the real truth of the matter eludes most everyone.

The trouble is that human affairs cannot be treated as a laboratory experiment. In abstract models, we can hold things the same, but in human affairs, there are no controllable constants. There are only established laws of cause and effect, precisely what empirical testing cannot discover on its own.

Empirical tests can illustrate principles, but in human affairs, unlike the physical sciences, they don't yield the principles themselves. To discover the effects of price and wage controls requires us to use economic logic of the kind the Austrian School has pursued.

And this is where seemingly arcane differences in methodology can have profound effects. While generally arriving at free-market conclusions, the Chicago School has made exceptions in a host of important areas. This is because, as a matter of principle, they have no fixed principles. To be true to their doctrine, all Chicago policy recommendations must bow to the latest empirical analyses, with the most elegant among them winning.

I recently heard a talk by Gary Becker, a Nobel laureate, true gentleman, and brilliant economist of the Chicago School. He was asked about the effects of gun control on crime. He hesitated, and then made it clear that he could give no *a priori* answer. He had no principle about whether people ought to be allowed to own guns. But, he said, in light of the empirical and econometric work of economist John R. Lott, and his nicely titled book *More Guns, Less Crime*, he would tend to say that we should not rush to think gun control is the answer to crime problems.

Becker came up with the right answer, thanks to the new book by Lott, who, incidentally, is influenced by the Austrian School, but when you hear this kind of answer, you can only be unsettled. If Lott's book had not been written, or had not received a huge amount of publicity, Becker would have had to rely on last year's empirical studies, many of which were designed to reach the opposite conclusion.

Moreover, we can't know with any certainty whether another book may appear next year, one even more technically sophisticated than Lott's, that would seemingly demonstrate the opposite. Someone once said that empirical studies in the social sciences are like government laws and sausages: you do not really want to see them being made.

The net result of this policy agnosticism on a base of empiricism is a tendency to embrace halfway schemes to inject market signaling into essentially statist institutions, with inferior results. The school voucher movement, whereby taxpayers fund not only the public schools but also the private ones, and do so in the name of competitive markets, is a scheme that originated with Chicago.

The negative income tax, the principles of which ended up in the hugely expensive earned-income tax credit, is another Chicago notion. So is the withholding tax, which disguises the true burden. And Chicago's refusal to provide a theory of justice to back its defense of property rights has led judges to toy with the institution of ownership the way they toy with the law itself.

Mises knew from his earliest years that economists who claim to do science on the model of physics were overlooking the distinctiveness of economics as a social science. Mises saw the task of economics as deducing from first principles of human action the entire workings of the market economy, and in this, he was only formalizing the *de facto* method of his predecessors in the history of thought.

He also saw that economists who abandoned the deductive method lacked a sure theoretical footing to oppose invasions by the State, since one can never know in advance of testing what the effect of a policy will be. And even after the supposed tests are run, you can never be sure about the data set chosen, the methods of analysis, or the subtle ways in which the bias of the author is built into the model.

Let me provide one final illustration of the problem of doing economics strictly by the numbers. In 1963, Friedman and Anna Schwartz published a history of the money supply in the US, in which they argued that if the money supply rises at the same rate as output, and velocity is relatively stable, prices will also be stable.

The policy conclusion was embodied in Friedman's proposed constitutional amendment that would have had the Federal Reserve increase the money supply at 3 percent per year, an idea that somehow eluded men like James Madison.

Had Friedman really discovered an empirical law with variables so simple that government officials could control them at will? In the first place, as the Austrians have long argued, there is a hidden assumption in the Chicago model that the money supply enters the economy evenly, as if dropped from a helicopter. But as we know, in real life, new money enters the economy from the banking system through the credit markets.

New credit infusions send false signals to borrowers who are led to make bad judgments about real economic conditions. The result is the business cycle, for which Friedman was never able to provide a causal explanation.

But the reason Chicagoite monetarism became unworkable as a theory goes to the heart of the empirical case. After financial deregulation and the internationalization of currency markets, their old reliable system for measuring the velocity of circulation and how much money was in the economy became unviable. The monetarists themselves couldn't agree on whether the money supply was going up or down, much less to what degree. This is akin to the builders of a new house not agreeing on how many inches there are in a foot. But in economics, if you live by the numbers, you eventually die by them.

Meanwhile, the Austrian money and banking theory has been used, in the pages of our journals and newsletters and books, and those of many others, to explain a host of recent money and banking problems arising in the US, Mexico, and Asia.

At the Mont Pelerin Society meeting where the famed blowup occurred, several economists were debating how to structure the tax system so the government could collect the most revenue while not distorting the operation of the market.

To Mises, this discussion presumed several wrongheaded notions. First, that the government is entitled to collect as much revenue as it can get away with collecting. Second, that the taxes of the 1950s were not fundamentally injurious to the market economy. Third, that economists should be in the business of giving advice with an eye to what is best for the State. Fourth, that there is a branch of economics dealing with tax theory that can be considered as separate and distinct from the whole of economics. Fifth, that economists should try to design measures of government interference to achieve optimal results.

To Mises, economists have a role in the political life of the nation. But it is not in making life easier for the State and the political class. It is not in becoming specialists in providing rationales for the expansion of State power. To Mises, this was a betrayal of economics.

The good economist is supposed to deliver uncomfortable truths that would likely make him unpopular to the political class. He is to explain to them how their high tax rates seriously damage the ability of entrepreneurs to make sound judgments about the future, how taxes prevent consumers from saving and investing for themselves, and how taxes hinder businessmen in serving consumers through innovative products and marketing. Moreover, a State receiving the maximum possible revenue would be an expansionist State that would never cease its interventions in the market. The good economist would point out that economic distortion can only be curtailed by minimizing the collection of tax revenue.

Yes, Mises thought that economists who attempt to make this possible, while failing to recognize that the postwar tax State and the market economy were at odds, are acting very much like the socialists of old. It was the socialists, after all, in the form of the German Historical School of institutionalists and empiricists, who first conceived of economics as a science in service to the State.

Mises had been through these struggles as a young man, had devoted a lifetime of teaching and writing to combating them, and had laid out a clear path for the future of economic science in his treatise *Human Action*. He wasn't about to be party to a repeat of the same errors, especially not when he saw the administrative State engulfing the West.

What was his vision for the economist? When the economist isn't making politicians angry at him, he should be raising up new generations of students and intellectual leaders, and educating the public in every way possible about the workings of the market economy.

He should be conducting research that applies market principles in new areas of history. He should be perfecting the theory and presentation of economic science consistent with the principles of logic and with an eye toward defending freedom above all else. He should be combating with all his might the legions of bureaucrats whose goal it is to maximize State revenue.

In quoting the passage from the Friedmans' memoirs, book reviewer David Brookes, an advocate of what is called "national greatness conservatism," was trying to make Mises look bad. But in our experience, the mention of Mises in this setting has the opposite effect.

Readers come across an anecdote like that, however inaccurate and incomplete it may be, and say: who is this uncompromising advocate of free markets, and why do the *New York Times* and its friends dislike him so much? My own view is that the *New York Times* can attack Mises as much as it likes. It's good for attendance at our teaching programs, and only increases the circulation of our journals and other publications.

This is hardly the first time Mises has been criticized for not toning down his criticisms of government. He never followed the advice of the people who said: You're a great economist, but you would be taken much more seriously if you were not so unyielding.

If Mises had listened to this advice, he would indeed have been much better off. He might have been appointed to a chair at the University of Vienna. Instead, he conducted his seminar from his offices at the Vienna Chamber of Commerce. He might not have been driven out of his country. Instead, the invading National Socialists regarded him as perhaps the most dangerous intellectual opponent of their ideology. Once arriving in the US, he might have been awarded a prestigious post at an Ivy League university. Instead, his salary came from outside sources, and he was never more than an unpaid visiting professor at New York University, relegated by the statist dean to a dank basement classroom.

So why did he do it? Why did Mises stick to principle above all else, even when he knew it was not in his self-interest? Murray Rothbard addressed this question in a powerful 1993 essay called "Mises and the Role of the Economist in Public Policy." He pointed out that Mises was often criticized for his engagement with political questions, but that engagement was not the cause of the criticism. After all, Keynes was steeped in political battles himself, and so was Irving Fisher, the godfather of the Chicago School.

The problem for Mises was that he bucked the fashionable opinions of the time, rejected the planning mentality, and persistently and consistently insisted on holding the purest free-market position, even when everyone around him was caving in. He stood as an exemplar of the scholar who speaks truth to power, an all-too-rare figure in our century.

Mises's perseverance in the cause of freedom cost him dearly. He writes in his autobiography that he was often reproached by his friends in Vienna "because I made my point too bluntly and intransigently, and I was told that I could have achieved more if I had shown more willingness to compromise."

But, Mises said, "I could be effective only if I presented the situation truthfully as I saw it." He concludes, "as I look back today. . . . I regret only my willingness to compromise, not my intransigence."

He wrote these words in 1940, at a time when he had good reason to regret his refusal to compromise. He had been driven out of Vienna and his home had been ransacked. He had left Geneva due to the growing pressure on Switzerland to harbor fewer refugees, especially prominent opponents of National Socialism.

His masterwork, *Nationalökonomie*, the predecessor to *Human Action*, had appeared in Geneva in the midst of the war. But his book was only sparsely reviewed, and made no impact on the German-speaking world. In 1940, he had no fixed place to live, and no means of support. He would not be made an American citizen for another six years. He had a new bride and no real future. All the evidence around him suggested that his teachings about the market economy had been soundly rejected from one side of the world to the other.

Almost anyone else, particularly an intellectual today, would have concluded that he had been wrong. He had been tilting at windmills, and as a consequence, had destroyed his career, his relationship with his colleagues, and his reputation in history. Anyone else would have had regrets at this time, but they would have been about how he should have changed matters so as to avoid the tragic fate in which he had found himself.

And yet, at the lowest point of his life, Mises had only one regret: that he had not been even tougher and less compromising.

This is a remarkable impulse, not only because it involves putting aside personal interest for the sake of a fundamental commitment to higher ideals. It is remarkable for the virtue of hope that it displays.

Mises understood that no matter how bleak the present circumstances, the future could be very different. Even as the world collapsed around him, he believed that freedom could triumph, provided the right ideas emerged at the forefront of the intellectual battle.

He was convinced that freedom did have a chance for victory, and—this is the crucial part—that he bore some measure of personal responsibility for bringing that victory about.

Keep in mind, too, that Mises would not have had to become a full-scale socialist to have kept some or even most of his troubles at bay. The State and the postwar establishment made good use of free-market economists who were willing to be flexible.

In the US, there were several students of Mises who had good positions—at Harvard, Princeton, the University of Chicago—and who were not on the margins of academia. They proved more career-minded than he, and their marketability in the world of ideas was increased by their willingness to abandon some part of Austrian theory. They all made important contributions to economics, but at the same time, they were all useful, in small ways and large, to the partisans of power.

Alone among them, Mises was not swayed by the Keynesian revolution or the rise of welfarist ideology. Instead, he attacked both as species of the same interventionist mind-set, one attempting economic sorcery, the other bringing about sheer robbery.

Mises didn't live to be rewarded for his intransigence. He died in 1973, at the height of the Keynesian-planning mentality, when the mainstream of the economics establishment was still promoting the Soviet economy as potentially the most productive in the world.

Even a few years later, with the basis of Keynesian fiscal planning in tatters, there would have been reason for hope. But Mises had no basis for thinking the truth would eventually triumph, other than this: he believed that the power of ideas is ultimately stronger than all the governments and armies and planning bureaucrats and even economics professors put together.

How ironic, then, to look back and notice that it is Mises who now stands as the worldwide standard bearer of the market economy. New editions of his books are selling in every major language and year by year, his reputation grows. Students return to him because they respect his case for the pure free market, and his unwillingness to compromise. Today, more than ever, the advocates of intervention know that it is Mises with whom they have to deal, in order to make their case.

What a remarkable body of work he left us. His book on monetary theory, written in 1912, still stands as the foundational work. His 1919 book *Nation, State, and Economy*, forecast the troubles that would rack Europe in the post-monarchical age, and held up secessionism as the only viable route out of the nationalities problems that still plague phony nations like Yugoslavia.

It was this book that also warned of the dangers that war posed to economic freedom, rightly identifying the militarized economy as a species of socialism. We are very pleased to have Leland Yeager, the translator of that brilliant volume, here with us at Auburn. Last year, he conducted a seminar on this book for us.

In 1922, Mises published *Socialism*, which among all the attacks on the totalitarianism of the century, remains the most comprehensive, deeply insightful, and devastating, from an economic, sociological, and political point of view. The answer to socialism was *Liberalism*, the title of his 1927 work that remains the most solid and compact statement of the classical-liberal view of society and economy.

As Ralph Raico has argued, it was this work that firmly entrenched the idea of private property at the very center of the classical-liberal agenda. In doing so, Mises was the first to clearly distinguish the old liberalism from the new, even as the new liberals were working to blur the lines for purposes of their own ideological advancement.

The trilogy was completed in 1942 with a book entitled *Interventionism: An Economic Analysis*. In it, he sees a world economy that is marooned between capitalism and socialism, and thereby buffeted mercilessly by the internal contradictions of the interventionist State.

He forecasted monetary crisis in essentially capitalist countries due to the deviation of central banking. He predicted the entrenchment of poverty due to welfare benefits. He forecast the artificial suppression of savings due to state pensions. He anticipated the burdens that would be placed on countries with governments that refused to rein in their imperialist international ambitions. Sadly, this book was not brought to print until this year.

In 1944, Mises wrote a brilliant essay on monopoly, in which he explained that the problem of monopoly was a problem of government, and that attempts by government to break up or curb the ability of businessmen to price and market their products in the manner most pleasing to consumers would only backfire to the detriment of prosperity. This essay also never saw the light of day, but fortunately, the summer issue of our *Quarterly Journal of Austrian Economics* will publish this important piece for the first time.

Lacking publishing venues, a full-time position, and even students to teach, Mises forged ahead to present his *magnum opus* to the English-speaking world. The result was *Human*

Action, which made its appearance in 1949. It was the culmination of the classical-liberal vision of economics that dated back centuries, tightly integrated with the scientific rigor of the Austrian School formally founded by Carl Menger.

It was the most complete statement of good economics ever to appear, and it should have become the mainstay of the profession. But by then Keynesianism had taken root, and Mises was again denounced for his intransigence. One of his critics was John Kenneth Galbraith, whose review showed every sign that he never got beyond the book jacket.

Mises did not expect to see his treatise sweep the profession. Indeed, the publisher feared that the book might not cover the costs of production. But the sales were surprisingly good, for there was already a growing Misesian movement, helped along by his friends in New York like businessman Lawrence Fertig and journalist Henry Hazlitt, who used his position at the *New York Times* to promote Mises and his ideas. (Both of them were later to become great benefactors of the Mises Institute.)

Yet Mises—then in his 80s—experienced personal tragedy over the book. Due to some larger than expected last-minute changes, the second edition was mangled by the publisher, and rendered all but useless.

To commemorate the 50th anniversary of *Human Action*, the Mises Institute is reissuing the pristine first edition. This Scholar's Edition will feature not only paper, printing, and binding for the ages, but also a new introduction by our senior scholars, three of whom are with us this weekend, Hans-Hermann Hoppe, Joseph Salerno, and Jeffrey Herbener.

In all, Mises wrote 25 books and hundreds of essays. In the future, we hope to publish a Collected Works. In the meantime, we are proud to have assisted in the republication of such great works as *Theory and History* and essay collections like *Money, Method, and the Market Process*, and to bring into print such classic works as "Liberty and Property" and "Economic Calculation in the Socialist Commonwealth."

And we are proud to have produced a film biography, sponsored many conferences centering on some aspect of his thought, and to have sponsored the world's leading teaching programs, scholars conferences, and journals on Misesian economics.

As we meet, our Mises biographer, Jörg Guido Hülsmann, is in Moscow immersed in Mises's papers, and those of Mises's colleagues from Vienna, stolen first by the National Socialists and then by the International Socialists. Guido has just returned from a trip to Mises's secondary school in Austria, where the carefully preserved records show the content of every class he took, and his grades. He was a straight-A student in everything from ancient Greek to higher mathematics. We expect Guido's biography, the first of Mises, to have a tremendous effect in advancing our knowledge and admiration of the man and his ideas.

But, in the 1970s, as the Austrian movement experienced renewed interest, the two books that had carried the School during the postwar period, Mises's *Human Action* and Rothbard's *Man, Economy, and State*, began to be pushed to the sidelines.

The Mises Institute was founded in 1982, in part, as an attempt to correct that. But as soon as I started to talk about such an organization, I heard the same old song and dance. Mises was too extreme. He was better left to the historians of thought. He could never be made palatable to the economics profession. He should be forgotten as an embarrassing figure. He had unnecessarily linked the Austrian School to radical politics.

Yet today, the power of Mises's ideas has mowed down his many detractors, and he is the undisputed godfather of the Austrian School. His name is cited by a broad array of scholars across disciplines and countries. His ideas are at last leading an international revival of classical-liberal scholarship and, simultaneously, driving forward a global movement against political control of society and economy.

But would Mises's influence be even stronger if he hadn't been so uncompromising? It might have been, but then that influence wouldn't have been all to the good. Let me explain.

Let's imagine how history would have been different if Mises had been a different sort of man. Let's say that somewhere in his writings, just for the sake of expediency, he had conceded the need for a welfare State, or antidiscrimination laws, or protectionism, or labor regulation, or old-age pensions, or some other socialist-inspired measure.

How useful these concessions would have been to the enemies of capitalism. These days, they would be inflicting on us the idea, for instance, that a social safety net is necessary. After all, even Mises conceded that this was the case. Such, of course, was never the case.

From time to time you see references in popular journals claiming that even Mises favored subsidies to the Vienna State Opera. This canard has been around for decades and has no basis in fact. The idea itself probably originated from a twisted interpretation of a passage in *Human Action* condemning such subsidies.

Why are so many so anxious to discover that Mises had actually compromised his position? Because for the power elite and the Left, free-market economists can add credibility to statist policies. If free marketeers can be caught in a contradiction or a compromise, surely it cannot be bad for the Left to favor the same thing, or so they say.

This is partly why so many have an interest in protecting the exalted status of Adam Smith as the primary theoretician of free enterprise. It's true that he made a devastating case against mercantilism and explained the working of the market economy better than most of his contemporaries. But as Murray Rothbard has shown, and as the Left has long trumpeted, he also made a huge number of compromises. Protectionists enjoy quoting Smith's periodic defense of tariffs and trade controls, for example. Smith can also be found defending controls on consumption, interest-rate ceilings, and government monopolies of all sorts.

So, yes, Mises could have been more famous in our time. In the short run, he could be cited more often and have his name invoked as frequently as others who were less tenacious and less unyielding. But, with the exception of the bogus opera anecdote, we can have assurance that most anytime the name Mises is invoked, whether in scholarly or popular culture, it is for his greatest virtue, whether or not it is being attacked.

What a joy to have as our hero a man whose ideas we can embrace so completely, without fear that his deviations or contradictions will be thrown back in our faces. He is a model and ideal, and his ideals are the standard which all principled proponents of liberty can be confident in celebrating.

In our own time, the problem of compromising free marketeers makes a very interesting study. Let's set the context. For a century, the Left has been defined by its advocacy to two possible positions. The first is that government should plan the economy using fiscal controls, monetary controls, and regulatory controls. It is hard to remember, but there used to be an elaborate philosophical apparatus to justify this.

The economy was supposed to work like a machine. Pull this lever, and a certain result comes about. Pull that lever, and a different result comes about. But this model has been discredited. Even more discredited is the second option, the pure socialist model, still favored by a huge part of the academic elite.

The cultural, economic, and political Left has been largely discredited in the eyes of the public. Where does the State go for vindication? Ideally, it finds intellectuals with credibility on the right who are willing to make compromises with State power. They are very useful in shoring up the propaganda edifice in service of State power.

I noticed that when Bill Clinton was arguing for Congress to shell out more money for the United Nations and the

International Monetary Fund, that he chose quotations from Ronald Reagan in which Reagan lavishly praised the UN and the IMF. This kind of tactic can be extremely useful.

Free marketeers beware. If you utter a word in support of the State and its interests, the Left and the elite will do all they can to make sure that word is all you're remembered for.

These days, for example, when you pick up a scholarly treatise in defense of the transfer society, you can bet there will be an entry for F.A. Hayek. It will not cite his crushing attack on egalitarianism, his case against managed economies, his defense of the common law and the gold standard, or his demonstration that the mixed economy is contrary to freedom.

It will note his defense of freedom, but also cite his periodic concessions to the welfare State. As much as I regret Hayek's concessions, he would surely be displeased to see his writings used in this manner. But free marketeers who make exceptions can earn a high return.

Of course, the use of market economists in the service of statism doesn't always take place without their consent. I know a talented economist who was also a leading critic of the national sales tax. He debunked the claims that the present tax code could be entirely replaced, dollar for dollar, with a bearable fee on all goods and services sold at the retail level.

Rather than refute his arguments, the proponents of the sales tax hired him. He then proceeded to write the opposite. (The Mises Institute has stayed out of this flat-tax/sales-tax cat fight, and instead promoted our own plan, which we call the lower tax.)

A free-market voice on the wrong side can really skew the debate. We learned this during the battle over Nafta, which we fought because it was a regulatory trade bloc, not the international free market.

In promoting Nafta, the Clinton administration made effective use of free-market intellectuals willing to back the treaty. Assembled in a well-funded "Nafta Network," they swayed the final debate. As a consequence, cross-border trade is now hampered with endless inspections, lines, labor and environmental restrictions, and regulations nobody seems to understand.

Let me give you another example. Robert Bork, for years a tough-edged critic of antitrust enforcement, recently signed up as a consultant with Netscape, the corporation that stands to benefit the most from an antitrust breakup of Microsoft.

He's doing very well. He could probably rack up a hundred billable hours, at $400 each, just on the responses he's written to Mises Institute editorials in the last month. No doubt his total take will be somewhat higher than if he had been just another pro-antitrust economist. But it illustrates a point: the personal advantages of compromise far outweigh those that come from sticking to principle. If your conscience can bear it, it's a good career move.

Like all our scholars, Dominick Armentano, the Rothbardian antitrust economist with us this weekend, would be very valuable to the Justice Department if he were willing to make the switch.

The defense of freedom has got to be made of tougher stuff than Bork. In a line from Virgil, which Mises, as a young boy, chose as his lifetime motto, we are told: "Do not give in to evil, but proceed ever more boldly against it." For Mises, this was not just an abstract tenet of personal morality. He thought this stance was essential to the preservation of civilization itself.

To understand why, we must know something about Mises's own view of what constitutes society. He saw all human action as choices by which we seek to bring about what we perceive as improvement. Since society itself is nothing more than the coming together of millions upon millions of individual choices, we can say, from Mises's perspective, that the kind of society we live in is a product of human choice.

Notice how different this is from the theory of society that sociology professors are always trying to drill into college students, and which we hear on radio and TV on a daily basis. In that view, our actions do not form society and our choices do not determine its shape; society somehow acts to form us and determine our choices for us. Thus no one can be held responsible for his actions—not criminals, not union workers, not failing entrepreneurs, not international bankers investing in foreign bubble-economies, and certainly not Bill Clinton.

This view of society also means that there is not much anyone can do to change the present structure of government.

But to Mises, this was a lie. Instead, he said, society is a product of conscious choices that we make, influenced by ideas we hold, and shaped by trends established and driven forward by human actions. This is how Mises understood the market. But it is also how he understood the crucial question of government.

Along with David Hume and Etienne de la Boétie, Mises saw that the State always rules with the tacit consent of the governed. That doesn't mean that at every step, everyone in society must approve of what the State does. Instead, it means that a sizeable majority have invested the State with a sufficient degree of institutional legitimacy to keep the political system running. Otherwise, the State and its programs would fall.

As Mises wrote in *Liberalism*, government is by its nature always ruled by "a handful of people" compared to the general size of the population. This small group cannot impose its will by force alone. No regime in human history has been able to accomplish its goals through force alone.

All regimes depend on the consent of the governed, what Mises called the general "acceptance of the existing administration." The people "may see it only as the lesser evil, or as an unavoidable evil, yet they must be of the opinion that a change in the existing situation" would make them worse off.

In Mises's view, then, government is always in a vulnerable position. Its rule can be challenged and even overthrown in a heartbeat, if consent is withdrawn. We can think of the colonial government in America, British rule in India, and the Shah of Iran. There is the example of Indonesia. Before that, we can think of Poland, East Germany, Romania, and even Russia.

The history of politics is an endless struggle between the forces of liberty and the forces of power. States that announce themselves to be invulnerable and eternal—the Roman Empire, the Third Reich—in retrospect appear to be on the verge of collapse. It puts the Clinton administration's announcement that it runs the "indispensable nation" in a new light.

What makes it possible for the largest government in human history—I'm speaking of the US government—to continue to rule in our own country? The answer is complex. But it involves an enormous apparatus of propaganda and legitimization by the media, the academic elite, bureaucrats on the payroll, and special interests anxious to provide a cover for their graft.

It also involves buying off potential critics and radical dissenters from the regime. And it involves the misuse of religion, whereby we are taught to treat national symbols as sacred, worship the presidency, and regard the political and bureaucratic class as some sort of exalted ecclesiocracy.

Mises proceeds to ask the profoundly important question of what happens when this system, designed to shore up confidence in the ruling regime, begins to weaken. His answer:

> once the majority of the governed becomes convinced that it is necessary and possible to change the form of government and to replace the old regime and the old personnel with a new regime and new personnel, the days of the former are numbered. The majority will have the power to carry out its wishes . . . even against the will of the old regime.

Now we gain insight into Mises's determination to stick to principle no matter what the personal cost. He understood that the preservation of civilization depends on establishing and protecting cultural, social, and economic freedom. And he knew that the enemies of freedom exercise power only with trepidation.

Their rule could be overthrown in an instant. And the instrument of that overthrow is the body of ideas that convinces people they would be better off under a radically different system, one where the government did not lord it over them. But to understand that, people must be shown the failure of the present system.

If Mises was optimistic about the eventual prospects for freedom, how much easier it is for us. The public is far less convinced of the merits of the present system than it was 25 years ago. Not a day goes by when I don't see some commentator, left or right, bemoan the dramatic decline in the public's confidence in the system of government that has waged war on economic and social liberty for much of this century.

They say we are losing our civic culture, when we are only regaining our private lives. They say we are losing our patriotism, when we are only recalling our love of liberty. They say we are losing hope in our nation's future, when we are only recapturing our hope in freedom's future. They say we are losing our faith in politics, when we are only restoring our faith in our families, our neighborhoods, our companies, ourselves, and our Creator.

I urge you to see through to the real agenda of the people who would restore a '30s-style loyalty in the central State. What they want is not just our allegiance, but our property and businesses to control, our children to indoctrinate, our culture to distort, our towns and cities to break down, and our futures to steal—for their own benefit.

To them we must say: No, you may not have our first loyalties. Our first loyalties are to things we love. And no, Mr.

Clinton, despite your injunctions, we do not love the government.

We are extremely fortunate to live at a time when the restoration of the classical-liberal society does not require a wholesale change of direction. In many ways, we are headed in the right direction now. Consider some old statist institutions, notions, and rules that have fallen into disrepute, are widely thwarted and ignored, or are in the process of crumbling before our eyes.

The monopoly of the media has crumbled. Even the highest rated shows on the networks would not have been in the top 25 two decades ago. Network news is vanishing from the radar screen. In the new world of the Web, Matt Drudge has more influence than Dan Rather. And the Mises Institute has as much influence over students all over the world as their own professors.

It's astounding for us to receive messages and questions and requests from all over Europe, Latin America, and even China. The Web has allowed us to break through the old information barriers we used to confront.

As for academia, the professorial ranks are still filled with socialists of every stripe. But students know better than to take them seriously. Meanwhile, we have had remarkable success in making inroads into the faculties themselves. For many years, our Mises University and other programs have trained economists, philosophers, legal scholars, and historians for faculty positions.

At the founding of the Institute, I was told that to send young free-market scholars out into the world was cruel. I was told they would be chewed up and spit out by the academic mainstream. That was never entirely true, but things were very tough in the early days.

Today, however, there is a huge network of young professors, and even some department heads and deans, who actively seek people who have graduated from our programs.

In particular, PhD economists with a Misesian bent are suddenly in high demand.

As an illustration of the current struggle, New York University Press just published a deluxe 100th anniversary edition of the *Communist Manifesto*, and it is the toast of the elite set. But we know that another book published this year by the same press will ultimately have a more profound impact on history: Murray N. Rothbard's the *Ethics of Liberty*.

There are many other signs of the crumbling of power and the bankruptcy of politics in our time. Formerly sacrosanct institutions of left-liberal academia—like multiculturalism, bilingual education, the devaluing of talent, the social security system, the attack on the family, the planned economy, the year-by-year socialization of our bank accounts, the love of the executive State—increasingly appear as anachronisms. In the future, they will be history.

Let me state for the record that I am not among those pining for a return of the days when every child aspired to be president. Let our children aim to think great ideas, found great companies, create ingenious software, make great investments, build great fortunes, run excellent schools and charities, have large families, raise great children, become great religious and moral leaders. But may we not fritter away another generation in the bankrupt field of politics and public administration. A mind is a terrible thing to waste.

So, when people say, Clinton is disgracing the office of the presidency, let's remember the upside. The desanctification of the executive is an important step in the depoliticization of society.

Mises never tired of telling his students and readers that trends can change. What makes them change are the choices we make, the values we hold, the ideas we advance, the institutions we support.

Unlike Mises, we do not face obstacles that appear hopelessly high. We owe it to his memory to throw ourselves completely into the intellectual struggle to make liberty not just a hope, but a reality in our times. As we do, let us all adopt as our motto the words Mises returned to again and again in his life. "Do not give in to evil, but proceed ever more boldly against it."

ARE WE ALL HISTORIANS OF DECLINE?

[This speech was delivered at the Mises Institute's "History of Liberty" Conference, Auburn, Alabama, January 29, 2000.]

The memoirs of the indefatigable economist Ludwig von Mises, written from his exile in Geneva, December 1940, contain this moving, even tragic, passage:

> Occasionally I entertained the hope that my writings would bear practical fruit and show the way for policy. Constantly I have been looking for evidence of a change in ideology. But I have never allowed myself to be deceived. I have come to realize that my theories explain the degeneration of a great civilization; they do not prevent it. I set out to be a reformer, but only became the historian of decline.

Reading the whole of Mises's works, it is clear what he means by decline: the deliberate wrecking of civilization itself, which occurs as a byproduct of the rise of the total State. In our own time, I believe, we are watching the opposite occur: the slow, systematic, intermittent, but relentless and glorious decline of the State, which is an essential condition for the restoration of civilization, the evidence of which can be read in the daily newspapers and seen all around us.

These trends, either in Mises's time or our own, are not determined by historical forces beyond the control of the intellectuals and people who shape the social order. There is no such thing as historical inevitability. The direction history takes in the next hundred years will be decided—as it has always been—by the ideas people hold about themselves and the choices they make.

Mises knew this as much as any of his enemies. In 1940, he wrote these words conceding that he had been defeated in the first half of scholarly life. It was a period of grave uncertainty and doubt that might have led any other scholar to total despair and retreat.

His masterpiece *Nationalökonomie* had been printed in Geneva, but sank without a trace. It is not clear how many, if any, copies made it to America. Europe was already consumed by war. The so-called wise men from the US, Britain, and Russia—would-be world planners now in their element—would soon be at the height of their power. The political ideology and economic theory to which Mises had devoted his life were fast becoming the stuff of historical interest only.

As for his personal life, hear the words of his wife Margit:

> The day we arrived in the United States was hot and humid. Behind us were four weeks of traveling, four weeks of anxiety, of heartache, and apprehension. We were admitted on a nonquota visa; but we had no home or family here to greet us. Like many other immigrants, we were to experience difficult times before we once against felt firm ground beneath our feet. Our belongings, among them his valuable library, had been packed and shipped before we left. Now they were lying somewhere en route, and we were not sure that we would ever see them again. Moving from one small hotel to another, with only savings to live on, and no teaching position offered that might interest him—such was the background when in the autumn of 1940 my husband sat down to write, as he originally planned, an autobiography.

Margit actually understates the problems Mises faced. He had already completed his masterworks—the *Theory of Money and Credit*; *Nation, State, and Economy*; *Socialism*;

Epistemological Problems; *Liberalism*; and *Nationalökonomie*
—but they were known mostly in a Europe that no longer
existed in 1940. Two had been translated into English, but circulated mainly in British academic circles. Most tellingly, the
intellectual tide had turned against him, with the rise of
socialism in Europe and Keynesian-style New Deal planning
in the US. To be a proponent of laissez-faire economics in
1940 was seen as a proponent of the telegraph would be today:
a quaint position at best, and a nutty and ill-informed
predilection at worst.

Mises's realization that he had been a historian of decline
comes two-thirds into his book, after telling of case after case
of a danger that presented itself, his warning, and the final
result, which was often contrary to his recommendation. Crucially, Mises recognized that he had played an important role
in preventing the communization of Austria and in ending
the Austrian inflation. But he had no illusions about the limits of his own power to change the direction of history.

No intellectual working alone can guarantee a future of a
certain path. Ideas can sway history, but there is no certainty
that good ideas will prevail over bad ones. No matter where
you looked in 1940, bad ideas were triumphant, while good
ones were seemingly discredited and crushed by the force of
events.

Mises also understood that he was a member of the second generation of European liberals to be faced with events so
ghastly that no 18th-century liberal would have ever predicted
them. Boundless hope was integral to the classical-liberal
worldview, and it was carried over in the mindset of the
Vienna economists, including Carl Menger in his youth.

When the optimism of the classical liberals turned out to
be unwarranted—the carnage and massacres of World War I
were the most convincing evidence that it was not true—
many despaired. Mises noted that pessimism had broken the
strength of Menger, who retired very early, robbing us today of
the further insights of the most brilliant economist of his age.

Despair colored his last two decades and crippled him intellectually.

One senses that Mises, in his youth, might have been troubled by the example of Menger. It might have been the case that nearly all was lost, Mises might have thought, but sitting and stewing about it accomplishes nothing. Engaging in the intellectual battle and fighting for truth comes with no guarantee that truth will triumph. But apart from such engagement, there is no hope at all. There is nothing an intellectual with principles can do when faced with a world in tatters but throw himself into the battle.

As Mises puts it in an inspiring paragraph:

> It is a matter of temperament how we shape our lives in the knowledge of an inescapable catastrophe. In high school I had chosen a verse by Virgil as my motto: *Tu ne cede malis sed contra audentior ito.* [Do not give in to evil, but proceed ever more boldly against it.] In the darkest hours of the war, I recalled this dictum. Again and again I faced situations from which rational deliberations could find no escape. But then something unexpected occurred that brought deliverance. I would not lose courage even now. I would do everything an economist could do. I would not tire in professing what I knew to be right.

"It is a matter of temperament" was Mises's theory on why some give up and others continue to fight. And truly we can only marvel at the fact that the second half of Mises's life, even in the face of astonishing personal, intellectual, and political calamities, was as productive as the first half, if not more so. Had he given up, there would have been no *Human Action*, which appeared in print 10 years later, no *Omnipotent Government*, a critique of national socialism even more devastating than Hayek's *Road to Serfdom*, and no *Bureaucracy*, books written during years when the State controlled all prices and production in most parts of the world, and killed some 56 million people in its bloodiest war. During that war, every day, another 30,000 died at the hands of the State, but

Mises did not give in. He fought with the most powerful weapon of all.

Had he not done so, there would be no Austro-libertarian intellectual movement today, and—one cannot know for sure—there might not have been a pro-freedom movement at all in America today. He continued to fight until the end, even though nothing in particular happened between 1940 and 1973, the year of his death, to give him a secure hope that liberty would prevail in the end. In those years, the redistributive State in the US exploded, the gold standard was finally destroyed, the US became a world military empire, the regulatory State intruded into the lives of average people more than ever before in history, and the Soviet Union, which claimed to practice the socialism that Mises said was impossible, seemed to most naïve observers to be secure, stable, and statistically prosperous.

Why did Mises persevere? We might say that he knew the truth when others did not. Sadly, that may be a necessary reason, but it is not sufficient. The other ingredients, besides having a good education and knowing the truth, are courage and tenacity, qualities that are actually just as rare if not more so.

For as long as I can remember, I have had people explain to me why I really should support this politician, student, or faculty member based on the fact that he is secretly a Misesian even if he doesn't announce it more broadly for strategic reasons. It was on these grounds that we kept being told we had to back Reagan's spending increases or Bush's tax increases: after all, he is really on our side.

Nonsense. For all I know, Janet Reno is a secret devotee of Lysander Spooner, and Hillary Clinton is still the Taft Republican of her youth. Maybe they are both just biding their time, working their way into the establishment until the time is right for them to act on their convictions. But, honestly, what does this matter? It wouldn't matter if President Clinton's economic adviser Sandy Berger revealed that he is actually a Rothbardian; in practice, he is the intellectual bodyguard of the House of Clinton.

A person must be judged by his actions and his willingness to face trials with courage. It is a great thing when a person holds the right views, when a politician favors freedom, and when academics have affection for truth. But it is only valuable to society when these same people are willing to follow through on their ideas with actions.

We've heard for years that ideas have consequences. But Richard Weaver did not mean that ideas have consequences whether or not they are acted upon. They must be advanced in public life, lived, and defended to make a difference in history, and even when there is no promise that doing so will make a difference, we must act anyway.

And here is where Mises excelled over all of his contemporaries, many of whom regretted the passing of freedom but were all too willing to ride the wave of statism to further their careers. Now, moral theology has never required heroism from anyone; but that doesn't mean we shouldn't recognize and praise heroism when it does occur. And Mises was a hero.

Rothbard himself puzzled over the question of what makes some men surrender and others fight when faced with near certainty of failure. Rothbard wrote,

> In the ultimate sense, no outside person, no historian, no psychologist, can fully explain the mystery of each individual's free choice of values and actions. There is no way that we can fully comprehend why one man trims his sails to the prevailing winds, why he "goes along to get along," in the infamous phrase, while another will pursue and champion the truth regardless of cost. We can only regard the nobility of the life and actions of Ludwig von Mises as an exemplar, as an inspiration and a guide for us all.

It is all the more noteworthy that Mises persevered despite his realization that he had witnessed little but civilizational decline in his time. If we are to follow his example, it should not matter to us whether, in our own times, we see our world as still thundering down the statist path or whether we can find evidence that we are actually living in a new dawn of liberty. I will try to convince you of the latter, but bear in mind that the case for principled intellectual activism does not depend on having realistic hopes for victory in our lifetimes.

Despite all evidence, then, Mises had hope for the future of liberty, and it was this hope that kept him engaged in the battle. Consider the contrast with Joseph Schumpeter, a classical liberal who won the hearts of the Marxists at Harvard by forecasting the death of capitalism. In Schumpeter's view, four things would lead to the permanent triumph of a fascistic-style of socialism in America.

First, he said, the business class would shrink with the rise of the heavily bureaucratized corporation. And yet, since his time, we have seen a virtual revolution occur in the Fortune 500, with old established firms being wiped out by younger, smaller, and more aggressive upstarts. The business class has swelled to become the more prestigious and most active sector of American society.

Second, Schumpeter predicted that a bureaucratized capitalism would lead to a loss of respect for private property. And while it is true that property in America is fully private in name only, and that Americans are far too lax in its defense, and that we live under the rule of the largest government in the history of man, dogged attachment to property has increased in recent years. For many in the former socialist world, the blessings of extensive property ownership are being discovered for the first time.

The tax revolt would not have become a permanent fixture of American politics, bureaucrats would not find themselves fearing for their lives when attempting to enforce wetlands regulations, and people's attachment to their stock portfolios would not have recently driven them to turn to the business section before the sports section of the newspaper every day. If anything, attachment to private property, or what remains of it, is more intense than in any period since the war.

Third, Schumpeter predicted that the intellectual class would become fully socialist. But he didn't predict that this intellectual class would undermine itself by burying its socialist moral system in deconstructivist relativism, thereby inadvertently encouraging students to be just as dismissive of socialist orthodoxy as any other. And neither did Schumpeter anticipate the rise of an alternative intellectual class that organizes itself around the principles of the Austrian and classical liberal tradition.

Schumpeter predicted that the American public would increasingly accommodate itself to a political environment that exalts social security, egalitarianism, and economic planning. What he underestimated was the propensity of so many to resent having their money stolen by equality-promoting racketeers with a social and economic record of unrelenting calamity. But Schumpeter's greatest error was in having dismissed Ludwig von Mises's argument that socialism is impossible.

Schumpeter opposed socialism but believed that with some effort, it could be made to work. Mises, in contrast, argued that socialism could never be realized economically, and that even halfway attempts could not achieve what it promised to achieve. This was one of the reasons that Mises had confidence and hope in the future of liberty. He didn't live to see the Berlin Wall come down or the Soviet Union fall apart, or the Western regulatory and welfare states begin to crack, but we have been privileged to live in just such times.

Today, while Leviathan is on the march, it has been delivered a number of setbacks relative to both the ambitions of the ruling elites to devour private life entirely, and even the reach of the State in past decades. Murray Rothbard says this began in the early 1970s, with Watergate in particular. He wrote that the event signaled the downfall of the State because it exposed the reality of the central State to the American people who had been conditioned since World War I to believe their leaders were benevolent, public spirited, intellectually superior men of courage, men who embodied the general will in the Rousseauian tradition.

If Vietnam discredited US foreign policy, Watergate was a serious blow to the administrative State on a domestic level. In the 1950s, it was considered nearly scandalous when Bob Hope poked fun at Eisenhower's golf game; now the jokes against the president are so ruthless (and deserved) that you have to ask the children to leave the room in advance.

I can well recall when it was not uncommon for American homes to sport a picture of the great leader. No longer. In wartime, support for the president can be high, but it does not last. Evidence that entrenched opposition to the State is vast and growing can be seen in the enormous spying apparatus that the White House believes is necessary to keep track of its enemies.

Rothbard saw that Watergate—however partisan and petty—represented a sea change in American politics. Instead of moral men looking out after the public, the political class was revealed as foul-mouthed, selfish, conniving, and ready to lie. From Watergate until the present, the trend has been relentlessly down. No president since JFK—the now-discredited JFK—has enjoyed immunity from widespread public antipathy. Even the great Reagan was caught in a scandal—now forgotten—that had him working with the CIA and supposed international terrorists in Iran to pay off would-be junta leaders in Latin America.

And yet the trend toward a decline in the moral, intellectual, and cultural credibility of government has dramatically accelerated since the end of the Cold War. Consider the long view of our century: As Robert Higgs has emphasized, it has been a period of crisis, from world wars to depressions to inflationary recessions, all of which conspired to instill a sense of dependency and loyalty to the central State.

For 40 years during the Cold War, the State kept us in constant fear of a nuclear holocaust. The only thing that stood between the people and total annihilation was the government and our political leaders. We were told that they were protecting us from Russia. Whatever you want to say about that assertion, it is undeniably the case that it benefited DC at the expense of our liberties. I recall noticing a distinct lack of jubilance on the part of the ruling class when it woke up one day and found its reliable enemy had ceased to exist.

Since then, the ruling class has engaged in a series of attempts to find some effective substitute for the Soviets, an enemy so formidable that it suppressed the libertarian impulse and inspired the old civic loyalties that the ruling class has come to know and love. But no matter what they have dreamed up—and how many Hitlers has Washington invented in the last 10 years?—nothing quite works like it used to.

Since the end of the Cold War, there is an emerging literature that addresses the astonishing decline of the State. Generally, it divides into two camps. The first is represented by those who cannot imagine social or international organization taking shape apart from some type of government, and thereby support the formation of ever more institutions of world government.

Among these thinkers, we can point to Stephen Krasner whose new book, *Sovereignty: Organized Hypocrisy*, takes the position that the future rests with agencies such as the IMF, the World Bank, the WTO, Nafta, the EC, and the like, which will come to replace the nation-State as the source of primary citizen allegiance. He is partially backed up in this by Henry Grunwald, whose article in the Millennium Edition of the *Wall Street Journal* forecast the wreckage of the State as we know it and its replacement by universal institutions, not excluding those of world government.

There are several reasons why these writers are not ultimately correct. First, the idea of world government is hardly new: it has been a dream of socialist writers and despotic rulers for centuries. It was never more close to becoming a reality than after World War II, when the Bretton Woods institutions were established with relatively little controversy. But today, every attempt to increase the power of the international bureaucracy is met with widespread hostility.

WTO meetings are routinely disrupted and wrecked, most conspicuously by the protesters outside, but more substantively by the delegates from developing nations who resent attempts by the US to impose a prosperity-crippling labor and environmental regulatory regime. Clinton has been constantly stymied in his attempt to bolster the power and authority of international institutions and his own personal power to represent the interests of the US to them. That, and not the fall of free trade, was the real story behind the defeat of fast-track trade authority. And whatever happened to the proposal to create a new world financial architecture, a global New Deal, an idea batted around by the Clinton administration? Does anyone in government really have the stomach or the energy for that type of world planning?

The power of the EC continues to be the most important political issue in Europe. Meanwhile, its North American counterpart in Nafta has been discredited throughout the hemisphere. When was the last time any politician in Canada, Mexico, or the US publicly claimed credit for Nafta? The silence is revealing.

There is another factor that suggests that world government institutions are not a viable replacement for the nation-State. The world government itself is a parasite on the nation-State: it has State-like qualities but is not itself a governing unit with autonomous power. For example, there is no sharp distinction between the power of the US government and the power of Nato or the World Bank. When you hear about threats to American sovereignty from the world government, remember that the US is the world government, the hidden hand in the glove of the global State. The good news about the prospect for world government is that when the host is wrecked, so is the parasite.

Far more compelling opponents of the nation-State, like Murray Rothbard, Hans Hoppe, Guido Hülsmann, and Martin van Creveld, argue that it needs no replacement. The international market economy is self-ordering, and political systems are best when they reflect the preferences and unique qualities of the people most affected by them. Combining the insights of the Austrian economists with the Catholic moral imperative of subsidiarity, you end up with Murray Rothbard's dictum: universal rights, locally enforced. This way, and not toward world government, is where we should be heading in this period of nation-State decay.

Just how intense is the present antigovernment feeling? It is interesting to note that not even at the height of the Cold War did Washington feel the need to become the complete fortress that it is today. We're told that this is to protect our leaders from attacks by foreigners, but the truth is that the fortress is designed to protect the government from retaliation by the governed—a situation that the Scholastic political thinkers said was *a priori* evidence of tyrannical rule.

Before he retired, Senator Daniel Patrick Moynihan was asked what can be done to restore the people's faith in government. He responded, "I've given up trying to restore faith in government. I'm just trying to get through the day."

Indeed, not since the Whisky Rebellion has the political class been so paranoid and fearful of the public. During the Clinton scandals, people on the right expressed astonishment that Clinton did not suffer at the hands of public opinion more than he did. But this observation assumes a preexisting public expectation that the presidency should be free of scandal and corruption. If expectations are rock bottom to begin with, revelations about corruption in the White House do not cause shifts in public opinion so much as confirm people's already low opinion of the ruling elite.

"Where's the outrage?" the neoconservatives kept asking. But they didn't mean where is the outrage against government itself; in fact, it is they who have been most vocal in condemning the persistent outrage against government in our time, which they decry as dangerous antigovernment cynicism. What they desired was outrage against Clinton personally, and there seems to be fully a third of the public that truly hates the man. But far more important than this is that two-thirds or more expect politicians to act exactly as Clinton acts. This isn't antigovernment cynicism; it is simple realism.

This goes a long way toward explaining other events that have shocked mavens of the political system. Voting is down to historic lows, not because of indifference, but because of the perception that the system is wholly owned by the power elite, designed and constructed to keep the current regime in charge. The New Left used to fulminate against the illusion of democracy, but hardly anyone believed that this critique would become mainstream in the next century.

In the current system, not voting is a form of protest, using the freedom not to vote to express disapproval of the current system. Already we are seeing public interest groups demand that the government institute an incentive system to increase voting, or even require voting as many other governments do. Never underestimate the desire of the State for symbolic evidence of citizen support. Never forget the insight of Thomas Hobbes, Etienne de la Boétie, Hume, Mises, Rothbard, and others that government ultimately rules not by force but by achieving something of a public consensus. Voting totals are one way to browbeat people into granting consent.

Neither is the perception that politics is one big racket restricted to the US. Even in Germany, where libertarian ideas have had a very difficult time gaining a foothold, public respect for the State is at a postwar low. Helmut Kohl stands discredited, but so do most other potential leaders of the German State. Commentators at the *New York Times* are already warning that the present political climate could end up uprooting an entire generation of German political leaders. The same is true in Britain, where Tony Blair gave up social- ist ideology, not because he wanted to, but because the prospects of nationalized industry no longer inspired voter interest.

We see the decline of the State reflected in a hilarious turn of events in the polling industry. I have seen only a few arti- cles on this subject—the polling industry understandably wants to keep it under wraps—but it turns out that pollsters are able to gain the cooperation of only one out of three peo- ple they talk to. Most people approached for their political opinions simply refuse to participate—a fact which makes a mockery out of their pseudo-scientific so-called margin of error. So taboo have some political opinions become that even those who answer the polls do not always tell the truth. Only this explains why every election season of the last three has featured huge political upsets.

Lying to the pollsters is one form of rebellion, but we are surrounded by many others. When the State says it is going to impose new restrictions on gun ownership, sales boom. When the State says we shouldn't smoke, especially not teens, smok- ing soars among teens. When the State says we shouldn't eat fast food, the stocks of Burger King and McDonald's take off. When the State says to vote, people stay home. We can only hope that the government never undertakes an advertising campaign on behalf of Austrian economics.

The prevalence of antigovernment cynicism is fast becoming like the weather: everyone complains about it, but no one does anything about it, because no one can. Govern- ment is having serious trouble recruiting people into its ranks. As van Creveld has pointed out, the rise of the State was in part dependent on the perception that the State offered its employ- ees the greatest financial prospects of any industry and offered a secure path to social advancement. This is no longer true. Even with the government's inflated salaries, it cannot compete with the private sector. The word bureaucrat, originating as a term of prestige, is now a swear word. The bureaucracy is no longer what Hegel praised as the "objective class" or what Max Weber said was the embodiment of "goal-oriented rationality."

When Clinton bragged that he has reduced the government to the smallest size in 30 years, he was referring to the number of people on the government's civilian payroll. But it was a trick. He came up with these numbers by deleting the numbers of unfilled positions from the payroll. What his statistic meant, then, is that the government is having a hard time recruiting and retaining employees—not exactly a flattering statistic when presented in that light.

A recent study of graduates from the Kennedy School at Harvard, set up to promote so-called public service, showed that only a third of its graduates enter the public sector. And no wonder. Parents used to want their kids to grow up to become president, but the wish now seems like the closest thing to psychological abuse I can imagine.

What about taxes? Yes, they are higher than ever and tax collection the most intrusive in history. But the technological revolution has raised the possibility of increased competition between tax jurisdictions. We don't have to go as far as David Laband of Auburn to predict that Web commerce will drive sales taxes to zero, but the possibilities are there that increased competition between political units impose serious downward pressure. And I think it is clear—and it has been true for some time—that while the public's appetite for freebies is high, its tolerance of tax increases stands at exactly zero. Liberal media commentators like to point out that politicians promising to cut taxes experience no great boost as a result. But this isn't because the public demand isn't there; it is because, more radically, no one believes them anymore.

The tax State will be dealt a mortal blow if the time ever comes when money and banking are taken out of the hands of the State and become the exclusive domain of market economies. Certainly, the prospects for genuine tax reduction coming via legislation seem low indeed. The best case scenario for tax reduction involves an increase in the present practice pioneered by the very rich: they shelter their money in financial forms that avoid extreme tax penalties, or even bank in places that guarantee privacy.

Richard Rahn, in his book the *End of Money*, has argued that the demand for bank privacy is far more widespread than is traditionally known—a case in point being the public outrage over Clinton's proposed and defeated "know your customer" regulations. In Rahn's view, online technologies will eventually come to meet the demand for bank privacy, making it very difficult for the nation-State to collect what it believes it is owed. Certainly, the tax State, like the antique Post Office, is closely tied to brick and mortar, and could eventually find itself outrun by digital means of avoidance.

The gold standard represents the ideal monetary arrangement, and the only one that erects a wall of separation between the means of exchange and the nation-State. Guido Hülsmann has argued that a truly free monetary arrangement—one free of legal-tender laws, taxes on gold, and free entry and exit—would result in a *de facto* gold standard. Further, Joseph Salerno has made the argument that the rise of nonbank banks represents a viable replacement for traditional banking services, ones which are far more sound because they keep 100-percent reserves and are therefore relatively more immune from panics or the contagion effect.

The unexpected change in monetary affairs in the last decade has been the startling effect that financial deregulation and internationalization have had on the ability of the Federal Reserve to monitor and control money. The Fed is no longer sure which monetary aggregate to watch, and it cannot be sure of the market's response to its actions, in either the value of the dollar on international exchange or on the shape of the yield curve. The Fed is flying blind—exactly the opposite of the all-knowing, all-seeing central bank it has pretended to be.

The problem of money and banking may be the most intractable problem we face in the future, and in this area, we can chronicle nothing but decline, and will probably continue to do so for some time, barring some amazing digital break-through. This is not so with Social Security, FDR's tax racket that hooked generations into dependence on Leviathan. The liabilities of the system are huge and growing—far too vast to allow some easy Chilean-style privatization to cure all woes. Fortunately, the unexpected has happened with the rise of 401(k)s and other forms of retirement accounts, created by Congress as a concessionary measure in the wake of relentless tax increases.

Young people today do not believe they will see a dime in Social Security, a perception which has caused tens of mil-lions to mentally secede from the system. Today, people are socking away money in these private accounts on the expecta-tion that the government will never give them a dime. Social Security is not an investment program, as is obvious from the abysmal returns the system pays. But the fact that the govern-ment continues to advertise it as an investment program only serves to discredit the State as a pension fund manager. Whereas people once were grateful to FDR for caring for them in their old age, young people today are wildly angry at Social Security for looting their earnings, and this growing anger explains why some in Congress are actually beginning to openly discuss this previously taboo topic.

Secession is taking a variety of forms, not just financial. Nation-States have multiplied since 1900, and secession remains an important political force in almost every one of the 200 nations in the world, even the US which sports active secession movements in every region. We should realize the implications of this. The more States there are, the more dif-ficult they are to manage, which is why the establishment is always sounding the alarm that it is a dangerous world. It is indeed dangerous for those who believe the world economy and political structure need top-down control.

In the old days, people knew why they wanted to be connected to the central State. It gave us security. It delivered the mail. It protected us from foreign invaders. It provided courts of law. First, what has become of the State's security? As Bruce Benson has pointed out, the drop in crime in recent years coincides with proliferation of gated communities, huge expenditures on home security systems, a boom in private security guards, and the vast increase in individual gun ownership.

Contra Hobbes, our security is due to our own efforts, not those of the State. And it is not only personal security at issue, but also financial security, which the State also purported to provide. But in the present economic environment, it is the State, with its constantly shifting rules on welfare provision and regulatory arbitrariness in general, which has become the major source of insecurity.

As for the government's mails, is there anything the feds do that is more laughably anachronistic? AOL's Instant Messaging program delivers twice as many communications today as the Post Office, and with online banking becoming easier, bill paying will no longer be a Post Office monopoly. In the end, the Post Office may find itself in business only to deliver Christmas cards.

What about defense? Just as the US government has failed to protect its own borders from relentless invasion, its foreign military adventures constitute defense in name only. I'll leave aside the crazy and murderous crusades from the 19th century through the end of the Cold War—so thoroughly chronicled in John Denson's book, the *Costs of War*— and only cite a few outrageous recent cases.

It turns out that US soldiers are being investigated for raping Serbian women during the Kosovo war—the exact charge the US made against Serbian soldiers in their dealings with Kosovars. As the news continues to trickle out about, for example, the US soldier who sexually assaulted and then killed an 11-year-old child, we can only expect the outrage to continue. This is to say nothing about the war crimes that continue to be committed against the Iraqi and Serbian people, not least by the so-called depleted uranium shells that spawn leukemia for decades afterward, the terror bombing of a pharmaceutical factory in the Sudan, the killing of 20 skiers in the Italian alps, and the spreading of debauchery and prostitution anywhere in the world that is unlucky enough to host a US military base.

The US military has been devastated by drastic changes in its management over the last 10 years. Inside reports indicate that it is now organizationally far more concerned with affirmative action, speech codes, and political correctness in general than military expertise. Promotions take place according to political standards having less and less to do with merit. This has demoralized the officer corps, which finds itself in entrenched opposition to the politics and priorities of its civilian masters.

Clinton had an idea in 1993 that he would institute an embryonic national service program to replenish the ranks of the volunteer military. But the program has been a bust, not because Congress has slashed its budget, but because of a lack of public interest, bureaucratic screw ups, and the usual looting by special interests. National service has not come back, and there no imminent danger of a reinstitution of the draft. Public resistance to a reimposition of the draft today would be extraordinarily high.

As for courts of law, the boon in private arbitration tells us something about the efficiency and efficacy of government courts. US corporations are loathe to even enter them for fear that they will get a judge like Thomas Penfield Jackson, a man who had never used a personal computer but who nonetheless presided over the most important software trial of our times. He is an incompetent and a malcontent lording it over a brilliant, productive company at the behest of less successful companies. And he is typical of the judges within the federal judiciary, almost none of whom inspire any respect.

What about schools? Here we have a hopeless case in which the level of government spending is directly correlated with declining scores and knowledge. The public schools have become such a disgrace that school districts are having to beg people to take positions like superintendent, which used to be considered high status. In the wake of Columbine, and all the other school shootings, parents are increasingly concerned for their children's safety. Even if irresponsible parents send their children to public schools and pay no attention to their academic decline, the prospect that their child might be gunned down by a drugged-up maniac tends to focus the mind.

And hardly anyone wants to talk about the real deadly effect of the public schools: what they have done and continue to do the students' character. Cramming thousands of kids in a prison-like environment saps their intellectual energy and puts the strongest in charge by default, exactly as in a prison. But the encouraging sign is the growth in alternatives, whether private schools or homeschools, which are increasingly being used by the most astute people. It's no wonder some members of the power elite have pushed the idea of government vouchers to hook these islands of genuine learning into the State nexus before the government loses control altogether.

In the business world, too, we are seeing the wonderful results of what happens when the entrepreneurial class circulates and rotates from one generation to the next. The entrenched, State-connected elites end up being replaced by new ones. The new class of technological elites is the least connected to government of any in our century. In their very work, they breath and thrive on the relative freedom of the technological sector, and are being shaped by a business setting the State neither understands nor can come close to competing with.

An article in *Vanity Fair* last month quotes a member of the Rockefeller family at their panic that the new millionaire class is richer and more culturally powerful than what remains of America's old families, which too often secured their social and political status by close proximity to the State. By the way, what a wonderful thing that the business school myth—the idea that only academic professionals can teach market success—is at last being demolished.

The thriving market for employment has devastated the ranks of the professional political activists. Thomas Sowell points out that any black with intelligence and drive is in school or in business, which leaves the ranks of the race hustlers seriously thinned of bandwidth. The quality of the people on the political front lines has been drastically diminished in the past 30 years. They may be more belligerent than ever, but they will be ever easier to outsmart in the years to come.

I've chronicled a whole range of areas in which the State is in decline, and have done so without excessive focus on the effects of the information revolution. Even though it has become a cliché, we shouldn't underestimate the effect of the Web in advancing the revolution. Murray Rothbard, in his famous essay on the nature of the State, pointed out that the thriving State must monopolize the command posts of society. Primary among them is the communications network. It is no accident that the government has always worked to build public-private partnerships in telegraphs, telephones, and the airwaves. The State is inherently pro-censorship, viewing its best interest as bound up with suppressing excessively critical judgments against it.

This has all come to an end, much to the shock of the power elite. You will notice that discussion of the information revolution, and the political issues it raises, has been largely missing from the campaign trail this year. The reason is that the political class is hopelessly behind. Each member steers discussion away from the topic for fear of making a brazen mistake.

Recall that a few years ago George Bush senior was skewered for not knowing that prices in grocery stores are usually read by bar codes. Today's politicians are terrified that they will be asked a question that mentions URLs, ISPs, bandwidth, or packet switching. Their advisers would like to help, but the political class is generally out of touch. For example, I know a major campaign manager who still refuses to get email in hopes that the whole thing will go away.

All of these factors combine to paint a fascinating picture of the State in decline. We would be foolish not to take heart in the denunciations of this trend printed in the daily newspapers. Everyone from Mario Cuomo to Bill Bennett to Garry Wills decries these trends and promises to reverse them with a newly invigorated public sector. Every national politician promises to restore the American people's faith in government. May they all fail, and miserably.

On the other side of the ledger, the list is just as daunting: government spending is at an all-time high, regulations are ever more intrusive, the middle class is ever more lackadaisical and nonchalant intellectually, the new generation of teens is lacking in moral character, and public schooling continues to drain people's brain cases. Democracy itself still remains what it has been since the turn of the century: a degenerate system whereby organized groups of special interests are able to exploit the majority of taxpayers for their own purposes. And no trend can more quickly inspire exasperation and pessimism than the overwhelming success of some lawyers in using the government's laws and courts to their own benefit.

The single most important factor of uncertainty is the business cycle. Some of these trends owe themselves to the economic growth of recent years, which is causing private markets to continually outrun the ability of governments to keep up. It provides no comfort to observe the Fed's loose credit policies that began in the first quarter of 1995, so that rates of growth in 1998 and 1999 have averaged 7 percent, with periodic spikes as high as 15 percent.

What will happen if the business cycle turns and we enter into another inflationary recession, one caused by the Fed's reckless monetary and banking policies? Some of these glorious trends will be reversed, while others will not. The State will attempt to use the crisis to bolster its own power, but it will confront a public that is socialized in a pattern of resistance, and it will be in a much weaker starting position than it has been in any previous economic crisis since the New Deal.

The habit of resistance recalls our forebears, whose history before the US Constitution was one long period of resistance to the central State. This is what the best part of American history is all about, and it is what is distinct about American culture. Recall too that history can turn on a dime, just as it did in the Soviet Union and all over Eastern Europe. Despotisms can be here today and gone tomorrow.

We must prepare in every way. We must ourselves become historians of decline: historians of the decline of the State, historians even of its fall, along with the fall of all its apologists, dependents, and sycophants. Until they become the mere stuff of history, we must fight in every way we know how to secure liberty with the strongest possible intellectual foundation, among this generation of faculty and students and every one that follows.

To the supporting Members of the Mises Institute, I pass on the warm thanks and appreciation of the thousands who have been educated in our seminars and the millions who use Mises Institute publications to inoculate themselves against error in political and economic theory.

We must prevail because the future of civilization itself depends on the triumph of the ideas of liberty. This is what Mises believed, and it is what kept him going even in our century's darkest hours. Nine years after Mises declared himself a historian of decline, *Human Action* appeared like a bright light on the intellectual horizon, and 50 years later, that light grows brighter every day.

There can be no way that Mises could have anticipated what the future held for that masterpiece. The pace of sales of our Scholar's Edition, produced on the 50th anniversary of its original publication, comes close to matching the startling sales rates of the first edition. And this is for a book that has never gone out of print.

But here is something else. Mises.org has put *Human Action* online, which permits anyone anywhere in the world, at all hours, day or night, to have access to a fully searchable and printable version of this 900-page book. In these two weeks, nearly 7,000 students and others from around the world have spent time reading the book or downloading it, and these are people who would not otherwise have access to such a book. Moreover, the online version has not hurt the sales of the hardback but rather the opposite: it has made it more popular.

Mises would be thrilled. Rothbard would be overjoyed. So would all our forebears who understood the meaning of freedom. We should be too. They would be happy to see you here today and they would remind us all of the extraordinary privileges that come with doing the work of liberty.

THE PROMISE OF *HUMAN ACTION*

[This speech was delivered at the Mises Institute, September 14, 1999, the 50th anniversary of the publication of Human Action.*]*

I n a 1949 memo circulated within Yale University Press, the publicity department expressed astonishment at the rapid sales of Ludwig von Mises's *Human Action*. How could such a dense tome, expensive by the standards of the day, written by an economist without a prestigious teaching position or any notable reputation at all in the US, published against the advice of many on Yale's academic advisory board, sell so quickly that a second and third printing would be necessary in only a matter of months?

Imagine how shocked these same people would be to find that the first edition, reissued 50 years later as the Scholar's Edition of *Human Action*, would sell so quickly again.

How can we account for the continuing interest in this book? It is unquestionably the single most important scientific treatise on human affairs to appear in the 20th century. But given the state of the social sciences, and the timelessness of Mises's approach to economics, I believe it will have an even greater impact on the 21st century. Indeed, it is increasingly clear that this is a book for the ages.

Human Action appeared in the midst of ideological and political turmoil. The world war had only recently ended, and the US was attempting to reshape the politics of Europe with a new experiment in global foreign aid. The Cold War was just beginning.

Virtually overnight, Russia went from ally to enemy—a shocking transition, considering that nothing much had changed in Russia. It had been a prison camp since 1918, and its largest imperial advances in Europe had taken place with the full complicity of FDR. But in order to sustain wartime economic planning in the US, and all the spending that entailed, it became necessary for the US to find another foreign foe. By 1949, the US began to fight socialism abroad by imposing it at home.

Indeed, on this day 50 years ago, the old idea of the liberal society was gone, seemingly forever. It was a relic of a distant age, and certainly not a model for a modern industrial society. The future was clear: the world would move toward government planning in all aspects of life, and away from the anarchy of markets. As for the economic profession, the Keynesian School had not yet reached its height, but that was soon to come.

Socialist theory enthralled the profession to the extent that Mises and Hayek were thought to have lost the debate over whether socialism was economically possible. Labor unions had been delivered a setback with the Taft-Hartley Act, but it would be many years before the dramatic declines in membership would take place. In academia, a new generation was being raised to believe that FDR and World War II saved us from the Depression, and that there were no limits to what the State could do. Ruling the land was a regime characterized by regimentation in intellectual, social, and political life.

Human Action appeared in this setting not as a polite suggestion that the world take another look at the merits of free enterprise. No, it was a seamless and uncompromising statement of theoretical purity that was completely at odds with the prevailing view. Even more than that, Mises dared to do what was completely unfashionable then and now, which is to build a complete system of thought from the ground up. Even his former students were taken aback by the enormity of argument and the purity of his stand. As Hans-Hermann Hoppe has explained, some of the shock that greeted the book was due to its integration of the full range of philosophy, economic theory, and political analysis.

When you read *Human Action*, what you get is not a running commentary on the turmoil of the time, but rather a pristine theoretical argument that seems to rise above it all. To be sure, Mises addresses the enemies of freedom in these pages—and they happen to be the same enemies of freedom that surround us today. But much more remarkable is the way he was able to detach himself from the rough and tumble of daily events, and write a book restating and advancing a pure science of economic logic, from the first page to the last. It contains not a word or phrase designed to appeal to the biases of the world around him. Instead, he sought to make a case that would transcend his generation.

To appreciate how difficult this is to do as a writer, it is useful to look back at essays we may have written last year or

10 years ago. Quite often, they have all the feel of their time. If any of us have written anything that can hold up 5 years later, much less 50, we should feel extremely happy at our accomplishment. And yet Mises sustained a 1,000-page book on politics and economics that doesn't feel dated in the least—or at least that was the consensus of the students we recently had in our offices to reread the entire work.

Consider Samuelson's *Economics*, which made its first appearance in 1948. It's no accident that it's in its 16th edition. It had to be continually updated to fix the theories and models that events rendered anachronistic in only a few years. Even as late as 1989, the book was predicting that the Soviets would surpass the US in production in a few years. Needless to say, that had to go. Last year, a publisher brought out the first edition—as a kind of museum piece, the way you might reproduce a 78-RPM phonograph record. In any case, it did not sell well.

Incidentally, when John Kenneth Galbraith reviewed *Human Action* in the *New York Times*, he called it a nice piece of intellectual nostalgia. Interesting. Does anyone read any of Galbraith's books today for any other reason? Our purpose in reissuing the first edition, on the other hand, was not nostalgia: it was to introduce a new generation to what it means to think clearly about the problems of social order. We still have so much to learn from Mises.

We need to reflect on what it required of Mises personally to write the book. He had been uprooted from his homeland, and much of his beloved Europe was in tatters. Well past midlife, Mises had to start over, with a new language and a new setting. It would have been so easy for him to look around at the world and conclude that freedom was doomed and that his life had been a waste.

Try to imagine the intellectual courage it required for him to sit down and write, as he did, an all-encompassing apologia for the old liberal cause, giving it a scientific foundation, battling it out with every enemy of freedom, and ending this huge treatise with a call for the entire world to change direction from its present course onto an entirely new one.

I'm sometimes accused of having an excessively pious devotion to the man Mises, but it is impossible not to notice, in the thicket of his dense argument, that he was also a singular character in the history of ideas, a man of uncommon vision and courage.

When we honor *Human Action* on this great anniversary of the book's publication, we must also honor the fighting spirit that led him to write it in the first place, and to see it through to its miraculous publication.

What are the political and economic trends that have come to pass in the last 50 years? The rise of new technologies, whose existence are best explained through a Misesian theory. The collapse of the Soviet Union and its client states, for the reasons explained in this book. The failure of the welfare state, again foretold in these pages. The widespread disappointment at the results of positivist methods in the social sciences, also addressed here.

Indeed, if we look at the failure of the welfare state, the persistence of the business cycle, the hyperinflation in Asia, the collapse of currencies in South America, the benefits we've derived from deregulation in our own country, and the meltdown of social insurance schemes, we'll see that each is addressed and predicted in *Human Action*. Again, each is discussed in terms of timeless principles.

But none of these issues touch on what I find to be the most encouraging trend of our time: the decline in the moral and institutional status of the central State itself. Quite often in the press these days, pundits decry the rise of cynicism and antigovernment feeling among the public. But what does this really mean? Surely not that Misesian theory has come to capture the imagination of the masses. We are a long way from that. What they are decrying is the end of the old intellectual and political regime that was just coming into its own when Mises's book appeared in 1949, and has been breaking apart since at least 1989.

The same level of respect is not shown to leaders in Washington as it was in those years. Involvement in politics or the civil service is not valued as highly. In those days, the State got the best and brightest. These days, it gets those who have no other job prospects. The public sector is not the place to look for bandwidth. Moreover, hardly anyone believes that central planners are capable of miracles anymore, and the public tends to distrust those who claim otherwise. The political rhetoric of our time must account for the rise of markets and private initiative, and acknowledge the failure of the State.

Now, there are exceptions. There is the Bill Bradley campaign, which, as far as I can tell, is driven by the idea that Clinton has cut the government too much! And then there are the conservatives at the *Weekly Standard*. Last week's issue called for something new: what they have dubbed "One-Nation Conservatism." The idea is to combine the conservative domestic statism of George W. Bush with the conservative foreign-policy statism of John McCain. This is what might be called the politics of the worst of all worlds.

The entire approach fails to come to terms with a central insight of Mises's treatise: namely, that reality imposes limits on how expansive our vision of government can be. You can dream about the glories of a society without freedom all you want, but no matter how impressive the plans look on paper, they may not be achieved in the real world because economizing behavior requires, most fundamentally, private property, which is the institutional basis of civilization.

Government is the enemy of private property, and for that reason becomes the enemy of civilization when it attempts to perform anything but the most minimal functions. And even here, Mises says, if it were possible to permit individuals freedom from the State altogether, it should be done.

People were not ready for that message then, but they are more ready for it now, because we live in times when government routinely confiscates one-half or more of the profits associated with entrepreneurship and labor. Politics consists of 100,000 pressure groups trying to get their hands on the loot. Why would anyone believe that it would be a good idea to expand this system?

Let me read you the rationale for this One-Nation Conservatism. It will inspire people to throw themselves into what they call public service. Public service has four main merits in their view: it "forces people to develop broader judgment, sacrifice for the greater good, hear the call of duty, and stand up for their beliefs."

These are all desirable traits. But I fail to see how they have anything to do with politics. Rather, a politicized society tends to produce the opposite: narrow judgment, selfishness, petty graft, and compromise. And that's putting the best possible spin on it.

Who are the real visionaries today? They are software developers, communications entrepreneurs, freedom-minded intellectuals, home schoolers, publishers who take risks, and businessmen of every variety who have mastered the art of serving the public through excellence, and doing it despite every obstacle that the State places in their way.

The real visionaries today are the people who continue to struggle to live normal lives—raising children, getting a good education, building healthy neighborhoods, producing beautiful art and music, innovating in the world of business— despite the attempt by the State to distort and destroy most of what is great and good in our world today.

One of the great rhetorical errors of Mises's time and ours has been to reverse the meaning of public and private service. As Murray Rothbard pointed out, private service implies that your behavior and your motivation is about helping no one but yourself. If you want an example, tour the halls of a random bureaucratic palace in DC.

Public service, on the other hand, implies a voluntary sacrifice of our own interests for the sake of others, and I

262　　　　　　　　　　　　　　　　　　　　　　　*Speaking of Liberty*

suggest to you that this is the most overlooked feature of a free society. Whether it is entrepreneurs serving their customers, parents serving their children, teachers serving their students, pastors serving the faithful, or intellectuals serving the cause of truth and wisdom, we find an authentic public ethic and a real broadness of judgment; it is in the voluntary nexus of *Human Action* where we find the call of duty being acted on. It is here we find people standing up for their beliefs. It is here we find true idealism.

It was Mises's firm conviction that ideas, and ideas alone, can bring about a change in the course of history. It is for this reason that he was able to complete his great book and live a heroic life despite every attempt to silence him.

The scholarly followers of Mises in our own time exhibit these traits, and inspire us every day with their innovative, principled, and radical approach to remaking the world of ideas. In their work for the *Quarterly Journal of Austrian Economics*, in their books, and in their teaching we see the ideals of Mises being fulfilled.

At a low point in his life, Mises wondered if he had become nothing but a historian of decline. But he quickly recalled his motto from Virgil: "Do not give in to evil, but proceed ever more boldly against it." With *Human Action*, Mises did just that. He was to die around the time that Nixon went off the gold standard and imposed wage and price controls, to Republican cheers. He didn't live to see what we see today—nothing short of the systematic unraveling of the statist enterprise of our century—but he did foresee that hope was not lost for the flourishing of human liberty. For that great virtue of hope, we must all be very grateful.

Let me also say how grateful I am to everyone involved in the production of the Scholar's Edition on this 50th anniversary, from our Members to our faculty to our staff. Mises smiles today.

HUMAN ACTION AND THE POLITICS OF FREEDOM

[This speech was delivered at the Mises Institute's Human Action Conference, Auburn, Alabama, February 6, 1999.]

The head of state makes a speech to a packed house of legislators, and is cheered to the rafters for his flurry of visionary policy ideas. He calls for the restoration of cities and towns, and the revival of the nation's industrial base through new spending programs. He makes more housing a national priority. He promises more education spending, new resources for the armed forces, a secure system of old-age pensions, and more equitable healthcare delivery. He takes the credit for a purported economic boom, and further promises to surpass all previous records in national productivity.

No, this isn't Clinton's state-of-the-union address. It was Stalin's 1946 speech, which concluded as follows: "The Soviet people are ready for it! Under the leadership of the Soviet government, with Stalin at its head, the Soviet people will transform the law on the new Five Year Plan into life."

If anyone still took Clinton seriously, this could be a chilling comparison. After all, there was a time when the state-of-the-union speech set the agenda for the nation. Now it is seen as little more than theater. Even the news media treated it like a movie premier, evaluating the script, the acting, and the emotional impact, but never confusing it with real life.

In Washington now, they only pretend to make grand new policy. In fact, as New York Senator Pat Moynihan pointed out last year, they're just trying to get through the day.

If we look at the present state of the war between government and the economy, it is clear that the economy is winning. Technological developments far outpace the ability of government to control them. The public is participating as never before in capital markets. Private arbitration is steadily replacing government courts. The sheer power of market forces overwhelms government power on an almost daily basis.

Books on freedom and against the corruptions of government are more available than ever before, even if today's professors are loath to see their students get their hands on them.

Through the Internet, the Mises Institute reaches a world-wide audience on a minute-by-minute basis. Journal articles that were once inaccessible are available at no charge to students and faculty around the clock. We hear from everywhere, from the University of California to the University of Beijing. The Austrian School has sympathizers in nearly every economics department in the country, and in such departments as history and philosophy as well.

Meanwhile, the moral legitimacy of government, its officials, and its policies has been on the wane for some time. Show me a student who aspires to enter the civil service these days, and I'll show you a failure.

Politicians as a group, and not just one party, are deeply distrusted and even detested. At all levels of government, the competent are leaving for the private sector. The military cannot retain pilots, the IRS cannot retain accountants, and the labor department cannot retain economists.

Politicians are dropping like flies, and the two parties are having trouble recruiting anyone respectable to put his name on the ballot. The Clinton administration cannot even retain cabinet members.

As for voting, few bother to do it any more. But far from being a sad commentary on the present state of the civic culture, nonvoting is actually a form of secession from a fraudulent system that offers the illusion of democratic participation but not its reality.

Nobody in Washington really believes in Keynesian fiscal planning anymore. Sure, they pay lip service to the idea, because it provides a rationale for their jobs. But the last hint that government spending should be used to boost macroeconomic aggregate demand came in 1993, just after Clinton was elected.

In the meantime, the growth in government spending has slowed dramatically since the 1980s, a decade in which a 163-percent increase in government spending was accompanied by daily talk of budget cuts.

A new high-tech corporate power elite is being raised up, disconnected from government. They make their fortunes by virtue of their terrific innovations and their extreme attentiveness to the needs of the consumer, and through a competitive struggle with others who are constantly attempting to do the same.

The members of this new corporate elite are far less connected to the idea and regulatory apparatus of the nation-State than any of their predecessors. They have witnessed firsthand the remarkable power of the market economy to transform society and individual lives, and have seen nothing but failure from government programs and consortiums.

Now, we must remember that we are in the midst of an economic boom. I would feel a lot more like celebrating the soaring stock market, and the rock-bottom unemployment rate, if the Fed hadn't been boosting the money supply, a fact which is already showing up in the declining value of the dollar on the international exchange.

In time, the boom will turn to bust, and market traders will receive a new lesson in what that old-fashioned word "recession" means. But the question we have to ask ourselves is this: in the next recession, will the forces of government be able to impose the kind of fiscal and regulatory planning that they once enacted as a matter of course?

I don't think so. To impose a dramatic step-up in government power requires a public consensus in favor of government "solutions" that simply no longer exists.

What we are witnessing is the continuation of a process that began to be revealed in the late 1980s, when socialist regimes crumbled despite every prediction that they would be permanent. The same forces are working themselves out in different and unpredictable ways right here at home. The ideological foundations of all-round statism are beginning to collapse. It has never been more likely that we will see a reflowering of classical freedom in our time.

What a distance we have traveled since 1949. In the year Mises's *Human Action* was published, capitalism had no future. The Great Depression was widely attributed to the failure of the free market, despite the valiant efforts of Henry Hazlitt to convince the world otherwise. The New Deal combined with wartime economic planning was said to have saved us from further ruin. The ideology of socialism was all the rage in intellectual circles—as it had been for decades.

The old idea of the liberal society was gone, seemingly forever. It was a relic of a distant age, and certainly not a model for a modern industrial society. The future was clear: the world would move toward government planning in all aspects of life, and away from the anarchy of markets.

The US had fought and won a European war against National Socialism, and an Asian war against a regional empire. The ideological lesson of this experience was not that the free society is superior. Recall that the US had been closely allied with Stalin's Soviet Union, a regime even more deadly and totalitarian than the foes the US had battled.

The experience reinforced New Deal statism. When the US government is given total power, the lesson ran, it can get the job done, so long as the government is granted discretion to choose its friends and enemies along pragmatic lines.

Moreover, the government must be allowed to make decisions over issues of life and death. It must be allowed to conscript, as the US did. It must be allowed to take innocent life with deliberate intent, as the US did in mass bombings of whole cities.

In terms of the ideological superstructure, this was the era of the total State. People the world over had been shaken to their souls at the awesome display of nuclear weapons at Hiroshima and Nagasaki, at the ability of three heads of state to meet and carve up Europe into spheres of influence, at the apparent central role that governments played as a force of history, and at the awful and undeniable reality that individuals appeared to be merely pawns in the new superpower-driven drama of world affairs.

In 1949, the State Department and the Defense Department drafted a document called "National Security Council Finding 68." NSC 68 was a blueprint for global US hegemony. It asserted that only the US government could muster the moral, political, and ideological resources to reestablish and maintain world order, which in turn required a massive munitions and covert-action buildup, and a permanent global military and CIA presence. It would be a new empire, and even more ambitious than the former British empire.

We had come a long way from the original American vision of a country uniquely situated to avoid international political conflicts. In 1949, the major concern of the US power elite was to cement its position by establishing global institutions of unprecedented power, such as a world court, a world central bank, a world economic planner, and a world police force. The only critics deemed respectable were Marxists, who said this planning apparatus was entirely too enthralled with capitalist ideals.

Meanwhile, the real resistance movements in the US, including the Southern Agrarians and the America First Committee, had been smashed and discredited, their leaders branded as reactionaries and Axis sympathizers. The election of 1948 seemed to confirm this, as the Dixiecrats were crushed and Truman reelected in an election that represented the highwater mark of voter participation.

What was left of the antisocialist element in American life was distracted into ignoring US socialism and focusing on the Soviets, a sentiment that was denounced and simultaneously used by the Truman administration to bring about a huge military buildup.

Anyone who doubted the glories of the escalating welfare-warfare national-security State was accused of having an "authoritarian personality," in Theodor Adorno's phrase that still has a prominent place in undergraduate abnormal psychology textbooks.

Freedom-minded intellectuals were dying off, and the few remaining ones had virtually no publishing outlets. Most of the dissident publications that survived the Depression had been killed off during wartime censorship. And shaped by years of war propaganda and fireside chats before that, radio networks and newspapers chose their programming based on nationalistic concerns.

Love of the nation-State had even come to displace traditional religion. The flag became an object of worship for the second time in American history (the first being during Wilson's invasion of Europe). Religious sentiments were added to the national pledge and to depreciating coinage, in acts that our forebears might have regarded as blasphemous.

The middle class was roped into a growing welfare State by virtue of expanding Social Security, school loans and grants from government, and the cult of the civil service.

In 1949, freedom seemed to have no future. The only serious dispute was over the degree to which choice and autonomy should be limited in government's pursuit of the planned world economy.

The State and the intellectual classes were one. The prophet of this new order was Keynes himself, who achieved an intellectual revolution of unprecedented completeness. As one writer said at the time without irony, "Keynes indeed had the Revelation. His disciples are now dividing into groups, each taking sustenance from the Keynesian larder. The struggle for the Apostolic Succession is on."

Seymour Harris, an economics professor at Harvard, whose 1949 book *Economic Planning* had a huge impact, sums up what was considered the empirical reality of Soviet socialism. "Twenty years ago," he wrote, "Russia presented her first five-year plan. Her phenomenally rapid rate of industrialization and economic growth in the years 1928–40 attracted the attention of all the major nations of the world."

As tens of millions were shot or starved to death in the charnel house of socialism, Harris wrote that the

> numerous advantages of the socialist state can not be denied. For example, it can achieve a distribution between production of essential and nonessentials apparently impossible for the capitalist state. . . . In its concentration on essentials prior to producing nonessentials, the economy of the USSR has much to recommend it.

Among the advantages that Harris lists is this: "The USSR is not troubled by excessive salesmen and advertisers."

And what of Hayek's 1944 criticism that planned economies and loss of freedom are all of a piece? Harris claims to show that Hayek has fallen victim to an elementary fallacy. "The fact of concomitant variations (e.g., planning and fascism in Germany)," writes Harris, "does not prove that the planning brought fascism any more than the concomitance of marriages and the appearance of ants in June suggests a causal relation."

That this flippant dismissal of any connection between big government and loss of freedom was considered persuasive is a measure of the ideological climate of the time.

As for the efficiency of the planned economy, there was no need to fear. Exhibit A in the intellectual arsenal of the pro-planning economists was World War II. In the US, production was planned, prices controlled, labor conscripted, and consumption regulated. And didn't we win the war? Even more impressively, didn't the war itself bring the gruesome realities of the Great Depression to a close?

The Supreme Court was busy shredding the Constitution and centralizing power in the executive State. In 1949, the court held in *Wolf v. Colorado* that the search and seizure provisions of the Bill of Rights applied to the states, and that the central government should be charged with protecting people from their respective state governments.

Of course, in the original design of the Constitution, the Bill of Rights was to protect the people of the states from the central government, an intention that was turned on its head with the doctrine of incorporation. But even aside from constitutional law, how absurd it is for the feds to claim to be the guardians of freedom. The centralization of power is one of the greatest threats to liberty ever known.

In these years, the State and the corporate classes were one as well. Every major company was now beholden to the planning State, having been shaped by FDR's Blue Eagle program, wartime price controls, and all-round unionization. The captains of industry were joined at the hip with the regulatory apparatus. The American worker was terrified for his family's livelihood, and in no mood to rock the boat.

Such traditional institutions as advertising and individual initiative were declared dead in plays such as *Death of a Salesman* and books like the *Organization Man*.

In retrospect, it is clear that the foundations for the massive step-up in State power of the 1960s, and the war on such countervailing institutions as private property, the family, and federalism, were laid in the late 1940s and early 1950s.

The Depression and the war had demolished traditional loyalties and demonstrated the massive power of government, and the 1950s effort to globalize and universalize the planning State set the stage for the continued socialization of society that followed.

Mises, who lived through it all, was singular because he had both the intellectual apparatus to fight what appeared to be an invincible foe, and the moral stamina to do so though he knew he would doom any future he had in academia. And yet he saw what needed to be done, and did it. The very basis of the market economy and the free society needed to be presented anew, and reestablished on a solid intellectual foundation for a new generation.

In the midst of the war, he had already written that the most important postwar priority was to fight the forces of statism on the battlefield of ideas. With *Human Action*, he would engage in that battle nearly alone. And yet one reason the book stands out is that it is not about politics as such. Rarely does he directly address the burning political issues of the day, and then only in a timeless way. Two-thirds of the book is a painstaking reconstruction of the theoretical foundations and applications of economic science.

Mises's intention was nothing short of magnificent. He had concluded from his study of history that the classical economists were the real heroes in the march of freedom. It was they who explained the workings of the free economy and the rationale for eliminating statist restrictions on trade and labor.

In Mises's words, they "reduced the prestige of conquerors and expropriators and demonstrated the social benefits derived from business activity."

While others attributed the rise of the glorious Industrial Revolution to mysterious forces or accidents of history, Mises said it was the economists who exploded mercantilism and made it possible for society to adopt the ideals of freedom.

The history of the American Revolution would seem to bear him out. We hear often about the political education of the founders. But just as powerful were their economic ideals. For example, Jefferson studied the economics of Turgot, whom Rothbard has identified as a founder of the Austrian School.

As Mises looked at the ideological landscape of 1949, he saw the philosophical foundations of freedom being destroyed. Austria had been engulfed in statist ideology, America too, and he was shocked and dismayed at the status accorded to totalitarian regimes like the Soviet Union.

But he also saw that the difference between the New Deal and Stalin's Five Year Plan was not one of kind but of degree, and he set out to do everything in his power to stop the encroaching darkness, and relight the flame of liberty.

In placing blame for the destruction, he again sought an explanation in the intellectual realm. In Germany, it began with fallacies concerning money creation and the supposed benefits of protectionist policies. In the US, it was the ideological baggage of Progressivist ideology working hand-in-glove with Keynesian economics, an import from Britain that had socialized much of the birthplace of the Industrial Revolution.

All around him, Mises saw assaults on the basic tenets of sound economics. It was said that the price system does not work, that property rights are a hindrance rather than the path to economic progress, that business does not serve society but exploits it, that laborers have a friend and not an enemy in government, that government can innovate better than the market, that the freedom of contract is a source of waste rather than the embodiment of efficiency.

Mises predicted that civilization "will and must perish if nations continue to pursue the course which they entered upon under the spell of doctrines rejecting economic thinking."

So strong was his faith in ideas that he dared begin at the very beginning, with the general science of human action, with the nature of man as a choosing agent, with the foundation of economic knowledge itself.

People who pick up *Human Action* for the very first time are perhaps startled to discover that the first 200 pages consist of a closely argued treatment of such foundational issues. It is not until page 201 that we find a discussion of market institutions like prices and money. And it is not until very late in the book that we find the ways in which government policy wrecks the operation of the market.

Clearly, Mises had tremendous confidence in his readership, a confidence that was confirmed when his massive treatise was made a selection of the Book of the Month Club, and became an academic bestseller nearly overnight.

More importantly, he believed that it was only through a painstaking reconstruction of economic science that the tide of history could be turned.

Mises lived to see the free-market movement reborn as a consequence of this book. He died knowing that he had given the Austrian School a new birth, and he was thrilled to see brilliant young students, especially Rothbard, picking up the torch. But he did not live to see how his ideas would have a broader impact in world affairs.

Human Action almost did not see the light of day. Only kind benefactors such as Lawrence Fertig, a friendly director of the Yale University Press, and good colleagues such as Fritz Machlup and Henry Hazlitt made it all possible. Mankind is very much in their debt.

But as we explore the political message of *Human Action*, I would first like to focus on an issue that was most pressing in Mises's time, and continues to affect our present dilemma. This concerns a section of *Human Action* that is not often discussed, Chapter 34, on "The Economics of War." He begins with this startling statement: "The market economy involves peaceful cooperation. It bursts asunder when the citizens turn into warriors and, instead of exchanging commodities and services, fight one another."

Now, in 1949, this statement flew in the face of conventional wisdom. It was widely believed that World War II, far from being contrary to economic efficiency, was the means by which the US and its allies had pulled out of the Depression.

Government had funded a massive amount of capital expenditure, boosted aggregate demand, provided work to millions, and eliminated idle industrial capacity. War was not economically destructive, it was said, but constructive and productive.

Mises argued that war and the market economy, war and high civilization, are incompatible. To be sure, he said, sometimes people must fight wars. But if it is necessary, only the classical form of warfare is acceptable.

International law still applies. Civilians must be left out of the battle. Neither must the civilian economy be touched. Prices are not to be fixed and production is not to be planned. Wars should be defensive and limited in duration and scope, and conscription is out of the question.

Today, he says, the ideology of the total State has given us total war as well. It involves the whole of the civilian population and the whole economy. As Mises writes,

> modern war is merciless, it does not spare pregnant women or infants; it is indiscriminate killing and destroying. It does not respect the rights of neutrals. Millions are killed, enslaved, or expelled from the dwelling places in which their ancestors lived for centuries.

Mises says this is a direct result of the ideology that makes the State the center of a nation's life and worship. Indeed, when you consider the US's aggressive war against Iraq, and the millions of lives that its bombs and embargo have cost, you gain a glimpse of what Mises was referring to.

This is why it is utterly preposterous for modern conservatives to pretend to combine love of the free society with love of the culture of warfare and military might. What too many conservatives mean when they invoke a strong national defense is not defense at all, but the preservation and expansion of empire.

But if we follow Mises, we see that if we want freedom, we must embrace a foreign policy that rose up with the advance of freedom in the 18th and 19th centuries. That is to say, we must reject militarism, imperialism, and foreign entanglements, and embrace trade instead of conflict as the basis of international relations.

The immediate retort from today's pundits is that the US cannot afford to withdraw from a dangerous world. People are dying in Kosovo, Somalia, Haiti, Liberia, Rwanda, Sudan, Angola, Nigeria, Congo, and everywhere else, and the US, as the world's indispensable nation, has a responsibility for doing something about it.

Left unexamined is the assumption that the US should destroy regimes that US political leaders dislike. Whence this impulse to free the world of State Department-defined sin, regardless of the cost in lives and freedom? Mises traces it to Wilson. "Under laissez-faire," he says, "peaceful coexistence of a multitude of sovereign nations is possible. . . . The tragic error of President Wilson was that he ignored this essential point."

Recall too that Wilson was no advocate of free markets. He was a progressivist academic and early socialist, as Rothbard argued so persuasively. It should not surprise us that the president who gave us the income tax, the Federal Reserve, and the direct election of senators would also be the first president to believe that the US government has a holy mission to rid the world of all heads of state whose values are different from those celebrated in the District of Columbia.

It is long past time for us to come to terms with the fact that our country is host to an imperial power. We are loved the world over for our people and commerce, just as our government is loathed and despised.

If you believe in the old ideal of America upholding the light of freedom for the whole world to see, this is an uncomfortable truth. But nonetheless it is a priority for us to come to terms with the deadly damage that the US government has inflicted throughout the world, and to oppose it with all our might.

Mises also addressed another crucial issue of our time, namely poverty. As he points out, there was no question about poverty or riches in the precapitalistic era. For the huge majority of the population, there was only poverty.

Capitalism made possible continuously rising living standards for the masses. As a result, the only people who are poor by any historical standard are those unable to care for themselves, or who refuse to do so.

Contrary to the stereotype, Mises was a strong advocate of private charity. He celebrated both religious and secular groups that care for those who cannot care for themselves, as well as the families that provide care in times of need. He praises them for accomplishing marvels. And he also points out that private charity is dependent on the flourishing of a market economy, since the more capitalism increases wealth, the more is available for giving.

But Mises refuses to take at face value the claims of politicians who say they want to abolish poverty, since they also desire equality. The goal of equality, Mises says, poses a huge danger to the market economy. If pursued far enough, it is capable of destroying the market, which depends on inequality. That is to say, it is the radical inequality of individuals, the fact that people are unique, that brings about the desire to exchange goods and services to the mutual betterment of everyone involved.

It is no coincidence, Mises says, that the "most despotic system of government that history has ever known, Bolshevism, parades as the very incarnation of the principle of equality."

In a similar vein, he writes that egalitarianism

> is very clear in its abomination of large fortunes. It objects to big business and great riches. It advocates various measures to stunt the growth of individual enterprises and to bring about more equality by confiscatory taxation of incomes and estates. And it appeals to the envy of the injudicious masses.

The result, says Mises, is an accumulation of power in the hands of a political elite, the destruction of private savings, and the dramatic curtailing of private initiative. Until we learn to celebrate natural inequality, we cannot appreciate the greatest virtue of the market economy: its ability to coordinate the needs and desires of all individuals through peaceful exchange.

In Mises's section on interventionism, he advances a theory concerning the inevitable exhaustion of the reserve fund, his phrase for the capital stock built up under capitalism. He predicts that as the reserve fund is increasingly looted by government, society will grow poorer and more stagnant and eventually the system will fail.

The market economy will then be reestablished only if the right intellectual conditions are in place. He confidently predicts in 1949 that we will exhaust the reserve fund in the United States, just as Britain had. And yet it does not appear that the interventionist State has exhausted itself. Government spending is at an all-time high and tax revenues are as well. Was Mises wrong?

Well, let's look at the sectors of the economy that are most unworkable, most dilapidated, and most stagnant. We can start with the public schools, the postal service, the government transit system, the military, the courts, and the inner cities that have received so much attention from government over the last few decades.

In every case we see stagnation, waste, vast bureaucracy, and lack of innovation, that is, we see the hand of the State. These institutions are incapable of rational economic calculation, and they look increasingly ridiculous and broken-down when compared to the market-driven sectors.

So Mises was right: these institutions have largely exhausted themselves. In the coming decade, and possibly sooner, they will crumble. Meanwhile, the sectors governed by market forces and voluntary choices, which thus enjoy the fruits of innovative human energy, will continue to thrive and grow and eventually displace the old, creaking interventionist apparatus. Mises was right: interventionism is not a permanent system of social organization.

If we set out to list all the areas in which Mises was prescient, we would be here all afternoon. Just for starters, he demonstrated the economic impossibility of the socialist economy and foretold its collapse. He saw early on in his career that central banking would lead to inflation and business cycles. He predicted that social welfarism would lead to social disintegration. He saw that socialized medicine would produce the ironic result of declining health. He foresaw that interventionism would lead to the opposite results of those promised by its proponents.

I would like to draw your attention to a paragraph on page 859. Here Mises talks about the role of public opinion, a subject much in the news today. He writes that one of the great benefits of the market economy is that members of the public can benefit from technical expertise that they themselves do not possess.

You do not have to know how to build a website to order a book from Amazon.com. You do not need to know how to pilot a 747 to fly coast to coast.

But matters are different regarding economic policies. The practical use of the teachings of economics presupposes their endorsement by public opinion, Mises writes. He is very emphatic on this point.

> [T]he best theories are useless if not supported by public opinion. . . . They cannot work if not accepted by a majority of the people. Whatever the system of government may be, there cannot be any question of ruling a nation lastingly on the ground of doctrines at variance with public opinion.

Because Mises held this view, he devoted enormous personal resources to teaching average people about the benefits of economic freedom. Here Mises was basing his practice on the theory of de la Boétie and Hume: that all governments—no matter how powerful they seem—are fundamentally fragile, and cannot rule solely by fear and coercion because the enforcers are always in the minority. They depend on some measure of public willingness to be ruled.

Thus all governments pursue policies that are in some measure—at least tacitly—supported by the people. Hence, the New Deal was only made possible by the dying public consensus in favor of the market economy. And hence, the always economically disastrous Soviet Union finally collapsed when the public turned against socialist theories and those who used them as a cover for their power.

But what can we say about our own time? What does public opinion support today? In the media, we hear that the public is very happy with the rule of Clinton. The polls seem to indicate support for his policies, a factoid which has caused supporters of the market much despair.

In an effort to sort out this mysterious subject, I would like to distinguish three methods of discerning public opinion. The first is that which Mises identified: the practical workings of the market economy. If we seek a society in which the desires of the public are manifest in the use of social resources, the market economy provides it. Only here do we have the means of discovering the values of the masses and signaling businessmen what to produce and in what quality and quantity.

The failure to understand this leads the likes of Janet Reno to complain that the wrong firm has temporarily won the software war, or that a toy retailer is too large. Others complain that the wrong products are chosen by the people. For example, cigarettes are more valued than copies of the state-of-the-union address.

But the truth is that the market is a daily and hourly plebiscite over who or what will be the winners and losers. The market has proven itself capable of serving a vast range of interests. Classical music afficionados are served as efficiently as those who prefer country music. Moreover, we can have some confidence in the outcome of this vote, because people are laying their own personal property on the line, and putting their money where their values are.

In all of human history, philosophers have sought to find a system of social organization that truly embodies the will of the people. With the market economy, we have that system.

How disgraceful that week after week on Sunday talk shows, we hear politicians explaining to us that the American people want this and the American people want that. How can they know? The polls they cite represent nothing but words in the air. Just once I would like one of these politicians to tell the truth: we know what the American people want based on which entrepreneurs and companies make the most money.

We cannot know whether the American people truly want national education standards, but we can know, because we have eyes to see, that they want imported cars that work, books delivered to their doorsteps overnight, and lots of do-it-yourself home improvement products. We know this because the companies that effectively deliver them are prospering.

Well, what about those public opinion polls? Their dirty secret is that they nearly always consist of random calls to people's homes, and two-thirds of the people who pick up the phone hang up without answering the questions. If you've received a call from a polling firm, you know why people are reluctant. There is nothing in it for you. It feels like an invasion of privacy. You have no way of judging the veracity of the caller.

If your political opinions are politically incorrect—that is, if you disagree with respectable media opinion—you are far less likely to talk. An official pollster might as well be from the Justice Department, for all the citizen knows. Hence, participants tend to have conventional opinions they feel safe in spouting off to a perfect stranger on the phone. Most people are unwilling to express an un-PC opinion at a cocktail party, much less to a pushy character interrupting their dinner.

The question of whether a president ought to be removed from office falls into the potentially dangerous category. If the person agreeing to the poll senses that he will be regarded as a kook for saying the president ought to be tried and convicted, on the margin he will say what he is supposed to say and not say what he is not supposed to say.

The most absurd public opinion polls are those on taxes. Now, if there is one thing we know about taxes, it is that people do not want to pay them. If they wanted to pay them, there would be no need for taxes. People would gladly figure out how much of their money that the government deserves and send it in.

And yet we routinely hear about opinion polls that reveal that the public likes the tax level as it is and might even like it higher. Next they will tell us that the public thinks the crime rate is too low, or that the American people would really like to be in more auto accidents.

When Mises writes of public support for market economics, he is speaking on a different level. He is addressing the most basic ideological preferences of the public. What kind of society do we want to live in? One planned by government or one in which free individuals have control over the means of production and can accumulate wealth through serving the consuming public? A society in which the government confiscates income or one in which wealth can be passed to new generations? These are fundamental questions, and the ways they are answered really do determine, in the long run, how a political system is organized.

The public's passion for a free society was destroyed by the intellectual class of the Progressive era, and this culminated in a dramatic shift in public opinion during the 1930s, away from market economics and toward a planning mentality. The years between 1930 and the mid-1970s were characterized by a notable lack of support for freedom among the intellectual classes.

The glorious news that I can report to you today is that this has begun to change. When the Mises Institute was founded in 1982, I was thrilled to find even one student interested in the thought of Mises and Hayek and Rothbard. Today, we are overwhelmed, and even lack the resources to serve them all as we would like. And these are not marginal students but rather the best, the ones so smart that even their left-wing professors dare not dismiss them.

Since 1982, we have developed a massive network of dissident intellectuals to fight the socialistic status quo on campus. And what thrills me most is not the numbers—after all, more will attend this year's Socialist Scholars Conference than our own Austrian Scholars Conference—but rather the trend.

The energy, the excitement, the new ideas, and the genuine scholarship are all working in our direction. Meanwhile, the left is tired, spent, and increasingly desperate.

The obvious objection to my thesis is that the government is not getting any smaller. The regulators are on the march, and the judges are monsters. Never before in American history, outside of world war, has the government controlled so much of our lives and taken so much of our property.

All true: but let me tell you about an insight passed on to me by Yuri N. Maltsev, who worked as a Soviet economist during the Gorbachev era. Contrary to what the US press said at the time, the sheer viciousness of the State was more on display in the 1980s than under Brezhnev.

Gorbachev's antidrinking campaign alone led to mass spying, mass arrests, and mass confiscation of income. Huge vineyards were plowed under. Distilleries were destroyed. People were frogmarched through the streets and dragged into jail in public humiliation. Moreover, Gorbachev raised instead of lowered taxes. Managers were granted less, not more, autonomy.

Yuri says that it was precisely this step-up in enforcement that led to the downfall of the Soviet system. The public consensus for Soviet statism was no more, and in a few years the apparatus of socialism came tumbling down.

His point is that at the end times for a regime, we can expect it to behave like a wounded rat, more vicious in its death throes than in full health.

Does that consensus against government really exist today? The seeds are planted and growing, but we have much work to do. At the Mises Institute, we are convinced, as was Mises, that it is far more important to raise up a new class of intellectuals than it is to get the right people elected to office.

It is also important to teach businessmen that what they do as a matter of course is extremely beneficial to their fellow man. As Mises says,

> Economics must not be relegated to classrooms and statistical offices and must not be left to esoteric circles. It is the philosophy of human life and action and concerns everybody and everything. It is the pith of civilization and of man's human existence.

And it is the natural commercial and professional elites of society, working with a liberty-minded class of intellectuals, that will ultimately tip the balance in favor of freedom, and bring about the end of the interventionist State.

It was the genius of Mises that he could even imagine this possibility in the dark days in which he wrote his treatise. But he knew that society was the product of a body of ideas, and to his mind, it was an unfortunate but reversible reality of 1949 that the wrong intellectuals and the wrong ideas had triumphed.

From time to time, I hear freedom lovers despair over our supposed lack of progress and the unlikelihood of victory. But the evidence of our eventual triumph is all around us. Mises, the master economist who showed us the way, did not have the benefit of seeing what we see, and yet he never gave up hope and he never stopped working for freedom.

The members and faculty of the Mises Institute have a special understanding of what it will take to succeed, and what it will require to defend the basis of civilization against those who would destroy it. Therefore it is our moral obligation, it is our intellectual duty, it is our profound privilege, to carry on the work of Mises, and to make proper use of the rich treasury of knowledge he left us, for the advancement of human liberty.

AGAINST DESTRUCTIONISM

[The following speech was delivered on the Mises Institute's 20th anniversary celebration in Auburn, Alabama, October 19, 2002.]

How wonderful to be here with so many Members and supporters, scholars in our academic community, students whom the Mises Institute has backed now teaching yet another generation, so many friends of our work. It offers us all a chance to step back and observe what can be done for an ideal even now. And of course we recall those who gave so much but have since died, including Murray N. Rothbard, and, of course, Ludwig von Mises himself.

Mises ended his great book on *Socialism*, a scientific treatise on economics published in 1922, with a call for a moral crusade against what he decried as the ideology of destructionism. This was the theory of politics that claims to favor a better world, but is in fact the spoiler of what our forebears worked so long to create. Destructionism disparages commerce and bourgeois life, exalts the State, and rejects the proposition that the blessings of civilization have come from one source, and one source only: human freedom, with its inseparable twin, peace.

In the place of freedom and peace, destructionism gives us institutions that consume wealth, consume human energy, consume capital, consume lives, and drain away civilization.

Destructionism can take many forms, from terrorism to the construction of imperial States to taxation to the fomenting of war, for all these acts represent attacks on wealth, property, and life itself.

In light of the intellectual and political threat of destructionism, which Mises saw gathering momentum in the early 1920s, he wrote of our moral obligations:

> Everyone carries a part of society on his shoulders; no one is relieved of his share of responsibility by others. And no one can find a safe way out for himself if society is sweeping towards destruction. Therefore everyone, in his own interests, must thrust himself vigorously into the intellectual battle. None can stand aside with unconcern; the interests of everyone hang in the result. Whether he chooses or not, every man is drawn into the great historical struggle, the decisive battle into which our epoch has plunged us.

Five years ago, at our 15th anniversary, I would not have begun a talk with that quotation, because much seemed to be heading in the right direction. We were in the upswing of the business cycle, the president was a laughingstock—always a good sign for human freedom—and the forces of liberty were racing ahead of the forces of tyranny. Free enterprise was making great strides in Russia and China. Public pressure was mounting for an end to the permanence of the welfare-warfare state. There were political controversies and movements calling for expansion of government power, but they were struggling more than they had in decades.

But here we are today, two decades after the founding of the Mises Institute, and many of the externals have dramatically changed. The recession continues a full 18 months after the experts said it was over. Government spending is increasing at a rate not seen since the days of LBJ, and deficits are back. The forces of mercantilism and socio-economic regimentation are experiencing political success.

The attacks on commercial enterprise as a profession rival the anticapitalist hysteria of the 1930s. Since 9-11, the march toward government control in every area of life has continued steadily, and the pace is quickening. The world is on the brink of war that is guaranteed to not bring peace but only more conflict, domination, and hatred. Most alarmingly, public attitudes appear to trope less toward love of liberty and more toward fear, nationalism, and deference to the State. If you are not inclined to defer, you risk being called a traitor.

Indeed, for many of us, these are hard times, times that tempt us to despair. Is there still cause for hope? Yes, I believe so. I've lived long enough to see dramatic political changes appear seemingly out of nowhere. How great it was when the expectations of nearly all political thinkers and commentators—not to speak of economists like Paul Samuelson—were thwarted by the sudden and thrilling collapse of the seemingly impenetrable structure of the Soviet government and all its international holdings.

In our own country, we have seen a loss of faith in the ability of the government to manage our economy. Daily we watch the forces of economic law beat back the central planners. As Mises demonstrated, statism of all varieties is unstable because it wars against human choice, and, moreover, contains within itself the seeds of its own destruction. All of this points to the truth that it is always a great mistake to despair for human freedom, even at the darkest hour. Mises did not, and neither should we.

Yet we must be realistic. The long-term changes required to preserve and further release the blessings of liberty require massive amounts of work, not so much in politics but in the world of ideas. This work must be both broad and specific, academic and popular, scientific and rhetorical. We must work with students, faculty, pastors, businessmen, and citizens. The target audience for education must not be artificially limited but all-embracing.

I am fortunate to live and work in a sector of our world that does just that and thereby provides great hope for liberty and learning in our time. I speak of course of the Mises Institute, which—thanks to men and women like you—has made immense strides in two decades, and, along with the Institute, the intellectual framework that we have daily worked to help grow and thrive.

The Mises Institute was founded to correct one of the great oversights in the history of the 20th century: the neglect of the ideas of Ludwig von Mises, those of his followers, and the Austrian School tradition that they represent. This neglect was mainly the consequence of a political-ideological turn that began before Wilson's war and was sealed in the 1930s. The classical-liberal tradition in intellectual life had been in decline for decades, despite Mises's attempt to give it a more rigorous foundation, and with the Great Depression, an ancient and yet new ideology arose to fill the vacuum.

It was the ideology of statism, and it was born in opposition to the market economy and with a political agenda that targeted private property, freedom in commerce, and decentralized political institutions. It flourished in what is wrongly called the Progressive Era, and its proudest achievement was World War I, which destabilized the old order that had helped protect society from the wiles of political fanaticism. The war also showcased a model of central planning that would inspire generations of would-be despots.

The new ideology was not called statism. In each country in which the revolt against freedom took root, the ideology took on a different permutation. In Germany, it was National Socialism, which sold itself as the only viable alternative to Communism. Russian Communism itself enjoyed a new vogue, as Stalin discovered the political benefit of uniting Marxism with an old form of Russian nationalism and diplomatic overtures. In Italy, the new creed was nicely summed up by Mussolini: "everything within the State, nothing outside the State, nothing against the State."

The links among socialism, fascism, and political developments in the United States were not lost on the intelligentsia. In 1933, the same year that Franklin Delano Roosevelt abolished the gold standard, created the Tennessee Valley Authority, established the Civil Conservation Corp, and regimented industry under the National Industrial Recovery Act, the *New York Times Magazine* published glowing reports on the brilliance and vision of Professor Mussolini, even as academic treatises heralded the advances made by the central planning movement from Moscow, to Berlin, to Washington.

We must not flatter ourselves into thinking that the poison of totalitarian ideology infected only Russia and European states. What has happened in the United States differs in degree, not in kind. New Deal planners looked to Russia as a model for organizing the agricultural sector, and were inspired by an Italian fascist theoretician in imposing the NIRA and its Blue Eagle. And by way of further illustration, consider that in 1936, the economic treatise by English economist John Maynard Keynes that provided the economic rationale for the New Deal, appeared in Nazi Germany, with a preface by Keynes himself, in which he wrote:

> The theory of aggregate production, which is the point of the following book, nevertheless can be much easier adapted to the conditions of a totalitarian state than . . . conditions of free competition and a large degree of laissez-faire. This is one of the reasons that justifies the fact that I call my theory a *general* theory.

No matter what name it happened to be called in any particular country, statism was indeed the new "general theory" of world politics. The justifications and details matter far less than this general theme. It was the first time in history that the West had come to believe that the State and the State alone should be charged with complete control over society, economy, property, culture, family, and faith. The degree to which the full program of totalitarianism was to be put into effect was to be left to the discretion of political leadership, determined according to the circumstances of time and place.

Evaporating from view was another general theory, one that had developed over millennia and which achieved its scientific apogee in the work of Mises: I speak of the general theory of freedom. Seeing the likely absorption of his beloved home into the imperial Third Reich in 1934, he fled Austria for a safer academic position in Geneva and then, in 1940, racing with his wife Margit across France just in front of the advancing Nazi armies, escaped to Lisbon, and then the United States.

He had completed the great book that would later appear in English as *Human Action*. It is a brilliant work, perhaps the most important book written in the history of the social sciences. It would deserve to be studied and celebrated had it been written in any epoch, war or peace, freedom or tyranny.

But what is not often appreciated is that Mises wrote this treatise in a strange land at a time when the world he knew was falling apart, in the midst of the consuming fires of war, at a time when all the world agreed on little else but that freedom was a relic and the future belonged to the State.

The core thesis of his book was that government planning is a destructive force, and that civilization needs liberty *from* the State—any State, all States—to thrive. This argument ran contrary to all conventional wisdom, contrary to the approved doctrine of the smart set in Russia, England, France, Spain, Germany, Italy, and the United States.

Complicating matters, Mises had no assurance that his 1940 book would ever receive a wide circulation. There was no guarantee that the publisher could print enough copies to get it into academic libraries, or that the libraries would even be interested.

All of us are accustomed to looking for signs of hope in the political world, so that we might believe we have a prospect for success in our efforts, but there were few, if any, signs of hope for Mises, as he wrote those six long years in Geneva, among many signs of impending doom. Why did he continue? Because he believed it was the right thing to do, and because he knew that if he did not do it, it might not be done. He carried an immense weight on his shoulders because he believed that this was his calling as a scholar and a man.

Having completed his masterwork, and awaiting its publication, he began an aggressively political book designed for a larger audience, and it was completed in 1938. Its original title was, *In the Name of the State*. It summed up all political trends of the time. It was this work, written six years before Hayek's *Road to Serfdom*, that identified the essentially shared ideological traits of the nationalist socialism of the Nazi variety and international socialism of the Communist variety. The book would later appear in English as *Omnipotent Government: The Rise of the Total State and Total War*.

Setting sail for the United States in 1940, with no assurance of a teaching position, very little money, and facing a career in another land where statism had also clearly taken hold, any other intellectual might have despaired or even cracked under the pressure. Mises, instead, continued to work and write. He wrote an autobiography of his European years and essays on economics and politics, both popular and scientific. And when an opening appeared in the United States, he published in rapid succession *Omnipotent Government*, *Planned Chaos*, *Bureaucracy*, and, in 1949, *Human Action*.

Bureaucracy in particular is an interesting case because it was clearly designed, not just as an attack on European bureaucracy, but also on the US bureaucracy that was then exercising astonishing control over all aspects of American life for purposes of the war. Clearly, Mises's ideas were destined to be no more popular with the US regime than they were in

Austria during the vogue of Communism and the rise of the Nazis.

Mises never stopped working and teaching, even after his ideas stopped reaching a large audience, even after it appeared that old-style liberalism had no future, even after he had been declared to be wrong about socialism, even after he was refused the academic status that he deserved. In the course of two decades, he had vastly expanded his range of academic work, established economics on a sounder scientific foundation than it had ever had been, and stood up courageously to the most evil political trends of his time, perhaps all time.

He had done amazing and heroic things, accomplishments that made him worthy to be included among the great intellectuals in the history of ideas. And yet look what it got him: in those same two decades, he had gone from being a celebrated intellectual force on the Continent to becoming almost an invisible person in the world of ideas, without even a university-paid teaching post.

When his manuscript for *Human Action* was sent out for review from Yale University Press, the publisher received highly skeptical comments, even from Mises's own former students. Why would they fail to help him? Well, many of them had moved on to high academic posts after making their peace with Keynesianism. Mises's vision of a society and economy that organizes itself without the guidance of omnipotent government seemed hopelessly out of date, and an unwelcome reminder of the gullibility of a previous generation of social scientists. Mises was not on the cutting edge, they believed, and in a world of ideas driven more by politics than by the demands of truth, this was the worst thing one could say about him.

Recently an economist who works for a federal agency commented that when you look at Mises's career, and the nosedive it took after the Second World War, it is clear that Mises was his own worst enemy. This economist suggested that if Mises had played his cards right, not been so dogmatic about his principles, had been more sensitive to the ideological constraints of his time, and had been less aggressively critical of the planning State, he would have done better in his career.

In one sense, this critic is right: Mises was surely aware that he was not advancing himself, and that every manuscript he produced, every book that came to print, was harming his career ever more. But he didn't back off. Instead he chose to do the rarest thing of all in academia: he chose to tell the truth regardless of the cost, regardless of the trends, regardless of how it would play with the powers that be.

Mises might have been his own worst enemy in terms of his professional career, that's true, but he was the friend of truth, of morality, of intellectual integrity, of principled attachments to certain fixed ideals. It seems to me that if we are going to place blame for the awful reality that one of the century's greatest intellectuals received such shabby treatment, it should not be with the man who dared to tell the truth, but with those who tried to make him go away precisely because they did not want to hear the truth or did not understand it.

Did Mises feel remorse about the manner in which he managed his career? In a posthumously published memoir, he repented only of one thing: what he thought of as his willingness to compromise! Never did he regret his intransigence.

The traits that led Mises to do what he did are so rare in academia that they cry out for an explanation. Murray Rothbard once wrote an essay in which he grappled with the issue of why some academics ride with the tide of politics or just keep their heads down during a storm, and why others stand up against trends, take political and personal risks, and fight. In this essay, Rothbard concludes that we cannot fully explain it:

> In the ultimate sense . . . no outside person, no historian, no psychologist, can fully explain the mystery of each individual's free choice of values and actions. There is no way that we can fully comprehend why one man trims his sails to the prevailing winds, why he "goes along to get along" in the infamous phrase, while another will pursue and champion the truth regardless of cost. . . .
>
> Economic science may be value-free, but men can never be, and Ludwig von Mises never shirked the responsibilities of being human.

As for Mises and his school of old-style liberalism, they did begin a long period of decline after World War II. But in considering the intellectual history of the last 50 years, I've long been struck by the place of Murray Rothbard in the constellation of events. Along with a handful of other academics during the late 1950s and early 1960s, he chose an intellectual path very different from his contemporaries. Rather than go along with the prevailing trends, he charted a different course, one that followed in the tradition of Mises, knowing full well that the choice was an enormously costly one.

When I think of Murray before his much-welcomed appointment to a named chair at the University of Nevada, Las Vegas, I think of him at Brooklyn Polytechnic, in an office smaller than the sound booth at the back of this room, trying to support a wife in Manhattan on a salary of $26,000 per year. With degrees in mathematics and economics from Columbia, and a vita that included a major economic treatise written before the age of 35, he was not lacking in academic credentials or accomplishments. What he lacked was a willingness to go along. Once having charted an independent course, with full knowledge of where it would land him, he never complained and never looked back.

From his tiny office, he reconstructed the historiography of the American Colonial experience, rewrote American banking history, founded modern libertarianism, extended the theoretical dimensions of the Misesian paradigm, wrote the first general treatise on economics since *Human Action*, pioneered a new typology of interventionism, pushed out the boundaries of the theory of the free society, corresponded with hundreds of intellectuals around the world, and spread his effective help and good cheer and optimistic outlook as widely as he could. Though he was never in a position where he could direct PhD dissertations, he had wide influence through his books and his personal friendships.

Rothbard faced dangerous trends in public life and battled them heroically. In his youth, he saw positivism and Keynesianism become the dominant paradigms in economic theory, and he set out to combat them. At the same time, the intellectual basis of American conservatism underwent a shift from a love of American liberty to an embrace of the warfare state and even the welfare state. He eventually became known as the State's greatest living enemy. And we know the fate of such people in all times.

But he never gave up. In fact, anyone who knew Murray will tell you that his life was filled with joy, in public and private. Always optimistic about the prospects for liberty, he relished every intellectual battle and inspired every student with whom he came in contact to take up the cause, and become an enthusiastic and relentless scholar for liberty.

Later, he helped the Mises Institute get its start, founded a new journal, wrote a massive history of economic thought, and dedicated himself to securing a place for the Austro-libertarian and Misesian schools in academia. We might ask what would have happened to the Misesian legacy—indeed the cause of liberty itself—had he not dedicated himself so completely to the task.

Conjectural history is always risky business, but I think we can say for sure that the Austrian School, not to speak of the Mises Institute, would not be what they are today, and a hope for the future of freedom would not be so much in evidence.

I single out these two men, not because they are the only ones, but because they are exemplars in how to conduct one's life in the face of adversity and very long odds. We gather here tonight facing similarly long odds, and we are all too aware of this fact.

I am often asked what the Mises Institute hopes to accomplish. Both Mises and Rothbard were undoubtedly asked the same question. I think their answer would have been very simple: they hoped to write what is true and do what is right, and to do it with enthusiasm and vigor. As an Institute, we have hoped to create opportunities for other intellectuals in this tradition to do the same. If we do nothing else, that is enough. And yet, it is everything.

It is often said of the Mises Institute what was said of Mises: we are our own worst enemy. We don't have many friends among the powerful. We do not court the media. We do not bend the knee to the political class. We refuse to buy into the political choices the regime presents us. Our intellectual ambitions are deeply contrary to the current trends.

We can plead guilty on every point. The Mises Institute was founded to carry out his vision of an independent source of intellectual support for young minds that have academic vocations. I think of the institute in Geneva that took in Mises during those hard times, when academia was so politicized that an entire generation had to find somewhere to practice the vocations of research and writing. In Geneva, there was sanctuary. In some ways today, the Mises Institute serves a similar role, and that role as a sanctuary could become more important in the days ahead.

As for our teaching programs, the goal has never been to indoctrinate anyone, but rather to make sure that young freedom-minded intellectuals receive the backing, encouragement, and teaching they need to pursue a rich life of writing and research. Their influence works toward overturning the reigning intellectual paradigm.

The Mises Institute has worked to bring this about, and today, the Institute is a life-support system for the worldwide libertarian movement, the top source for scholarship in the tradition of the Austrian School, the leading publisher of free-market materials, and a promoter of the best new books on history, economics, and philosophy.

Have we made a difference? There can be no doubt. Working one-on-one for two decades, the influence of the Institute has been growing exponentially. Whereas we were once grateful to place one new faculty member per year, such placements are now so common that we can barely track them all. Whereas we once took a leap of faith with every teaching conference we scheduled, we now enjoy the luxury of select-ing from the piles of applications for every program we offer. And many of our best applicants are students of our former students, now teaching.

Our journals and books achieve a wider circulation than ever before. Mises.org is indisputably the most highly-traf-ficked, market-oriented research site on the Web, easily beat-ing any comparable organization in the world and crushing even mainstream professional associations. Academic honors granted by our faculty are highly regarded the world over. And most incredibly of all, association with the Mises Institute has become an asset even in job searches.

We couldn't be more pleased about the progress so far, and it inspires us to look to the next 20 years, which are cru-cial. Many of the most hard-core socialists now teaching will be retiring. Many others will just lose faith in their ideals. The question is: what worldview, what theory of economics, what political ideal, will replace what the left once held out as a model? The Austrian School, in the tradition of Mises and Rothbard, offers precisely the radical and attractive alterna-tive.

Every day we see minds being changed. Three years ago, it was hard to find economists at major investment houses who even noticed Austrian business cycle theory. Today, many of the top ones are busy educating themselves. So too in departments of finance, economics, philosophy, history, and political theory. In the marketplace of ideas, our ideas are on the march. The journals, the books, the students, the daily hard work of our faculty and staff, all add up to create something much larger than the sum of its parts, and much larger than we ever dreamed all those years ago.

Anyone who works with or for the Mises Institute can confirm that our goal was never growth alone, never attention alone, never public relations alone, never large conferences alone. We never set out to build a great institution as an end in itself. The goal, the driving passion, of the Mises Institute has been to create the conditions for truth to be told, to make available a setting where freedom is valued and practiced.

If there is anything to be said for the difficult times in which we live, it is that they are a reminder that our mission is far from complete. The forces of destructionism are always waiting for an opportunity to rob us of the blessings of civilization. They do not always hail from far-flung terror groups. Many are tenured in American universities. Many work as editors and producers in our nation's media. Many hold high positions in government. Mises believed that the best way to defeat them was to say what is true. Against the idea of liberty, he said, the fiercest sword of the despot is finally powerless.

The many supporters of the Mises Institute are what make it possible. How grateful we are to them, and to all of you here tonight, and to the thousands of others, from around the country and the world, who are with us in spirit.

All have dedicated themselves to achieving what may appear improbable. To seek such a thing requires a leap of faith. But it is precisely those who take that leap who represent the best hope for the future of the world. As we look to the next 20 years, thanks to the Mises Institute and those who support her, we need not despair, but rather look to a future in which liberty and learning triumph against all odds.

Your faith is evidence of freedom unseen, but, God willing, our children, their children, and every generation after, will live and breathe it. May they never take it for granted.

4. Ideas

An American Classical Liberalism

[This talk was delivered at the Scott L. Probasco Chair of Free Enterprise Seminar on Classical Liberalism, University of Tennessee, Chattanooga, June 6, 1996.]

Every four years, as the November presidential election draws near, I have the same daydream: that I don't know or care who the president of the United States is. More importantly, I don't need to know or care. I don't have to vote or even pay attention to debates. I can ignore all campaign commercials. There are no high stakes for my family or my country. My liberty and property are so secure that, frankly, it doesn't matter who wins. I don't even need to know his name.

In my daydream, the president is mostly a figurehead and a symbol, almost invisible to myself and my community. He has no public wealth at his disposal. He administers no regulatory departments. He cannot tax us, send our children into foreign wars, pass out welfare to the rich or the poor, appoint judges to take away our rights of self-government, control a central bank that inflates the money supply and brings on the business cycle, or change the laws willy-nilly according to the special interests he likes or seeks to punish.

His job is simply to oversee a tiny government with virtually no power except to arbitrate disputes among the states, which are the primary governmental units. He is head of state, though never head of government. His position, in fact, is one of constant subordination to the office holders around him and the thousands of statesmen on the state and local level. He adheres to a strict rule of law and is always aware that anytime he transgresses by trying to expand his power, he will be impeached as a criminal.

But impeachment is not likely, because the mere threat reminds him of his place. This president is also a man of outstanding character, well respected by the natural elites in society, a person whose integrity is trusted by all who know him, who represents the best of what an American is.

The president can be a wealthy heir, a successful businessman, a highly educated intellectual, or a prominent farmer. Regardless, his powers are minimal. He has a tiny staff, which is mostly consumed with ceremonial matters like signing proclamations and scheduling meetings with visiting heads of state.

The presidency is not a position to be avidly sought but almost granted as honorary and temporary. To make sure that is the case, the person chosen as vice president is the president's chief political adversary. The vice president therefore serves as a constant reminder that the president is eminently replaceable. In this way, the vice presidential office is very powerful, not with regard to the people, but in keeping the executive in check.

But as for people like me who have concerns besides politics, it matters little who the president is. He doesn't affect my life one way or the other. Neither does anyone under his control. His authority is mainly social, and derived from how much the natural elites in society respect him. This authority is lost as easily as it is gained, so it is unlikely to be abused.

This man is elected indirectly, with the electors chosen as the states direct, with only one proviso: no elector may be a federal official. In the states that choose their electors by majority vote, not every citizen or resident can participate. The people who do vote, a small percentage of the population, are those who have the best interests of society at heart. They are those who own property, who head households, and have been educated. These voters choose a man whose job it is to think only of the security, stability, and liberty of his country.

For those who do not vote and do not care about politics, their liberty is secure. They have no access to special rights, yet their rights to person, property, and self-government are never in doubt. For that reason and for all practical purposes, they can forget about the president and, for that matter, the rest of the federal government. It might as well not exist. People do not pay direct taxes to it. It doesn't tell them how to conduct their lives. It doesn't send them to foreign wars, regulate their schools, pay for their retirement, much less employ them to spy on their fellow citizens. The government is almost invisible.

The political controversies that involve me tend to be at the level of the city, town, or state. This is true for all issues, including taxes, education, crime, welfare, and even immigration. The only exception is the general defense of the nation, although the standing military is very small with large state-based militias in case of need. The president is commander in chief of the federal armed forces, but this is a minor position absent a congressional declaration of war. It requires no more than insuring the impenetrability of the borders by foreign attackers, a relatively easy task considering our geography and the ocean that separates us from the incessant feuding of the old world.

In my daydream, there are two types of representatives in Washington: members of the House of Representatives, a huge body of statesmen that grows larger as the population does, and a Senate elected by state legislatures. The House works to keep the federal Senate in check, and the Senate works to keep the executive in check.

Legislative power over the public is nearly nonexistent. Congressmen have little incentive to increase that power, because they themselves are real citizens. My House member lives within a square mile of my house. He is my neighbor and my friend. I do not know my federal senator, and do not need to, because he is responsible to the state legislators I do know.

Thus, in my daydream, there is virtually nothing at stake in this coming presidential election. No matter which way it goes, I retain my liberty and my property.

The politics of this country is extremely decentralized, but the community is united by an economy that is perfectly free and a system of trading that allows people to voluntarily associate, innovate, save, and work based on mutual benefit. The economy is not controlled, hindered, or even influenced by any central command.

People are allowed to keep what they earn. The money they use to trade is solid, stable, and backed by gold. Capitalists can start and close businesses at will. Workers are free to take any job they want at any wage or any age. Businesses have only two goals: to serve the consumer and make a profit.

There are no labor controls, mandated benefits, payroll taxes, or other regulations. For this reason, everyone specializes in what he does best, and the peaceful exchanges of voluntary enterprise cause ever-widening waves of prosperity throughout the country.

What shape the economy takes—whether agricultural, industrial, or high-tech—is of no concern to the federal government. Trade is allowed to take place naturally and freely, and everyone understands that it should be managed by property holders, not office holders. The federal government couldn't impose internal taxes if it wanted to, much less taxes on income, and trade with foreign nations is rivalrous and free.

If by chance this system of liberty begins to break down, my own political community—the state in which I live—has an option: to separate from the federal government, form a new government, and join other states in this effort. The law of the land is widely understood as allowing secession. That was part of the guarantee required to make the federation possible to begin with. And from time to time, states threaten to secede, just as a way of showing the federal government who's boss.

This system reinforces the fact that the president is not the president of the American people, much less their commander in chief, but merely the president of the United States. He serves only with their permission and only as the largely symbolic head of this voluntary union of prior political communities. This president could never make light of the rights of the states, much less violate them in practice, because he would be betraying his oath of office and risk being tossed out on his ear.

In this society without central management, a vast network of private associations serves as the dominant social authority. Religious communities wield vast influence over public and private life, as do civic groups and community leaders of all sorts. They create a huge patchwork of associations and a true diversity in which every individual and group finds a place.

This combination of political decentralization, economic liberty, free trade, and self-government creates, day by day, the most prosperous, diverse, peaceful, and just society the world has ever known.

Is this a utopia? Actually, it is nothing more than the result of my initial premise: that the president of the United States is so restricted that it is not even important that I know who he is. This means a free society that is not managed by anyone but its members in their capacities as citizens, parents, workers, and entrepreneurs.

As you may have already assumed, my daydream is what our system was designed to be in every detail. It was created by the US Constitution, or, at least, the system that the vast majority of Americans believed they were getting with the US Constitution. It was the world's great free republic, however unrecognizable it is today.

This was the country where people were to govern themselves and to plan their own economy, not have it planned by Washington, DC. The president never concerned himself with the welfare of the American people because the federal government had no say over it. That was left to the people's political communities of choice.

Before the Constitution was ratified, there were some doubters called the anti-federalists. They were unhappy with any move away from the extreme decentralism of the Articles of Confederation. To placate their fears, and to ensure that the federal government was held in check, the framers further restricted its powers with the Bill of Rights. This list was not designed to restrict the rights of the states. It did not even apply to them. It confined to the ultimate extent what the central government could do to individuals and to their communities.

As de Tocqueville observed about America even as late as the 1830s,

> [i]n some countries a power exists which, though it is in a degree foreign to the social body, directs it, and forces it to pursue a certain track. In others the ruling force is divided, being partly within and partly without the ranks of the people. But nothing of the kind is to be seen in the United States; there society governs itself for itself.

and "scarcely an individual is to be met with who would venture to conceive or, still less, to express the idea" of any other system.

As for the presidency itself, de Tocqueville wrote that, "the power of that office is temporary, limited, and subordinate" and

> [n]o candidate has as yet been able to arouse the dangerous enthusiasm or the passionate sympathies of the people in his favor, for the simple reason that when he is at the head of the government, he has but little power, little wealth, and little glory to share among his friends; and his influence in the state is too small for the success or the ruin of a faction to depend upon his elevation to power.

That America would never have tolerated such an atrocity as the Americans with Disabilities Act. Here is a law that governs the way every local public building in America must be structured. It holds a veto power over every employment decision in the country. It mandates that people take no account of other people's abilities in daily economic affairs. All of this is arbitrarily enforced by an army of permanent bureaucrats working with lawyers who get rich quick if they know how to manipulate the system.

The ADA is merely one example among tens of thousands that would have been considered appalling, and, indeed, unimaginable, by the framers. It's not because they didn't like handicapped people or thought that people should be discriminated for or against. It is because they held to a philosophy of government and public life that excluded even the possibility of such a law. That philosophy was called liberalism.

In the 18th and 19th centuries, the term liberalism generally meant a philosophy of public life that affirmed the following principle: societies and all their component parts need no central management and control because societies generally manage themselves through the voluntary interaction of its members to their mutual benefit. Today we cannot call this philosophy liberalism because the term has been appropriated by the democratic totalitarians. In an attempt to recover this philosophy for our own time, we give it a new name, classical liberalism.

Classical liberalism means a society in which my day-dream is a reality. We don't need to know the president's name. The outcome of elections is largely irrelevant, because society is ruled by laws and not men. We don't fear the government because it takes nothing from us, gives nothing to us, and leaves us alone to shape our own lives, communities, and futures.

This vision of government and public life has been destroyed in our country and in almost every country in the world. In our case, the president of the US is not only extremely powerful, especially given all the executive agencies he controls; he is probably the most powerful man on earth—excepting, of course, the chairman of the Federal Reserve Board.

There is a public myth in this country that the office of the presidency sanctifies the man. For all the browbeating that Richard Nixon took as president, and the humiliation of his resignation, the testimonials and tribute at his funeral spoke of a man who had ascended to godlike status, like some Roman emperor. Even with all of Clinton's troubles, I have no doubt that he would be treated the same way. This sanctification process applies even to cabinet appointees: Ron Brown, a corrupt fixer, ascended to godhood status despite the fact that his legal troubles were on their way to sweeping him into jail.

Of course my comments might be denounced as antigovernment. We are told on a daily basis that people who are antigovernment are a public menace. But as Jefferson wrote in the Kentucky Resolutions, free government is founded in jealousy, and not in confidence. "In questions of power, then, let no more be heard about confidence in man, but bind him down from mischief with the chains of the Constitution." Or as Madison said in the *Federalist*, "All men having power ought to be distrusted to a certain degree." We can add that any government that employs three million people, most of them armed to the teeth, ought to be distrusted to an enormous degree. This is an attitude cultivated by the classical liberal mind, which puts a premium on the liberty of individuals and communities to control their own lives.

We could multiply the "antigovernment" statements by the framers without end. For they spelled out their theory of public affairs, that of classical liberalism, because in the mid- and late-18th century, it had come under fire by a new brand of absolutism, and Rousseau was its prophet. In his view, a democratic government embodied the general will of the people, this will was always right, and therefore government should have absolute, centralized power over a militarized and unified egalitarian nation-State.

This has been Rousseau's century. And with the help of the statist doctrines of Marx and Keynes, it has also been the bloodiest in human history. Their views of government are the very opposite of the classical liberal. They allege that society cannot run itself; instead the general will, the interests of the proletariat, or the economic plans of the people need to be organized and embodied in the nation and its head. This is a view of government that the framers rightly saw as despotic, and tried to prevent from taking root here.

Of course, they were not entirely successful. Two centuries of war, economic crisis, wrongheaded constitutional amendments, executive usurpation, congressional surrender, and judicial imperialism gave rise to a form of government that is the opposite of the framers' design, and the opposite of classical liberalism. The ability of the federal government, with the president as its head, to tax, regulate, control, and completely dominate national life is practically without limit today.

When the Constitution was written, Washington, DC was a marshy cow pasture with a couple of buildings, and American society was the freest in the world. Today, the DC metropolitan area is the richest on the face of the earth because it is host to the biggest government in the world.

The US government has more people, resources, and powers at its disposal than any other. It regulates more and in finer detail than any government on the planet. Its military empire is the largest and the most far-flung in the history of the world. Its annual tax take dwarfs the total output of, for example, the old Soviet Union.

As for the federal system, it is more a slogan than a reality. From time to time, we hear about returning power to the states or banning unfunded mandates. Bob Dole says he carries a copy of the Tenth Amendment in his pocket. But don't take this rhetoric too seriously. The states are virtual adjuncts of national power, by virtue of the mandates they are under, the bribes they accept, and the programs they run.

The individual, the family, and the community—the essential units of society in the pre-statist era—have been reduced to federal serfs, having only the freedoms the government allows them to have, but otherwise required to act as part of an overall national collectivist order. No major national political figure proposes to change that.

The reality, however, is that people are not satisfied with this arrangement. During the Cold War, the public was persuaded to hand over a surprising amount of their freedoms for the sake of the larger mission of rolling back Communism. Before that, it was World War II, then the Depression, then World War I. For only the second time in this century, we live in absence of any crisis the government can use to suppress the rights the framers intended to guarantee.

As a result, public opinion now overwhelmingly favors reductions in government power. Practically every politician in this country who wins an election has promised to do something about it. That goes for both major parties. This year, both Clinton and Dole will run on platforms that promise, in one way or another, to reduce the size and scope of federal power.

If we think back to November 1994, we heard some of the most radical anti-Washington rhetoric from politicians since 1776. Unlike the media, I found this to be a wonderful thing. The results, however, were less than impressive. Taxes and spending are higher since the Republicans took over. The foreign aid budget is up. The regulatory State is more invasive than ever. The centerpieces of the Republican legislative agenda—including the farm bill, the adoption bill, and the medical bill—expand, not shrink, government power.

There are many reasons for this, not the least of which is the duplicity of the congressional leadership and the talents of their allies in the conservative press, who give them an ideological cover. Yet the freshmen themselves, whom the media describe as ideological firebrands, deserve some of the blame, for they lacked a consistent philosophical logic to oppose the monster they encountered.

Consider for example the issue of the balanced budget. Every politician claims to want one. The freshmen promised to vote for one. But they were immediately snookered by the political class. When they wanted to cut taxes, the elites pounced on them and said that this would increase the deficit. Immediately, they were confronted with a problem: how to reconcile their fiscal conservatism with their desire for lower taxes?

This confusion results from intellectual error. The priority is to shrink government. That means taxes should be cut anywhere and everywhere. And well-schooled classical liberals know that governments can use the trick of balanced budgets to keep themselves large and growing. Higher taxes do not typically lessen the deficit, and even if they did, that is no way for men of honor to proceed. The federal budget is not a household's writ large. It is a giant redistribution racket.

This fact raises a central insight of the classical-liberal intellectual tradition. Government has no power and no resources that it doesn't first take from the people. Unlike private enterprise, it cannot produce anything. Whatever it has, it must extract from private enterprise. Although this was understood well in the 18th century, and most of the 19th as well, it has been largely forgotten in our century of socialism and statism, of Nazism, Communism, New Dealism, welfarism, and total war.

As we approach the next century, what lessons have we learned from this one? The most important refutation of socialism came from Ludwig von Mises in 1922. His treatise called *Socialism* converted good people away from bad doctrines, and was never refuted by any of the thousands of Marxists and statists who tackled it. For this book, he is now hailed as a prophet even by lifelong social democrats who spent years attacking and smearing him.

Much less well known is another treatise which appeared three years later. This was his great book *Liberalism*. Once having attacked all-out statism, he found it necessary to spell out the alternative. It was the first full-scale revival of the classical-liberal program in many decades, this time from the leading political economist on the continent.

In his introduction, Mises noted that the 18th and 19th century version of liberalism had made a mistake. It had attempted to speak not only to the material world, but also to spiritual matters. Typically, the liberals had positioned themselves against the church, which had the unfortunate effect of influencing the church against the free market and free trade.

To try to avoid this polarizing effect, Mises makes clear that liberalism

> is a doctrine directed entirely towards the conduct of men in this world . . . it has nothing else in view than the advancement of their outward, material welfare and does not concern itself directly with their inner, spiritual and metaphysical needs.

Of course men's lives concern more than eating and drinking and gaining material advancement. That is why liberalism does not pretend to be a full-blown theory of life. For that reason, it cannot be reproached by theologians and conservatives for being a purely secular ideology. It is secular only in the sense that it deals with matters appropriate to the political world, and no more. There is nothing in the liberalism of Mises to which any religious person should object, provided that he agrees that the material advancement of society is not morally objectionable.

Another change Mises made in traditional liberal doctrine was to link it directly to the capitalist economic order. Too often the older liberalism offered a magnificent defense of free speech and the free press, but neglected the all-important economic dimension.

Mises's direct linkage of liberalism and capitalism also helped divorce the liberal position from the fraudulent form that was emerging in Europe and America. This phony liberalism claimed that there was some way to favor both civil liberties and socialism, as the ACLU said then and now.

But as Mises argued, liberty is all of a piece. If the government is big and powerful enough to stamp out the freedom to trade, to inflate the money, or to fund massive public works, it is no large step to also control speech and press, and to engage in military adventures abroad.

Thus Mises's most famous line from his book, the one that both alarmed and inspired intellectuals the world over: "The program of liberalism," if "condensed into a single word, would have to read: property." By property, Mises meant not only its private ownership at all levels of society, but also its control by those same owners.

With that one demand, that property and its control be kept in private hands, we can see how the State must necessarily be radically limited. If the government can only work with resources it takes from others, and if all resources are owned and controlled by private parties, the government is restricted.

If private property is secure, we can count on all other aspects of society to be free and prosperous. Society cannot manage itself unless its members own and control property; or, conversely, if property is in the hands of the State, it will manage society with the catastrophic results we know so well.

If property rights are strictly guarded, the State cannot take advantage of social crises to seize power, as it has during wars, depressions, and natural disasters. The limits on government apply regardless. There are no exceptions. Thus a classical-liberal society would not have built the TVA, it would not bail out Texas farmers in a drought, it would not send men on space missions, and it would not have taxed Americans six trillion dollars and poured it into a failed war on poverty.

The second pillar of the liberal society, Mises says, is freedom. This means that people are not slaves of each other or of the government, but are self-owners who are at liberty to pursue their interests so long as they do not violate the property rights of others. Most importantly, all workers are free to work in the profession of their choice, establishing free contracts with employers or becoming employers themselves.

Combining liberty and property, people are able to exercise the all-important right of exclusion. I can keep you off my property. You can keep me off yours. You do not have to trade with me. I do not have to trade with you. This right of exclusion, along with the right to trade generally, is a key to social peace. If we cannot choose the form and manner of our associations, we are not free in any authentic sense.

The breakdown of the freedom of association, especially in the form of antidiscrimination law, is a main reason why social acrimony has so increased in our time. Although hardly ever questioned, antidiscrimination law cannot be reconciled with the classical-liberal view of society. No association that is forced can ever be good for the parties involved or society at large.

Any discussion of this subject invariably raises the issue of equality. And here we find yet another improvement that Mises made over earlier models of liberalism. They were too much in love with the idea of equality, not only as a legal construct, but also in hoping and working for a society without classes, which is nonsensical.

As Mises said, "All human power would be insufficient to make men really equal. Men are and will always remain unequal." He argued that people cannot be given equal wealth or even equal opportunity to become wealthy. The best society can do for its members is to establish rules that apply across the board. These rules do not exempt anyone, including the rulers in government.

The very rich will always be with us, thank goodness, and so will the very poor. These concepts are bound up with particular societies and settings, of course, but from the standpoint of policy, they are best ignored. It is the job of charity, not government, to care for the poor, and to protect them from being drafted into demagogic political campaigns that threaten essential liberties.

Government in a liberal society does not protect individuals from themselves, strive for a particular distribution of wealth, promote any particular region or technology or group, or delineate the distinction between peaceful vices and virtues. The central government does not manage society or economy in any respect.

The third pillar of classical liberalism is peace. This means that there can be no love of war, and, when it occurs, it cannot be seen as heroic, but only as tragic for everyone. Yet we continue to hear how war is good for the economy, even though it always and everywhere misdirects resources and destroys them. Even the victor, Mises pointed out, loses. For "war," said Randolph Bourne, "is the health of the state."

So is empire. Americans opposed an alien Soviet presence in our hemisphere. Yet we never consider how people in Japan, to take just one example, may feel about large numbers of American troops in their country. By far the largest cause of crime in Okinawa and the rest of Japan is American troops. But do our troops and planes and ships and nuclear weapons "defend" Japan? From whom? No, we continue to occupy the country 51 years after the end of World War II for purposes of control.

If you want to discover the real character of a man, forget about what he says about himself, and look at his dealings with other people. The same is true of a government. We can forget its claims; simply look at how it treats others. The classical-liberal state is one that protects the rights of its citizens to trade with foreign peoples. It does not pine for foreign conflicts of any kind. It does not, for example, demand that foreign countries buy the products of influential US manufacturers, as Kodak is demanding, backed by US military power, that Japan buy its film.

Neither does the truly liberal society send government aid to foreign countries, bribe or arrest or kill their rulers, tell other governments what kind of country they should have, or get involved in global schemes to impose welfare rights on the world. Yet these are all actions the US has undertaken as normal policy since the 1930s. Our rulers seem to think that they must be bribing someone, bombing someone, or both. Otherwise we risk falling into the dreaded "isolationism."

Jonathan Kwitney illustrated American foreign policy this way: he asks us to imagine that every few months we take a walk down the block, knocking on every door. At one house, we announce to our neighbor, "I like you, I approve of you, here's $1,000." At the next house, we do the same thing. But at the third house, we say, "I don't like you, I don't approve of you." Then we reach under our coat, pull out a sawed-off 12 gauge shotgun, and blow him and his family away.

So we go, down the block, every few months, handing out money to some people, death to others, and making our decisions based on the interests we have at the moment, with no clear rules.

My guess is that we would not be very popular. Think about that the next time you see some "anti-American" rally on television. These people might be receiving our foreign aid, but they might also think they could be the next Iraq, Haiti, Somalia, or Panama. For a classical-liberal foreign policy is no foreign policy at all, except, as George Washington said, of commerce with all and belligerence toward none.

These three elements—property, freedom, and peace—are the basis of the liberal program. They are the core of a philosophy that can restore our lost prosperity and social stability. Yet I have only begun to scratch the surface of the liberal program. There is more to be said about monetary policy, about trade treaties, about social insurance schemes, and so much else. Yet if our political class could understand this core of freedom, property, and peace, we would be much better off, and I would feel more confident that the next class of freshmen we send to Washington would keep their eye on the prize, which is not redistribution or special rights, but liberty.

"Liberalism," Mises wrote,

> seeks to give men only one thing, the peaceful, undisturbed development of material well-being for all, in order thereby to shield them from the external causes of pain and suffering as far as it lies within the power of social institutions to do so at all. To diminish suffering, to increase happiness: that is its aim.

Would classical liberalism work in our time? Think about the contentious issues in society today. Every one involves some area of life that is wrapped up in some form of government intervention. Today's conflicts revolve around the desire to grab hold of someone else's property using the political apparatus of compulsion that is the State. Would our society be more peaceful and prosperous if it followed the liberal program? The question answers itself.

Now back to my daydream. I don't know or care about presidential politics because they don't matter either way. My liberty and property are so secure that, frankly, it doesn't matter who wins. But to arrive at this goal, none of us can eschew the political or intellectual battles of our time. Even once the classical-liberal vision has been restored in this country, as I believe it can and will be, we cannot afford to rest.

Goethe's Prometheus cries:

Do you fancy that I should hate life,
Should flee to the wilderness,
Because not all my budding dreams have blossomed?

And Faust answers with his "last word of wisdom":

No man deserves his freedom or his life
Who does not daily win them anew.

IN DEFENSE OF PUBLIC INTELLECTUALS

[Adapted from an address on the dedication of the Mises Institute's
new campus, Auburn, Alabama, September 28, 2001.]

In the last two weeks, I've heard some people comment that this is a difficult time to be a libertarian. I disagree. The events of September 11 and its aftermath only reinforce the case for a free society, a point to which I will return shortly. What is difficult is to defend freedom and peace when everyone around you is crying out for unprecedented statism, central planning, and ever more bloodshed. Indeed, many public intellectuals, backed by the enormous megaphone of the mass media and the immense power of the State, have used the occasion of the attack to call effectively for the end of freedom itself.

The chorus went like this. The reality of September 11 suggests that there are some values, namely security and unity, that are more important than liberty and rights. Our predilection for liberty presupposes that people are basically well intentioned. Because we have come face to face with evil, an evil from which only public authority can protect us, we must now recognize that our attachment to liberty is anachronistic, even dangerous, even life threatening.

Consider Francis Fukuyama's comments. "Peace and prosperity," he theorized,

> encourage preoccupation with one's own petty affairs and allow people to forget that they are parts of larger communities. [During] the long economic boom . . . many Americans lost interest in public affairs, and in the larger world beyond its borders; others expressed growing contempt for government. . . . In this respect, the September 11 attacks on Wall Street were a salutary lesson.

Now, Fukuyama may find people's desire to be free and to be able to provide a good life for themselves and their families to be petty. He is, after all, part of an intellectual tradition that longs for the reinvention of the pre-Christian, Greco-Roman *polis*, in which State and society are one, where individual rights are unknown, where the merchant class is expendable, and where the head of State becomes a god after his death. But it is the later ideas of liberty and individual rights, and the free-enterprise economy that are implied by both, that are the very foundation of the rise of Western civilization.

It is this freedom that makes authentic community, based on voluntarism and contract, possible in the first place. To provide for ourselves materially means to build family security, purchase the best education and medical care for our children, invest in new businesses that serve people with ever-better goods and services, give to charity and educational causes, fund the arts, and have time and space for the contemplative life. Prosperity is not a petty concern but the very pith of what it means to thrive and grow in peace.

The social cooperation engendered in the market economy is not only local but international, and symbolized by the activities that went on in the World Trade Center towers. Here were people who, in pursuit of their allegedly petty affairs, managed to facilitate trade and cooperation among two hundred countries and just as many language groups and currencies, and also to make a profit by doing so. Government has nowhere accomplished any of the miracles that are the daily business of free enterprise.

I would gladly compare the creative productivity of any business in the world to the goings-on in the highest councils of any government. If you have ever examined government closely, you know that the ideal of the all-encompassing *polis* as the ancients conceived it is actually a horror; any attempt to reimpose it, using wartime as the excuse, would result in a massive reduction in freedom, a trampling on human rights, further invasion of family and property, and a complete repudiation of everything the founders of this country worked to achieve.

But in these times, many are prepared to do just that. Letters to the editor of the *New York Times* scream that taxes must be raised, industry must be nationalized, privacy must be ended, and citizens conscripted. They say we should rally around the flag, and in doing so abolish everything that is good and right and true about America.

Yet that view was widely held long before the attack. Partisans of the statist model have been saying exactly this for centuries. Whether war or peace, prosperity or poverty, security or anxiety, there are some people who always find a good reason to justify Hegel's conception of the State as God walking on earth.

When prosperity and security prevail, they say we are losing our sense of civic duty and need the State to restore it. They claim that the State must grow in order to check our natural tendencies to focus selfishly on ourselves and our families. In peace, they say we need the State to prevent war. In war, they say the State is the only answer. In times of crisis and upheaval, they see the answer as nothing short of what Mises called "omnipotent government," total war and total State. For many of these intellectuals, there is never a good time for freedom and peace. For them, the State must always be on the move, or history is regressing.

And make no mistake: the logic of the State apparatus is always to expand. As Mises says,

> governments . . . have always looked askance at private property. Governments are never liberal from inclination. It is in the nature of the men handling the apparatus of compulsion and coercion . . . to strive at subduing all spheres of human life. . . . [S]tatism is the occupational disease of rulers, warriors, and civil servants.

As for those who believe that the State is the instrument by which we raise ourselves above our petty concerns to deal with crisis, Mises asks us to remember that

> The state is a human institution, not a superhuman being. He who says "state" means coercion and compulsion. He who says: There should be a law concerning this matter, means: The armed men of the government should force people to do what they do not want to do, or not to do what they like. He who says: This law should be better enforced, means: The police should force people to obey this law. He who says: The state is God, deifies arms and prisons. The worship of the state is the worship of force.

The worst aspects of a State are made worse in war. Says Rothbard,

> In war, State power is pushed to its ultimate, and, under the slogans of "defense" and "emergency," it can impose a tyranny upon the public such as might be openly resisted in time of peace. War thus provides many benefits to a State, and indeed every modern war has brought to the warring

peoples a permanent legacy of increased State burdens upon society.

It is never more important to remember this than in a crisis, when people are so apt to give up their remaining liberties. Stalin once explained why he scrapped Lenin's New Economic Policy, which permitted primitive free enterprise when the entire urban population was starving, and replaced it with a total command economy that he surely knew would cause chaos.

He explained,

> Crisis alone permitted the authorities to demand—and obtain—total submission and all necessary sacrifices from its citizens. The system needed sacrifices and sacrificial victims for the good of the cause and the happiness of future generations. Crises enabled the system in this way to build a bridge from the fictional world of utopian programs to the world of reality.

As much as peace and prosperity is in our interest, it is not always in the interest of our rulers. In the 18th century, Voltaire observed that "the peoples are indifferent to their rulers' wars" because then, after many centuries of just-war teachings, armed conflicts took place between rulers and did not affect the civilian population to any great extent. But that was before the modern State, beginning with the French Revolution, which draws the entire civilian population into every conflict, and targets them, as the pagans did.

One victim of modern war is commercial freedom. And all other freedoms are made vulnerable and attacked once this one falls. Notice that in all the tributes offered to the victims of the attack, precious little has been said about the people who worked in the World Trade Center, about the traders, brokers, insurers, speculators, money managers, stock analysts, and economists who lost their property and their lives. Some were friends of the Mises Institute.

On every other day, after all, the contribution of such people to society is denigrated. Government treats their jobs like crimes waiting to happen. Popular culture considers them parasites as Soviet propaganda demonized the kulaks. No fewer than three rap groups had CDs already in production featuring covers with the World Trade Center towers on fire. One of the CDs had a song called: "Five Million Ways To Kill a CEO." The director of sales explained to the *Washington Post* that the group didn't mean any harm; they were just carrying forward their desire for the "destruction of corporate America."

That is precisely the message imbibed by students around the country in their classes, where assaults on free enterprise are core dogma. Students who come to us constantly express amazement and relief just to be out from under the tyranny of this intense indoctrination, which reflects the attitudes of the ruling regime toward the capitalist class.

The actions of the federal government after the terrorist attack have only contributed to the assault. Its first impulse was to ground all airplanes, close all flight schools, shut down the stock market, force foreign exchanges to prohibit trading in US stocks, harass and fine so-called price gougers, and spy on Internet service providers. In short, the war on terrorism began exactly as you might expect: as a war on capitalism. Even worse, the new regulations and spending will make it more difficult for the economy to recover from the attack, much less climb out of the recession into which it was already heading after the bubble of the late 1990s.

Consistent with Mises's theory of intervention, in which one action against market freedom seems to make others necessary, the federal government then bailed out both the financial markets through the creation of new money and the airline industry with direct subsidies. And this is just the beginning. The demands for wider circles of subsidies, bailouts, and every manner of central planning, will continue.

Not surprisingly, the very same people supporting this have also claimed that the terror attack was good for the economy. The absurdities began with Timothy Noah of *Slate* Magazine, who said that the rebuilding would spur an economic boom. Paul Krugman, a reliable and faithful Keynesian if there ever was one, said the same in the *New York Times*. But the claim wasn't limited to the left. On the right, *National Review* echoed the same sentiments.

Austrian economists find it exasperating to have to explain again and again what Henry Hazlitt presented in his 1946 book, *Economics in One Lesson*. Picking up on a theme developed by Frédéric Bastiat in the nineteenth century, he said that such a rationale—that catastrophe is good for the economy—ignores the alternative uses of resources had the destruction not occurred. This is the simple idea of opportunity cost, the very beginning of good economic analysis. But as Mises said, Keynes and his followers are wrong from their very first assumption.

Going further down the list of economy-killing devices, the federal government now has the power to impose eavesdropping on email. Then there are the preposterous regulations on the airlines. There is no more curbside check-in, no more parking near the terminal, no more metal utensils, and a physical search of bags. Never mind that none of this relates to anything having to do with the attack. The malicious people in this case used plastic box cutters, which were effective only because they were the biggest weapons on board.

The thing to do, then, to end hijacking, is to assure that pilots and crew are armed. Yet this continues to be opposed by the government. Why? For the same reason that nothing was done to arm teachers and principals after Columbine. The State is willing to consider any measure that takes away property rights and freedom, including the right to defend yourself against attack, but unwilling to consider reasonable suggestions that might actually solve the problem.

With every other war serving as precedent, the Federal Reserve has opened the monetary spigots, and is promising a total bailout of the banking system and stock market if necessary. Then there is the Office of Homeland Security, whose creation didn't relieve a single anxiety anywhere in the country. The US Constitution enumerates only a few functions of the central government, among which is to provide for the common defense. The feds tax and spend $2.1 trillion per year, and only now does it occur to anyone in Washington that it is time to secure the homeland.

Compounding the problem is that the new department will not protect us. The emphasis in the press is that this is a new "cabinet-level" agency, as if giving its director access to cabinet meetings is going to protect it from becoming what every other agency in DC already is: not only a waste of money, but a threat to life and property and real security.

A march through the sorry history of war shows the same pattern again and again. Taxes, inflation, industrial planning, control of opinion, censorship, and brutality against civilians is a pattern. As for the problem of rampant militarism abroad, some of the best minds in the military and economic sciences have warned about the problem of blowback for years. Murray Rothbard did in the early 1990s. The historian Martin van Creveld foresaw this as well. Among our own scholars, Robert Higgs, David Henderson, and Jon Utley issued many warnings. Hans-Hermann Hoppe has said again and again, at conferences that you may have attended, that the State's security is an illusion.

But you haven't read about this in the mainstream press, and, in fact, you have read very little about the relationship between the rise of the terrorist threat and US policy. The self-censorship of our free press is truly a wonder to behold, and it applies whether the government is pursuing a war on terrorism or a war on poverty, drugs, tobacco, homelessness, disease, ill health, racism, ignorance, and a hundred other ills.

We are told about the alleged progress, but rarely the setbacks. We are told about the supposed victories but not the costs.

Rarely are the initial ambitions compared with the actual results, for in each case we find that the program did not achieve what its designers claimed, and usually made the original problem worse. For example, it took a war on tobacco to actually increase the rate of teen smoking, a war on discrimination to actually increase unemployment among disabled people, a war on poverty to entrench an impoverished class, and a war on ignorance to cause the illiteracy rate and the cost of education to rise proportionally. I shudder to think what a full-scale war on terrorism is going to bring.

But there will be some unintended effects too. In the coming days and years, everything about our political system will be coming into question. Even now, when public opinion strongly supports political initiatives—at least that's what people are willing to tell strangers phoning them—no one seriously believes that government action is going to make us more secure. We may look back at our current plight as the beginning of a sea change in attitudes toward the federal government, and the ideas of individual freedom and responsibility. The first impulse is always to expand the State. The next may be the rational one: to recognize that the State has failed us in every way, from employing Osama bin Laden, to creating the Taliban, to fueling international hatreds, to disarming pilots, to failing to provide promised security.

We were told that the FAA was providing security on planes, but it turns out that the FAA was preventing it from being provided. We were told that the military would protect US cities, but they couldn't even protect their headquarters. We were told that a vast intelligence apparatus kept a watchful eye on terrorists, but the large group involved in this attack either went unnoticed or was ignored. We were told that US foreign policy was designed to deter aggression, but it turns out to inspire it.

If the US government were a private security agency, it would be fired and sued. But because it is a monopoly provider without voluntary customers, it can't be. So it takes the opposite course after massive failure: it extracts even more money and grabs even more power.

The ultimate lesson is that we cannot trust the State to do what it says it will do. This truth is not going away, no matter how much they spend, regulate, propagandize, and control. The growth of international trade, the collapse of formal socialism abroad, the rise of a sense of solidarity among the taxpayers of all nations, the ability of the market to outperform the government in every area of life, the advance of libertarian theory—all have combined to make it very difficult for the nation-State to operate as it once did.

Many people look to the 1930s or the 1950s as the model for the current wartime mode. In those days, the intellectual movement that backed a consistent application of libertarian principles at home and abroad was very small indeed. But during the last 20 years, this too has changed. We have a huge commercial class that has seen how politics poses a deadly threat to trade, commerce, and enterprise. We have a burgeoning middle class that knows better than to believe that any sort of central planning will be good for them. We have a large and growing movement of intellectuals for freedom in universities who are teaching more and more students in the Misesian tradition of thought.

We have centers of thought springing up all over the United States, but also in Paris, Madrid, Bucharest, and even Moscow. The translations of works are proceeding so quickly it is difficult to keep track. There is now enough quality scholarship in our tradition to support several major journals and publishing programs. It was Jeffrey Herbener, director of our Austrian Scholars Conference, who called our movement the largest intellectual global conspiracy since Marxism.

Indeed, a new book by a Marxist blames free marketeers and the Mises Institute for stopping the progress of socialism by clouding the minds of the masses and preventing them from seeing their true interests. We would say clarifying, not clouding, but it is not difficult to be flattered by his claim, for that is precisely what the ideas of liberty do indeed accomplish.

It was Mises's view that the role of intellectuals is to boldly dissent from conventional wisdom, and proclaim what they know to be true, especially in the most difficult circumstances. You believe that too, and that is why you have been so supportive of our work. You have taken up Mises's challenge to throw yourselves into the intellectual battle.

What does this accomplish? Everything in the world. Just stating what is true can cause minds to change, conventions to collapse, and even States to decline. Just saying what is true is the most powerful weapon in the history of liberty. It is what terrorists and despots fear, and it is ultimately the very basis of freedom itself.

Tomorrow is the 120th anniversary of Ludwig von Mises's birth. What better way to celebrate that than the dedication of this campus to his memory and ideals? In the conservatory you will notice that we reprint his lifetime motto, adopted from Virgil when he was in high school. We have it in many languages because ours is truly an international school. The words in Latin are *"Tu ne cede malis, sed contra audentior ito."* In English, they are: "Do not give in to evil, but proceed ever more boldly against it."

We should never tire in our mission to point out that there is an alternative to the Politically Correct Left and the Militarized Right: that there is freedom itself, the genuine article, and a tradition of thought in defense of freedom unmatched by any other in its rigor and dedication. This ideal will continue to rise from the ashes, again and again, to point the way forward to peace, prosperity, and liberty.

THE SINFUL STATE

[The following article is based on a talk delivered for Thomas Dorman, M.D., in Federal Way, Washington, on November 26, 2002.]

Hardly anyone talks of the table of virtues and vices anymore—which includes the Seven Deadly Sins—but in reviewing them, we find that they nicely sum up the foundation of bourgeois ethics, and provide a solid moral critique of the modern State.

Now, libertarians don't often talk about virtues and vices, mainly because we agree with Lysander Spooner that vices are not crimes, and that the law ought only to address the latter. At the same time, we do need to observe that vices and virtues—and our conception of what constitutes proper behavior and culture generally—have a strong bearing on the rise and decline of freedom.

Let me illustrate. A speaker at a Mises Institute conference two years ago was explaining how problems of welfare, charity, and support for the poor could be handled through voluntary means; that is, through philanthropy. His explanation was brilliant, but a hand shot up.

A student from India had a question. What if, he said, one lives in a society in which the religion says that a person's lot in life is dictated by God, and thus it would be sin to change it in any way. The poor, in this view, are supposed to be poor, and to help them would violate God's will. In fact, a charitable person is committing a crime against God.

The speaker stood there in stunned silence. The students around the room looked at the questioner with their mouths open. We were all amazed to confront a reality too often ignored; namely, that the ethics undergirding our culture, which we so often take for granted, are essential to the functioning of what we call the good society, based on the dignity of the individual, and the possibility of progress, freedom, and prosperity.

In our country and in our times, a productive free-market economy, one supported by a strong sense of personal responsibility and a moral commitment to the security of property rights, has one great enemy: the interventionist State. It is the State that taxes, regulates, and inflates, distorting a system that would otherwise operate smoothly, productively, and to the great benefit of all, generating wealth, security, and peace, and creating the conditions necessary for the flourishing of everything we call civilization.

The name that Karl Marx gave to this system was capitalism, because he believed that the free market was the system that empowered the owners of capital—the bourgeoisie—at the expense of the workers and peasants of the proletarian class.

The name capitalism is somewhat misleading, because free enterprise is not, in fact, a system of economics organized for the sole benefit of the property-owning classes. And yet, the advocates of free markets have not been entirely unhappy with having to use the term capitalism, precisely because capital ownership and accumulation is indeed the engine that drives the operation of a productive free market.

While the system works not to the sole benefit of the capitalists, it is certainly true that private ownership of the means of production, and the creation of this class of citizens, are crucial for us to enjoy all the glories of a productive economy to bestow themselves on society.

Along with the creation of this class comes the formation of what are called bourgeois ethics—a term used derisively to describe the habitual ways of the business class. Hard-core Marxists still use the phrase as if it described the exploiter class. More commonly, it is used by intellectuals to identify a kind of white-bread sameness and predictability that lacks an appreciation for the avant-garde.

Usually it is used to describe people who have an affection for hometown, faith, and family, and a suspicion of lifestyle experiments and behaviors that skirt commonly accepted cultural norms. But those who use the term derisively are not generally appreciative of the extent to which bourgeois ethics make possible the lifestyle of all classes, including the intellectual class.

The bourgeoisie is a class of savers and contract keepers, people who are concerned for the future more than the present, people with an attachment to family. This class of people cares more for their children's welfare, and for work and productivity, than for leisure and personal indulgence.

The virtues of the bourgeoisie are the traditional virtues of prudence, justice, temperance, and fortitude. Each has an economic component—many economic components in fact.

Prudence supports the institution of saving, the desire to get a good education to prepare for the future, and the hope to pass on an inheritance to our children.

With justice comes the desire to keep contracts, to tell the truth in business dealings, and to provide compensation to those who have been wronged.

With temperance comes the desire to restrain oneself, to work before play, which shows that prosperity and freedom are ultimately supported by an internal discipline.

With fortitude comes the entrepreneurial impulse to set aside inordinate fear and to forge ahead when faced with life's uncertainties. These virtues are the foundation of the bourgeoisie, and the basis of great civilizations.

But the mirror image of these virtues shows how the virtuous mode of human behavior finds its opposite in public policies employed by the modern State. The State sets itself against bourgeois ethics and undermines them, and the decline of bourgeois ethics allows the State to expand at the expense of both freedom and virtue.

In the Western religious tradition, the Seven Deadly Sins are not the only ones. They are called the deadly ones because in traditional teaching, they result in spiritual death. Let's take each one in turn.

VAINGLORY. This is also called pride, or, more precisely, excessive or disproportionate pride. We know what it means for a person to be excessively vainglorious or prideful. It means that he puts his interests before that of anyone else, even if doing so may cause harm to another. It is the overestimation of the worth of oneself and one's interests and entitlements at the expense of others.

In public policy, we can think of many pressure groups who believe their interests are more important than anyone else's. In fact, this trait of vainglory describes the appalling clamor for all sorts of new rights. We have disability lobbyists who believe they are entitled to violate everyone else's property rights and freedom for their own sake.

The same is true of many groups identified by various racial and sexual categories. They are convinced by their own pride to believe that they are owed special privileges. The rule of law and its equal application becomes distorted by the demands of the few against the many.

This is hardly the route to long-term social peace. Consider the issue of discrimination in hiring. Why anyone would want to work for an employer who does not really want to hire him is beyond me. In a competitive market, employers are permitted to discriminate, but the costs of discriminatory hiring are wholly born by the employer, whose success or failure is determined by the consumer.

Because employers are in competition with each other, everyone can find a place for himself within the vast network of the division of labor. The pride that leads to short-circuiting this process is not in the long-term interests of society.

The same is true of nations. There is nothing wrong with having a natural and normal pride in one's nation. But to be vainglorious and to overestimate the merit of one's nation can have bad economic effects. Among these bad effects may be chauvinism and belligerence in foreign affairs, as well as mercantilism in international trade policy.

If, for example, we are so convinced that American steel is so much better than foreign steel that we must punish any foreigner who would attempt to sell us steel, we are guilty of vainglory. We are also doing ourselves economic harm by forcing consumers of steel—at all stages of production—to pay higher prices for lesser quality steel than would prevail in a free market.

This is an unsustainable state of affairs. Any industry that is protected from competition becomes ever less efficient. The nation that comes to practice this form of mercantilism can end up producing all sorts of things inefficiently, and displacing new lines of production that would be efficient but are not being undertaken.

Pride in public policy can result in a failure to use critical intelligence in assessing our system of government. We might say, for example, that the United States is the greatest nation on earth. But does that mean that our tax and regulatory polices are what they should be, and that to criticize them is somehow anti-American? Not by any means. To say so is to be guilty of vainglory.

The truth is that the US system of government is gravely flawed and woefully contrary to most of what the founders hoped to bring about when they set up a new government.

The framers never imagined such a thing as the monstrous Department of Homeland Security, or an income tax, or a Federal Reserve, or a far-flung military empire that spends more than most of the world's other nations combined.

These institutions and the change of public-policy culture generally have created the most vainglorious State in the history of the world, especially under the leadership of the current president, whose speeches and statements give new meaning to the word messianic.

ANGER. Western civilization over the last 2,000 years has regarded anger as a grave vice because it leads to destruction rather than peace and productivity. Thus the institution of courts in domestic affairs and diplomacy in foreign affairs.

But in our own country, the taboo against anger in public affairs came to be violated, in particular by the war crimes of federal armies during the civil war. Civilians were deliberately targeted. Homes were looted, crops were burned, livestock killed. This was an expression of anger.

The institutionalization of anger has persisted ever since, in massacres of civilians in the Philippines, in the hunger blockade of World War I, in the bombing of cities in World War II, in the destruction of churches in the war on Serbia, and in the war on Iraq, 11 years running.

When officials say they are angry and plan to unleash Hell on some foreign country, they are partaking in this deadly vice, which also has cultural effects.

The man who was behind the bombing of the Oklahoma City federal building developed his taste for violent anger during the first Gulf War. Many of the killers who have shot up public schools were later revealed to be obsessed with military means and wars.

What lesson is the current generation learning from the speeches and attitudes of the current ruling class and its taste for blood? I shudder to think.

The modern military arsenal, combined with a shredding of all restraints on what is permissible and impermissible in warfare, has unleashed the angry State on the world. Its relentless mode in foreign policy is vengeance, and its main product is human suffering and death.

ENVY. Again, this is a word hardly heard anymore. Envy is not the same as jealousy. Jealousy is merely wishing that you enjoyed the same property and status as another. Envy means the desire to harm someone else solely because he enjoys some quality, virtue, or possession, and you do not. It is the desire to destroy the success or good fortune of another.

In the current round of corporation bashing, I fear the unleashing of envy against people because of their personal accomplishments. And we see the work of envy in the redistributionist welfare State.

Some people say that what matters most is not that the welfare State helps the poor but rather that it hurts the rich. So too with the inheritance tax, which collects relatively little revenue, but does grave damage to would-be family dynasties.

How many Congressional speeches against the business class and the rich are driven by this deadly sin? All too many. Antitrust policy that seeks to smash a business solely because it is big and successful is a working out of envy. I recall an article by Michael Kinsley several years ago in *Slate* Magazine that honestly asked the question: what is wrong with envy?

Nothing, he concluded. In fact, he rightly observed, it is the foundation of much modern public policy. Even so, it is a deadly sin. It is one that will destroy society if it is fully unleashed. And nowhere is it more relentlessly unleashed than within the culture of the State itself, which attacks success in business and private life in every way.

A century ago, many private dynasties had more wealth at their disposal than the federal government. Would the modern Envy State tolerate such a thing? Not likely. All wealth apart from the State's own is up for grabs, but particularly dynastic wealth.

COVETOUSNESS. The related sin of desiring to grasp what belongs to another, through whatever means one can assemble, is also socially harmful. Through taxation and welfare programs, the State is effectively blessing the sin of covetousness.

Now, let us be clear. To covet something is not the same as an innocent desire to improve one's lot in life. This is a good impulse, one that drives people to succeed. Covetousness is different because it cares nothing for the means used to achieve one's goals.

Instead of productive exchange, covetousness resorts to theft, whether private theft or public theft that uses the government. We saw covetousness turn to a public clamor after the collapse in stock prices in 2000 and following, when the public demanded that the Fed do something to stop their investments from going belly-up.

Here again, we see the desire for money outstrip the moral consideration of how precisely this money is to be acquired. And the more the State feeds the sin of covetousness, the more of it we are likely to see, and the more bourgeois ethics fall into disuse.

The modern State is nothing if not covetous. It has its gaze constantly fixed on our liberty, privacy, wealth, and independence, and desires to take through any means possible. In the covetous State, liberty is always declining, the percentage of wealth subject to taxation always growing, and the ability for institutions and individuals to thrive apart from government blessing always in doubt.

GLUTTONY. We think of gluttony as solely related to eating. But it can also mean the excessive desire for comfort, luxury, and leisure at the expense of work and productivity. Senior citizens' lobbies, when they demand that the public provide comfy living for all septuagenarians at the expense of young workers, are playing into the deadly sin of gluttony.

The problem doesn't only afflict seniors. It is a problem among the poor, who have been conditioned by the welfare state to believe they are entitled to live well without earning their money. Interestingly, rates of obesity among the poor far outstrip those among the bourgeoisie.

The pervasiveness of gluttony also shows up in the appalling consumer debt load. This implies a desire to consume now regardless of the later consequences. The gluttonous consumer cares nothing about the long term, only that his appetite is satisfied today.

The Federal Reserve encourages this deadly sin through loose credit policies and bailouts, which create the illusion that there is no downside to living for the present at the expense of the future. So too with the policy of inflation, which encourages us to spend money today because it will have less buying power tomorrow. Inflation institutionalizes the sin of gluttony and makes it appear rational.

It only takes a quick look at a detailed map of Washington, DC to see the ultimate display of gluttony, for land, money, and power. From the point of view of the State, it never has enough land, money, and power. It eats and eats, grows ever fatter, and you take a risk in merely pointing this out.

SLOTH. The story of how the welfare State has created a slothful class is an old one, hardly disputed anymore, but no less true. The promise of something for nothing at others' expense has corrupted the poor, but also the aged and another group as well: students between the ages of 18 and 25.

On the aged, it is pathetic to see how a class of people that should be leading society with wisdom and through experience, to the highest ideals, has become a grasping group of vacationers with ever more time on their hands. Let us be clear: in a free society, there is no right to retirement, and certainly no right to a comfortable retirement. The concept itself was invented by the late New Deal. Before then, sloth was something to be purchased with one's own money. Now, one can enjoy it via the tax State.

As for students, our school system has socialized them into believing that the more official credentials one earns, the more one has the right to extract from society, a payment in return for blessing the world with one's mere presence. Talk to anyone who is in the hiring business these days. He will tell you that it is extremely rare to find a young person who understands that employment is not a tribute paid but an exchange of work for wages. All these trends are worse in Europe, where school welfare is more generous—but we are catching up.

The subsidization of sloth creates a vicious circle. The more the State rewards not working, the less people have by way of personal and financial resources to live independently from the State. The slothful are naturally inclined to develop dependencies, which is exactly the way the State likes it.

Meanwhile, consider the slothfulness of the State itself. There is no more risk-averse class than the bureaucratic one. Whether it is in the FDA process of approving drugs or the loan-application department at HUD, getting bureaucrats to work is like getting hogs to run a race.

Some years ago, a federal bureaucrat sent us the following article, to which he refused to attach his name. It noted:

> What draws people to government work? What keeps them there for a lifetime? It's simple: overcompensation, huge benefits, and great working conditions. It's attractive to sign up and nearly impossible to leave. . . . What would I lose if I left the government? The short work week would be out the window. . . . Right now, I can spend 8.7 percent of my work time on vacation. That's six weeks per year in perpetuity. . . . I could also forget about the unofficial "bennies": for example, I take an hour-long jog every day, followed by a shower and a leisurely lunch. It keeps me in tip-top condition for my vacations. And shopping excursions during work are always possible. What about stress? If relaxation lengthened life, bureaucrats would live to be 150 years old.

And yet, in this one area, perhaps we should be grateful. The only thing worse than the slothful State is an energized one that awakes early to take away our liberty.

LUST. This is thought of as a personal problem only. But we see its destructiveness at work in any government policy that fails to appreciate the family as the foundation of bourgeois society. In public life today, we pretend as if the family is dispensable, when it is the essential bulwark between the individual and the State.

Thoughtful economists like Ludwig von Mises and Joseph Schumpeter saw that the family is the training ground for the ethics of capitalism. It is here where we learn about the evil of theft and to respect others' property, to save and to plan for the future, to keep our word.

It is no accident that Marxists have long sought to smash the family as an institution, and reduce all of society to atomistic individuals who lack the resources to provide security for themselves and who inevitably turn to the State, instead of parents and kin, for help.

These are the Seven Deadly Sins, and in each case, and in a hundred ways I have not mentioned, current government policy encourages them at the expense of bourgeois ethics, which are the ethics of a free market, of a society that is productive, peaceful, and secure from arbitrary power.

Why do we hear so little of the Seven Deadly Sins? Perhaps because no institution is more gluttonous, covetous, prideful, or angry than the State itself. In the private sector, market institutions correct these abuses over time. In the State, with no market test and no check on unethical behavior, these deadly sins thrive with a vengeance.

I am by no means despairing of the future of the bourgeoisie. If there were a danger that this class could be destroyed, 60 or so years of government policy designed to kill it would have accomplished its goal by now.

And yet, we should not become complacent. To the same degree that so many current political struggles are reduced to a conflict of cultures, our best means of fighting back is to live and practice bourgeois ethics in our homes, communities, and businesses.

Let us instead recall the four great bourgeois virtues of prudence, justice, temperance, and fortitude, and, in doing so, do our part to build freedom and prosperity, even in our times. May we never take these cultural foundations of our civilization for granted.

THE REAL STATE OF THE UNION

[Delivered at the Mises Institute's Supporters' Summit in Palm Beach Gardens, Florida, February 5, 1994.]

L udwig von Mises was once asked how we can distinguish a nonsocialist economy from a socialist one. He thought a bit, and then answered: the presence of a stock market. It is this that indicates that the nation's capital stock, or at least a portion of it, is in private hands.

America's stock market—inflated as it may be due to central-bank credit expansion—demonstrates that we are not a socialist country. But a realistic assessment of our current predicament would have to conclude that in almost every other area, our government operates on one of socialism's principal claims.

That claim is this: in the name of equality, fairness, and helping the poor, the central State should loot and obstruct bourgeois property owners and independent producers. Just as the Communists tried to organize the proletariat against the bourgeoisie, so it is in our country. The names have been changed, but the drama remains the same. The bourgeoisie is the middle class. The proletariat is the underclass. The capitalist exploiters are those who "discriminate" against accredited victim groups. The five-year plan is the Economic Report of the president and the libraries of regulations that appear every year. The one-party State is the two-party cartel, both of whom have a stake in the status quo.

As in the USSR, the intellectual classes are in the pay of the ruling elite, or act so as to be worthy of such beneficence. The cultural tone is dictated by our own Pravda and Izvestia, the manipulative, statist media.

So let's forget the rubbish we've heard recently about the wonderful (in the Democratic version) or the pretty good (in the Republican version) state of the union. The union is in crisis, a crisis caused by an explosion in the size and scope of federal power.

Statism has enormous and complex effects on every aspect of national life. It separates work from production, destroys our communities, and politicizes our culture. It shreds our history, wastes our resources, and attacks our families. It feeds off public vice and private envy, promotes crime, and transforms education into indoctrination.

Every day, our markets are less free, our property less secure, our laws more arbitrary, our officials more corrupt, and the ideal of liberty a more distant memory.

Federal regulators are grasping for control over every sector of the economy. Medical care is the most obvious example. Both parties seem to have settled on one or another mandatory national plan for universal access, a euphemism for socialism. This is despite the sorry fiscal record of Medicare and Medicaid, the source of present industry problems.

Every Republican alternative to medical socialism accepts the dominant assumptions of Clinton's program. They may not go as far as Ira Magaziner would, but Clinton is correct in thinking that the final bill need not. So long as the new health care system is universal and mandatory, it will eventually become totalitarian. And as far as private practice goes, it will be targeted and drafted into the State apparatus.

Another mandatory national plan with universal access is Social Security. That too is in crisis. Demographic trends ensure that the program will eventually go belly-up. The younger generation knows it will never see the promised benefits. Yet there is no serious effort toward reform.

The term "insurance" itself has been corrupted. In the private model of insurance, the underwriter is supposed to make a profit by correctly assessing risk and premiums. The new model of insurance is welfare and redistribution. In the name of insurance, the government routinely practices what was once called insurance fraud.

The family is being nationalized. The administration is pushing for starting school earlier, more federally funded babysitting services, and more after-school programs, so as to keep children in the hands of State-approved therapists. Eventually, every three-, four-, and five-year-old is supposed to enter Head Start.

The danger is not the cost, although it is exorbitant. It is not even its failure rate, which is high. It is that it takes the responsibility for raising children away from parents and gives it to bureaucrats.

The family serves as the primary bulwark between the individual and the State. That's why the State relentlessly attacks it. This administration sees parents as expendable at best and abusers at worst. If we get a health security card from the Clinton bill, children's lives will be monitored from birth.

The Department of Education is developing politically correct national standards to be imposed on every school. The new curriculum includes not only environmental and other statist propaganda, but also sexual reeducation.

American history, as taught in the new federally approved classroom, is so dumbed down and left wing as to be a parody of itself. Here it is in a nutshell: America was founded by patriarchal white males who oppressed women and killed Indians; they also enslaved African blacks, broke up their families, and whipped them unmercifully as the slaves built America; Lincoln freed the slaves; women got the vote; labor unions got rights; Roosevelt saved the country from a greed-caused depression; Martin Luther King, Jr. finished freeing the blacks; Reagan unleashed greed and racism; but Clinton is giving rights to blacks, women, gays, unions, the disabled, and the uninsured. That's about it.

In this type of system, a real education involves first unlearning everything you've been taught in the government schools. The National Service program passed by Congress was a deception. Under it, the government agrees to pay for college, provided the recipient of the money gives, as they say, "something back to the community." In concrete terms, this means the taxpayers fund not only schooling, but also a make-work job.

It would be cheaper for taxpayers if the students never gave anything back to the community, and instead got real jobs. This program will start small, but unless stopped, it will balloon into a full-scale European model.

Old standards of merit are being destroyed and replaced with affirmative-action mandates and quotas. We cannot overestimate the damage this has inflicted on our society. There was a time, for example, when a smart student could get an academic scholarship regardless of his income level. Those days are gone. Scholarship money is reserved for the politically correct.

This form of redistribution can be devastating. While middle-class parents struggle to make ends meet and get their kids through school, others get unjust favors, which in turn increases social division.

Businessmen suffer from the constant threat of victim-group lawsuits. Pity the businessman in a large city who has a frequent turnover in his staff. The more he must hire, the more he exposes himself to lawsuits.

Denny's and Shoney's, for example, were the targets of hate campaigns alleging that their waitresses and managers were turning away paying black customers. This was non-sense, of course, but fearing the cost of litigation, and the cost of worldwide media condemnation, the companies paid millions to a few lawyers and their recruited plaintiffs. There's a word for this: extortion.

Then there's the Americans with Disabilities Act. Thousands of complaints have already been registered with the Equal Employment Opportunity Commission, but we haven't begun to see the damage the ADA will do. Under the ADA, business is required to accommodate so-called disabilities like drunkenness, drug addiction, AIDS, forgetfulness, and dim-wittedness. This has to do with the government's effective definition of disability: "any physical or mental limitation."

Notice that a surprising number of new jobs being created in the private sector are in temporary employment. This can be through temporary employment agencies or direct contracting with the individual. In the last 12 months, it may be as high as 28 percent of all new jobs.

Why is that? The mandates on business for full-time employees are just too high, and they can be avoided by hiring temporary employees, who do not have to be paid medical insurance or unemployment insurance, and who do not have tenure through victimology. That is, temps can be easily fired. The businessman is much less likely to face charges of discrimination and be bankrupted by lawsuits.

The temporary industry is a wonderful market innovation, but it is also largely a response to the socialization of the labor pool. So it is not surprising that Congresswoman Pat Schroeder and Labor Secretary Robert Reich hate the temporary employment market. If they follow the pattern of their counterparts in Europe, and her legislation in Congress, they will crush this growing market.

The Environmental Protection Agency is completely out of control. As I speak, it is conducting the so-called National Biological Survey to take a full accounting of every plant, animal, bug, weed, stick, and dirt ball in the country, to make sure all are frozen in place and not "endangered."

The Senate was barely able to pass a binding resolution forbidding the EPA from intruding on private property without the owner's knowledge. Now, at least, they have to notify you before they trespass on your land with the hope of finding plants or animals that will enable them to steal it.

There are enough Green laws on the books to destroy the economy overnight if they were all enforced. The Endangered Species Act is only one of many examples. The National Biological Survey will extend it nationwide.

Clinton's new head of OSHA promises a reign of terror against business. The FDA wants to control the wording of every food label and drive out alternative health remedies. And HUD is sending out spies to mortgage companies and apartment buildings all over the country to check for so-called discrimination. These swarms of roaming testers have a chilling effect, of course.

HUD uses a statistical measure called the Index of Dissimilarity to target areas that are too homogeneous, so coercive therapy can be administrated. This was tried in the 1970s with Chicago's Gautreaux Demonstration Program. The result was 700,000 people fleeing Chicago altogether.

In international trade, with Nafta, we got a total of 43 new bureaucracies. The bill pretended to be about trade, but instead merely cartelized regulatory agencies across borders. Congress can no longer easily lighten labor and environmental regulations. Any such effort would face a challenge from the Nafta commissions on the environment and labor.

Now we are confronted with the prospect of Gatt, another regulatory bill being promoted as free trade. In April, the US Trade Representative will sign this agreement to create a World Trade Organization. It institutionalizes the environmental agenda, Keynesian fiscal planning, redistributionism, and "full-employment" policies. This is the Keynesian dream come true, but it's a nightmare for national sovereignty and economic liberty.

Incredibly, the wording of the WTO charter is almost identical to that of the failed International Trade Organization, which the postwar planners tried to foist on the country in 1948. It was killed by Mises's student and free-market businessman Philip Cortney, with his great book the *Economic Munich*. Almost single-handedly, Cortney proved the power of ideas. Similarly, we should do everything in our power to expose the WTO.

This is not easy, of course. The ideological climate is intolerant of libertarian ideas. For example, in an age of email, faxes, FedEx, and UPS, hardly anybody is considering privatizing the postal service or repealing its monopoly status. The private sector has achieved miracles in information distribution, but it is not allowed to carry the mail. Meanwhile the government mandates, and controls. Instead of obeying customers, entrepreneurs now have to spend much of their time obeying politicians and social workers.

Even personal liberty is in free fall. In the name of crime control, private gun ownership is under attack as never before. And the administration of the post office raids companies to make sure they are not using FedEx in violation of the law.

Similarly, even after the S&L fiasco, which was created by government deposit insurance, there are no efforts underway to put banking on a sounder footing. Instead, the banking industry is slipping into a mire of victimology.

A bank can no longer conduct mortgage policy based on merit. It must first consider race. Indeed banks are paying millions of dollars in ransom to pressure groups. The old values of saving money and paying bills no longer apply.

We have nearly lost the traditional American principle that liberty is the best organizing force for society. It's no longer simple, for example, to start a business, so costly and twisted are regulations and taxes. The Clinton administration has announced its intention to drive most gun dealers out of business through higher taxes.

Maybe we should be thankful that the administration has admitted, for once, what taxes do to thriving enterprises. Yet a columnist who is supposed to favor tax cuts recently suggested a nationwide confiscation of handguns, a position well-received at the White House. I speak of Bill Buckley.

Then there are the FBI, the US Marshals, and the Bureau of Alcohol, Tobacco, and Firearms. They killed 86 religious dissenters in Waco, Texas. The survivors are now on trial for defending their lives and property. And the media is rooting for their conviction.

There's also the exploding debt, Washington's phony budgeting, the sorry state of education, foreign aid, domestic aid, tax-funded condom ads, and foreign adventurism.

But what about the good economic news we've been hearing recently? Inflation is down and economic growth is up. Yet Mises taught us to look behind these numbers. The growth is almost entirely fueled by low interest rates.

There would be nothing wrong with that if these rates were based on increased savings and a longer-term outlook by the public. But savings remain historically low and the public is increasingly short-term oriented. Given these conditions, we should have much higher interest rates than we do.

One of the many hallmarks of the Austrian School is warning about the damage that artificially low interest rates do to the capital structure. They cause the capital goods sector (residential housing, for example) to over-extend itself, an extension which is reflected in the official data.

We are on the upswing in a government-manufactured business cycle. The inevitable result of a Fed-induced boom is a market-driven recession. That doesn't mean that people shouldn't be buying homes. Market signals suggest they should. It means the punch has been spiked and will eventually run out. And the after-effects are worse than a steady state of sobriety.

But what economic school will be prepared to explain this when the downturn comes? How can we turn our next economic crisis into an opportunity for the advancement of freedom? And is there anything that can be done before a collapse to improve our lot, and lessen the arrogance of the central State?

That brings me to the role of the Mises Institute. The truth about what is being done to our economy and society is being suppressed by a kept media and a political class that benefits from allowing only marginal criticism of the status quo. Part of the Institute's efforts are therefore devoted to public education.

We are anxious to use every forum available to us to explain sound economics, identify its enemies, incite anger against the State, and urge that something be done. We don't attempt to persuade politicians or lobby for legislation. That has proven a dead end in many cases.

Instead, we strike when we see the opportunity. Through public education, we battled last year against new administration appointees, against the trends of race quotas for banking, against trade bureaucracies, and against the spending trends in Washington. We've learned that when the trumpet sounds a certain tone, the troops will swing into action. But our work in public affairs is only the beginning. We also attempt to address the underlying problem of our country's economic ignorance, bolstered by the academic establishment for at least 40 years.

Within the academy, statism is newly in vogue. The media have again beatified John Maynard Keynes just as volume two of his hagiographic biography appears. The *New York Times* praises "Socialism's Noble Aims." All reports from the meetings of the American Economic Association said it was overrun with socialists and would-be central planners. The eighties' enthusiasm for tax cuts was completely unrepresented.

A recent dispatch from the Associated Press names the economic guru of our age: John Kenneth Galbraith. "At age 85," the AP reports, "he's back in vogue." There's no denying the truth of that statement. In the early 1980s, we thought we had gotten rid of him. When socialism collapsed in Eastern Europe, we hoped he would become an object of ridicule. If there were justice in this world, he would have.

Galbraith should do penance for his lifetime advocacy of State power, price controls, budget deficits, inflation, and central economic controls. Instead of listing among his greatest achievements his stint as Franklin Roosevelt's price control czar, he should be redfaced about it. He should, in fact, be out on the street with a sign reading: "Will work for food."

The public figure he admires most, Galbraith says, is Franklin D. Roosevelt, and he comments about himself and other economists: "We didn't make up our minds on an issue until we knew what Roosevelt wanted."

Imagine: "We didn't make up our minds on an issue until we knew what Roosevelt wanted." That's a Harvard professor describing his profession as being in the business of serving the State.

Times have not changed. Most economists are political weather vanes. Whichever way the wind is blowing in Washington, they go in that direction, although they are particularly excited about moving to the left, because it gives them status and power.

Today economists ask, what does Clinton want? You only have to look at the transcripts of Clinton's economic summit. One by one, on bended knee, economists told the incoming president what he wanted to hear. And the students who learn under them are indoctrinated into the reigning ideological regime.

The Austrian School is different, however, and always has been. Carl Menger fought the statist and nihilistic trends of his time when he founded the Austrian School on the view that economics is about acting individuals. His colleagues and students did, too.

Ludwig von Mises, the father of the modern Austrian School, battled his whole life against statism and for economic truth. Though he sometimes won acclaim for his brilliance, he faced unremitting hostility and opposition to his writings. But it didn't stop him. This prophet of socialism's collapse was a Rock of Gibraltar, as his students are in our time.

The Institute that carries on his work desires a society where the central government is neither seen nor heard. When that day comes, we can all live as Americans were supposed to

live: secure in our property and freedom, and with optimism
for the future. That is why we are so grateful for your support—spiritual, intellectual, and material. You enable us to
carry on. Ludwig von Mises never gave up the fight, and neither will the Institute privileged to be named in his memory.

THE TRANSFORMATION OF AMERICAN OPINION

*[Delivered at the Mises Institute's Supporters Summit, "Liberty
and Public Life," Newport Beach, California, February 2, 2001.]*

W e live in times that are both despotic and revolutionary. We know what despotism means. Never
before has any people lived under a government
this well-funded, this technologically sophisticated, this well-
armed, which daily undertakes activities that would have
been inconceivable to governments of ages past. The great tax
and political revolts in history occurred under regimes that
mostly look like paradises of liberty by comparison.

We shell out 40 percent and more of our income to fund
a government to oppress us with its regulations and routine
invasions of our private life, to erect and run schools to which
we are loath to send our children, to engage in far-flung wars
that create nothing but wreckage and death, to gouge us with
their mail and utility services, to seize our guns, to fund welfare schemes and entitlements that drain life from economic
affairs.

An even greater loss consists in what we do not see.
How many innovations have been lost due to regulations?
How many businesses have left their plans unfulfilled due

to discrimination lawsuits and taxes? How many good minds have been lost to the public-school system? These are the sunk costs of statism, and they are incalculable.

What's more, the defenders of this system posture as the nation's moral elite, and are nearly wholly in control of the establishment media and educational institutions. On a day-to-day basis, it is this aspect of the present despotism, the endless prattle from the Left, that drives us all bonkers.

Who can stand to listen to National Public Radio pose as a voice of moral authority as it spews out repackaged press releases from the Democratic National Committee? Who can bear another solemn proclamation from the *New York Times* that Jesse Jackson's plan to redistribute wealth should be immediately implemented? Who can stand to hear another election analyst tell us that the Republicans must curb their extremist rhetoric, or that no living soul ought ever again to speak at Bob Jones University, or that no person who aspires to national office should ever again take a principled stand on anything?

Most of this nonsense is made up out of whole cloth, and has no connection to what any real American is thinking about these issues. These statements reflect media etiquette, which is nothing but a repackaging of the etiquette of the State. In that etiquette, one must never say anything that would cast a poor reflection on the left-liberal agenda, and must always treat any alternative as morally suspect.

The etiquette needs no conspiracy to enforce it. It is the backdrop of the entire profession. It is pervasive because the corruption begins at the top and journalists are professionally ambitious. If the crime reporter for the local paper hopes to make it to the national news desk of a major daily, he had better start thinking like a reporter thinks. And he finds out very quickly what this means. It means adopting the official etiquette of the profession.

Thank goodness for the advent of Web communications, which has liberated so many of us from the tyranny of this tiny elite and their insufferable and intolerable bias against normalcy and good sense. The promise that talk radio offered in the early 1990s has exploded into something unimaginable in the past: the possibility of being, at the same time, completely informed on public affairs and completely independent of established channels of information.

More on the media despotism and what to do about it later. What about this word, "revolution"? I fear that we no longer know what it means. Newt Gingrich called himself a revolutionary. But his only lasting legacy was to impose term limits on House committee chairmen. Whatever you think of that idea, it is not revolutionary. These days political figures have watered down the word so much that we hear calls for a revolution every few months. What they mean is a more compelling version of the status quo.

That is not what I mean by revolution. In 1969, when the New Left was proclaiming its desire for revolution, Murray N. Rothbard wrote a short but extremely powerful essay on the subject, one that penetrates to the essence of the issue. In those days, the word revolution still had an edge. It still caused people to sit up and listen. It was not used to describe a new line of toiletries or a new congressional spending bill. It meant a wholesale turning over of political affairs marked by direct acts against the State, some nonviolent, some not. Often revolutions led to war. But they certainly ended in an entirely new state of affairs.

The word revolution recalled Lexington and Concord, the storming of the Bastille, and the murder of the Czar—all three of which were directed against government power, but only the first of which ended by establishing liberty. Today, we have other examples that keep within the American tradition: the fall of the Berlin Wall, the trial and execution of Nicolae Ceausescu, the flight of Gorbachev loyalists from the

Politburo. These are all examples of revolutions that turned out much better for the cause of human liberty.

Rothbard emphasized that such events are just the *culmination* of a long, mighty, complex process with many vital parts and functions. A revolution necessarily begins with small acts on all fronts. The seeds of the American Revolution, for example, were planted centuries before when scholars in Spain and France in the High Middle Ages began to radically question the need for the State as a social and political manager. They were the first moderns to see the potential for individuals, and voluntarily formed associations to serve as the foundation for a prosperous and peaceful society. They were the first to formulate systematic objections to coercion as a means of social organization.

These ideas became the basis of the great liberal movements of the 17th and 18th centuries, movements that involved everyone who cared about ideas: intellectuals, pamphleteers, journalists, teachers, philanthropists, churchmen, students, agitators, businessmen, propagandists, and statesmen. Not one of the groups could do it alone, but inspired by an idea and driven by a moral agenda—carried out over the generations—they finally overthrew mercantilism and perpetual war, and replaced them with the foundations of social peace, the free market, and a free society. We owe the prosperity and freedom we have today to these movements that took a great idea and acted on it.

In passing, Rothbard also exposed the phoniness of the idea of socialist revolution. He argued that socialism is neither genuinely radical nor truly revolutionary. True, it claims to achieve classical liberalism; that is, bring about economic progress and the withering away of the State. But it does so using collectivism and State control. Socialist ideology, he said, is not revolutionary but rather a new form of Toryism that seeks to take the present system of government and entrench it so deeply and expand it so far that it cannot be questioned or challenged.

His insight here helps us understand why many of us feel so uncomfortable with the word *conservative* to describe our agenda. The last thing we need today is to conserve the collectivist and socialist victories of Clinton, Johnson, FDR, Wilson, and Lincoln, or keep in place the present media elite that are constantly telling us how wonderful these people are.

And as Rothbard further emphasized in this piece, there is no one predetermined path to achieving a revolutionary victory. Rather, each individual uses the talents he has to delegitimize and fight the present structure of mainstream opinion. The action could be introducing a friend to a book or article he may not otherwise have seen. It could be writing the definitive treatise reinterpreting a historical event, or one improving our understanding of economic theory. It could be a letter to the editor, a speech to a civic organization, an article, a scholarship to the promising student of liberty, or education you provide your own children and grandchildren. These actions produce a cumulative effect, maybe not in one year or one generation. The key is that the movement behind them endures to the end.

Rothbard also underscored a point Mises often made in his writings. The difference between a revolution that is building and one whose time has come can be found in the shape of public opinion. By that, I do not mean polls, though they are variously helpful and misleading, depending on the methodology. I mean the assumptions about political and economic life shared by the majority of people. As long as public opinion generally supports a regime, so that the system has more friends than enemies, it survives. But when the situation reverses, so that the regime has more enemies than friends, the path of history can turn dramatically. The regime must either conform to the turning of the tide, or risk its very existence.

It is no accident that the art of molding and shaping public opinion has been the preoccupation of governments from time immemorial. Their very existence depends on it, simply because—as de la Boétie, Hume, Mises, Rothbard, and many others have shown—the State cannot rule by coercion alone. It needs consensus if it is to have control. It follows, then, that the prospects for a genuine overthrow of the current despotism depends heavily on access to information. Not just any information but the kind of information that tells the truth about the State and its apologists.

Consider the place of Tom Paine's *Common Sense*, the pamphlet that circulated in the months before the American Revolution. Published in 1776, an incredible 120,000 copies sold in three months. Nearly every literate home in the country could quote its contents. It was more than an attack on the British monarchy; it was an exegetical treatment of the origin of the State itself. He distinguished between society, which he called our patron, and government, which he called our punisher.

> Society in every state is a blessing, but government, even in its best state, is but a necessary evil; in its worst state an intolerable one. . . . Government, like dress, is the badge of lost innocence; the palaces of kings are built upon the ruins of the bowers of paradise.

Incidentally, Paine was sound on a whole host of issues from taxation to inflation. He was an advocate of the gold standard and even 100-percent reserves in banking.

Just as Paine's pamphlet emboldened the radicals, it terrified the Tories. The work was called artful, insidious, pernicious, and seditious. It was said that this pamphlet could lead to ruin, horror, desolation, and anarchy. These days, such language seems to be lost on our media elite, who would be satisfied to dub it racist, sexist, homophobic, anti-Semitic, hateful, and generally meanspirited. But the fact remains that the pamphlet triggered a revolution, without which America might have sunk into the historical ditch.

Why have there been so few decisive pamphlets since Paine's? It wasn't long after the Constitution was ratified that the American elite worked to suppress such radicalism, and took up the Tory line that anyone who wrote such things was crazy, cranky, dangerous, and flirting with anarchism. Indeed, if you look back over the course of American history, it is actually quite surprising how far the radicalism of Tom Paine has faded into memory.

Tom Paine-style thinkers have been especially rare in the last century, when the intellectual classes and the approved journalistic voices have tended to sympathize with the State. If you leaf through the library for American books on liberty between the years 1900 and 1920, for example, you will find precious few authors who understood the essential issues. There were virtually no economists denouncing the income or inheritance tax on principled grounds, and virtually none warning of the dangers of central banking.

These watershed years also gave us World War I and the embryonic version of the New Deal. What strikes you when studying this time was the lack of a coherent opposition movement. Yes, there were people who resisted the drive for war and people who resented the income tax. But still, the libertarian movement was small and lacked a firm intellectual foundation. It had virtually no institutional apparatus of support and precious little presence in the universities.

But as the State continued to grow, so did its opponents, so that each new generation created a crop of thinkers, activists, and statesmen that had been influenced by the last generation of dissidents. There were the anti-New Dealers, a vibrant movement that fought FDR at every turn, but which was later almost destroyed by the war. Their successors made something of a showing in the 1950s, and again in the 1980s. Thus, parallel with the rise of the State in our century has been the growth of a radical opposition movement, a revolutionary movement, one that continues to build today.

The Mises Institute was founded in 1982 with the goal of encouraging that opposition, as well as becoming the vanguard intellectual movement to further antistatist trends in academic and public life. And today that revolution is proceeding in ways that should make us hopeful for the future, most noticeably in the manner in which public opinion has been transformed in recent years by the explosion of quality information available.

The explosion of Web access has also created an effect that I couldn't have imagined.

Outstanding writers from all walks of life are coming forward with excellent articles on a wide range of political and historical subjects. I run a daily news site, and I can tell you that I have far more excellent copy than I could ever run. And the irony strikes me daily that the difference between my one-man news site and the massive MSNBC is nothing more than a click.

At a time when Web traffic is highly competitive, Mises.org is receiving 2 million hits per month. Users range from students and professors doing deep research, to classrooms using journals and articles, to businessmen simply reading the latest commentary. And the traffic is international and truly interdisciplinary.

This reality has contributed to the threat of accountability to the press and their allies on campus. No longer do their lies and distortions go uncorrected. Reporters find themselves flooded with email when their biases get out of hand. And when they cover up a story, there is always a site out there to pick it up and get the truth out. The speed at which this happens on a daily and hourly basis is truly breathtaking. And this change has contributed to the brewing revolution. Indeed, access to information may in the long run prove to be the critical turning point.

Now, the Left uses the Web as well, but not with nearly the degree of success that real dissidents have. Salon.com, for example, was deluded into thinking that it could actually make a profit by combining hit pieces on Clinton's opponents with pornography. They even went so far as to hold an IPO, selling shares for $40 a pop. Today that stock is in the penny

category, with the site plagued by lack of traffic and unim-
pressed advertisers.

It is due in part to the new technologies that no excres-
cence of government enjoys the uncritical public support they
all did from World War I until the mid-1970s. The new media
have helped encourage and embolden the trend away from
State worship and have dramatically accelerated the process
of discrediting the old media.

The election of 2000 illustrates what I mean. For years
leading up to this election, we were told by the pundit classes
that the American people had once again fallen in love with
big government. People didn't want tax cuts. Indeed, we were
told, people would be glad to pay higher taxes in exchange for
more government "services." The spirit of 1994 was gone forever because, thanks to Clinton, we have at last made our
peace with Leviathan.

Again, this was sheer nonsense. In the waning days of the
campaign, both candidates declared themselves opponents of
big government. Gore probably told the biggest whopper of
his life when he said, on national television: "I'm opposed to
big government. . . . I don't believe any government program
can replace the responsibility of parents, the hard work of
families, or the innovation of industry."

Bush refined his message down to his claim that he is for
the people, not the government—a version of Tom Paine's
essential message. Now, if it is really true that the American
people have abandoned that old libertarian spirit, if people
had really come to love Leviathan, why were the candidates
talking this way? Of course, they and their pollsters knew
what the voters on the margin wanted to hear.

The lack of public confidence in the State is evident in
these large areas but also small ones. The post office, for
example, was recently forced to cut a deal with Federal
Express to help maintain its overnight delivery service. The
post office is on life support as it is, and with the march of

electronic communication, we can confidently predict that it probably has no more than a decade of life left.

There was a rush after the rolling blackouts in California to place the blame on deregulation. But this was absurd because price controls were never fully repealed and environmental controls prevented the construction of new power plants and shut down old ones. Once again, the government showed itself unable to perform even the most basic function of keeping the power on.

There was a time when we had to wait for publishers to correct these errors in articles that came out months later. No more. We are now able to respond within hours to such nonsense, posting pieces on our sites, sending messages to our lists, and broadcasting the response to major media outlets. Such responses are taken up in classrooms and newsgroups around the world where current events are discussed. We are also able to anticipate the left-wing line and counter it before it takes hold of the public mind.

The free-market position, the truly revolutionary position, is getting a hearing.

And the effect not only works in the popular press. When an antigun historical tract by a professor at Emory University appeared last year, gun experts from around the country started to rip it to shreds. It was only a matter of weeks before large archives of rebuttals, including some from LewRockwell.com and Mises.org, were available in an instant, and the professor ended up whining to the press about how horribly he had been treated.

The Left is worried about all this activity. They have taken note of where the energy is in American life. They grow bitter at developments like the massive growth in private arbitration, the explosion in private security guards and gated subdivision living, and they see all these trends as indicators of a decline in public confidence in their beloved government. They are as aware as anyone that the ideological forces in American life that oppose government control are huge, diverse, and young, while the defenders of the old order of government control, while retaining power, lack intellectual confidence.

Recently, ex-*New York Times* writer Anna Quindlen, writing for MSNBC, tried to console leftists by assuring them that they are merely out of power and not irrelevant. She cited the example of the delayed nomination of John Ashcroft as US Attorney General as proof of the kind of mischief the Left can cause.

It is a good example because it illustrates how fundamentally thin and absurd the Left has become. Instead of being a robust intellectual movement, it is nothing but a collection of grasping, screaming, hysterical special interests who come nowhere close to representing anything normal. Given Ashcroft's public positions, and the extent of leftist power in the media, it is something of a shock that he was nominated at all.

And yet, this powerful apparatus, involving many sectors of society, has a weak hold on power and a very thin margin of public support, and they grow weaker and thinner by the day. That fact in large part accounts for the increasingly hysterical tone of left-wing rhetoric and the maniacal behavior of interest groups that depend on the welfare-warfare state.

No longer do the Left and its media backers consider people who oppose wealth redistribution and support local self-government and free enterprise to be merely mistaken or misguided. No, we've seen a change in tone in the last few years. Even the slightest deviation from left-wing orthodoxy is decried as hate, and any man who dares think unapproved thoughts is pounced on as an enemy of society. This is true in politics, academia, the business world, and many other sectors.

To be sure, this type of rhetoric has a long historical precedent. In the 1960s, books were already appearing that purported to unearth hate and danger on the Right. The tactic was always the same: linking people through association. If a conservative politician had once taken a phone call from a donor who was friends with someone who was on the board of an alleged Nazi group, the politician was said to be secretly allying himself with Nazis.

Now, you might think that such tactics actually date from the McCarthy era of the 1950s. That's not entirely accurate, because it is impossible to understand McCarthyism without seeing it as partial response to FDRism of the 1930s, in which every opponent of the New Deal and the run-up to war was smeared as a proto-fascist. Many of the anti-New Deal writers and activists lost their jobs and had their lives ruined by the Roosevelt administration's determination to shut up all its critics by any means necessary. The McCarthyites, who often had a strong case to make, simply regarded turnabout as fair play.

We can keep going back further in American political history, to see that Wilson decried his political opponents as reactionaries or Germanophiles, and ended up jailing quite a few of them. German teachers were even lynched. And before that, there was Reconstruction, in which every white Southerner was treated as a political criminal by virtue of his birth and race, not to speak of Lincoln's jailing of his opponents and shutdowns of dissenting newspapers. In truly Stalinist fashion, Americans were jailed for the crime of being present when Lincoln's policies were criticized, and remaining silent.

In fact, we can trace the use of smear tactics back all the way to the Federalists, who used vicious rhetoric against any partisans of the Articles of Confederation, and later attempted to shut down political opposition with the Alien and Sedition Acts. All opponents of the regime have received the same treatment given Tom Paine by the Tories in 1776.

Today, contrary to conventional wisdom, Marxism is more, not less, mainstream than in the past. Instead of defining people according to class, the new Marxists define people according to race, sex, religion, and, now, sexual orientation. History, in their eyes, is nothing other than the working out of a great struggle within these categories.

The philosophical method by which this transition took place is complex, and I don't want to go into it here, but it involves a several-stage process by which old-fashioned standards of logic and reason and truth are thrown out. To paraphrase G.K. Chesterton, people are first encouraged to believe in nothing, and then are fully prepared to believe in anything. What the Left, particularly that which runs the mainstream media, believes in today is power and little else, because, to them, only power, exercised in the interest of group identity, has meaning.

Today, if a free-market economist makes an argument against taxes, he is called a tool of the rich. If he argues against race and sex quotas, he is called a racist and a sexist. If he argues against trade sanctions, he is called a tool of Saddam or Castro. If he argues against disability or environmental regulations, he is called an enemy of the disabled and clean air. These are not arguments but attempts to shut people up, which is just about all the Left can come up with. This is Marxism at work, throwing out rationality in favor of identity demonization.

This approach is pervasive in today's political culture, but far from being an indication that we are losing the battle of ideas, it is actually a measure of how much we are winning, and how close we are coming to the day when the regime's enemies outnumber its friends. Increasingly, the State and its allies resort to intimidation and power as their means of maintaining their grip on the sectors of national life they control.

Think of all the old liberal clichés that are hardly ever invoked anymore. Remember this one from Voltaire? "I disagree with what you say, but I will defend to the death your right to say it." This has been transformed, so that the new left-wing message, on campus and in public life, is: if you say the wrong thing, I'm not only going to run you out of polite society, I'm going to call the federal cops.

Recall the phrase "academic freedom," once so sacred to the Left? Today, people who invoke it are dismissed as dangerous rightists attempting to bypass the thought police on curriculum and human rights committees.

Now, there is some truth to the Marxist idea that a type of struggle characterizes history. In fact, Marx himself stole the idea from the classical liberals, who saw that a struggle between the taxeaters and the taxpayers, the producers and the dependents, the market and the State, is at the heart of politics, and no more so than in our heavily interventionist society. In the days after the national election, *USA Today* produced a county-by-county map of the US, with the areas that voted for Bush colored in red and those that went with Gore colored in blue.

If you have seen this map, you know that it is worth more than any lecture in politics or sociology you ever heard. What it showed was nothing short of a sea of red, from top to bottom and left to right. The red zone represented five times more land mass than the blue. What's more, the division perfectly summed up the deep split between the taxeaters and the taxpayers.

The blues were inner cities, the state capitols, the government-funded intellectual class on the east coast, the leftist cultural elite on the California coast, immigrant areas on the borders, and the environmental crazies. And who are the reds? Everyone else. If you believe that we live in a stable political system, one look at this map and you will see that it is wildly unstable, and unworkable over the long run.

Now, this is not to say that Bush somehow represents a pure case of political revolt, but when you are aware of how hard the press worked to defeat him, and how the media did this work for 12 months leading up to the election, you begin to realize just how entrenched mainstream American opinion is against the ideological orientation approved by the media elite.

The Mises Institute recently came under fire from one of these watchdog groups that claims to oppose intolerance and hate. What was our offense? We have published revisionist accounts of the origins of the Civil War that demonstrate that the tariff bred more conflict between the South and the feds than slavery. For that, we were decried as a dangerous institutional proponent of "neoconfederate" ideology. Why not just plain old Confederate ideology? The addition of the prefix neo is supposed to conjure up other dangers, like those associated with the term neo-Nazi.

These are desperate tactics of people who know, in their heart of hearts, that they are on the wrong side of history. Their day has come and gone, and now they will do anything to hang on to the only source of life they have, which is not intellectual or popular, but rather rooted only in government power.

The Left and the partisans of government power are surrounded on all sides by dissidents. In the media, only one of four networks, Fox, offers anything close to a balanced view of current events, and it recently zoomed past the other three networks in total viewership.

This is a change most of us never expected to see in our lifetimes. In the universities, Mises Institute faculty members report that it is precisely their political *incorrectness* that draws students to their classes and drives young people to devour the literature they recommend. When they get in trouble with the thought police on campus, it is the students who come to their defense.

As for the attack on us, distributed by a major leftist organization to every important media outlet in the country, we received all of two phone calls. Neither resulted in an article.

Someday, perhaps even Republicans will figure this out. An amusing exchange occurred the other day during the hearings on John Ashcroft, who once correctly wrote that the most important reason for private gun ownership was to protect against tyranny. Ted Kennedy exploded in a tyrannical rage at Ashcroft for suggesting that the United States system of government could ever be tyrannical—this coming from an architect of the tyranny.

Ashcroft, in keeping with the instructions he received from the Bush transition team, didn't respond to Kennedy's harangue. But wouldn't it have been nice to actually hear him explain what he meant? He could have quoted the founders on the issue of gun ownership. He could have upbraided Kennedy's strange arrogance in thinking that the US government is somehow, unlike any government in the history of the world, incapable of tyrannical acts. How glorious to have heard Ashcroft say what we hope he believes: that the Kennedys of this nation are personally responsible for the present tyranny, and that Ted stands as the living embodiment of why it is so important that the citizens be armed.

Alas, Ashcroft did not. And though we may be disappointed, we are no longer surprised that Republicans acquiesce to left-liberal claims of moral and intellectual superiority. We've seen it for so long. Anyone who expects the Republicans to set out to reverse the tide of statism ushered in by Democrats hasn't been paying attention to the course of American politics for the last century. The Democrats and Republicans have played the role of Good Cop and Bad Cop in the statist enterprise, each putting a face on despotism that can be accepted by their loyal constituents.

A good example is Clinton's program of Americorp, an embryonic system of national service. This program was passed by a Democratic Congress in 1993 with nearly universal Republican opposition. Over seven years, it has paid young people to become servants in a political army whose job it is to entice families and businesses to get on welfare, and otherwise agitate to sell big government to the grass roots through grants to left-wing organizations.

So committed has Americorp been to big government that its enlistees have even distributed the much-hated low-flush toilets to households that still have old-fashioned toilets that use enough water to keep them clean and working. On the other end, Americorp enlistees have worked to round up and crush older toilets, to make sure that they do not become part of the burgeoning black market.

What are Republicans saying about the program today? In the last week of its term, the Clinton White House sent out a press release quoting Republicans—including John McCain, Rick Santorum, John Kasich, Robert Bennett, Orrin Hatch, Thad Cochran, Chuck Grassley, Mitch McConnell, Conrad Burns, Mike DeWine, Pete Domenici, among many others—testifying that the program is wonderful, efficient, and should be preserved and expanded.

Another example: the Republican Congress is going wild for President Bush's education proposal. The *New York Times* announced the proposal with the following lead sentence: "President Bush proposed a significant increase today in the federal role in public education." That's really all you need to know to make a judgment about it. It spends more money, grants more power to the Department of Education, imposes a national testing scheme on schools for the first time, and pushes a new spending program that will put willing private schools on the federal dole.

The GOP is intimidated by the media and always looking for an occasion, if not a good reason, to sell out, only to be shocked that the much-anticipated praise from the Left never arrives. A bigger problem is that, while Republicans are blessed with some degree of sense, and they are less reliant on parasitic special interest groups than the Democrats, they lack any kind of ideological sophistication, and thus are not prepared to make any kind of serious argument against government intervention.

In all my years of observing Capitol Hill, I've known of only one man who did not succumb to the temptations of power. He is Ron Paul of Texas. And still, there is little chance of cloning him, no matter how many think tanks move their offices to Capitol Hill, no matter how many seminars are held for legislative aides, no matter how many cocktail parties are held for our rulers.

In the end, political involvement and activism of the conventional sort will not be enough to reverse the tide. What is needed, and what is occurring right now, is an underlying intellectual and cultural shift. For years, libertarians and conservatives have placed their hopes in politicians and political forces, only to be disappointed again and again. It's time that we understand that these people are often late barometers of shifts in public opinion; they tend to follow, not lead.

Now, whether you are optimistic or pessimistic about the prospects for the Bush presidency depends a lot on your starting point. If you start with the assumption that these people will govern like many other Republican administrations, it means you expect no serious decrease in any area of big government, and fear massive increases. We need only think about the Hoover, Eisenhower, and Nixon administrations.

People look back on the Reagan years with some degree of fondness but, in fact, his reputation is wildly overblown. At the end of the 1980s, taxes were higher, spending had quadrupled, the welfare state had doubled, and regulation on the private sector had dramatically increased. Was it all the Democrats' fault? These things took place with a Republican Senate.

A serious problem also presents itself when you look at the legacy of George W. Bush's father, who not only gave us a tax increase but also the Americans with Disabilities Act, some disastrous amendments to civil rights law, and the first major post-Cold War war, which set a precedent for Clinton's warmongering during the 1990s. We can only hope that the son does not follow his father in this respect.

One reason many of us are not woefully pessimistic about this administration, of course, is that whatever it is, it is not the Clinton administration, a regime implacably opposed to the ideals of a free society. And yet, when you consider what the administration wanted, and measure that against what it actually did, there are some surprising results.

Despite its desire, expressed by Hillary when she complained there were no gatekeepers on the Web, the Clinton government was never able to regulate or tax the Internet. In fact, the Clinton regime was pressured into accepting legislation that guaranteed a measure of freedom. Many plots to read our email, tax our mail-order and Internet transactions, and spoil our privacy were foiled by the enormous public outrage that each attempt provoked.

Despite the Clinton administration's socialist ideological orientation, it was not able to raise taxes after its initial increase in Clinton's first term. You might chalk that up to increased revenue due to the economic expansion. And yet it is interesting that the rate of discretionary domestic spending actually slowed during the Clinton years.

It is preposterous that Clinton claimed to have shrunk the government to its smallest level in postwar times. Yet it does remain true that the employed workforce of the federal government is smaller than anytime since World War II. That is due to a major problem that faces government: people are quitting, and recruits to government work are fewer every year. This reflects no deliberate change in policy, but rather a dramatic shift in public opinion that is working itself out in ways that are going to change our future.

What do the ideological convolutions of our age tell us? I believe they tell us which way the wind is blowing, and it is toward freedom and away from government planning. The Left continually claims that government has never been weaker or more downtrodden than today. They see the triumph of capitalism everywhere and bemoan it. They cry and wail that there are no more New Deals, Great Societies, or grand socialist experiments abroad. They say this represents the end of political idealism, a word used to mask an essentially totalitarian agenda.

Now, the Left is obviously exaggerating for political effect. Nonetheless, there is truth in what they say. The socialists control the universities, the labor unions, the nonprofit world, most special interest lobbying organizations, the international bureaucracies, the public schools, and nearly all positions in the permanent bureaucracy. And yet, strangely, they complain that they have no power and no influence.

This is because they sense that they do not and cannot control those things which are most determinative of the shape of the future: the pace and direction of technological change, the explosive growth of the private sector worldwide, the antigovernment trendline in public opinion, and, most importantly, the imaginations of the new generation of intellectuals.

There is a revolution that is brewing and building slowly, systematically, but relentlessly. And it is a revolution against that ideological centerpiece of the 20th century, the omnipotent State. It is taking the form of a renewal of private life and the establishment of a new generation of natural elites and intellectuals who have no interest in allying themselves with the State. Indeed, they are working for a society in which society is left to flourish in the State's absence.

How long it will take for this revolution to run its course, and turn the world we live in upside-down, cannot be known. It may be this year or it may be 50 years. But this much we do know: those of us committed to the building of an intellectual infrastructure necessary to overturn the despotism of a government-managed society must never let up. Never let anyone tell you that what you believe is an anachronism. The Left does not own the future.

If we get discouraged we also need to remember that our efforts are not in vain even when they are not victorious. I'm reminded of something C.S. Lewis said in response to the example of a man who is both very bad and very religious. Lewis asked us to imagine how much worse he might be without religion. In some ways, we might also imagine how

much worse off we would be today without efforts of our forebears.

What if Mises had never written his attack on socialism
when it was universally popular, or if Rothbard hadn't come
to the defense of property rights at a time when they were universally traduced? Knowing the ways in which ideas affect the
course of events, we can say that we would be much worse off.
All great revolutions in history had an ideological basis that
took generations to build up. That is the stage we are in today.

The times are also right. We are not in depression and we
are not in war. We are not locked into any Manichean international struggle. It has never been easier to see that the
enemy of American freedom is not overseas, but within the
Beltway. It has never been easier to find out the truth, and the
tellers of truth have never told it with so much evidence and
moral conviction.

We have every reason to celebrate the political and cultural constellation of our time. These days, supporters of less
government at home also tend to be those who doubt the wisdom of globalist nation building, while those who favor big
government at home are also most likely to push for the glob-
alization of government authority abroad. This is a huge step
in the right direction: our side is working to shed the ideological baggage of imperialism, and approaching something like
a consistent set of principles.

The rise of homeschooling and gated communities gives
the middle class a strong interest in the protection of the sanctity of the home and private property. As Mises explained,
these are as much issues of capitalism as complicated questions of corporate finance. Also, the new generation of Web
users and people whose livelihoods and essential sources of
information are connected with the new technologies are with
us as well.

There is much work left to do. The judiciary needs to be
desanctified. The history of statism and its evil needs to be

constantly researched and published. Economic theory needs to be separated from its positivist research program that fits so well with the needs of the State, and good economic theory restored to its proper foundation in the social sciences. Students need ever more opportunities to escape the ideological prisons of their universities and colleges, and to be exposed to alternative modes of thought. The need for funding for books, conferences, teaching materials, journals, and scholarships is immense.

If we approach our task with vigor and continue to build on our victories, we can win. This victory will not take a conventional path, or even a path we can expect. But we know that victory is impossible unless we continue to raise up and encourage a new generation of intellectuals, whose work with future students can build a powerful force for change, and continue to sway public opinion for freedom and against the State.

That is the mission of the Mises Institute. Throughout history, the strongest defense of liberty has come from the natural elites in society who own property, form families, establish dynasties, worship God, and serve as the backbone of the business class. As in past revolutions for liberty, they must link arms with the dissident intellectuals who refuse to become mouthpieces for the ruling regime, and have the courage to defy conventional wisdom.

When freedom is finally secured, and big government brought to its knees, it will be the consequence of a revolution led by this coalition. It is this intellectual and political movement that can speak a radical language that embraces the free economy and the prosperity that comes with it, and tolerates no more government interference in family, community, business, or any other aspect of our lives.

As Tom Paine concluded his pamphlet, "we have it in our power to begin the world over again. The birthday of a new world is at hand."

DAWN WILL FOLLOW THIS DARKNESS

[This speech was delivered at the Mises Institute's "Boom, Bust, and the Future" conference in Auburn, Alabama, January 19, 2002.]

In arguing that dawn will follow the present darkness, I must first establish that the darkness exists at all. If you believe Robert Bartley of the *Wall Street Journal*, the dawn has already arrived with the government's response to September 11, and its political and economic aftermath.

Now, Bartley's a supply-sider, and if you know something of that school, it is a mixed bag. It can be very good on the need for tax cuts and the fallacies of zero-sum thinking. However, it is dismissive toward debt and public spending, and all-too-friendly toward inflation and State intervention generally.

Bartley writes that before the Bush administration's bombing campaign, America was consumed with guilt "at being too powerful, too prosperous, and . . . too assertive." Now, however, with the war, we can consolidate "a new century of safety, peace, and spreading prosperity."

Now, the supply-siders can be an absurdly Panglossian bunch, so long as stock prices are rising. And for many years, the *Wall Street Journal* editorial page has never found a low stock price that it didn't believe could and should be raised with an injection of new liquidity. That leads the writers to celebrate any event that will prompt the Fed to lower interest rates. War, for example.

But the *Journal* is hardly alone in the opinion that war and prosperity go together. The whole media hold that the overthrow of a tottering and thuggish regime in dirt-poor Afghanistan represents some sort of triumph of the national will, a foreshadowing of the government-run utopia of peace and prosperity headed our way.

The tactic here is an old one: the identification of military prowess with economic health, which conflates the voluntary sector of private productivity with the coercive sector of central planning. It accepts fallacies from Keynes's view that government spending boosts productivity, to Lenin's view that capitalism thrives on military conquest.

But Bartley goes further. His point is not only that prosperity and military assertiveness stem from the same political priorities, which is not true in any case. He actually suggests that militarism itself is what brings about prosperity. After all, his column is not a tribute to enterprise but to war planners.

Bartley should know that it is not the military that makes prosperity possible. It is prosperity that makes it possible for the military, like all government programs, to exist in the first place. Government revenue that funds the military is seized from the private sector, the way a parasite lives off a host. The healthier the host, the happier the parasite, which is allowed to become fatter and stronger than ever.

Thus, it is capitalism and the astounding productivity of the free economy alone that accounts for the power and influence of the US. As to the government, when it isn't taxing the markets, it is draining their productive power in other ways.

The current war on recession, for example, is being funded through credit expansion, which has led to massive debt accumulation. Meanwhile, the Fed's 12-month campaign to keep the economic expansion going has been a spectacular failure. It has pushed interest rates so low that saving, already at historic lows, is punished in favor of stock speculation.

In the second half of 2001, American politicians got into the act by urging consumers and businesses to go on a spending spree. This was an attempt to stymie the good instincts that people have to get their financial house in order during recession. Instead of dumping debt, debt of all kinds has reached very dangerous highs. Americans have driven up total consumer credit, as well as corporate credit, to record highs.

Neither cheerleading nor an artificial injection of liquidity is a viable substitute for old-fashioned rebuilding. As we've learned at this conference, real economic growth can't be created by a printing press. At a time when the political establishment is using happy talk to generate the appearance of happy days, and spending untold billions on war and welfare, no one wants to hear the message that there is a price to pay for this fiscal and monetary profligacy.

"War prosperity is like the prosperity that an earthquake or a plague brings," Mises wrote.

> The earthquake means good business for construction workers, and cholera improves the business of physicians, pharmacists, and undertakers; but no one has for that reason yet sought to celebrate earthquakes and cholera as stimulators of the productive forces in the general interest.

Government power and market productivity work at cross purposes. As Mises wrote:

> History is a struggle between two principles, the peaceful principle, which advances the development of trade, and the militarist-imperialist principle, which interprets human society not as a friendly division of labor but as the forcible repression of some of its members by others.

He goes on to point out that: "The military state is a state of bandits. It prefers to live on booty and tribute."

In Mises's view, there are times when employing the military is necessary, but he pleads with us not to be naïve about the consequences. "Not only economic but moral and political conditions will be affected," he writes. "Militarism will supplant democracy; civil liberties will vanish wherever military discipline must be supreme." Hence, says Mises, the use of the military always comes at the expense of liberty, and there's no reason to pretend otherwise.

We see the erosion of liberty taking place in our own time. Thanks to legislation passed this fall and winter, the federal police now enjoy unprecedented rights against the people. And our supposedly free media have been ignoring this—or, in the most abject, toadying fashion—heralding it.

Right now, political deviants are being rounded up without probable cause. In recent days, students said to hold antigovernment views have been visited by the FBI and the Secret Service at their dormitories. So have business professionals, overheard making cynical remarks at, for example, the local gym. As for Congress, it has become utterly useless in curbing the executive State. By congressional decree, the chief executive has been granted unprecedented power and autonomy, in complete violation of the Constitution.

That only begins the catalog of interventions. In economic affairs, we now have a conservative administration calling for a vast expansion of unemployment benefits, new restrictions on the use of cash, food stamps for foreigners, stepped-up federal spending and control of public schools, more foreign aid, and more Federal Reserve money and credit to make it all possible.

We can look forward to another round of international bailouts, possibly even of Japan, where banks are holding $1 trillion in bad debt, and officials are burning up the phone lines to DC. And don't forget the billions headed toward Afghanistan to fund a massive rebuilding of what the US just destroyed.

No one should believe the *Wall Street Journal*, that the dawn has arrived because the government believes itself to be more powerful than anyone or anything on earth. No, as Jefferson said, the opposite is true: the more latitude the government has at home and abroad, the more we ought to be concerned for the future of freedom.

Interestingly, Bartley pens a chilling sentence that would appear to indicate some knowledge of this. Listen to his choice of language:

A new era . . . cannot be consolidated in the foreign arena
alone. In the new year, Mr. Bush will have to make the point
that the serious minds who can so ably run a war are also
the best minds *to run an economy*, nurture better education,
make environmental trade-offs, and save a faltering Social
Security system. [Emphasis added.]

Of course, he favors central planning by Republicans as
opposed to Democrats, but from the point of view of the free
society, it doesn't matter whose calling card the State is carrying.

That free enterprise is capable of funding a huge military
empire creates something of a problem for those of us who
advocate freedom, for we know that the more wealth society
produces, the more tempted governments are to steal it. This
is why it is morally and intellectually incumbent on believers
in free enterprise to take the lead in warning against expansions of government, of all sorts.

One may argue, of course, that to the extent that the US
military assists in keeping peace and stability in the world,
this is good for free markets and prosperity. But is this what
the Pentagon does? The terrorists who attacked the World
Trade Center were striking out at wealth and those who produce it, just as many bureaucrats in Washington strike out at
market productivity on a daily basis. The damage done on
September 11 was dramatic and compressed into one instant;
the damage done by Washington bureaucrats is spread out
over years and decades, and less visible to the eye.

But both forms of violence constitute the use of coercion
against peaceful people. So by hating and attacking the market economy, the terrorists share a profession in common with
the political class in this country, though the latter is in good
standing with the law; indeed, it makes and enforces the law.

Moreover, there is more than enough evidence, including
the statements of the terrorists themselves, that they were
not only protesting economic freedom but also specific US
military policies that would not exist in a free market, for

example, a deadly embargo against Iraq, and US troops on what is to them the holy sand of Saudi Arabia. I don't believe that US foreign policy ought to change because terrorists demand it; I believe it should change because it is the right thing to do.

The US government somehow managed to do more than simply provide terrorists with motivation. With policies dating back decades, it made it very difficult for Americans to protect themselves against terrorist attacks, by, for example, preventing privately owned planes from arming themselves against hijackers, and leading us to believe that a military budget larger than that of every other developed country combined might actually be all the protection we would need.

A government at war always uses the occasion to expand its power over the economic and social lives of its citizens. To be sure, some of its excuses are quite plausible: everyone favors justice for those involved in killing the innocent. But unleashing the dogs of war leads to unpredictable consequences. Even after adding to Afghanistan's miserable lot, and killing some 4,000 civilians who had no part in September 11, the US still hasn't caught Osama bin Laden. There were better ways than war to pursue justice, but there was no better way to increase the grip of the central State over America, which is what the government actually aims at.

That we have always known, but events of recent months have reminded us again of why it is so urgent to join the intellectual battle in defense of the free society, particularly in the field of economics, and for the sake of our personal well-being and that of society as a whole.

If there is new faith in government today, it is not a faith that government can completely manage society, as tracts from the 1930s claimed. Instead, it is a faith that government can pulverize its enemies with ease, and to that degree the faith is not entirely misplaced. The human mind has always been impressed by the ability of power to accomplish spectacular acts of destruction.

Yet the Fed has proven itself powerless as a tool of macro-economic stimulus during this recession. Its impotence has startled everyone, especially the Fed's own economists.

Think of it: we live in times when the government cannot point to a single one of its programs and call it a success. We are faced with several huge fiscal crises in the future involving retirement benefits, rising debt, and the overvaluation of stocks. Because politicians destroyed the gold standard, we have a currency that is fundamentally unsound and unchecked by any limits on the central bank. We have collapsing public schools, public transit, and public services of all sorts, which no amount of cash infusions are going to fix.

Yet there are positive signs that have emerged recently. I would name the shredding of the Kyoto treaty and the hampering of environmentalism as a political movement, the inability of the left-liberals to enact more gun laws, the sucker punch that September 11 gave to the multicultural movement which claims that there is something inferior and inherently awful about the Western mind, the relentless march of the homeschooling movement, the well-documented trend among students to reject the left-wing prattle of their professors, the rise of a new bourgeois cultural sensibility, and the continued growth of a diverse Internet as an alternative source of news.

The realization that the government, despite the Department of Homeland Security, cannot protect us is probably a good thing too. It can only increase the use of market means of providing the security we all seek. These things are not enough to bring about a new dawn, of course. But we will also be helped by one thing we can be one hundred percent sure of: the State will continue to get egg on its face wherever it intervenes, in terms of spectacular scandal, and spectacular failure.

Before talking about what we must do, however, let me explain what I mean by dawn. For all of us, it is the free society, one in which we are secure in our property and privacy from a grasping government, when our families and community lives are permitted to flourish in absence of the belligerence of State officials, when the US government no longer believes itself the master of the country and the world, but rather begins to observe the Constitution's limits on its power.

That dawn will require, first, an ideological change in public opinion, where people's latent distrust of government is hardened into a hard-core love of liberty itself. This change must begin in the world of ideas, the world to which the Mises Institute is dedicated.

Through it all, the Mises Institute's intellectual work proceeds apace and with astounding results. Our teaching and resident fellow programs prepare the cadre that any revolution needs. Our journals overflow with outstanding scientific and historical scholarship. All of this, which you help make possible, is laying a foundation for the future, just as Rothbard and Mises did.

However, that doesn't mean that good scholarship in the Austrian tradition goes unnoticed today. The IMF, for example, just released a working paper that does a credible job of presenting the Austrian theory of the business cycle. If you think about this, it is astounding for a theory that was supposedly killed off in the 1930s to be emerging into discussion again today. But it is happening, and at far more places than the IMF. This is the power of ideas at work.

Recently, Gene Callahan mentioned that there are so many articles appearing in the popular press that discuss Mises that you can't swing a dead cat without hitting one. This would have been unthinkable 20 years ago.

Every summer we bring in hundreds of brilliant and dedicated students, leaders on their campuses, to receive systematic instruction in economics, history, ethics, law, and social theory. They leave telling us that their time here had a greater impact on their education than anything at their colleges and universities. Dozens of dissertations and books have been completed based on ideas sparked at these conferences.

We have hundreds of young professors, teachers, researchers, and writers doing the hard work of liberty. Our daily editorials reach tens of thousands of the world's smartest students, educators, and business professionals. The intellectual movement backing our ideas has become nothing short of a well-oiled international machine spreading truth and good sense at all levels of academia, society, and culture. I submit to you that this trend should make us more bullish on liberty, despite any political or financial crisis.

The time is ripe for the Austrians to be heard. Only the Austrian School has coherently explained what is happening right now in Argentina and Japan. Only the Austrian School has provided a full account of what brought us to the present economic downturn in America, and why welfare and warfare and inflation only make things worse. Only the Austrian School has offered a consistent vision of a radical alternative, one that is capable of attracting young minds and appealing to society's cultural and intellectual leaders.

Our greatest patron in this battle is the free economy itself, which daily astonishes us with its ability to provide, innovate, and expand in the midst of so many attacks. The creative power of commerce dumbfounds even the leftists who have foretold its death. The State may pave, but the flowers of enterprise break up the concrete. And by commerce and enterprise, what I really mean is human action, the choices of individuals to embrace their own self-interest, and that of their families and communities, rather than to live for the political aims of the omnipotent State.

For hundreds of years, and more so now than ever, the market has outrun the ability of interventionist governments to make it conform to some predetermined plan. And despite the boom and bust of dot-coms—thanks to the Fed—the Internet continues to grow as a source of commercial strength, and as an alternative source of news and analysis not cleared with DC in advance. The success of LewRockwell.com, the libertarian daily news, is only one example.

With the aid of human motivation and innovation, and human action in the marketplace, aided by all those institutions that sustain it in society, we will see our way out of the mire.

We must be aware, of course, that those of us who champion a consistent vision of a free society, without apology or compromise, are going to continue to come under fire. These criticisms can be brutal, but they are no different in character from what they have always been. The fundamental tactic is to question our motives, and to disparage our cause as only another special interest. But liberty is not the demand of a pressure group. It is a plea for the good of the entire society. That makes it unique.

Ours is not a mass movement, of course, and it need not be so. Throughout history, the true friends of freedom, the ones who believe in it as a matter of hard-core principle, have always been few. We have been reminded of this in recent days.

How much more important, then, to stress and restress our continuing theme: liberty for everyone, State privilege for no one. This is the social framework of a market economy.

This is a message that no faction within the ruling class wants to hear. No matter how divided the factions are among themselves, they form a united front against the libertarian idea.

That's why to sign up with the cause of liberty is to take a principled step. It means rejecting the dominant strain of politics, that the State ought to be used to promote the agenda of some special interest, whether it be those who benefit from welfare, regulation, inflation, or war.

The cause of liberty rejects all this, not because we have a special interest but because we stick by the most unpopular claim of all: that society ought to be permitted to organize itself so that it benefits everyone in the long run. There is only one system that does so, and that is the competitive market economy operating under the natural order of liberty.

We must never, even now, underestimate the power of ideas. The State, with its attacks on freedom and peace, is ultimately no match for the truths we love and defend with all the energy we have.

Our tradition of thought is deeply rooted in European and American history. It flourishes today among students, faculty, and professionals all over the world. Those who seek to stamp it out through intimidation are no match for a body of thought that has withstood every crisis that has befallen it for centuries, survived and flourished, as new young minds join its cause.

One of the blessings of prosperity is that it permits serious scholarship and teaching—in addition to art and music and all the humane studies—to flourish. In this way, through the intellectual means, civilization perpetuates itself.

There will always be crises: financial, economic, social, and political. But there will also be great opportunities for change. If we adhere to the spirit as well as the ideas of freedom, there will indeed be a new dawn. As Mises said, "Ideas and only ideas can light the darkness." We have the ideas, and they will light the way to victory.

THE PATH TO VICTORY

[This talk was given at the Mises Institute Spring Seminar Series, Auburn, Alabama, March 5, 2003.]

The Mises Institute was founded as a research center based on classically liberal ideas that have always been under fire: the ideas of Mises and the tradition of thought he represents. That means a focus on the Austrian School of economics, and, in political philosophy, individual liberty and the need to prevent the State and its interests from crushing it, as all States everywhere are inclined to do.

The first priority of such an institute is to keep a body of ideas alive. Great ideas have no inherent life of their own, especially not those that are opposed by the powers that be. They must circulate and be a part of the academic and public mind in order to avoid extinction.

And yet we must do more than merely keep a body of thought alive. We don't just want our ideas to live; we want them to grow and develop, advance within the culture and public debate, become a force to be reckoned with among intellectuals, be constantly employed toward the end of explaining history and current reality, and eventually win in the great ideological battles of our times.

What is the best means of achieving such victory? This is a subject that is rarely discussed on the free-market right. Murray Rothbard pointed out that strategy is a huge part of the scholarship of the left. Once having settled on the doctrine, the left works very hard at honing the message and finding ways to push it. This is a major explanation for the left's success.

Our side, on the other hand, doesn't discuss this subject much. But since some sort of strategy is unavoidable, let me just list a few tactics that I do not believe work. The following, I'm quite sure, will fail for various reasons:

QUIETISM. Faced with the incredible odds against success, there is a tendency among believers in liberty to despair and find solace in being around their friends and talking only to each other. This is understandable, of course, even fruitful at times, but it is also irresponsible and rather selfish. Yes, we may always be a minority, but we are always either growing or shrinking. If we shrink enough, we disappear. If we grow enough, we win. That is why we must never give up the battle for young minds and for changing older minds. Our message has tremendous explanatory power. We must never hide our light under a bushel.

RETREAT. One mark of the liberal tradition is its intellectual rigor. It contains more than enough intellectual substance to occupy the academic mind for several lifetimes. There is a tendency, then, to believe that retreating into academia and eschewing public life is the correct path. The idea is that we should just use our knowledge to pen journal articles and otherwise keep to ourselves, in the hopes that someday this path will pay off in terms of academic respectability. But this has not been the path of brilliant minds from Turgot and Jefferson, Bastiat and Constant, Mises and Hayek, Rothbard and the adjunct scholars of the Mises Institute. They are all engaged at some level in public debate. They believed that too much is at stake to retreat solely to private study. We cannot afford that luxury.

HOLDING CHAIRS IN THE IVY LEAGUE. I've seen this related error take a real toll on otherwise good minds. A young person can start out with real commitments, but he may fear the marginalization that comes with holding unpopular ideas. He tries to pass himself off as a conventional scholar, while sneaking in libertarian thoughts along the way. He may intend to reveal his true colors eventually, but then there are the demands of tenure and promotion, and social pressures to boot. Eventually, in short, he comes to sell out.

CONVINCING THE POLITICIANS. Another type of problem stems from the belief that political organizing is the answer. But this can only lead to despondency, as effort after effort fails to yield fruit. Despite what you hear, the political class is not interested in ideas for their own sake. They are interested in subsidizing their friends, protecting their territory, and getting reelected. Political ideology for them is, at best, a hobby. It is only useful insofar as it provides a cover for what they would do otherwise. I'm generalizing here, and yes, exceptions are possible. In fact, I can think of one in our century: Ron Paul.

PLACING HIGH-PROFILE ARTICLES. I know think-tank people who would do just about anything to get in the *New*

York Times or *Wall Street Journal*. This is a snare and delusion. Once you put a priority on the medium over the message—and this is inevitable once you begin to think this way—you are forgetting why you got in this business to begin with. If these venues come to you and ask you to offer an opinion you hold, by all means do so. But that is not the way it works.

GETTING ON TV. The same applies here. I know people who were once dedicated to the ideas of liberty who developed a hankering for media attention, and eventually forgot why they got into the ideas business in the first place.

STARTING MORE THINK TANKS. I know this sounds silly but some people on our side of the fence believe that the more nonprofit organizations there are, the more likely we are to win the battle of ideas. To me, this amounts to confusing the success that franchising represents in the commercial marketplace with ideological success, which is not guaranteed by the proliferation of websites and institutes. Indeed, ideology is not solely a commercial enterprise. We are a nonprofit research institute for a reason. What we do pays huge returns for civilization but not in the form of accounting profits. Our reward comes in other ways.

BUILDING AN IMMENSE ENDOWMENT AND HIRING A HUGE STAFF. Funding and staff alone will solve nothing. Funding is crucial and heaven knows the Mises Institute needs more of it. Staffing is great, so long as the people are dedicated and competent. But neither is an end in itself. The crucial question is whether the passion for ideas is there, not just the financial means. Amazing things are possible on small budgets, as I think the success of the Mises Institute shows.

WAIT FOR THE COLLAPSE. We know that socialism and interventionism cannot work. We know they fail, and we suspect that they might finally fail in a catastrophic manner. This may be true, but we are mistaken if we believe that the ideas of liberty will naturally emerge in such a setting. Crisis can present opportunities but no guarantees.

Finding errors such as these is easy, and I could list a dozen more. Let me offer a few points I think we should remember.

Our ideas are unpopular. We are in the minority. Our views are not welcome by the regime. They often fall on the deaf ears of an indifferent public. Big newspapers don't often care what we think. In fact, they want to keep us out of their pages. Politicians will always find us impractical at best, and threatening at worst.

In short, we fight an uphill battle. We must recognize this at the outset. We are what Albert Jay Nock called the remnant, a small band of brothers who have special knowledge of theory and history, and a concern for the well-being of civilization. What we do with that knowledge and concern is up to us. We can retreat or sell out, or we can use it as our battle cry and go forward through history to face the enemy.

Let me offer just a quick outline of some principles I use:

EDUCATE EVERY STUDENT who is interested in what we do. Never neglect anyone. One never knows where the next Mises or Rothbard or Hayek or Hazlitt is going to come from.

ENCOURAGE A PROLIFERATION OF TALENTS. Some people are great writers. Others are great teachers. Still others have a talent for research. There are other abilities too, like public speaking and technological competence. It takes all these abilities to make up the great freedom movement of our time. There is no need to insist on a single model; rather, we should make use of the division of labor.

USE EVERY MEDIUM we can to advance our ideas, from the smallest newsletter to the largest Website. Never believe that a medium is beneath you, or above you. We must be in the academic journals and we must be in the pages of the local newspaper. Along these lines, the Web has solved the major problem we faced throughout history, namely finding a medium to communicate our ideas in a way that makes them available to everyone who is interested. But it never happens automatically.

It requires tremendous effort and creativity to bring about change.

ADHERE TO WHAT IS TRUE. This means avoiding fancy ways of pitching your ideas in keeping with current trends. It's fine to be attentive to sales techniques. But never let this concern swamp your message.

SAY WHAT IS TRUE. Never underestimate the power of just stating things plainly and openly. Whatever the topic, the ideas of liberty have something to add that is missing from public debate. It is our job to make that addition.

DON'T NEGLECT ACADEMIA. Yes, colleges and universities are corrupt. But they are where the ideas that rule civilization come from. We must not neglect them. We must publish journals, sponsor colloquia, help faculty and students. Never let academia believe it has the luxury of forgetting about our ideas. This is why the Mises Institute holds seminars for professors and students, as well as financial professionals and interested people of every sort.

DON'T NEGLECT POPULAR CULTURE. Yes, popular culture is corrupt, but not entirely. We must not neglect it because it has a huge impact on the way people see themselves and learn about their world.

USE YOUR MINORITY STATUS TO YOUR OWN BENEFIT. There is no sense in duplicating what others already do. If you publish, publish something radical and surprising. If you produce a book, make it a book that will change people's minds. If you hold a seminar, say things that are worth saying. Never fear the unconventional. It is possible to be conventional in form and radical in content.

REMEMBER THAT INFLUENCE CAN BE INDIRECT. The effect of ideas on a civilization is like waves on water. By the time they reach the shore, no one remembers or knows for sure where they came from. Our job is to stick to the task. We should use every means at our disposal to get the ideas out there; what happens after that is as unpredictable as the future always is.

SUCCESS CAN TAKE MANY FORMS. I am often asked how we can think we are succeeding even as the government keeps growing. To me, this poses no great quandary. All governments want total control. What stops them, primarily, is ideological opposition. Without it, the government would grow much quicker and civilization would be doomed in short order. To what extent has the circulation of the ideas of liberty slowed down the growth of the State? How much worse off might we be?

CHANGE CAN HAPPEN QUICKLY. The ideological foundations of statism weaken in ways that are not always detectable. Change can happen overnight, after which all becomes clear in retrospect. If you had told the average Russian in 1985 that in five years, the Soviet Union would be defunct, you would have been dismissed as a madman. It's my opinion that statism in America may have run its course. We should all do our best to speed up the process.

In the history of warfare, there have always been armies that are ruled by the center and emphasize drills, lines, and discipline. They tend to treat their soldiers as expendable. They can win but at a huge price.

The other model is guerrilla warfare, usually undertaken by the underdog in the battle. Guerrilla armies usually consist of volunteers; every soldier is considered valuable. Their tactics are unpredictable. They are not ruled by the center but rather exploit the creativity of each member. Such armies have proven remarkably effective in the history of warfare.

I believe that the guerrilla model is what suits us best—a campaign of ideological guerrilla warfare conducted by the remnant. This is no guarantee of success but it is the best guarantee against failure that I know.

Mises.org receives 15 million hits per month, and LewRockwell.com is the most popular liberty-minded site on the net. This week 250 scholars will present papers at our annual scholars conference. Our journals circulate like never before, in academia and public culture. Our books have changed history in so many ways.

The key to our success, I believe, is that the Mises Institute is all about being attached to principle and truth before anything else. We've never traded short-term attention for building for the long term.

Mises did not either, and he paid a personal price. But his ideas are changing the world. We must all follow his lead, never giving in, never giving up, fighting for truth until our last breath. We have the passion and energy. Most importantly, we have truth on our side. I believe we can have the victory.

5. Interviews and Tributes

ROCKWELL-DOHERTY INTERVIEW

[An interview by Brian Doherty which appeared in the May 12, 1999 issue of SpintechMag.com *as "Libertarianism and the Old Right."]*

Doherty: *How and under what circumstances did you first become interested in political philosophy/work? Was it of an individualist/libertarian orientation from the beginning?*

Rockwell: I've been interested in ideological matters from the earliest age. My father was a Taft Republican, and trained me well. A good thing too, for even as a schoolboy, I argued with my teachers over the New Deal, public accommodations laws, US entry into World War II, and McCarthy's questioning of the military elites (I'd still like to know who promoted Peress).

I told them that Tailgunner Joe should have been attacking the US government all along, because it was the real threat to our liberties. That drove my teachers crazy. None of them would be surprised that I grew up to be a full-time gadfly against the conventional wisdom.

My influences included Taft, Garrett, Flynn, Nock, Mencken, Chodorov, Tansill, and the scholastic just-war tradition. Though a Yankee, I never subscribed to the Lincoln cult, and I admired the Southern secessionists for taking the original constitutional compact seriously.

For my twelfth birthday, a friend of my father's gave me Hazlitt's *Economics in One Lesson*. That book taught me how to think in economic terms, and I have been reading in economics ever since, with a special appreciation for the old French Liberal School and the modern Austrians from Menger to Rothbard.

Once oriented, I gained reinforcement from a wide range of literature in high school and as an English major. I found property rights in German literature, skepticism against the State in English literature, and a love of liberty in American literature.

I was also taken with Cicero: his love of liberty and the old republic; his celebration of natural elites and opposition to egalitarianism; and, most of all, his fighting, indefatigable spirit. I believed that he was no less right because his principled stand did not prevail. There is virtue in the fight regardless of the outcome. The eloquence and courage of Tacitus influenced me for the same reasons.

Over time, I became aware that I was not only dissenting from the left but also from the conservative establishment, which was embroiled in the Cold War as a first principle. I grew increasingly skeptical of the official right, especially during the war on Vietnam.

Back then, the establishment meant *National Review*. There were some good people on the masthead, and it wasn't as neoconservative domestically as it later became, but the magazine's position on the Cold War came close to calling for a murderous first strike use of nuclear weapons. I could never understand how a person claiming to understand the merits of liberty and property, much less a person schooled in Christian ethics, could entertain such a bloody fantasy.

In the 1960s, like Murray, my sympathies were with the antiwar crowd (but not the unrelated Age of Aquarius bunch). I liked the willingness to resist, the commitment to principle, the moral tone, the defiance of the power elites. I had been a reluctant Goldwaterite in 1964, but by 1968 I worked briefly for Gene McCarthy.

There were some very sophisticated antistatist writings coming out of the left at that point. This is what distinguished the New Left from the Old Left. The Old Left, at least since the Stalin-Hitler pact, had become cautiously pro-empire and unflinchingly pro-DC bureaucracy. To believe in any central planning, as the Old Left did, is to cease to be a radical, of course. It means to love what the bureaucracy was doing and aspired to do.

This is why the New Left was a breath of fresh air. Its orientation was antigovernment. It focused on a fundamental moral issue—whether the US government should be waging war on foreign peoples—and it was open to historically revisionist scholarship that demonstrated the evils of the corporate State in American history. The focus was also correct: on the war profits being garnered by the munitions manufacturers, exactly as the Old Right had done in the interwar period. If you read Mises's *Liberalism*, you see the same ideological disposition at work at a different time and a different place.

In some ways, there was a dovetailing of the New Left and the little that remained of the Old Right. For instance, hardly anyone remembers this, but the right was actually divided on Vietnam.

I remember when Robert Welch of the John Birch Society, harkening back to a praiseworthy Americanist impulse, criticized the war. It was then that *National Review* turned its guns on the JBS, citing a book Welch had written on Eisenhower some 10 years earlier. It was sheer farce. Buckley tolerated dissent on a wide range of issues—even allied himself with anti-Soviet Marxists like Max Eastman and Sidney Hook—so long as he could consolidate a consensus for the buildup of the military State.

The civil-rights movement of the 1960s complicates the picture. My ideological sympathies were and are with those who resisted the federal government's attacks on the freedom of association (not to mention the federalist structure of the Constitution) in the name of racial integration. At first I didn't like Martin Luther King, Jr. I thought he was a fraud and a tool. But when he turned his attention to the evils of the US war on Vietnam, I began to like him. That's also when the establishment turned against him, and soon he was murdered.

These days, the neocons say the 1964 Civil Rights Act was an attempt to remove barriers to opportunity, and only later was distorted with quotas. That's absurd. Everyone, both proponents and opponents, knew exactly what that law was: a statist, centralizing measure that fundamentally attacked the rights of property and empowered the State as mind reader. To judge not only our actions, but our motives, and to criminalize them.

The good folks who resisted the civil-rights juggernaut were not necessarily ideologically driven. Mostly they resented horrible intrusions into their communities, the media smears, and the attacks on their fundamental freedoms that civil rights represented. The brighter lights among the resistance movement correctly forecasted quotas, though few could have imagined monstrosities like the Americans with Disabilities Act. Of course, they were and continue to be viciously caricatured by the partisans of central power.

By the way, I've recently noticed that mild neoconish critics of the ADA are saying that it too was passed with the best of intentions, and only went wrong later. This is a fantasy based on an impulse to always believe the best of the State and its edicts.

In the early 1920s, Mises said that no man who has contributed to art, science, or letters has had anything good to say about the State and its laws. That is exactly right. Intellectual secession from the ruling regime is the first step to clear, creative thought.

How can all these threads in my personal history be reconciled? What was missing in those days, that the ascendancy of libertarian theory in Rothbard's hands later provided, was an overarching framework to explain why war resistance, opposing forced integration, and celebrating individual enterprise were all of a piece. Liberty rooted in private property is the highest political virtue, and its enemy is the consolidated State. I have made that my lifetime credo.

But those were frustrating days and ideological confusion was everywhere. When Nixon was in power, I could not stand him (though I will admit to once having had a sneaking appreciation of Agnew). Like many later political leaders on the right, he talked a good game but expanded government power in ways the left never could have gotten away with.

Affirmative action, the EPA, the CPSC, the CFTC, destruction of the gold standard, massive inflation, welfarist ideology, huge deficits, price controls, and a host of other DC monstrosities were Nixon creations—not to mention the bloodiest years of the war. Nixon's carpet bombing of Cambodia, for example, destroyed the monarchy and brought the Khmer Rouge to power. Nixon, Kissinger, and the rest have the blood of millions on their hands.

In intellectual circles, you could find conservatives who would write passionate articles and give riveting speeches on the glories of free enterprise. But then the other shoe would drop. Nixon is the answer, they said, because at least he has his priorities straight: before restoring free enterprise at home, the US needed to be a world empire to defeat the Russian army. The Russian army was defeated, or rather fell under its own weight, and all we're left with is another evil empire. We're still waiting for free enterprise.

Doherty: *How did you get involved with Arlington House?*
When did Arlington House begin, who financed it, what was its
philosophy, and why did it die?

Rockwell: In the early 1930s, most libertarian literature was
published by mainstream houses. There wasn't much of it,
but our ideas did get a hearing. Hazlitt was published in
Nation and the *American Century*, Garrett appeared in the
Saturday Evening Post, and Nock was in the *Atlantic*, while the
Southern Agrarians were at the height of the literary profession and Mencken had the *American Mercury*. American Austrian economists like Benjamin Anderson and Frank Fetter
had very high profiles in academia and business. And there
was Colonel McCormick's *Chicago Tribune*.

But a decade of the Depression and the New Deal killed
off most mainstream outlets. Opposing the federal government became politically incorrect, and publishers didn't want
to take the risk of calling down the price-control police or
being accused of sedition. The generation that opposed the
New Deal's welfare-warfare State did not reproduce itself on
any serious scale, and those who remained couldn't get a
hearing.

After Roosevelt tricked the Japanese into firing the first
shot, the America First Committee, which had been a major
vehicle for the resistance, shut down, and after the war, dissident, pro-liberty publishing houses survived only in a handful of places.

Our professors had mostly retired, and our journalists
were reduced to the status of pamphleteers. The left enjoyed
ridiculing libertarian political commentary because it was so
unmainstream, and they were able to point to the existence of
all these cranky pamphlets to prove it wasn't serious material.
Of course, Trotskyite pamphlets were never similarly
attacked.

The only real publishers out there were Caxton, Regnery,
and Devin-Adair, which did heroic work, but their distribution

channels were limited, and in the latter case, some of the material cranky and tainted. Think about it: it was something of a miracle that Mises's books were able to come to print at Yale University. But we should appreciate the fact that there was massive internal and external resistance to each one.

In the middle fifties, as a consequence of Russell Kirk's book *Conservative Mind*, the word "conservative" came to describe anyone who was a nonsocialist skeptic of federal policy. I was unhappy with the word, because I was a conscious disciple of the pre-war Nock-Mencken-libertarian school.

There was a fundamental difference between the Old and New Right of Kirk's making. Kirk's book celebrated some good writers and statesmen. But he distorted what it was that drove them, which was not the "politics of prudence" but implacable moral and philosophical conviction. The main thrust of Kirk's influence, I believe, was to turn the right against its best pre-war instincts.

In Kirk's hands, conservatism became a posture, a demeanor, a mannerism. In practice, it asked nothing more of people than to acquire a classical education, sniff at the modern world, and privately long for times past. And if there was a constant strain in Kirkian conservatism, it was opposition to ideology, a word that Kirk demonized. This allowed him to accuse Mises and Marx of the same supposed error.

In fact, ideology means nothing more than systematic social thought. Without systematic thought, the intellectual shiftiness of statist impulse gets a free ride. You can't fight the massive and organized powers of statist, centralist, and generally destructionist social forces armed only with a watch chain and an antique vocabulary. Ultimately, the question that must be asked and definitively answered in the world of ideas was posed most famously by Lenin: What is to be done?

On the answer to that question rides the fate of civilization itself. And if those of us who believe in the magnificence of the classical-liberal vision of society do not answer it definitively, we will lose. Seeing this, men like Frank Meyer—who was a libertarian on all matters but war and peace—blasted Kirk as a statist and an irrationalist. In the end, however Kirk's moderatism and escapism prevailed because it was an easier path.

Rejecting this easier path was Neil McCaffrey, an extraordinary man who later became my friend and professional mentor on many levels. He was a very close friend of Meyer's, as was Murray. Neil had founded the Conservative Book Club in 1964, and built a booming market among *National Review* and *Human Events* readers. But he soon noted that there were not enough books for people to buy.

That's why Neil founded Arlington House in 1965, and named it after Robert E. Lee's ancestral home, stolen by Lincoln for a Union cemetery. (I still hope to see it returned some day.) McCaffrey had hoped to create a major publishing house that would bring conservative classics and contemporary titles to a broad public for the first time in the postwar period.

There was a series of books forecasting the death of the gold standard and its consequences, by Bill Rickenbacker and Harry Browne, preeminently. The only bestseller Arlington ever had was Harry's *How You Can Profit From the Coming Devaluation*, and I worked as his editor. I also edited George Roche's books, and the works of many other conservative leaders. I was peripherally involved in the publication of Hazlitt's books.

Preeminently, I served as editor for new editions of Mises's *Theory and History*, *Bureaucracy*, and *Omnipotent Government*. Reading those books, I became a thoroughgoing Misesian. I was so thrilled to meet him at a dinner in 1968. He was already in serious decline, but it was still wonderful. That is also when I got to know his wife, Margit, who later helped me found the Mises Institute.

Neil and I disagreed about foreign policy, and it was an uncomfortable topic. He was opposed to US entry into the two world wars, and sound on the so-called Civil War, but he was a complete cold warrior, like most people of his generation. However, on economics, Mises was his guide. One of his favorite topics was the moral and economic justification of charging interest. He was also a brilliant student of Catholic theology, literature, and history, and a saintly man.

Intellectually, I was a libertarian, but I stayed out of the movement, mainly because I had other interests in the publishing world, and the libertarians struck me as a strange bunch in the early 1970s. It seemed to be more a lifestyle movement than a political one, a problem that still persists. There was a very clear distinction in those days between libertarian intellectuals like Murray Rothbard, whom I admired, and the developing movement at large.

Neil had partners in the business, and he lost control, with Buckley playing a malicious role. The company was sold to Roy Disney in the mid-1970s, and eventually phased out.

By this time, I had gone to work for Hillsdale College. I had known George Roche while at Arlington, and admired the fact that he was both antiwar, having written his doctoral dissertation on 1930s war resistance on the right, and a free enterpriser with Austrian sympathies. At Hillsdale, I started *Imprimis* and Hillsdale College Press, set up a speakers' series, oversaw public and movement relations, and helped with fundraising.

It was clear to me at the time that Murray Rothbard was Mises's successor, and I followed his writings carefully. I first met him 1975, and knew immediately that he was a kindred spirit. Like all the other living intellectuals I respected, he was on the margins, laboring at a fraction of the salary he deserved, and excluded from conventional outlets of academic and political opinion.

I cannot remember the day that I finally came around to the position that the State is unnecessary and destructive by its nature—that it cannot improve on, and indeed only destroys, the social and economic system that grows out of property rights, exchange, and natural social authority—but I do know that it was Rothbard who finally convinced me to take this last step.

Unfortunately, I could only admire his writings at a distance. I tried to get Hillsdale to invite him to speak, but that was ruled out immediately. I was told that he might be a fine economist, but he was a loose cannon, unconnected from an organized apparatus of conservative thinking.

But what really did Murray in was not his conviction that the State was unnecessary, but his position on the Cold War. Libertarians were said to be tacit supporters of the Sovietization of the world. It was utter nonsense, but this accusation that Rothbard was a "fine economist" but nothing else would dog him until the end. I always saw this as a rationalization to justify fear of a fundamental rethinking of political philosophy and world affairs.

After Hillsdale, I turned to editing a journal of socioeconomic medicine called *Private Practice*. I worked to integrate the work of the Austrians and apply it to health economics and government intervention in that industry. It proved to be a fruitful mix, and in my mind demonstrated the possibilities of using the Austrian tradition to explain the way the world works in a very practical way.

Doherty: *How did you end up working with Ron Paul?*

Rockwell: In those days, unlike today, I had a keen interest in the affairs of Congress: the members of each committee, the legislation that was being considered, and the like. Being a congressional aide had always been a dream of mine, as absurd as that may sound today. When Ron won his first full term, he asked me to work for him.

We never saw his office as a conventionally political one. It was a bully pulpit to get the message out. We sent out hundreds of thousands of tracts on freedom, inserted amazing articles in the *Congressional Record*, and drafted libertarian legislation as an educational effort.

As for his voting record, Ron had a clear standard: if it meant stealing people's money, he was against it. If it gave people back the liberty and property the government had taken, he was for it. Most of the lobbyists eventually stopped visiting our offices.

He was always respected by fellow legislators, but they thought of him as a bit off-kilter. It was *Mr. Paul Goes to Washington*. Politicians view their job as trading votes, getting their share of pork, expanding government, and generally playing the game. They believe they are being productive when they have helped pass more spending and regulatory legislation, and the price for their vote gets high indeed.

Ron was the opposite. He was a standing rebuke, not only to his colleagues but to the entire system. He still is.

Not many people in DC understood what Ron was up to. I remember once when a lobbyist came by and demanded that Ron oppose foreign aid to the Philippines on grounds that people there killed dogs for food. Ron was glad to support cutting foreign aid for any reason. He introduced the bill, and overnight he was celebrated by animal-rights activists all over the country.

Of course, the bill didn't pass. It's important to remember that ideology plays a very small role in legislative affairs except as a kind of public relations gloss. If a farming bill is passed by a Republican Congress, it is called the "Freedom To Farm Act." If it is passed by a Democratic Congress, it is called the "Family Farm Fairness Act." The text can be identical; only the coloring changes.

Watching this system up close, all my worst suspicions about government were confirmed. When I later started the Mises Institute, I swore that it would not function the way party think tanks in Britain do: as intellectual veneer to a gruesome system of legislative exploitation.

Washington has its own version, of course, and if anyone thinks congressmen or their aides study some group's "policy report" on this or that bill, he knows nothing about the imperial capital of the world. Its animating force is not ideas but graft, lies, and power. Those policy studies are for PR. On the other hand, there is a cost to treating the policy game as if it were some sort of intellectual club to which we all belong: it imbues the process with a moral legitimacy it does not deserve.

A scam was perfected in the early 1980s among leading politicians and the think tanks. A group celebrates a politician's supposed achievements in exchange for which the politician pretends to be influenced by the group. It's all a public-relations game. This is a major reason why Murray was never able to work within that system. He had an irrepressible urge to tell the truth regardless of the consequences. Sure, he was a loose cannon, as any cannon should be on the ship of an imperial State.

Doherty: *What was the genesis of the Mises Institute? How difficult was it to get off the ground?*

Rockwell: When I was in DC, my happiest moments were receiving calls from students who wanted to know more about Ron and his ideas. He had a huge amount of support on Texas campuses. He struck students as smart, principled, and radical. But sending students speeches and pamphlets only took matters so far. I wanted to do more, but as I looked around, I didn't see any libertarian organization that focused on advancing academic scholarship specifically focused on the Austrian School.

Also, I worried that Mises had been losing status as a thinker since his death. Hayek's place was secure because of the Nobel Prize. But the rationalism of Mises, the tough-edged quality of his thinking and his prose, the conviction that economics is a logical system that can justly claim the mantle of science, seemed to be fading.

The free enterprisers were turning toward murkier thinkers, monetarists, positivists, and even institutionalists who had no interest in the grand Misesian project. This also seemed to go along with an unwillingness to consider difficult and radical questions on grounds that they were politically unviable.

There was overlap here with what was happening in politics. Since the early 1970s, the conservative movement was increasingly dominated by former members of the Old Left who had made their way over to the Right. These so-called neoconservatives made the switch in opposition to George McGovern's foreign policy "isolationism," but they had not really changed their views on domestic issues.

To give them credit, the neocons always admitted that they hadn't left the Democrats; the Democrats had left them. They openly celebrated the legacies of Wilson, FDR, and Truman—mass-murdering would-be dictators all.

That position needed to be refuted and fought, but instead, a military-minded conservative movement embraced the neocons as allies on the only issue that really mattered to them, the expansion of the warfare state. There was no place for Mises, whose writings on war and statism were numerous and profound, in this new consensus.

There were few alternatives to the Reaganized right. The Beltway libertarians were drifting more and more toward policy and a generalized concern with respectability (the two go hand in hand), and away from Austrian economics and anything that smacked of idealism or a high theoretical concern. Hosting Alan Greenspan at a cocktail party became the goal.

I noticed a similar tendency among scholarship-granting institutions. They seemed interested in subsidizing only Ivy-League students of a soft classical-liberal bent, rather than promoting the concrete development and application of radical thought.

Another approach I rejected was quietism. I've never been impressed with the idea that we should sit back in complacent satisfaction that we constitute the remnant, while others eventually join us or not. Surely ideas do have consequences, but reality dictates that they need passionate scholars to advance them on every front.

Hence, Mises as a thinker, who had done so much to resuscitate old-fashioned, tough-minded liberalism, was falling by the wayside, a victim of a movement that eschewed all such unrespectable thinkers. Misesian theory and practice were fading fast. I set out to change that, and to serve a neglected generation of students. Idealism is what stirs the young heart, and the only idealism that seemed to be available to students in those days was from the left. I harkened back to my lifetime love of Mises, of his brilliance and his courage, and talked with Margit about the project. She was thrilled, made me promise to make it my lifetime work, and we got busy.

When I asked Murray to head academic affairs, he brightened up like a kid on Christmas morning. We agreed that the goal should be to provide a support system that would revive the Austrian School as a player in the world of ideas, so that statism of the left and right could be fought and defeated.

The main criticism directed against Austrian economics in those days was that it was not formal or rigorous because it rejected the use of mathematics as the tool for constructing economic theory. But this is absurd. In fact, Murray actually had two majors as an undergraduate: one in economics and the other in math. What was at stake here was not the competence of the Austrians but a fundamental methodological question: can the methods of the physical sciences be imported to the social sciences via economics? The Austrian answer was no.

At the same time, there was a grain of truth in the criticisms. American academia provided no formal setting to study economics from the Austrian perspective. Most of the then-current practitioners were self-taught, so even they had a limited perspective on the possibilities of creating an alternative formal system of economics.

I wanted to make up for this deficiency by creating a shadow university setting in which students could study economics under the post-Mises generation of Austrian scholars, especially Murray.

Murray loved our programs. He would teach all afternoon and stay up until 3:00 and 4:00 A.M. talking to students about ideas. He was always accessible, laughed easily, and was never foreboding. He learned from everyone around him and rejected the "guru" persona he could have so easily adopted.

Students who came to us expecting a stern setting of judgmental theorizing were shocked to discover something closer to a salon where intellectual inquiry was free and open-ended. It had to be that way to balance out the rigor of the content. Murray's spirit still animates all our programs.

The funding problem was one I dealt with from the beginning. I had wanted to give Murray a platform, but I quickly discovered that old-line foundations would not help so long as he was on board. They certainly would not support an organization that argued for positions like the abolition of central banking, or funded revisionist historical scholarship and disagreed with the two-party consensus in Washington.

Corporate foundations, meanwhile are not very interested in ideas generally, particularly not ones that threatened the status quo. It's a cliché now, but I also found that big corporations are not the strongest supporters of free enterprise.

I also found that most old-line foundation and corporate money comes with strings attached. And if there is one institutional feature I desired for the Mises Institute, beyond its ideological stance, it was independence.

I did not want to get roped into supporting cranky policy projects like vouchers or enterprise zones, and I did not want to be forced into emphasizing some aspects of Misesian theory simply because they were trendy, while feeling compelled to deemphasize others. I never wanted to find myself censoring an associated scholar because some foundation bigshot didn't like what he was saying.

I wanted to see the fullness of the Austrian program funded and represented, consistently, fearlessly, and regardless of the fallout. The Mises Institute needed to do work that is deep and wide. It needed to be free to support research in areas like economic methodology, which doesn't interest corporations, or blast the newest policy gimmick, a stance that doesn't interest foundations. Finally, government money was not ever a consideration.

In the end, our support has come from individual donors and nearly exclusively so. I had a good-size Rolodex, so I started there. Ron Paul and others signed letters to their lists, which was a big help, and I had enough savings to work a few years without a salary.

We've been in business now for 17 years, and it took a long time to become viable. But we built slowly and carefully, brick by brick, and now have a solid edifice. And we still have our independence, and we still have an edge.

Doherty: *I've heard intimations that Koch interests attempted to stymie the Mises Institute's development. Is this so, and if so, specifically how?*

Rockwell: It wasn't exactly subtle. In the early eighties, Charles Koch monopolized the libertarian think-tank world by giving and promising millions. That's fine, but he was gradually edging away from radical thought, which included Austrian economics, and toward mainstreaming libertarian theory (as opposed to libertarianizing the mainstream) that attracted him in the first place.

I have never understood this type of thinking. If being mainstream is what you want, there are easier ways to go about it than attempting to remake an intellectual movement that is hostile to government into a mildly dissenting subgroup within the ideological structure of the ruling class.

Murray and Charles broke at this point, and I won't go into the details. But it was clear that Koch saw their break as the beginning of a long war. Early on, I received a call from George Pearson, head of the Koch Foundation. He said that

Mises was too radical and that I mustn't name the organization after him, or promote his ideas. I was told that Mises was "so extreme even Milton Friedman doesn't like him." If I insisted on going against their diktat, they would oppose me tooth and nail.

Later, I heard from other Koch men. One objected to the name of our monthly newsletter, the *Free Market*. The idea this time was that the word "free" was off-putting. Another said that   idea of an Austrian academic journal was wrong, since it implied we were a separate school, and mustn't be. All urged me to dump Murray and then shun him, if I expected any support.

I was taken aback by what I interpreted as pettifoggery, and I had no idea what we would yet face. I negotiated a contract with Lexington Books for an annual journal, and put together a pretty good list of editorial advisers with Murray as the editor. Soon after, what came to be called "the boycott" began. Letters and calls poured in from those associated with Koch-dominated organizations. They resigned and swore eternal enmity. We even lost some big donors. It was my baptism by fire into the world of research institutes.

It may seem absurd to talk about this as if it were some sort of conspiracy against the Mises Institute. Why would a multi-billionaire care if the Institute existed or not? I mean, we were a gnat compared to his water buffalo. It's a mystery that even today I do not entirely understand. In any case, there was blood all over the place by the time it was over.

Among threatened programs, the *Review of Austrian Economics* was nearly killed, but Murray persevered and the first issue came out in 1986. We went through 10 volumes of that journal, and it was the key to building up the Austro-Misesian movement as we know it today. The entire collection is on Mises.org, and downloaded by students all over the world. And now we have the higher-profile *Quarterly Journal of Austrian Economics*.

Today, I regard all these early conflicts as water under the bridge. The Koch Foundation uses our texts in their seminars, and the old antipathies are dwindling. Koch organizations are no longer shocked to see us taking different views in areas like vouchers and trade treaties. They serve one agenda with a particular style, approach, and audience, and we serve another with a different style, approach, and audience.

One note about competition among nonprofits. From time to time, well-meaning people suggest that the Mises Institute join with other like-minded groups. By pooling our resources, we would have a greater impact. But this rationale is flawed. Competition is as essential in the nonprofit world as it is in enterprise generally. The early opposition spurred us on to do a better job, never to give up, and never to give in.

I still get harassed from time to time about something someone connected to us has written or said. I'm told that I should do something to shut him up, and indeed policy institutes can be very restrictive in the way they treat their scholars. If they are pursuing a political agenda, I suppose they have to be. But I don't believe in telling any of our associated scholars—and there are fully 200 of them—what to think or what to write.

That's because I founded the Mises Institute to provide a setting for unrestricted intellectual exploration in the Austrian tradition, no matter how radical the conclusions may be. There are no speech controls at our conferences. There is no fear that someone will say something that lies outside the preset boundaries of respectable opinion.

I cannot let the temptation to get along with everybody, or fit into someone else's strategic agenda, stand in the way. In the political and academic worlds, taboos are piling up by the day, but they are enemies of serious thought.

The Mises Institute has a unique place in the division of labor, and it is to make possible a radical reevaluation of the intellectual foundations of the modern statist enterprise. Our senior scholars—Walter Block, David Gordon, Jeff Herbener,

Hans Hoppe, Guido Hülsmann, Peter Klein, Yuri Maltsev, Ralph Raico, Joe Salerno, and Mark Thornton—lead the way. Some people say our approach is reckless. I can only hope that it always remains so.

Doherty: *Relate to me what you think the Mises Institute's greatest successes have been.*

Rockwell: Most recently, I'm thrilled with the restored *Human Action*. I was astounded when I first realized how far later editions of this book had strayed from the original. I mean, the third edition has Mises endorsing conscription, which was not only not in the original, but Mises had specifically and persuasively condemned conscription in his writings.

There were other problems. Important passages on Nazi economic planning were eliminated as were whole paragraphs from the section on monopoly. By comparison, the first edition is a seamless web and I'm so pleased that it is back in print in a Scholar's Edition. It's been flying out of our offices.

By the way, what economics text of 900 pages is still a huge seller 50 years after it first appeared? I can't think of one. Facts like this tell me that Mises is here to stay. In the next century, I'm convinced he'll have a much higher profile than he did in this one. He was a prophet and a fantastic genius. Not that his work shouldn't ever be improved or criticized. We have such papers at every session of our Austrian Scholars Conferences. But we have to have the material available to learn from before it can be revised, improved, and reinterpreted.

The first book the Mises Institute printed was Mises's *Theory and History*, with an introduction by Murray. It is still a big seller. We have brought Murray's *Ethics of Liberty* back into print, along with two dozen monographs on the Austrian School that we have distributed all over the world.

Our book *Costs of War* has been called the most important piece of antiwar revisionist scholarship in the second half of this century. Our book *Secession, State, and Liberty* is a success. We brought *Man, Economy, and State* back into print, as well as a dozen other books.

We even have a new edition of Murray's *America's Great Depression*, with an introduction by Paul Johnson, and an Austrian economics text for smart high-school students in the works.

Oddly, I never envisioned the Mises Institute as a publishing house, though it could easily be mistaken for one. We are funding the research and writing of a major intellectual biography of Mises, a massive two-volume project. We want one of Rothbard as well. And we have five regular periodicals: a newsletter on current trends, an interview publication, a literary review, a scholarly journal, and a news and information sheet on the Austrian School.

Meanwhile, our summer Mises University has put a host of PhD students in economics through a rigorous program that would otherwise be unavailable. We've trained plenty of historians, philosophers, theologians, and others too. We've also started a summer Rothbard Graduate Seminar for advanced PhD students and post-docs, and been overwhelmed by the worldwide response. There's also our weekly Austrian Economics Workshop.

We spend the bulk of our money on students and student programs. When we take on a graduate student in economics, we stick by him or her for up to six years. That's a huge investment, but look at the results. We now have professors honeycombed through academia, and they have made Austrian economics a vital part of their curricula.

Our Mises and Rothbard Fellows are in demand, and not only because more and more departments seek genuine diversity at a time of Austrian renaissance. They are among the best young economists working today. Not only can they run rings around the mainstream with the mainstream's own tools, but their praxeological grounding gives them a real leg-up in understanding actual economic events. They are also blessed with the vocation to teach, to be scholars in the classical tradition. This is no way to get rich, and it's not for everyone, but in the secular world, there is no higher calling.

Over the long term, this will be where the Mises Institute makes the biggest difference. Seventeen years ago, Austrians had a hard time finding positions, much less holding on to them, but these days, we run out of candidates long before the requests for our students stop. Demand is outstripping supply.

Hazlitt told me that he thought the great success of the Mises Institute was providing a forum for Rothbard at a time when everyone else had turned his back on him. I am indeed proud of that. I also think that the Mises Institute has helped raise up an alternative intellectual framework as freedom of thought and speech has played a smaller and smaller role in academia.

The faculty at our conferences speak of their elation at escaping the stultifying political rules of their home campuses. Our students feel it too. That kind of freedom and collegiality is what a university is supposed to be about.

But I think the key achievement of the Mises Institute is the one Murray pointed to. Before the Institute, Austrian economics was in danger of becoming a hard-money investment strategy or an antirationalist process analysis—ironic indeed for a school rooted in Aristotelianism. The Institute rescued the praxeologically based main trunk of the school, and restored it to prominence and fruitfulness. Thus the Austrian School of Menger, Böhm-Bawerk, Mises, and Rothbard lives and grows and has increasing influence.

Doherty: *Tell me about your involvement with the Libertarian Party, and the specific reasons for your disenchantment with it.*

Rockwell: I was never an LP person, though I generally like the platform, which was largely written by Murray. People say that he wasted his time in the LP. That judgment presumes that geniuses like Murray should not be allowed to have hobbies and amusements. He loved Baroque church architecture and 1920s jazz. He loved soap operas and sports. He loved chess and 18th-century oratorios. And he enjoyed, for many years, his activities with the LP, particularly since it was a hobby that intersected with his professional interests. It certainly didn't distract from his scholarly work, which continued unabated through this entire period.

For years, as close as we were, I largely ignored what Murray was doing in the LP. But Ron Paul decided to run for the 1988 presidential nomination, and he announced in 1986. That's when I got involved. I feared he wasn't going to get the nomination. To my astonishment, Russell Means, who didn't seem to be a libertarian at all, had a real shot at it. I swung into action, and helped manage Ron's bid for the nomination. But that pretty much burned me out.

I wasn't pleased with what I saw in the party. I sensed a lack of interest in ideas and an absurd obsession with petty organizing details. There was a lot of waste of time and money. I also felt like the party was creating a false hope of successfully bringing about reform through politics. And yet, in all these ways, I suppose it was no different from any other party.

What bugged me the most, however, was a general tendency among the party types to downplay libertarian theory in a host of areas. They were generally sound on tax cuts and drug policy and the like. But there was no interest at all in foreign policy. In fact, the largest faction in the party was actually hawkish on war and strangely conventional on policy particulars. Then there was the perpetual focus on living a life of liberty. A life of liberty meant, in the first instance, never wearing a tie or a white shirt.

The last time I had any contact with the LP was the summer of 1989 in Philadelphia. Sweet, sweet Murray, eternally optimistic and good-hearted Murray, rose to the platform to make the case for electing this chairman over that chairman. I forget the details. In any case, they hissed at him. They booed him. They shouted him down and denounced him. I thought: this is just amazing.

The greatest libertarian thinker in history, and they can't even treat him politely? Even more astounding, Murray thought nothing of it. To him, this was just life in the LP. It was then that I thought: This is it. I reemphasized to Murray my views on these people, which he had come to share, and suggested we get out. We did, and his wife Joey cheered.

Again, this is water under the bridge. I'm perfectly happy for the LP to go about its business. Harry Browne said some good things in the last election. He's generally a man after my own heart. I'm just not cut out for politics, and I don't think politics holds out much hope for the future of human liberty.

Doherty: *Tell me about your relationships with Pat Buchanan and the Randolph Club.*

Rockwell: Before I do that, let me just emphasize that all these political goings-on were a mere sidelight in Murray's life. His main project in these years was the magisterial *History of Economic Thought* that came out just after he died. For most academics, these two volumes would be more than enough to show for an entire career. But for Murray, they were just a slight piece of a massive literary output.

His output was huge, even aside from scholarship. On a typical morning, I would find a 20-page article on politics on my fax, and a five-page article on strategy. For him, pounding out these gems was just a way to pass the time between 100-page scholarly articles and whole book manuscripts. His output was beyond human comprehension.

That's why Burt Blumert and I started the *Rothbard-Rockwell Report*, whose name Murray was kind enough to suggest. At the Mises Institute, we could have spent all our time marketing his material to newspapers and magazines. Instead, we needed a steady place to publish all his short pieces on political and cultural topics, and—as Joey has mentioned—it was one of the joys of his last years.

At the same time, Murray needed practical ideological recreation to make his scholarly work possible and add leaven to his life. Leaving the LP lifted a burden off Murray's shoulders, but I worried that it would also leave something of a hole in his life. A part of him loved ideological organization on a grand scale.

Our first contacts with the paleoconservatives came after their huge break with the neoconservatives, the most warlike and statist intellectuals in the country. Murray and Tom Fleming, editor of *Chronicles*, exchanged letters and found they agreed on the intellectual errors on the right. Some people say Murray was becoming more conservative and conventional. This is unbelievably uncomprehending.

Murray rejected what Mises called the cultural destructionism of the Left because he saw it as a back-door to State building. If you attack the family by impinging on its autonomy, the family can no longer serve as a bulwark against State power. So it is with leftist rhetoric that ridicules the habits, prejudices, traditions, and institutions that form the basis of settled, middle-class community life. He saw the relentless attacks on these as paving the way for government managers to claim more territory as their own.

Moreover, it was Murray's conviction that government power is the greatest enemy that a rich cultural heritage has. It is not capitalism that wrecks the foundations of civilized life but the State. In this, he was in full agreement with Mises, Hayek, and Schumpeter. And incidentally, this line of argument, which Murray had long used, has been picked up by other libertarians in the meantime.

But the real bond between Tom and Murray was their shared hatred of the statism, centralism, and global warfarism of the conservative movement. They were both fed up with a Buckleyized conservatism, and now, at last, here was a chance to do something about it.

Together Murray and I watched as the Berlin Wall came down and the Soviet Union dissolved, and we were intensely curious as to how the conservatives would respond. Would they return to their pre-war, antiwar roots? Or would they continue to push for the American empire? Well, we got our answer in 1990 with the beginnings of the Gulf War. It seemed obvious that this was Bush's attempt to keep the warfare State fat and thriving.

The US gave permission to Iraq to annex Kuwait, and then suddenly reversed positions. The US paid off countries around the world to be part of its "coalition" and waged a bloody war on Iraq, burying innocents in the sand and proclaiming victory over the aggressor.

We waited for the conservatives to denounce the war, but of course it didn't happen, although I'll always treasure Kirk's last letter to me, in which he called for hanging the "war criminal Bush" on the White House lawn. Too bad he never wrote like that in public. But the neocons were entirely in control of the right and cheered Bush to the Heavens.

These were disgusting days. Bush dragged out all his tax-funded missiles and other weapons of mass destruction and put them on the Washington, DC, mall for the booboisie to admire. Yellow ribbons were everywhere.

But the paleos were a different matter. Paul Gottfried, Allan Carlson, Clyde Wilson, Fleming, and others associated with the Rockford Institute blasted the war without qualification. They openly called the US an imperial power and made the argument that we had always made: that the greatest threat to our liberties was not overseas but in the District of Columbia.

Meanwhile, we were alarmed that not even the libertarians seemed prepared to go this far. *Reason* magazine and the Republican Liberty Caucus were for the Gulf War, and *Liberty* magazine, for whom Murray had written, was ambivalent on the question. In general, there was silence from the people who should have been our natural allies. To us, that merely underscored a more deeply rooted problem in libertarian circles: the strange combination of cultural alienation and political conventionality.

We began to write about the errors of the "modal" libertarians. They were soft on war, sanguine about centralization of power, and friendly toward the rise of the social-therapeutic aspects of the State inherent in civil-rights egalitarianism. They were uninterested in scholarship and unschooled in history. They were culturally fringy and politically mainstream, which is precisely the opposite of what Murray and Mises were. I couldn't imagine the old libertarian school of Nock, Chodorov, Garrett, Flynn, and Mencken at home with this.

The best of the paleoconservatives, in contrast, were old-fashioned constitutionalists who took libertarian positions on a range of issues. They wanted the troops home and the government out of people's lives. They wanted to abolish the welfare state, and had a very telling critique of it. Their critique was not based on rights, but it was serious and sophisticated.

The Center for Libertarian Studies cofounded the John Randolph Club, which I named for the aristocratic, antiegalitarian battler of centralized power of the early nineteenth century. The word "paleolibertarian" was mine too, and the purpose was to recapture the political edge and intellectual rigor and radicalism of the pre-war libertarian right. There was no change in core ideology but a reapplication of fundamental principles in ways that corrected the obvious failures of the *Reason* and *National Review* sets.

I remember people at the time saying: "Oh no! You're falling in bed with a bunch of religious rightists!" I would just rub my eyes in dismay. In the first place, if a person believes in liberty and also happens to be religious, what is wrong with that? Since when did atheism become a mandatory view within libertarian circles? Also, the point was not to fall in bed with anybody but to organize a new intellectual movement precisely to do battle with the statists on all sides.

Much good came out of this. We took out ads in the *New York Times* attacking war and we gave the neocons a run for their money. We had some very good and fun meetings, and Murray had the chance for a productive exchange of ideas with some of the smartest thinkers in the country.

But there were limits to what could be accomplished. As old-fashioned Burkeans, somewhat influenced by Kirk, they resisted ideology in principle. That meant an impatience with the rationalism of economic theory and libertarian political theory. That eventually caused us problems on issues like trade. All sides opposed Nafta, which was mercantilist, but we couldn't agree on the urgency of eliminating trade barriers. Still, the debates were fun. We agreed to cooperate where we could, and disagree where we must.

Another problem was that usual evil force in the world: politics. Nearly alone among Republicans, Pat Buchanan was a strong opponent of the war on Iraq, denouncing it up until the troops actually landed. He then began to offer a radical critique of the interventionist State in a host of areas. In 1991, he challenged Bush for the nomination, speaking out against Bush's tax increases and welfarism. In some ways, it appeared that he could become a dream candidate, uniting a passionate concern for both free enterprise and peace.

Conventional libertarians didn't like Pat, in part because he was against open immigration. But it seemed obvious that the patterns of immigration since 1965 have increased rather than decreased the government's control over the economy. And there is no obvious libertarian position on this subject: whether immigration is peaceful or invasive depends entirely on who owns the property onto which they immigrate, and whether they make their own way once here. The welfare state and public schools complicate the picture enormously.

Unfortunately for everyone, as the campaign progressed, Pat got more and more protectionist and nationalist. Murray saw that Buchanan was in danger of jettisoning all his good principles. If the State can and must plan trade to protect the nation, then why not the rest of the economy? Sure enough, by 1996, Pat's protectionist theories mutated and took over his economic thinking entirely. For example, he advocated a 100-percent tax on estates over $1 million. Pat still says good things on foreign policy, but the lesson for me is an old one: never hinge the hopes of a movement on a politician.

Chronicles is open to libertarians, and the Randolph Club still meets. But, for me, this chapter in the history of ideological organizing came to a close with Murray's death. With Murray, anything seemed possible. We could dabble in practical tactics and strategy, write on every topic under the sun, and keep cranking out the students and academic conferences and publications. But without Murray, I needed to concentrate on what I do best, which was and is internal development. At the same time, the Mises Institute began to develop the resources to expand its horizons as broadly as Murray had always wanted.

Doherty: *Do you feel you succeeded in creating the paleo movement you speculated about when you departed from the "modal" libertarian movement?*

Rockwell: To some extent, I would say the present decline in the moral legitimacy of the executive State represents a paleoization, if you will, a systematic radicalization of the middle class. As Frank Rich has pointed out in the *New York Times*, all the real political dissidents and radicals, the people who are raising fundamental objections to the status quo of the American civil project, are on the right.

They are homeschoolers fed up with the propaganda in public schools. They are average Americans who fear and resent anyone with a federal badge and gun. The pro-lifers are pushing the boundaries of permissible civil disobedience. Antiwar rallies are as likely to be populated by old-line constitutionalists as aging New Lefties.

Meanwhile, the mainstream left is increasingly censorious. It is there that you find the book burners, the taboo enforcers, the thought police, and the apologists for federal tyranny.

On the other hand, and despite the continued growth of the State, we are seeing the flourishing of enterprise across the country and the world, an intense and renewed interest in the art of private life, and a continuing secession from establishment political institutions. Another way of putting this is that the classical ideal of liberty and private life is again gaining currency, and a major reason is the successes that an intellectual vanguard of Austrian scholars and political dissidents have had in undermining the ideological foundations of the State.

Murray anticipated all this with his outreach efforts to marginalized conservatives. Contrary to the conventional wisdom, he had an outstanding strategic sense. It's just that he was always ahead of everyone else in his thinking, and so he suffered detraction and calumny. Not that it mattered to him. Early in his career, he decided to take a certain path, inspired by the example of Mises, and he stuck with it to the end.

Doherty: *What about plans for the future?*

Rockwell: These days, we have more than enough work to do in publishing, funding, and supporting Austrian and libertarian scholarship, both of which are in a boom phase. People on the left thought that the collapse of socialism would mean that antisocialist intellectual forces would decline as well. The opposite has happened. At last, it is clear to anyone who cares about liberty that the real enemy is the ruling regime in government and academia, and that this ruling regime resides within our own borders.

The Internet has been a tremendous boost to the Austrian School and the classical liberal perspective. Since World War II, the biggest hurdle our side has had is in getting the message out. At last, the Net evens the score. Not a day goes by without hosts of people around the world discovering the world of Misesian-Rothbardian theory for the first time, just because they run across our Website at Mises.org. Our goal always is to provide the resources that keep people's attention on the conceptual fundamentals: liberty and property versus the State and its power.

Right now, we are faced with a historic opportunity. In academia, the old guard no longer has the same credibility among students. The Left has surrendered the mantle of idealism and radicalism. The Austrian School is perfectly suited to be the new and fresh alternative. And in public affairs, we need to take advantage of the declining status and moral legitimacy of the central State to make a major push for libertarian ideas. The revolution that struck Eastern Europe a decade ago has come home in surprising ways, and we need to work to encourage these trends and direct them toward a consistent stand for liberty and property.

Many years ago, Hazlitt gave a speech in which he said it is our moral obligation to continue the battle no matter what the odds. What he said then is still true today: we are not threatened with bankruptcy or jail for holding the opinions we do. All we risk is being called nasty names. Surely that is not too high a price to pay for defending the very foundations of civilization.

ROCKWELL-KANTOR INTERVIEW

[Myles Kantor interviewed Lew Rockwell on March 12, 2002, for the pages of Frontpagemag.com, *on "September 11 and the Anti-Capitalistic Mentality."]*

Kantor: *Ludwig von Mises entitled one of his books the* Anti-Capitalistic Mentality. *What did Mises mean by this title?*

Rockwell: It's a marvelous book, written in 1956. It still holds up. Mises addressed the question: why are the cultural elites so biased against the free-market economy, and all it represents, despite the evidence that it is the only system compatible with a developed civilization?

He took it for granted that huge sectors of the intelligentsia and media are deeply ignorant of economics. In this book he addresses the problem not of ignorance but hate: hatred of the businessman and entrepreneur, and the assumptions that the business class is secretly criminal, that the rich never deserve what they own, that businesses that rake in profits by serving others through enterprise somehow "owe" something to the "community," so, if they don't give it up voluntarily, it should be taken from them.

We see this on display in these disgusting Enron hearings, lovingly reported by the echo-chamber press. It's one thing to prosecute crime, but this is anticapitalism running wild. Nobody remembers that during the '90s boom phase of the market created by loose credit, investors cared only about accounting in order to sell companies with real earnings and buy those without. The conventional wisdom on the street was that any company that paid dividends was worthless. That's the topsy-turvy world that easy money created in the late 90s.

So Enron was typical of major corporate high-flyers during the boom phase of the business cycle, but in 2001 the free market struck back with a dose of reality. Unviable businesses melted. Thank goodness for that! And now investors are wary, as they should be. There is a wonderful witch hunt on for companies that bury debt as subsidiaries, and there is 'fessing up all over the place. Truth at last, courtesy of the market economy.

Now contrast this process with HUD, the post office, or any other federal bureau. The GAO comes out with regular reports showing that these agencies' books are in complete chaos, with tens of billions missing, unaccounted for, or uncollectible. There are no earnings. There are no dividends. And who cares? No one. In Washington, GAO reports are used for scrap paper and birdcage lining.

And so now we have these politicos who specialize in public relations and wealth redistribution putting Enron on trial for alleged accounting malpractice. And why? Because the company went belly-up. But the market is supposed to punish unviable enterprises by shutting them down. Lord knows that would never happen to a government agency. Government specializes in keeping unprofitable operations going: look at the history of industry in the Soviet Union, or at American farming, or the TVA.

Kantor: *What type of anticapitalism did Mises draw attention to?*

Rockwell: All of the same types of bias were present 46 years ago when Mises wrote his book. He noticed in those days that detective novels, for example, frequently made the rich businessman the villain. In movies, bureaucrats are heroic and public spirited while businessmen are greedy, racist, and vaguely criminal. In popular music, the "suits" are the ones 'dissed.

As for academia, outside one or two economics professors, nearly the entire liberal arts faculty of the typical university is reliably anticapitalist. As a class, liberal arts academics can be depended on to oppose economic development, support high taxes, and latch on to every anti-enterprise cause that comes along.

Some of the anticapitalism of the intellectuals is self-interest at work: those paid by the State identify with the State and its interests. There's also snobbery at work—most intellectuals hate commercial culture. Well, folks, the glory of capitalism is that it permits you to choose what to consume and what not to consume. If intellectuals prefer the music of Anton Webern to Britney Spears, fine. Tower Records offers both.

But Mises's analysis goes further to identify the problem of envy at the root of anticapitalism. Whether in the arts, entertainment, or academia, the dominant players are talented people who believe that they are wiser and better than the masses. They are appalled that capitalism permits a B-school dropout to become a billionaire while they scrape by for a measly raise when promoted from assistant to associate professor. They set out to cripple the system that brings this about.

And yet this is not new. Since ancient times, the merchant has been scorned and his profession considered ignoble. The philosopher who strolls around speculating on the meaning of life is seen as the highest form of humanity, while the man who risks his own money to make available food, shelter, medicine, clothing, and all the other material goods that make life livable is despised.

Now I'm all for philosophy and other academic disciplines; like the priesthood, this is a vocation that requires sacrifice, and that is essential. But celebrate the risk-taking merchant too. He is a benefactor of mankind.

Kantor: *Radical environmentalists in Europe often vandalize and perpetrate arson against McDonald's restaurants. Is there a parallel between this aggression and the attacks on the World Trade Center?*

Rockwell: Notice that whenever looting of businesses occur, at these antiglobalist events or in Europe when McDonald's restaurants are burned, the press will frequently write that no violence has occurred, on grounds that no one was hurt or killed. No violence? What do you call it when gangsters destroy property for ideological reasons? You can call it violence, or you might even call it terrorism. The Earth Liberation Front has been doing this for years in the US, wrecking research labs and burning the cars of scientists. It's hardly ever reported.

Think about the people who worked at the WTC—traders, insurers, speculators, retailers, lenders—all financial experts whose contributions are essential to our daily lives. They labored every day to overcome linguistic, cultural, and regulatory barriers to unite the world in a great commercial project to improve the lot of mankind. But public schools teach that they are exploiters, Hollywood regards them as somewhat criminal, and not one person in ten thousand can tell you why what they do matters.

When the hijackers were choosing targets, they figured that they would smash these buildings because they somehow represented the "money power." Well, not many among the culture elites in this country or the rest of the world would really disagree with them. The urge to destroy business and finance as a sector plays itself out in politics and the media every day.

The attack on the WTC put into action what millions of students are taught every day in their college classrooms, what prime-time television suggests night after night, what the sociology journals seek to prove year after year: entrepreneurs and what they create are antisocial and wholly dispensable.

Yet enterprise and its symbols do not represent "money power" or any other kind of power. They represent the coming together of people to trade voluntarily with the hope of achieving material advancement and progress.

The watchwords of capitalism are persuasion and contract. Buying and selling is a cooperative act. No one ever forced a Parisian to eat a Big Mac. The urge to smash the system that makes it possible for people to have more choices in life stems from ignorance and evil. Without free enterprise, civilization would crumble and we would all starve and die.

Kantor: *Has popular culture's appreciation of these individuals increased since September 11?*

Rockwell: I wouldn't say so. We've gained a greater appreciation of rescue workers, and that's great, though I notice that many of them are seizing the opportunity to sue the city for personal damages. But what about the people and the occupations that were actually targeted by the killers?

Hardly anyone can name a single business that was smashed. Among them: Morgan Stanley, Fred Alger Management, Cantor Fitzgerald, MassMutual, Fiduciary Trust, Harris Beach & Wilcox, OppenheimerFunds, Bank of America, Kemper Insurance, Lehman Brothers, and Credit Suisse First Boston.

I don't recall a single tribute to these institutions printed in the popular press. I don't even rule out that many people among the US intelligentsia thought that because these people were on the front lines of capitalism, they had it coming. Yet these are the brokers who worked every day to invest our savings and channel resources to their most profitable uses. These insurance companies provide the valuable service of securing our lives and property against accidents, and did far more to achieve their aims than the Office of Homeland Security, which in fact has no real stake in the security of anything but its own budget.

Kantor: *Have federal policies after September 11 reflected a greater appreciation of capitalism?*

Rockwell: Again, the opposite has happened. At the World Economic Forum, held in New York in memory of September 11, you couldn't tell the protesters from the main speakers. The podium always seemed to be held by some demagogue railing against the wealth of the West. Not one speaker bothered to give a tribute to free enterprise, not even the corporate people there. In all, it was a disgusting show.

The conventional wisdom now is that multinational corporations are just elaborate shell games covering every manner of criminality. The recent talk is not about whether there should be new regulation of business, but how severe should it be.

Just recently, Pat Buchanan announced that the Enron collapse shows that "capitalism may contain the seed of its own destruction." That's a good summary of the Marxian view. Next he'll endorse a dictatorship of the proletariat and the expropriation of the Kulaks.

Kantor: *To what extent was September 11 facilitated by domestic anticapitalism, namely, regulatory impositions?*

Rockwell: This is an interesting case. Of course the FAA has long prevented airlines from defending their own property. I know many pilots who saw the need for guns on planes long ago. But the regulatory view was that this was unthinkable. They were told that hijackers need to be placated and talked to by experts on the ground, while passengers and crew should be compliant.

This is what all the terrorism experts were saying before September 11. If you think about it, this entire war and the huge increase in government power that has resulted, including the thousands dead and the billions in destroyed property, might not ever have occurred had the pilots had the right to protect property from invasion and theft.

So, yes, regulators are to blame in part. Of course that doesn't remove responsibility from the hijackers themselves. But let's say you have a town council that forbids banks from installing alarm systems, and then all the local banks are robbed. Should the town council be held morally culpable along with the robbers? I think so.

There is also the interesting case of asbestos and the WTC. Might the steel in the building have weakened more slowly if asbestos had been able to be used on the upper floors as it was on the lower? Might that have given people more time to leave the buildings? Some engineers have said so.

As for restrictions on trade, those who support ongoing sanctions against Iraq and other countries need to consider that these policies violate free trade, and give rise to hatreds that can fuel terrorism. Long before the terrorists cited these sanctions as an excuse, people from groups like the Institute of International Economics had raised serious questions about the effects of these sanctions. Remember too that this is a region rich with oil profits made possible in part by domestic restrictions on energy production. This is why a policy of free trade with all peoples of the world needs to be matched by loosened energy regulations at home.

Kantor: *Despite the devastation inflicted by socialism from Russia to Ethiopia to Cuba, its apologists maintain these regimes have perverted socialist principles. Is socialism inherently hostile to freedom? Is capitalism a precondition for peace?*

Rockwell: That's right, there's always a new form of socialism being proposed in some new books. A bestseller on the college circuit called *Empire*, for example, calls for a new communism which, the authors promise, will be different from the old. But anything other than free enterprise always means a society of compulsion and lower living standards, and any form of socialism strictly enforced means dictatorship and the total State. That this statement is still widely disputed only illustrates the degree to which malignant fantasy can capture the imagination of intellectuals.

What the socialists hate most is that the masses have never risen up to overthrow the free-enterprise society. This had already frustrated them by the turn of the 20th century, so many of them hatched a new scheme to impose socialism by crisis. In Europe, and to some extent in the US, war was their preferred method of getting rid of the market economy. They saw that war puts the government in charge of economic life. They knew that if they ever stood a chance to impose central planning, it was to be through war socialism.

This is why the socialists and the Left generally were such strong advocates of entry into World War I, and why FDR so badly wanted to enter World War II. Hitler too believed that war was the best way to bring about National Socialism. Mussolini felt the same about fascism. Dictators love war. We even saw elements of this in the Clinton years; he turned to war when his collectivist domestic programs weren't panning out. And the left is correct in this—people are more prone to give up liberty in wartime.

Ludwig von Mises, who saw his country and civilization wrecked in two world wars, used to say, "The first condition for the establishment of perpetual peace is the general adoption of the principles of laissez-faire capitalism." People on the left and right today reject that view, and we live with the destructive aims and policies of anticapitalism, and we have perpetual war.

This is why, so far as the Mises Institute is concerned, we will keep doing what we have always done—defend the economics of capitalism against its myriad enemies—because it is the very foundation of peace, prosperity, and civilization, and the best, and perhaps only, source of effective security as well.

THE WISDOM OF LEFEVRE

[A tribute to Robert LeFevre at the Mises Institute Conference "The Philosophy of a Free Society," Auburn, Alabama, September 28, 2001.]

In 1957, a businessman and radio personality named Robert LeFevre (1911–1986) founded a very special institution in Colorado Springs, Colorado. In his private studies, he had discovered the libertarian intellectual tradition. He noted the dire need for an institution that would educate people from all walks of life in the philosophy of freedom. He took it upon himself and named it the Freedom School, later changing the name to Rampart College before it shut down in 1968. Afterward, he carried on his work in South Carolina under the patronage of business giant Roger Milliken.

The Freedom School in Colorado was one of the most important institutions for teaching free-market economics in its day. Among its rotating faculty were Rose Wilder Lane, Milton Friedman, F.A. Harper, Frank Chodorov, Leonard Read, Gordon Tullock, G. Warren Nutter, Bruno Leoni, James J. Martin, and even Ludwig von Mises. Among its graduates were Roy Childs, Fred and Charles Koch, Roger MacBride, and many other intellectual activists still working today.

It is a testament to the power of ideas—and the fruit of the personal initiative of this intellectual entrepreneur—that Robert LeFevre could have sought to create a new teaching institution devoted to liberty, and succeed in so many ways.

He wanted to be remembered for what he believed. The individual actor was at the heart of his political worldview. He saw that civilization stemmed from the voluntary actions of men, not the laws of the State. Through their interactions in voluntary associations, of which the free market is only one of many, people build the structures of security and prosperity. That is the basis of cultural flourishing. Once created, civilization "breeds further desire and necessity for voluntary individual action. The one aids and abets the other."

He recounted how legions of historians have failed to understand this fundamental point. They write about the rise and fall of civilizations, of prosperity and famine, of peace and war. While noticing that government is often responsible for bad things, they incorrectly conclude it must be credited for all good in society as well. This leap of logic is what keeps the truth of freedom under wraps.

Crediting government for the good in society was, to his mind, like crediting the criminal class whenever it leaves us alone to go about our affairs. If we build a house, landscape it perfectly, and raise a wonderful family, we don't say: thanks be to the criminals who didn't interfere with our family's domestic bliss! Neither should the State be praised for the flowering of civilization, which is always and everywhere the result of individual action.

So important was this truth to him that he founded a school to explain it and apply it. He was an expert teacher with a razor-sharp understanding of the ways of government. He liked to distinguish between its true and artificial forms. True government is made up of the customs (habits, manners, folkways) and institutions (family, workplace, church) that regulate our daily life. Artificial government (the State) is the institution that steals our property, restricts our freedom, and endangers our lives in the name of protecting us.

He saw his main role as a teacher as dislodging the false consciousness that keeps so many from seeing artificial government as a parasite. Whether the form is democratic or autocratic, the State adds nothing to the development of civilization but rather hinders it. The extent to which it hinders freedom and prosperity depends on its size and its reach, which in turn depends on how much abuse people are willing to tolerate.

He astutely observed that all States are prone to expansion and always at the expense of liberty. Neither did he see socialism as a special form of social organization. It is just a word that indicates control of society by the State instead of individual actors. "All governments tend to move toward socialism," he said. "The larger and more vigorous they become, the more surely are they practicing socialism."

His views on patriotism (and remember that he was writing during the Cold War) followed logically:

> Patriotism cannot be a love of government. Patriotism rises
> above the government as a mountain towers above a blade
> of grass. When we think of our country and a feeling of love
> and devotion wells up within us, it should spring from the

reality of what our country is and means, and not from the government, which is the least of all our blessings.

The most obvious retort to the LeFevreian vision is that the State may be an unfortunate institution but it is nonetheless necessary to provide protection. But LeFevre had great faith in the power of the market to provide every service that is usually monopolized by government. He applied the Austrian insight concerning entrepreneurship to see that defense and protection services, precisely because they are so necessary, can also be provided by the market.

How? He spoke about the role of insurance companies as businesses that have a strong incentive to secure insured property against invasion. He talked about the possibilities of private security police and private arbitration. In our own time, when the failure of the State to protect us is so obvious, we see that he was remarkably prescient. There are more police and court services available in the private sector than the State sector.

But LeFevre also understood the limitations of looking for examples of private services that equal that of government.

> [W]henever a government invades any normal field of human endeavor, the tendency of human beings is to surrender that field and to make no further effort in it. Had market entrepreneurs been free all these ages to examine and explore adequate means of defense rather than relying upon the government to provide it, who can tell what marvelous means of protecting ourselves and our property might now be available to all?

LeFevre did not believe that all States are morally equivalent. He had a particular admiration for the American system, and he became an outstanding interpreter of American history. Whereas most others view the Constitution as the event that marks the "founding," he saw the American separation from Britain as the decisive event for liberty. It was the Declaration of Independence that firmly established the right of a people to resist and secede from State control.

So important is the right and duty of the people to dispense with despotism, this great Declaration contains the sentence not once, but twice. In its final utterance, the choice of words does not call for the formation of a government. Rather, it calls for "new guards" which may or may not entail such a unit as an artificial agency.

He further said that "the bill of grievances contained in the immortal Declaration of Independence could be extended by our own citizens in modern times, had they the stomach for it."

He went so far as to draft an excellent preamble to a new Declaration. He included this witty and wise sentence:

> That to secure these rights, each man is qualified to select for himself that agency or those agencies which seem to him best suited to protect his life and his property, to maintain his freedom, and which lie within his ability to afford.

To underscore the voluntarism at the heart of individual rights, he added: "that whenever any agency evinces characteristics of tyranny, he is well within his rights and his powers to discharge that agency and to find another more suitable to his inclinations and his finances."

Though he was concerned with political topics, his hope was a world without politics, which to him meant a world without the coercion inherent in all collective action. It was his own creative interpretation of the message of his intellectual mentors, among which he counted Ludwig von Mises.

The Mises Institute is honored and thrilled to be entrusted with the literary legacy of Robert LeFevre and the Freedom School, and grateful to Ross and Charlotte Anderson for making it possible. There are 10,000 books, and among the papers are transcripts of lectures by many giants of the libertarian cause, Mises among them. What a collection it is. Here is one piece of his legacy.

HANS SENNHOLZ: MISESIAN FOR LIFE

[Delivered at Grove City College on the 81st birthday celebration of Hans Sennholz, February 3, 2003.]

Hans F. Sennholz is one of the handful of economists who dared defend free markets and sound money during the dark years before the Misesian revival, and did so with eloquence, precision, and brilliance. From his post at Grove City College, and his lectures around the world, he has produced untold numbers of students who look to him as the formative influence in their lives. He has been a leading public voice for freedom in times when such voices have been exceedingly rare.

This much is well-known about him. But there are other aspects to his life and career you may not know. Sennholz was the first student in the United States to write a dissertation and receive a PhD under the guidance of Ludwig von Mises. Mises had only recently completed *Human Action*. Imagine how having such an outstanding student, and a native German speaker no less, must have affected Mises's life, how it must have encouraged him to know that his work could continue through outstanding thinkers such as this.

When Mises arrived in New York, determined to make a new life for himself after having first fled Austria and then sensing the need to leave Geneva too, he had no academic position waiting for him. He had no students and no prospects for students. But then came Sennholz. Here was living proof that ideas know no national boundaries, that even in the darkest hour there was hope for a new generation of economic scientists who cherished freedom, and were not fooled by the promise of government planning.

And think of the crucial time in which he entered the Austrian picture. Mises was by now carrying the school by himself. Most of his students had moved on to other things, whether Keynesian economics or social theory. For the Austrian School to survive in a profession now fully dominated by interventionists, it needed economists. The School desperately needed the new life that only new faces, names, books, and ideas provide.

When Sennholz began studying with Mises, it would still be another 12 years before Rothbard's *Man, Economy, and State* would appear, and nearly a quarter century before Kirzner's *Competition and Entrepreneurship* would be published. Sennholz provided exactly what was needed: that crucial bridge from the pre-war School to the postwar School in America, where the Austrian School would now make its home.

His dissertation became the book *How Can Europe Survive?*, published in 1955. It remains the best and most complete critique of European political union ever written. Sennholz demonstrated, some 50 years before others even cared, that political union under the interventionist-welfare state was only a prescription for chaos and bureaucratic rule. True union, he demonstrated, comes from free trade and decentralized States that do not attempt to plan their economies.

Europe today has a burgeoning movement of intellectuals who realize this same thing, and are working to curb the power of Brussels even as they attempt to preserve the free-trade zone. But we must remember that Sennholz anticipated this critique and agenda by nearly five decades. By taking a detailed look at all the programs for unification that were then being batted around, he saw precisely what was ahead for Europe: not prosperity and peace, but stagnation and conflict. So it is and will continue to be, so long as Sennholz's final chapters, which present a blueprint for authentic unity, are not followed.

Sennholz followed up this treatise, which included an account of the Great Depression and the onset of war, with a long string of trenchant writings on monetary theory and history, on employment, on fiscal policy, and even on the moral basis of freedom. Truly he followed in Mises's footsteps, and, like Mises, he refused to let the ideological hostility of his age and ours deter him from speaking truth to power, using every means at his disposal.

Let me provide one example of just how he carries the torch. During the 1980s, there were two camps on fiscal policy: the left, which wanted more spending and no tax cuts, and the supply-siders who wanted tax cuts plus spending increases. Sennholz became the voice for sanity: in Misesian terms, he called for tax cuts to be matched by spending cuts. In doing so, he dismissed the magic fiscal dust called "dynamic scoring" as well as the socialist demand for bigger government, while warning against the dangers of inflationary finance. Here was a lone voice for fiscal conservatism! During the early eighties, too, he wrote an extended Austrian critique of supply-side economics that anticipated all future trends of the decade.

At Margit von Mises's request, Sennholz was the translator of Mises's *Notes and Recollections*, which is the closest thing we have to an autobiography. It has been this book, above all else, that has shaped the way the generations that never had the chance to meet Mises have come to know the way an economist thinks about science and life amidst personal tragedy. Sennholz and his wife and partner Mary produced the first Mises *Festschrift*, presented to Mises on February 20, 1956, before Mises's fame in the United States would grow. Sennholz alone took the initiative to do Mises this honor.

Sennholz acquired Mises's papers for Grove City College, where they have been guarded as the treasures they are. He made Grove City stand out among American colleges as one of the few places where economic sense was taught during the heyday of Keynesian orthodoxy.

Sennholz did not only work to promote the Misesian school. He has been the great benefactor to all economists and scholars by being the translator and promoter of the work of

Mises's teacher, Eugen von Böhm-Bawerk. This was an act of great intellectual piety, since the market was not exactly clamoring for 100-year old books on interest-rate theory. And he did it all on the urging of Mises.

And though an outstanding theoretician, Sennholz placed a strong emphasis on the application of Austrian theory to the timing of the business cycle, and to explaining the current state of affairs. This is, by itself, highly unusual in the economics profession. If you know anything about academic economists, you know that they are the last people you want to ask about the state of the economy. But Sennholz made it his job to explain the world around him, a trait which drew many to his thought.

The Mises Institute, for which he serves as an adjunct scholar, is grateful to Professor Sennholz for his early support of our work. He wrote a wonderful paper on Carl Menger, later published in a volume on the gold standard, in which he showed that Menger was not just a theorist, but an activist in the cause of sound money. That paper changed the way we viewed Menger. We came to see him more clearly for what he was: an old-world liberal concerned about the fate of his country in difficult times—much like Sennholz himself.

Finally, I must add that Sennholz has never been shy about insisting on the centrality of ethics in the study of economics. He has decried the welfare state as confiscatory and immoral. He has called inflation a form of theft. He has identified government intervention as coercion contrary to the true spirit of cooperation. He did this at a time when saying such things was taboo in the profession. Here again, he was keeping alive the spirit of Mises, and the spirit of truth.

Sennholz told the *Austrian Economics Newsletter* that he has long been at work on his autobiography, which I'm sure will settle all scores. It cannot come too soon.

Nobody can ever gauge the full impact of a great intellectual in the development of culture. His influence spreads like waves in a lake; by the time the waves hit the shore, few are in a position to remember the source. But this much I'm sure of: We are in Hans Sennholz's debt far more than we know.

THE HAYEK MOMENT

[Delivered at the Mises Institute's Rothbard Graduate Seminar, Auburn, Alabama, June 2, 2003, to inaugurate the Hayek Lecture Series at the London School of Economics.]

Lecturing at the London School of Economics from 1931 to 1950, F.A. Hayek was nicely positioned to counter the rising influence of John Maynard Keynes. Keynes's new vision of macroeconomics was a resurrection of old fallacies, but with a modern twist: an open call for a consolidated State to manage investment. More than anyone else, and under the pretense of explaining the economic crisis of the time, Keynes gave intellectual credence to the rise of managerial States in America, the UK, and Europe during the 30s and the war.

Hayek countered with a defense of laissez-faire beefed up by the insights of the Austrian School of economics. He had worked with Ludwig von Mises in Vienna after the period in which Mises first laid out his business cycle theory. The danger of central banks, wrote Mises, is that they exercise power over interest rates, and can thereby distort the production structure of an economy. They can create artificial booms, which either lead to hyperinflation or economic bust.

Hayek advanced this theory as the alternative explanation for the global depression, and worked mightily all those years to show how the stock market crash was not the onset of the crisis, but rather the much-needed liquidation of a preceding boom. He further showed how the actions of the British and American governments were prolonging the crisis.

In the great debates of the period, it was said that Hayek had lost to the New Economics of Keynes and his followers. It was more precisely true that the Keynesians had won not by having a better argument, but by force of government policy. The Misesians and Hayekians of the time decided that they would fight the battle of ideas, and thus sprang up a host of institutions that would continue the work of liberty, despite all political impediments.

In a series of lectures named in honor of Hayek and sponsored by the Mises Institute and businessman Toby Baxendale, the spirit of those years at the London School of Economics is back. The Mises-Hayek explanation for economic booms and busts is receiving new attention during this current period of recession and market meltdown. The usual Keynesian prescriptions of more consumer spending, ever cheaper credit, and government spending have done nothing to solve the problems in the US, Europe, or Japan. The series begins with lectures by Roger W. Garrison, who has provided the most extended and comprehensive elaboration on the Mises-Hayek theory of the business cycle.

The relevance of Hayek in our times extends beyond just business-cycle analysis. In later years, Hayek turned his attention to other matters concerning the methods of science (he decried the "pretense of knowledge" affected by social scientists) and the uses of power in society. His *Road to Serfdom* warned that the regimentation of totalitarian societies can only come to Britain and the US through central planning. What is at stake, he wrote, is not just productive economies but freedom itself.

In our time, that freedom is threatened by intervention in every aspect of economic life, but also through the uses of the military power. Government not only claims it is smart enough to manage the economy, fix up our communities, run our schools, but also to decide which foreign politicians deserve to be protected and which deserve to be destroyed.

The implicit assumption is always that government knows more and better than the rest of us, and that this knowledge is sufficient to give it rights the rest of us do not have. It is often said that knowledge is power. In the case of government, however, its power vastly exceeds its knowledge.

When Alan Greenspan of the Fed (a branch of government in every important respect) testifies before Congress, legislators listen attentively to find out what he knows about the state of the economy, as if he has some privileged access to high-level data not reported elsewhere. It is further assumed that he knows precisely how to act on it. It is this knowledge that allows him to operate the gears and levers of the economy, so it is believed.

The same assumptions are made about many aspects of government. Many people who have backed war with Iraq assume that the government must know something awful about Saddam that it cannot share with the general public. It's true, they admit, that Saddam does not have nuclear weapons and that there is no public information that suggests he is plotting the destruction of America as we know it. But surely the White House must know something we do not, and know what to do about it, or else why would the administration be so intent on removing him from power?

The belief that powerful people know more than the rest of us is a main source of their power. It's true only to this extent: powerful people are likely to know when they are telling the truth and when they are not. The rest of us are put in a position of having to guess or dig to verify their claims point by point. Experience teaches that politicians often lie. But there's an even more important point: because government activity takes place outside the framework of the market economy, government has no idea how to use the information it does have to achieve social good.

Think of all the bits of information the government had been collecting to assess the likelihood of a terrorist incident. A few warnings among tens of thousands of tips did not suffice to prevent this destructive attack. The accumulation of information has grown steadily more voluminous. The government is in no better position to make judgments about it today than it was two years ago.

In contrast, insurance companies are in the business of assessing risk all the time, and they do this by means of a system of profit and loss, which Mises demonstrated is essential to a rationally organized society. Government, on the other hand, just collects piles of data and is completely at a loss on how to assess the relative likelihood of any particular scenario, or what to do about it.

Remember this winter's now-famous announcement that Americans should stock up on duct tape to protect themselves from chemical warfare. People rushed to the stores and cleaned out the shelves. Later it turned out that duct taping windows can be very dangerous and even cause asphyxiation. Not only that: the tip concerning the coming bioterrorism was a hoax. The "high alert"—as if that means anything to regular people—that government told Americans to be on was not justified.

In contrast, the private sector enhances security through peaceful and normal means. Home insurance companies give premium breaks for people who install alarm systems. Health insurers charge more for people who live dangerously. Premiums go up when risk is high, and they fall when it is low. Through this mechanism, people are encouraged to adopt safe ways of living or pay the difference if they choose not to. Those who contract to provide security face competition and have the incentive and means to provide what they promise. What a contrast with the chaotic and fumbling ways of government security provision!

But failure does not deter the State. Indeed, we are now asked to believe that the White House is not only omnipotent but omniscient as well. These people in government presume to make definitive judgments about the entire Iraqi ruling class, even going so far as to say that they know the secret hostility of a huge range of people toward Saddam, which thus qualifies them (who just happen to have essential technical knowledge) to help in administering the country. They can't possibly know this. That they believe they can, or they believe we will believe their claims to know, is incredible and frightening.

The alarming reality brings to mind Hayek's Nobel Prize lecture in 1974. With great courage, Hayek spoke of the tendency of economists to presume that they know things about human behavior that they do not and cannot know. They do this because they try to apply the models of the physical sciences to explain human action, always with an aim toward controlling the outcomes of human choice.

In truth, human action is too complex and subjective to be accessed by social scientists, and the attempt will always lead to abysmal failure. Hayek went on to explain how his critique of positivist economic modeling applies more broadly to anyone who would attempt to imitate the form while missing the substance of scientific procedure.

> But it is by no means only in the field of economics that far-reaching claims are made on behalf of a more scientific direction of all human activities and the desirability of replacing spontaneous processes by "conscious human control."

He mentions that the point applies to sociology, psychiatry, and the philosophy of history.

Hayek was raising an objection to the idea not of omniscience but of the possibility of accessing even mundane knowledge. No small group in government, much less a single person, can accumulate and sort through the kinds of information necessary to administer society, much less destroy and reconstruct one, as the Bush administration proposes to do throughout the Gulf region and the Middle East.

The attempt to assemble such a list is an act of power, not intelligence. We are being asked to make an enormous leap of faith that the Bush administration has somehow solved the great problem that afflicts us all: the limits of human comprehension. Because of those limits, we are right to try to limit the ability of men to exercise power over their fellows, at home or abroad.

Thus does Hayek's point apply to politics, especially to politics, even more especially to the politics of the military machine. The social scientist who believes he has the master plan to run the world is enough of a menace. But the politician who believes this, and is contemplating war, can bring about massive amounts of destruction and death. In these nuclear days—and let us say what we don't like to contemplate but which is nonetheless true—he can bring about the end of the world as we know it. As Hayek notes, a tyrant who carries the pretense of knowledge too far can become "a destroyer of civilization."

"If man is not to do more harm than good in his efforts to improve the social order," said Hayek, "he will have to learn that . . . he cannot acquire the full knowledge which would make mastery of the events possible." To believe otherwise is foolhardy and dangerous.

> The recognition of the insuperable limits to his knowledge ought indeed to teach the student of society a lesson of humility which should guard him against becoming an accomplice in men's fatal striving to control society.

MURRAY N. ROTHBARD: IN MEMORIAM

[Delivered at a memorial service at the University of Nevada, Las Vegas, January 20, 1995.]

Murray N. Rothbard (1926–1995) was just one man with a typewriter, but he inspired a worldwide renewal in the scholarship of liberty.

"Give me a short description of his thought and contributions," said the reporter when this free-market giant died at the age of 68. But how do you sum up Beethoven's music or Dante's poetry?

In 45 years of teaching and writing, Rothbard produced 25 books, thousands of articles, and three generations of students. He was a teacher who never stopped learning, an intellectual prize fighter who always punched cleanly. He battled every destructive trend in this century—socialism, statism, relativism, and scientism—and awakened a passion for freedom in thousands of scholars, journalists, and activists. At once a genius and a gentleman, his causes were honesty in scholarship, truth in history, principle in politics, and—first and foremost—human liberty itself.

Filled with laughter and principled beyond measure, Rothbard rejected the compromises and pretensions of the modern world. He was unaffected by intellectual fashion, undeterred by attacks, and untempted by opportunism. Quite simply, nothing stopped him. And as the Happy Warrior of economics, as *Forbes* called him, he made singular contributions to banking history, price theory, monopoly and antitrust, and business cycles, to name just a few areas.

For many years, he taught economics at Brooklyn Polytechnic Institute, working in a dingy, windowless office on the fifth floor, surrounded by Marxists. He never once complained, except to wonder why an engineering school couldn't make the elevator work. His admirers celebrated his appointment as the S.J. Hall distinguished Professor of Economics at the University of Nevada, Las Vegas.

Teaching in New York, Las Vegas, Auburn, and at conferences around the world, Rothbard led the renaissance of the Austrian School of economics. He galvanized an academic and popular fight for liberty and property, against the omnipotent State and its court intellectuals.

Like his beloved teacher Mises, Rothbard wrote for the public as well as professionals. "Civilization and human existence are at stake, and to preserve and expand it, high theory and scholarship, though important, are not enough," he wrote in 1993. "Especially in an age of galloping statism, the classical liberal, the advocate of the free market, has an obligation to carry the struggle to all levels of society."

Rothbard's theory was his practice. He was involved in nearly every political and social development of his time, from Robert Taft's presidential campaign to the 1994 elections. His last article, appearing in the *Washington Post*, warned that Newt Gingrich is more likely to betray the revolution than lead it.

The Mises Institute is honored that Rothbard headed our academic programs for 13 years. He spoke at all our conferences and teaching seminars, edited our *Review of Austrian Economics*, consulted on our books and monographs, and wrote for our *Free Market*. Most of all, he taught and inspired our students, who will carry his ideas into the future.

Rothbard has been compared to the greatest minds in social science, but his wisdom and character led him to show gratitude to his predecessors. His formative intellectual event was the 1949 publication of Mises's *Human Action*.

"I had gone through all the doctoral courses at Columbia University," Rothbard wrote, "without once discovering that there was such a thing as an Austrian School, let alone that Ludwig von Mises was its foremost living champion." But this book "solved all the problems and inconsistencies that I had sensed in economic theory."

Rothbard attended Mises's seminar at New York University from its first meeting, and became the student who would defend and extend Mises's ideas, push the Austrian School tradition to new heights, and integrate it with political theory. He taught the movement how to write, and was also an important cultural influence.

The Austrian School had previously been a largely European intellectual movement. Mises changed that with his migration to this country. Rothbard completed this process, so that the locus of the school is no longer Europe, but America, the nation whose founding principles Rothbard and Mises so deeply admired.

Man, Economy, and State, Rothbard's great work, was the key to the resurgence of Austrian economics after Mises's death. Beginning with the philosophical foundation, Rothbard built an edifice of economic theory and an unassailable case for the market. In many ways, the book rescued economics from its mostly deserved reputation. Instead of the dismal, statist, and incomprehensible pseudoscience students are used to, Rothbard gave us a tightly reasoned, sweeping case for the free market that is still used in classrooms all over the world.

The book treated economics as a humane science, not as a branch of physics. Every page took account of the uncertainty of economic conditions, the certainty of change, and the central place of the entrepreneur, while never losing sight of the implacability of economic law. No wonder Henry Hazlitt, writing in *National Review*, called it "brilliant and original and profound."

Since its publication, the treatise has only grown in stature. Through it, Rothbard has taught countless students to think like real economists instead of number crunchers. He explained and applied the logic of human action in economic exchange, and refuted its opponents. Like Mises, he looked not at "economic man," but *acting* man who deals with the scarcity of time and resources.

Rothbard breathed life into economic theory with his historical works, and refuted the charge that Austrians are only concerned with high theory. He was also one of the few intellectuals on the Right to champion revisionist history. Other historians have since picked up his works and built on them to create entire schools of thought.

He wrote *America's Great Depression*, applying the Misesian theory of the business cycle to refute the most common anticapitalist slander: that the market caused the crash and economic downturn of the 1930s. He showed that the villain was government intervention, in the form of credit expansion and Herbert Hoover's high wage policies. Paul Johnson adopted the thesis for his *Modern Times*. He also refuted the then-dominant view of Herbert Hoover as a laissez-faire conservative, by showing that he was actually a premature New Dealer. In journal articles, he showed that the New Deal followed logically from the economic regimentation of World War I and the Progressive Era, which gave us central banking and the income tax.

Rothbard was once asked to write a short book of American history. He agreed, and it eventually appeared. But *Conceived in Liberty* was four large volumes on the period 1620–1780. His purpose was to highlight forgotten events that demonstrate the libertarian character of our history and people. It is masterful, revisionist, and a pleasure to read. But what happened to the original project? Rothbard explained that he had discovered so much (tax revolts! uprisings! betrayals! power grabs!) that was left out of conventional accounts.

The American revolution threw off tyranny, he argued. It was not simply a continuation of British-style statism in another guise, as Hamilton claimed. The new social order would protect communities, properties, and essential rights. Rothbard also proved to be as proficient a military historian as he was an interpreter of ideological history.

Rothbard hardly let a moment go to waste, teaching through the day and writing through the night. His wife of 41 years, JoAnn, tells of being awakened once by his newest discovery: "That bastard Eli Whitney didn't invent the cotton gin after all!"

In his work, as in his life, he always sided with the pro-liberty forces against the welfare-warfare State. He especially liked the anti-New Dealers, the anti-imperialists, the Confederates, the anti-federalists, the tax resisters, the underground businessmen, the anti-State pamphleteers, and other unsung heroes. Throughout history the power elite has found profitable uses for the State. Rothbard never passed up a chance to name them, to explain how they did it, and to show how their actions harmed everyone else in society.

Conflict was the central theme of Rothbardian political economy: the State vs. voluntary associations, and the struggle over the ownership and control of property. He showed that property must be in private hands and owners must be free to control it as they see fit. The only logical alternative is the total State. There is no room for a "third-way" like social democracy, the mixed economy, or "good government," and the attempt to create it is always disruptive.

Power and Market, another enduring contribution, zeroed in on this conflict, and attacked every form of government intervention, confounding one antimarket cliché after another, and defending market competition as essential to social peace. Where others looked for "market failure," Rothbard found only government flops.

The book discussed the most common intervention in the market: taxation, the direct taking of someone's property by a group claiming a monopoly on coercion, i.e., the State. The taxing power defines the State in the same way that theft defines a robber.

He also showed that there can be no neutral tax, that is, one that leaves the market exactly as it would be without the tax. All taxes distort. And all taxes are taxes on production and hinder it, even so-called consumption taxes.

Taxation takes capital from private hands and prevents it from being used to serve private interests and the consuming public. This is true regardless of the type of tax. Also, the government spends taxes in ways that alter the production patterns of the market. If money is spent on market-oriented projects, it unjustly competes; if it is spent on nonmarket projects, it is economically inefficient.

Taxes are never "contributions," he argued. "Precisely because taxation is compulsory there is no way to assure—as is done automatically on the free market—that the amount any person contributes is what he would otherwise be willing to pay." As Rothbard said, it is not utopian to work for a society without taxation; it is utopian to think that the power to tax won't be abused once it is granted.

No principle of taxation, he argued, can equal a market system of fairness. A progressive tax discriminates on the basis of income; the rich aren't forced to pay more for bread than the poor. A flat tax forces the same result, since higher incomes contribute a greater dollar amount than lower ones. The least harmful tax is a head tax or equal tax: a flat fee low enough for even the poorest to pay.

As a steadfast believer in free trade, Rothbard argued that peace between nations cannot rest on negotiations between State managers. Peace is kept by the network of exchange that develops between private parties. This is why he opposed false "free trade" such as Nafta and Gatt, which have more in common with neomercantilism, and he was the first to forecast the disaster Nafta has become.

Interventionists have long used the language of markets to advance statism. Consider antitrust law enforced in the name of "competition." Rothbard showed that the only authentic monopolies are those created by law: the government subsidizes a producer at others' expense (public hospitals and schools) or forbids competition altogether (the postal service).

Other forms of monopoly include licensure, that is, deliberately restricting the supply of labor or number of firms in a certain industry. Government monopolies always deliver inferior service at exorbitant prices. And they are "triangular interventions," because they subsidize one party while preventing others from exchanging as they would in a free market.

He showed that unemployment insurance (actually, unemployment subsidies) increases the number of people out of work. Child labor laws, a favorite of unions and the Department of Labor, subsidize adult employment while preventing young people from gaining valuable work experience. Even eminent domain ("a license for theft") fails under Rothbard's property-rights strictures.

What about "intellectual property rights"? Rothbard defended the copyright as a contract made with consumers not to reprint a work, resell it, or falsely attribute the source. A patent on the other hand, is a government grant of monopoly privilege to the first discoverer of certain types of inventions to get to the government patent office.

And under public ownership, he argued, the "public" owns nothing, and the ruling officialdom owns all. "Any citizen who doubts this," Rothbard suggested, "may try to appropriate for his own individual use his allotted part of 'public' property and then try to argue his case in court."

The government sector focuses on the short run, he argued; there is no such thing as "public-sector investment." It is only the private sector, which is the *real* public sector, Rothbard said, where property owners take long-run considerations into account. Unlike government, they preserve the value of resources, and do not plunder or waste them.

In his last scholarly article, he developed the idea of the nation as something separate from either the State or the individual, a collective identity based on language, ethnicity, race, and religion. Rothbard celebrated the post-Cold War emergence of the nation as a countervailing power to the State, and presented the hope that "the brutal and repressive state will be gradually dissolved into a harmonious and increasingly prosperous social order." It was the final hope of a lifetime of hopes.

Many economists think numbers are the sum of the discipline. Rothbard turned the tables to argue that government data are gathered and used for piecemeal planning and the destruction of the economy. Whatever information markets need about economic conditions can be garnered privately.

A good example is the "trade deficit" between nations, which he said is no more relevant than the trade deficit between towns. There is no justification for assuming that trade must equal out in accounts. The important point is that people are benefiting from exchange, whether across the street or across the world.

Aren't historical statistics useful for research? Many are misleading. The Gross Domestic Product counts government spending as production, when it should be counted as consumption. Also, government taxing is considered neutral when it's destructive. Deficits, which drain savings and crowd out production, also need to be accounted for when assessing productivity.

Rothbard looked at private production by subtracting out the government component. The result is the Private Product Remaining, or PPR, which has served scholars as a basis for more accurate historical work. Using the PPR, for example, we see national product increasing at a much slower rate than the GDP, thanks to big government.

Even money-supply statistics were in need of revision in Rothbard's view. Long before people gave up on the Fed's ability to generate anything useful (the "M's" are laughable these days), Rothbard proposed his own measure based on the Austrian School theory of money. It counts cash, deposits easily turned into cash, and all other liquid financial assets.

The State and its banking cartel is the worst possible money manager, Rothbard argued, and free enterprise is the best. He produced many studies on the abuse of money and banking by central bankers and the central State. They include his doctoral thesis, *Panic of 1819*, *Mystery of Banking*, and papers on the banking debates of the mid and late 19th century, the monetary debauchery of FDR, the fiasco of Bretton Woods, and the following age of inflation and monetary chaos. Just out is his *Case Against the Fed*, the best book ever written on the subject.

View the Federal Reserve as a counterfeiting syndicate, and we have Rothbard's theory of the central bank. But, he pointed out, at least the counterfeiter doesn't pretend to be working in the public interest, to be smoothing out business cycles, and to be keeping prices stable. He was also the first to analyze in depth and from a free-market perspective the special-interest groups that created the Fed.

Rothbard added to Austrian theory a systematic model for how money is destroyed. The State conspires with the central bank and the banking industry to enhance their mutual power and wealth by devaluation, the equivalent of coin clipping. Little by little, society's money has less to do with its original form, and eventually it is transformed into paper created out of thin air, to best serve the State's interest.

As a part of this process, the State intervenes to forbid customers from insisting on 100-percent reserves in checkable deposits. From there, it is progressively easier to move from gold to paper, as has happened in this country from the turn of the century.

Like Mises, Rothbard saw inflation as a policy pursued by the banking industry in league with the government. Those who get the newly created money first—banks, government, institutional securities traders, and government contractors, for example—win out because they can spend it before prices go up and investments are distorted. Those who get the new money later lose.

A Rothbardian gold standard is no watered-down version. He wanted convertibility at home and abroad. Only that system—which would put depositors in charge of insuring the financial soundness of the banking system—can prevent the Fed's monetary depredations, which have reduced the value of the 1913 dollar to 5 cents today.

The ultimate guarantor against inflation is a private banking system with private coinage, a great American system that was squeezed out by the central State. Rothbard's writings on money and banking—extensive and deep—may eventually become the single most influential aspect of his thought.

Economists rarely talk about liberty and private property and even less about what constitutes just ownership. Rothbard did, arguing that property acquired through confiscation, whether by private criminals or the State, is unjustly owned. (He also pointed out that bureaucrats pay no taxes, since their entire salaries are taxes.)

Ethics of Liberty was his moral defense. "Liberty of the individual," Rothbard wrote, is "not only a great moral good in itself" but "also as the necessary condition for the flowering of all the other goods that mankind cherishes": virtue, the arts and sciences, economic prosperity, civilization itself. "Out of liberty, stem the glories of civilized life."

Once we understand why private property should be inviolable, troublesome notions fall by the wayside. There can be no "civil rights" apart from property rights, because the necessary freedom to exclude is abolished. "Voting rights" are also a fiction, which—depending on how they are used—can also diminish freedom. Even the "right to immigrate" is phony: "On whose property does someone else have the right to trample?" he asked.

Thus, the Rothbardian social order is no ACLU free-for-all. The security of property provides lines of authority, restraints on behavior, and guarantees of order. The result is social peace and prosperity. The conflicts we face today, from affirmative action to environmentalism, are the result of false rights being put ahead of private property.

In defense of capitalism, Rothbard was uncompromising. But he did not see the market as the be-all and end-all of the social order. For him, capitalism was not a "system," but a consequence of the natural order of liberty. Neither "growth" nor "greed" is the capitalist ideal. In the free economy, leisure and charity are goods like any other, to be "purchased" by giving up alternative uses of time and money.

And with growing prosperity the need for material goods falls relative to nonmaterial goods. "Rather than foster 'material' values, then, advancing capitalism does just the opposite." No society has ever been as grasping and greedy as the

Soviet Union, although the Left is still trying to convince us that State power equals compassion.

A Rothbardian world would be a world without politics. But Murray was no dropout, and in fact loved politics. Who else could write a 5,000-word essay on a random week of electoral life in New York City, and make every word fascinating?

His political writings date from the early 1950s, when he wrote for *Faith and Freedom*, a hard-Right, isolationist publication. In articles on the evils of the military buildup, he warned that American liberty would be sacrificed to the Cold War.

That led to his break with the Buckleyites, who ridiculed him and his ideas. They never took him on directly; they were smarter than that. Instead, they smeared him in private, and tried to deny him publishing and speaking opportunities.

As editor of *Left and Right* and *Libertarian Forum*, Rothbard also predicted that the Cold War would someday end because Soviet socialism would collapse. But, he said, the American military machine would keep on cranking out the planes and bombs. The real threat, he maintained, was not foreign Communism, but US militarism and socialism, which would do what the Soviets never could: steal our liberty.

Rothbard developed a large and growing audience for such views, and continued with this theme for the *Rothbard-Rockwell Report*, writing against US military interventions in Panama, the Gulf, Somalia, Rwanda, and Bosnia. As the official Left and Right pushed for a New World Order, Rothbard, exasperated, suggested we save time and just invade the entire globe.

Well, here we are 40 years after Rothbard began his foreign-policy writings. The warfare State is as big as ever, and so is the welfare State. *National Review*—which has always cozied up to power, and, like other neoconservatives, even holds up the dictators Lincoln and Roosevelt for our admiration—is still cheerleading the Republican establishment to new levels of hypocrisy. And we can see that Rothbard was right all along: right about the military, right about politics, right about the Buckleyite conservatives and their love of State power.

That is why Rothbard has triumphed in the end. Despite its attempt to purge and destroy him, *National Review*'s influence on the intellectual world hasn't come close to Rothbard's. And when the Buckleyites are long forgotten, Rothbard's authority will not have begun to peak.

For Rothbard, politics and criminal behavior are largely the same enterprise, to be treated with the same investigative rigor. Every day required another whodunit. His motivation in political writing was exposing crime and denouncing criminals.

Some people say that Rothbard's politics were all over the map. That is not true. He set the political standard as liberty itself, and worked with anyone who pursued it. At the height of the Vietnam War, for example, when the official Right was countenancing mass murder, he looked to the New Left as a vehicle for stopping this most vicious form of statism.

But as the Cold War ended, Rothbard was overjoyed to reunite with the remnants of the Old Right. After he was in paleoconservative circles only a few months, we began to witness new ideological hybrids springing up: anarcho-Southern agrarianism, anarcho-anti-federalism, anarcho-protectionism, and anarcho-monarchism. Their advocates were his colleagues, and he was their conscience.

Rothbard's political thought is simple at its core but astounding in its application. He believed that common moral strictures, and standards of evaluation, should apply to the State.

If theft is wrong, it is wrong. The same goes for murder, kidnapping, lying, and fraud. They are as wrong for the State as for everyone else.

"Always and ever," he wrote, "the government and its rulers and operators have been considered above the general moral law." It is this that Rothbard's right-wing "anarchism" was devoted to ending: he wanted to make government subject to the rule of law. But Rothbard was no Utopian; his view was that government power should be limited in any way possible, and he worked to make it so.

His pioneering studies of private courts predated the popularity of private arbiters. (Rothbard wanted to abolish "jury slavery" and force courts to pay a market wage.) His work on private law enforcement predated the popularity of home protection and private security. His promotion of private roads predated their wide use in suburbs and malls. His promotion of private schools predated the anti-public school revolt.

What Rothbard wrote about Mises applies in his case as well:

> never would Mises compromise his principles, never would he bow the knee to a quest for respectability or social or political favor. As a scholar, as an economist, and as a person, Ludwig von Mises was a joy and an inspiration, an exemplar for us all.

Like Mises, Rothbard gave up money and fame in academic economics to promote what is true and right. And he set all who knew him an example of how a man should live his life.

The Mises Institute was blessed to be associated with him, and he credited the Institute with having "at last forged an Austrian revival that Mises would be truly proud of."

Rothbard's ideas and character, like those of Mises, must be always before us, and before new generations as well. The Mises Institute will ensure that it is so. We are still discovering the breadth and depth of Rothbard's literary legacy, with the publication of volumes one and two of Rothbard's history of economic thought, put out by Edward Elgar shortly after his death. It is the most important work of its kind since Joseph Schumpeter's.

Whereas other texts pretend to be an uninterrupted march toward higher levels of truth, Rothbard illuminated a history of unknown geniuses and lost knowledge, of respected charlatans and honored fallacies.

Later in 1995, a two-volume compilation of his important economic articles, totaling more than 1,000 pages, will appear in Elgar's "Economists of the 20th Century" series edited by Mark Blaug. In addition, there are unpublished manuscripts, articles, and letters to fill many more volumes.

From Menger to Rothbard, Austrian School economists have argued that man is motivated by much more than mere self-interest and profit maximization. If the neoclassicals emphasize *homo economicus*, the Austrian School studies *homo agens*, the person who acts for a wide variety of reasons, including those that have nothing to do with material gain.

Murray N. Rothbard was empirical proof that the Austrian theory is correct. In his professional and personal life, he always put classical virtues ahead of his private interest. His generosity, his constancy, and his faith helped make him not only a giant among scholars, but also a giant among men.

His acts of charity were uncountable. How many times have I seen a student approach him at one or two in the morning at a teaching conference and ask a question about the gold standard, or economics as a purely logical science? He had been asked the same thing a thousand times before, but that student would never know it, as Rothbard enthusiastically explained everything.

Many, myself included, were schooled in economics, politics, philosophy, history, and much more at his feet. If his beneficiaries defaulted on their debts to him, as they so often did, he would shrug it off.

In an age of Limbaughvian self-promotion, Rothbard always pointed beyond himself, and never tired of extolling the greatness of his beloved teacher, Ludwig von Mises.

He never wanted, nor would he have tolerated, a cult of Rothbard. He lived to see the emergence and development of

Rothbardian political economy, but he never once acknowledged its existence. Even his demeanor suggested this. Was there ever a genius with so little pretension?

Rothbard took ideas so seriously that he refuted even the most idiotic thoughts from the most irrelevant sources. How few of these people realized that he was paying them the ultimate compliment: treating them as if they were his equals.

Rothbard never sought academic or popular prestige. A first look at his bibliography seems to reveal a prolific genius with little marketing sense. But that was the point: despite his promotion of the free market, Rothbard never let the market determine what he would think or say. He adhered to what is right regardless of self-interest.

Imagine, for example, the courage it took to carry on the American isolationist tradition—almost single-handedly—in a time of hysterical pro-war propaganda.

He could have given up his anti-interventionism in foreign policy and been a big shot in conservatism. He might have been *National Review*'s favorite intellectual. Who knows? He might have even made the pages of *Commentary*. Or he could have given up his free-market and strict private-property views, or at least downplayed them, and been rewarded by the Left. At the height of the Vietnam War, this would have made him a star at the *Nation*.

Some say that Rothbard's constancy was a vice, that he refused to change his mind. In fact, no one was more ready for correction. In recent years, to take just one example, he wrote that he had neglected the cultural foundations of liberty, and cheered those who hadn't.

In a contradictory accusation, others have said that Rothbard's consistency is a myth, that in his long political life he swung from Right to Left to Right. This is a smear. In moral and cultural matters, he was always a reactionary. In politics, Rothbard's constancy was based on his belief in the primacy of foreign policy. When a nation becomes an empire, he argued, the prospects for liberty are nil. Look for the opponents of war and imperialism during his life, and there you would find Rothbard.

One final trait of Rothbard's: he was a man of faith. He believed that there is order in the universe, that natural law is real and intractable, that truth exists and that it can set us free. His faith was the faith of all men who have put ideals ahead of selfish concerns.

If we are to live up to Rothbard's example, what must we do? Read and research and produce quality scholarship, commit ourselves to promoting liberty and fighting the State, act on our convictions with tireless energy, never sell out, never give in, and never forget that we will win in the end.

We have one other duty. Without him here to object, we can at last tell the truth about the world-historical figure that was Murray N. Rothbard, who now belongs to the ages.

THE JOY OF JOANN

[Delivered at the memorial service for JoAnn Rothbard at the Madison Avenue Presbyterian Church, New York City, February 26, 2000.]

The trouble with socialism," Oscar Wilde once wrote, "is that it takes too many evenings." Indeed, the private lives of socialists are highly politicized. They must not be interested in anything—not even their families—other than socialism. The theory must inform every aspect of their lives, which must be a microcosm of a socialist society: there must be no escape from the All-Embracing Theory.

The lives of Murray and JoAnn Beatrice Rothbard illustrated the opposite principle. He was the premier antisocialist of our time, the greatest economist of his generation, a philosopher and historian who made immense contributions.

She was his lifetime helpmate, an excellent manager, an opera aficionado with a scholar's level of knowledge, an enthusiast for liberty, a woman of remarkable personal patience, and, above all else, a wife supremely in love with her husband, as he was with her.

Together, their lives were a microcosm of liberty, with interests spanning an extraordinary range, and a private life just as rich and varied as what they accomplished together in their public life. In the months following her death, I came across a beautiful correspondence between them during their courtship, she at home in Virginia and he in graduate school at Columbia. His letters are hilarious and charming, and hers warm and witty. They corresponded about New York baseball, and why it was important to love the Yankees and launch a boycott against the Giants. He shared his view of child rearing, in particular the proper technique for teaching a child how to swim. Murray's view: throw them in the water! She took a more moderate view. These were two bourgeois students in love with life, and they adored each other.

Murray was blessed with an astonishing brilliance and intellectual creativity, but he was never one for fitting into the usual social conventions of young adulthood. Joey appeared to have understood him like no one else. She loved his creativity, his humility, and his unrelenting laughter. He found her kind, gracious, and beautiful, the first person whom he could really pour his heart out to, and whom he thoroughly respected. She used to draw up schedules for him to prevent breakfast from overlapping with dinner hour. She would signal him when it was time to get off the phone, or write a paper for that next conference. What must it have been like to have lived with Murray, to have seen him work, to enjoy his insights and humor every day for so long? In some way, I think, we all felt a bit of jealousy.

Many of us were fortunate to be a part of their private life to some extent. And as many of us know, a Rothbardian evening was not like Wilde's steely-eyed socialist one. They constantly entertained guests from all walks of life, freely talked to any callers curious about libertarian ideas, and spent endless hours with students and friends. They were generous with their time, food, and books, and as anxious to learn from others as others were from them. If the socialist evening served as a fearful look into the sternness and regimentation of a centrally planned society, a Rothbardian evening seemed to suggest the limitless possibilities and hope of freedom.

For them, it wasn't always about the great political struggle of our time. They also attended concerts, plays, and films, and took classes in German baroque church architecture, the paintings of Caravaggio, early music, and American history. Like many great intellectuals—G.K. Chesterton comes to mind—Murray was somewhat disorganized. JoAnn was the practical partner of the team. She hosted all the parties, cooked all the food, and kept his schedule. She proofed and typed all of Murray's manuscripts, inspired him in his research and writing, and sponsored a salon in their home that was crucial for the birth of the libertarian movement. Where he was naïve, she was knowing. Service of this variety is an old-fashioned virtue, not nearly as appreciated as it should be these days.

Once when Murray was discouraged from attending a Messiah sing because he would mistakenly attempt to sing all four parts, Joey began her own sing in their home. It became an annual staple for their always large and growing set of friends in New York City. Joey later developed and cultivated an intense interest in opera—more intense than Murray could ever muster—so she would frequently fly to large and important performances that couldn't be missed, especially those of Wagner.

When Murray got to know novelist Ayn Rand, he was told by one of her devotees that he had a problem: Joey appeared to believe in God, a self-evidently irrational impulse. Joey was given time to listen to a tape series in atheism, and was not convinced. The Randians told Murray that if he wanted to be part of their group, he had to divorce her. Murray took her arm and they walked out, together.

Joey loved to tell stories about Murray: how they were once tossed out of the Columbia University library for laughing, and how she knew how to find him in a dark theater on their first date—by following the laughter. Indeed, to spend even a few minutes with Murray and Joey was to find yourself laughing uproariously. Frequently the laughter concerned politics, but it might also concern anything else. Their joy together was boundless, their intellectual curiosity deep, and their love of life complete.

Murray could not have accomplished what he did without her. He wrote tens of thousands of articles and 25 books, and developed the first, fully integrated science of liberty—with her by his side, providing indispensable encouragement and support. She made his breathtaking level of productivity possible. But even more importantly, they lived good and faithful lives, to each other, to the principles they shared, and to never letting their passion for politics squeeze out the moral obligation to care for others and to embrace life to its fullest.

His unexpected and untimely death in 1995 was a devastating blow to JoAnn. Her health was failing and her main source of joy gone. But she knew what Murray would have her do. She stayed constantly in touch by phone. She threw herself into reading and research, becoming a real expert on the depredations of Lincoln. She gave classes at our student conferences, and lectured about Murray's thought at the Austrian Scholars Conference.

On the fourth anniversary of Murray's death, she suffered a terrible stroke, and died months later. We are left with warm memories of their happiness together, and the multitude of ways in which she and he touched our lives. They had their priorities straight, and in their public and private lives, exemplified the spirit of liberty, and changed our world. Thank you Joey, for all you did to make everything possible.

A TRIBUTE TO TRADE

[Delivered at the Mises Institute, September 12, 2001, in memory of those who died in the World Trade Center disaster the day before.]

T he sight of New York City's twin World Trade Center towers falling to the ground, the result of an act of deliberate aggression, seems to symbolize two points that seem entirely forgotten today: the magnificent contribution that commerce makes to civilization, and just how vulnerable it is to its enemies. If the enemies of capitalist commerce are hell-bent on the destruction of the source of wealth, there are few means available to prevent it.

From the two towers soaring 1,300 feet above the city, a person on the 110th floor enjoyed a panoramic view stretching 55 miles: a broad vision of human civilization. Much more important for the flowering of civilization is what went on there: entrepreneurship, creativity, exchange, service, all of it peaceful, all of it to the benefit of mankind.

What kind of service? The financial firm of Morgan Stanley took 20 floors, and at the time of the explosion, the firm was hosting a meeting for the 400 members of the National Association of Business Economists. Fred Alger Management, a training ground for young traders and stock analysts, occupied the 93rd floor of the North Tower. Bond dealers for Cantor Fitzgerald took up floors 101 through 105 of the North Tower.

Fiduciary Trust, a wonderful money management company, employed 500 people who worked on five floors at the very top of the South Tower. Other companies there included Network Plus, Harris Beach & Wilcox, OppenheimerFunds, Bank of America, Kemper Insurance, Lehman Brothers, Morgan Stanley Dean Witter, Credit Suisse First Boston, and Sun Microsystems.

Here were the brokers who invest our savings, trying their best to channel resources to their most profitable uses. Here were insurance companies, which provide the valuable service of securing our lives and property against accidents. Here were many retailers, who risk their own livelihoods to provide us with goods and services we as consumers desire. Here were lenders, lawyers, agents, and architects whose contributions are so essential to our daily lives.

Some of us knew men and women who are now dead. But most of them will remain anonymous to us. Whether we knew them or not, they were our benefactors nonetheless, because in the commercial society, the actions of entrepreneurs benefit everyone, in mostly imperceptible ways. They all contribute to the stock of capital on which prosperity itself is based. They work daily to coordinate the use of resources to eliminate waste and inefficiency, and make products and services available that improve our everyday lives.

Think especially of the remarkable people in that place who facilitated international trade. They daily accomplished the seemingly impossible. Faced with a world of more than 200 countries, and hundreds more languages and dialects, with as many currencies and legal regimes, and thousands of local cultural differences, and billions of consumers, they found ways to make peaceful exchange possible. They looked for and seized on every opportunity that presented itself to enable human cooperation.

No government has been able to accomplish anything this remarkable. It is a miracle made possible by commerce, and by those who undertake the burden of making it happen.

We often hear platitudes about the brotherhood of man. But you don't see it at the United Nations or at the summits of governments. There you see conflicts, resolved usually by the use of other people's money taken by force. But at the World Trade Center, the brotherhood of man was an everyday affair.

It didn't matter if you were a small rug merchant in Nepal, a fisherman off the Chinese coast, or a machine manufacturer in the American Midwest, the people who worked here put you in contact with others who valued what you did and what you could give to others. Consent and choice, not conflict and coercion, were at the core of everything. Their watchword was contract, not hegemony.

True, the objective of all these merchants and traders may have been their own personal betterment, but the effect of their work was to serve not just themselves but everyone else as well. Because the beneficial effects of trade are not just local but national, and not just national but international, the inhabitants of these buildings were in many ways the benefactors of all of us personally. The blessings we experienced from their work came to us every time we used a credit card, withdrew money from the bank, bought from a chain store, or ordered something online.

In short, these people were producers. Frédéric Bastiat said of them: they are the people who

> create out of nothing the satisfactions that sustain and beautify life, so that an individual or a people is enabled to multiply these satisfactions indefinitely without inflicting privation of any kind on other men or other peoples.

Yes, they earned profits, but for the most part, their work went unrewarded. It was certainly unappreciated in the culture at large. They are not called public servants. They are not praised for their sacrifices to the common good. Popular culture treats these "money centers" as sources of greed and corruption. We are told that these people are the cause of environmental destruction and labor exploitation, that the "globalists" inside the World Trade Center were conspiring not to create but to destroy. Even after all the destruction wrought by socialism, capitalists must still bear the brunt of envy and hatred.

The impulse to hate the entrepreneurial class shows up in myriad ways. We see it when franchise restaurants are bombed, as they frequently are in France. In the United States, the government works to "protect" land from being used by commerce, and increasing numbers of our laws are built on the presumption that the business class is out to get us, not serve us. The business pages more often report on the villainy, rather then the victories, of enterprise. Or take a look at the typical college bookstore, where students are still required to read Marx and the Marxians rather than Mises and the Misesians.

All the enemies of capitalism act as if its elimination would have no ill consequences for our lives. In the class-room, on television, at the movies, we are continually presented a picture of what a perfect world of bliss we would enjoy if we could just get rid of those who make a living through owning, speculating, and amassing wealth.

For hundreds of years, in fact, the intellectual classes have demanded the expropriation and even the extermination of capitalistic expropriators. Since ancient times, the merchant and his trade have been considered ignoble. In fact, their absence would reduce us to barbarism and utter poverty. Even now, the destruction of the property and people at the once-mighty towers of the world has already impoverished us in more ways than we will ever know.

Those who understand economics and celebrate the creative power of commerce understand this higher truth, which is why we defend the market economy at every opportunity. That is why we seek to eliminate the barriers that governments and anticapitalists have erected against the business-men's freedom. We see them as the defenders of civilization, and so we seek to guard their interests in every way we know how.

We mourn the lost lives of those who worked in the World Trade Center towers, which are no more. We mourn their lost vocations. We owe it to them to appreciate anew their contribution to society.

As Mises wrote,

[No] one can find a safe way out for himself if society is sweeping toward destruction. Therefore everyone, in his own interests, must thrust himself vigorously into the intellectual battle. None can stand aside with unconcern; the interests of everyone hang on the result. Whether he chooses or not, every man is drawn into the great historical struggle, the decisive battle into which our epoch has plunged us.

6. Bibliography

READING FOR LIBERTY

As this is a collection of speeches, I've avoided footnoting in this volume, but all quotations have been checked for reliability. The quotations from Ludwig von Mises are from *Socialism, Liberalism, Human Action,* and *Nation, State, and Economy,* all of which are online (a Google search reveals precise sourcing information), as well as *Notes and Recollections* and *Omnipotent Government.* Quotations from Murray N. Rothbard are "The Anatomy of the State," "Mises and the Role of the Economist in Public Policy," "Invade the World," and *Ludwig von Mises: Scholar, Creator, Hero,* all of which are online. The quotations from John Randolph are from his "Speech on Executive Powers"; V.I. Lenin from *The Collected Works*; Isabel Paterson from the *God of the Machine*; J.M. Keynes, the *General Theory*; F.A. Hayek, "The Pretence of Knowledge"; from Joseph Schumpeter, *Capitalism, Socialism, and Democracy*; from Robert LeFevre, *This Bread Is Mine*; and from Frédéric Bastiat, *Economic Harmonies.* Other sources, from new and old popular sources, are generally clear from the text.

Aside from those directly mentioned, there is the broader and more important list of books and ideas that form the ideological foundation of this book. This volume would be a lot longer if I listed all the books I love and heartily recommend. But I offer this short account as a list of volumes essential to my understanding of the world.

In economics, there are two pillars: *Human Action: A Treatise on Economics* by Ludwig von Mises, Scholar's Edition (Auburn, Ala.: Mises Institute, [1949] 1998) and *Man, Economy, and State*, by Murray N. Rothbard, Scholar's Edition (Auburn, Ala.: Mises Institute, [1962] 2004). The Scholar's Edition of *Man, Economy, and State* is joined for the first time with *Power and Market* (Kansas City, Mo.: Sheed Andrews and McMeel, 1970) as Rothbard originally had intended. What's in Mises's book? Enough to ignite a revolution in the social sciences and in the political realm as well. It's hard to believe that one mind could produce such a treatise.

Rothbard's book, meanwhile, began as a textbook on *Human Action* but became its own independent treatise, one especially valued by economics students who require a rigorous theoretical apparatus to counter fallacies taught in the classroom, as well as a wonderful account of everything that is wrong with State intervention. I would say that both need to be thoroughly understood but, in fact, that is unrealistic for most people in a lifetime. In any case, they both should be read.

Continuing with Mises, his volume *Bureaucracy* (South Holland, Ill., Libertarian Press, [1944] 1994) applies his argument against socialism to explain why the public sector does not work. His *Economic Policy: Thoughts for Today and Tomorrow* (Irvington-on-Hudson, N.Y.: Free Market Books, [1959] 1995) is a transcript of lectures and has proven very popular over the years. His *Socialism: An Economic and Sociological Analysis* (Indianapolis, Ind.: LibertyClassics, [1922] 1995) is more than an economic attack on collectivism; it counters a huge range of social, cultural, and political arguments for socialism. And it is written with an intellectual exuberance that could have only come from the ferment of interwar Austria.

Mises's first book, *Theory of Money and Credit* (Indianapolis, Ind.: Liberty*Classics*, [1912] 1995), still goes a long way toward explaining the monetary disorders of our time. Finally, his *Theory and History: An Interpretation of Social and Economic Evolution* (Auburn, Ala.: Mises Institute, [1957] 1985) is a systematic exposition of the place of economics within the social sciences and a systematic argument against antieconomic ideologies.

Continuing with Rothbard, *An Austrian Perspective on the History of Economic Thought*, 2 vols. (Cheltenham, U.K.: Edward Elgar, 1995) shows that economics predated Adam Smith and that the British School was something of a comedown from the Continental tradition.

Rothbard's *What Has Government Done to Our Money?* (Auburn, Ala.: Mises Institute, [1964] 1990) has been translated into many languages for a reason: it is the single best account of how the free market can manage money better than the State. His *History of Money and Banking in the United States: The Colonial Era to World War II* (Auburn, Ala.: Mises Institute, 2002) applies the lesson to American history. For shorter articles on applications of Austrian theory, and to see why he is so esteemed as a writer, see the shorter items that comprise his *Making Economic Sense* (Auburn, Ala.: Mises Institute, 1995).

For an introduction to Austrian economics, see Gene Callahan's *Economics for Real People: An Introduction to the Austrian School* (Auburn, Ala.: Mises Institute, 2002), and for the origins of the science in the High Middle Ages, see Alejandro A. Chafuen, *Faith and Liberty: The Economic Thought of the Late Scholastics* (Lanham, Md.: Lexington Books, 2003).

David Gordon provides *An Introduction to Economic Reasoning* (Auburn, Ala.: Mises Institute, 2000) while Henry Hazlitt's famous *Economics in One Lesson*, 50th Anniversary Edition (San Francisco: Fox & Wilkes, 1996) still holds up. For further elaboration on the implications of economic science for the world, I recommend Hans-Hermann Hoppe's *Economics and Ethics of Private Property: Studies in Political Economy and Philosophy* (Norwell, Mass.: Kluwer Academic Publishers, 1993) and *A Theory of Socialism and Capitalism* (Norwell, Mass.: Kluwer Academic Publishers, 1989).

On the history of taxation, see Charles Adams, *For Good and Evil: The Impact of Taxes on the Course of Civilization* (Lanham, Md.: Madison Books, 2001), in which he shows the central role that taxes play. For understanding the current moment in politics in light of the last 400 years, nothing beats Martin van Creveld's amazing *Rise and Decline of the State* (New York: Cambridge University Press, 1999).

For American history in particular, I recommend Robert Higgs's *Crisis and Leviathan: Critical Episodes in the Growth of American Government* (New York: Oxford University Press, 1987) and John V. Denson, ed., *Reassessing the Presidency: The Rise of the Executive State and the Decline of Freedom* (Auburn, Ala.: Mises Institute, 2001). On the founding, see *The Anti-Federalist Papers and the Constitutional Convention Debates*, Ralph Ketcham, ed. (New York: Mentor Books, 1996). It turns out that the skeptics of the Constitution were exactly right! On the Civil War, read Thomas DiLorenzo's the *Real Lincoln: A New Look at Abraham Lincoln, His Agenda, and an Unnecessary War* (New York: Prima Publishing, 2002) in which he shows that Lincoln was an inflationist, mercantilist, and all-round proponent of big government, and Charles Adams's *When in the Course of Human Events: Arguing the Case for Southern Secession* (Lanham, Md.: Rowman & Littlefield, 2000), which defends the right to secession, while deprecating the war.

Rothbard's *America's Great Depression* (Auburn, Ala.: Mises Institute, [1963] 2000) remains the definitive account of what caused the calamity (it wasn't the free market). And if you really want to understand American history, you must start long before the Constitution, and your best guide is

Rothbard's *Conceived in Liberty*, 4 vols. (Auburn, Ala.: Mises Institute, 1999).

On war, a wonderful and sweeping treatise is John V. Denson, ed., the *Costs of War: America's Pyrrhic Victories*, 2nd ed. (New Brunswick, N.J.: Transaction Publishers, 1997). On World War I, see Paul Fussell, the *Great War and Modern Memory* (New York: Oxford, 2000); Thomas Fleming, the *Illusion of Victory: America in World War I* (New York: Basic Books, 2003), Niall Ferguson's the *Pity of War: Explaining World War I* (New York: Basic Books, 2000), and Ludwig von Mises's *Nation, State, and Economy: Contributions to the Politics and History of Our Time* (New York: New York University Press, [1919] 1983).

On World War II, see Thomas Fleming's the *New Dealers' War: F.D.R. and the War Within World War II* (New York: Basic Books, 2001); John T. Flynn's *As We Go Marching* (Garden City, N.Y.: Doubleday, 1944); Garet Garrett's the *People's Pottage* (Belmont, Mass.: Western Islands, 1965); and Ludwig von Mises's *Omnipotent Government: The Rise of Total State and Total War* (New Rochelle, N.Y.: Arlington House, 1969), which is the best attack on national socialism ever written. Mises writes of those who would romanticize war; two outstanding antidotes to such nonsense are Paul Fussell's *Wartime: Understanding and Behavior in the Second World War* (New York: Oxford University Press, 1990) and Chris Hedges's *War Is a Force That Gives Us Meaning* (New York: Public Affairs, 2002). On postwar politics, see William Appleman Williams's the *Tragedy of American Diplomacy* (New York: W.W. Norton, 1988).

For a political outlook, I'll again stick with books that depart radically from the mainstream. Hans-Hermann Hoppe's *Democracy–The God That Failed* (New Brunswick, N.J.: Transaction Publishers, 2001) will change your thinking about freedom and the vote. Mises's *Liberalism: In the Classical Tradition* (San Francisco: Cobden Press, [1929] 1985) remains the best modern statement of the classical ideal, with an appropriate emphasis on peace and property.

On statism generally, reading Albert Jay Nock's *Our Enemy, the State* (Tampa, Fla.: Hallberg Publishing, 2001) is a transforming experience, and the same is true of Herbert Spencer's *The Man Versus the State: With Six Essays on Government, Society, and Freedom* (Indianapolis, Ind.: Liberty-Classics, [1884] 1995). Etienne de la Boétie's *Politics of Obedience: The Discourse of Voluntary Servitude* (Montreal: Black Rose Books, 1998) was written in 1552, but it explains why people go along with the birds that are ruling us today (the Rothbard introduction is indispensable).

Secession, State, and Liberty (New Brunswick, N.J.: Transaction Publishers, 1998), edited by David Gordon, is your guide to breaking up the consolidated state. John T. Flynn's the *Roosevelt Myth* (New York: Fox & Wilkes, [1948] 1998) remains the essential debunking of his icon (the Ralph Raico introduction is crucial). Murray N. Rothbard's *Egalitarianism as a Revolt Against Nature and Other Essays* (Auburn, Ala.: Mises Institute, 2000) is Rothbard at his applied best, while the *Ethics of Liberty* (New York: New York University Press, 1998) is the best modern treatise on political theory. Rothbard's *For a New Liberty: The Libertarian Manifesto* (New York: Fox & Wilkes, 1989) is the libertarian manifesto, and still the best introduction to the libertarian worldview.

Two other Rothbard books offer spectacular commentary on our times: *Freedom, Inequality, Primitivism, and the Division of Labor* (Auburn, Ala.: Mises Institute, 1991) and the *Irrepressible Rothbard* (Burlingame, Calif.: Center for Libertarian Studies, 2000). To understand neoconservatism, see Justin Raimondo's *Reclaiming the American Right: The Lost Legacy of the Conservative Movement* (Burlingame, Calif.: Center for Libertarian Studies, 1993). For a frightening look at the social and cultural consequences of modern statism, see Paul Gottfried's *After Liberalism: Mass Democracy in the Managerial State* (Princeton, N.J.: Princeton University Press,

2001) and Helmut Schoeck's magisterial book *Envy* (Indianapolis, Ind.: Liberty Fund, [1966] 1987).

My own Website (LewRockwell.com) offers detailed bibliographies on history and war, while Mises.org keeps its Study Guide constantly up to date. For war coverage see antiwar.com, for economic commentary and books see Mises.org, and for political commentary see LewRockwell.com. By the way, many of the books listed above are available online.

Comments on *Speaking of Liberty*

"Socialism in distant lands collapsed, and it will collapse in the US too if this book gets a wide hearing. Omnipotent government has rarely faced as fierce an intellectual opponent."
—— PAUL CRAIG ROBERTS, HOOVER INSTITUTION

"Like great American oratory from the 18th and 19th centuries, this book of speeches on economics and public affairs is capable of inspiring an entire generation."
—— THOMAS J. DiLORENZO, LOYOLA COLLEGE IN MARYLAND

"Austrian economics has never been made more accessible. Lew discusses technical economics with the rhetorical flair you find only in the best teachers."
—— JOSEPH T. SALERNO, PACE UNIVERSITY

"In this book, Lew Rockwell shows that he is the leading spokesman for the free society in our time."
—— WALTER BLOCK, LOYOLA UNIVERSITY NEW ORLEANS

"In Congress, the speeches I hear are dull and disposable. These are eloquent, timeless, and true. If I could, I'd enter this entire book in the *Congressional Record!*"
—— RON PAUL, U.S. CONGRESS

"If you value wit, learning, and eloquence in the service of liberty, read this book. It is a body blow to the managerial state."
—— PAUL GOTTFRIED, ELIZABETHTOWN COLLEGE

"One of our 19th-century classics is Herbert Spencer's *The Man vs. the State*. In the 21st century, The Man is Lew Rockwell, and this is his classic."
—— BURTON S. BLUMERT, CHAIRMAN, LUDWIG VON MISES INSTITUTE